INVITATION TO PRACTICAL THEOLOGY

Advance Praise

"*Invitation to Practical Theology* is an important book both for programs aimed at preparing people in ministry to be practical theologians and for academic theologians seeking fresh insight into how attention to practice can enrich their thinking. Contributors have been chosen from among the best U.S. Catholic theologians, and the topics they address ring true to the concerns and cultures of the Catholic world. As such, the book represents a true 'coming of age' for Catholic practical theology. It will be read with great interest not only by Catholics, but by all who are passionate about the dialogue between practice and theological traditions."

—Mary Frohlich, RSCJ, director of the Ecumenical Doctor of Ministry Program, Catholic Theological Union at Chicago

"The resurgence of practical theology has long needed a wide-ranging contribution from U.S. Catholic perspectives. Thanks to Claire Wolfteich and her superb group of collaborators, now we have one."

—Timothy Matovina, professor of theology and executive director of the Institute for Latino Studies, University of Notre Dame

Invitation to Practical Theology does indeed invite us to a diverse table of plenty, one in which refreshing, embodied, ecumenical, and interdisciplinary hands have prepared a meal where the Kingdom's laborers from the working fields of chaplaincy, liturgy, spiritual direction, ethics, teaching, and social activism can share not only food but also the sacred faith it engenders.

—Eduardo C. Fernández, SJ, professor of pastoral theology and ministry, Jesuit School of Theology of Santa Clara University and Graduate Theological Union in Berkeley, California

"A powerful and highly creative contribution to practical theology by one its foremost contributors. Certain to be widely discussed in the church and academy."

—Richard Osmer, Ralph B. and Helen S. Ashenfelter Professor of Mission and Evangelism, Department of Practical Theology, Princeton Theological Seminary

INVITATION TO PRACTICAL THEOLOGY

Catholic Voices and Visions

EDITED BY
CLAIRE E. WOLFTEICH

Paulist Press
New York / Mahwah, NJ

Cover image by saicle/Shutterstock.com
Cover and book design by Lynn Else
Photographs in Chapter 7 by Kathleen Dorsey Bellow

Library of Congress Cataloging-in-Publication Data

Invitation to practical theology : Catholic voices and visions / edited by Claire E. Wolfteich.
pages cm
Includes bibliographical references and index.
ISBN 978-0-8091-4890-5 (pbk. : alk. paper) — ISBN 978-1-58768-413-5 (ebook)
1. Pastoral theology—Catholic Church. 2. Theology, Practical. 3. Catholic Church—Doctrines. I. Wolfteich, Claire E., editor.
BX1913.I58 2014
230`.2—dc23

2014012787

ISBN 978-0-8091-4890-5 (paperback)
ISBN 978-1-58768-413-5 (e-book)

Published by Paulist Press
997 Macarthur Boulevard
Mahwah, New Jersey 07430

www.paulistpress.com

Printed and bound in the
United States of America

For the great "cloud of witnesses"—past, present, future—that surround us and teach us the practice of faith

CONTENTS

ACKNOWLEDGMENTS

This book is a collaborative effort, with many who have contributed to its conception and development. First, of course, are the authors who have met for conversation and interaction about their respective chapters at various points along the way. In earlier stages of brainstorming about this project, we benefitted from the input of multiple scholars and pastoral leaders. Too many to name here, we acknowledge these important contributions in clarifying the aims and framing of the book. The editor also gratefully acknowledges financial and logistical support from the Center for Practical Theology at Boston University School of Theology, with funding from the Lilly Endowment. Marc Lavallee, Tara Soughers, Holly Benzenhafer Redford, and Miracle Ryder made important contributions as research and editorial assistants. A sabbatical grant from the Louisville Institute also provided space and time for the development of this book project, along with other writing. Nancy de Flon at Paulist Press provided consistent support and encouragement for the book project. For these and other professional contributions, and for the constant and critical support of families, we are grateful.

CHAPTER 1

INTRODUCTION

An Invitation to Practical Theology

CLAIRE E. WOLFTEICH

✦ *The Feast of Our Lady of Guadalupe arrives on December 12 with singing and dancing, the strains of "Las Mañanitas" greeting the day as communities reenact the story of Juan Diego's surprising and transforming encounter with La Morenita. Red roses fill the churches to invite the community's participation in the liberating revelation of God in beauty…known in the meeting of the poor Indian and the dark-skinned Lady.*

✦ *A rangy group—sinners, the ritually impure, outcasts, and foreigners—gathers around a table to eat with Jesus. The praxis of table fellowship shapes a new community aligned with a God who loves to eat and welcome.*

✦ *With drums and the singing of spirituals, water flowing, dance, and recitation of names, the gathering lifts up the ancestors in prayer and thanksgiving—remembering them, seeking their guidance, and honoring their active presence within the communion of saints.*

✦ *Parishioners of Our Lady of Angels Parish gather with neighbors, tenants, local politicians, and community organizers for a candlelit prayer vigil in front of an apartment building in the Bronx. With song, prayer, scripture readings, and testimonies about inadequate housing conditions, the gathering joins together in solidarity as the suffering body of Christ—seeking, praying, and strategizing for change.*

✦ *A family tries to stay faithful in the midst of consumer pressures, time demands, children's many needs, and differences in beliefs within the home...struggling to pray together, to eat well together, and to give money and time.*

These are glimpses into the practices woven throughout this book, practices through which Christian faith is lived, learned, embodied, and passed on in complex ways. *Invitation to Practical Theology: Catholic Voices and Visions* explores practice—an increasingly significant focus of study across disciplines and traditions—from the particular lens of Catholic theology. This book aims to show the vitality and unfolding possibilities of Catholic voices and visions in practical theology. Put simply, practical theology entails critical thinking about what we do and how we live out our faith. It entails the study of practices, contexts, cultures, and communities in dialogue with faith traditions and informed by the best human knowledge available. In Catholic perspective particularly, practical theology entails a "reading of the signs of the times in light of the Gospel"[1]—a move that involves serious engagement with and discerning interpretation of contemporary experience and practice; deep remembering and critical analysis of the tradition; imaginative theological envisioning of future practice; and a hopeful and prophetic tending to the ongoing life of the faith community.

This book invites you, the reader, into the work of practical theology. We hope that you will catch our excitement for practical theology and bring your intellect, your studies, and a discerning heart to this work. *Invitation to Practical Theology* provides a much-needed resource in practical theology that is grounded in Catholic theology and attentive to issues of practice in Catholic contexts. This kind of resource is vital for pastoral formation programs; practical theologians bring essential tools and expertise in shaping religious leadership and faith communities. Yet this text also is intended for broader use in theological education: as this book shows, practical theology is not only for ministry programs but is also central to the work of theology per se.

AIMS OF THIS BOOK

This volume aims to make a Catholic contribution to practical theology and to explore the import of practical theology for Catholic theology. These dual aims are quite significant at this juncture. The Catholic contribution to practical theology is growing in robust ways—though it still is underdeveloped in what historically has been seen as a largely Protestant guild. The book demonstrates that practical theology, in various forms and names, actually has deep and distinctive roots in Catholicism. Catholic theologians thus have much to offer to the contemporary academic discipline of practical theology. At the same time, practical theology as a scholarly discipline has much to offer to Catholic theology and theological education. While practical theology is well established as an academic discipline with international scope[2]—with an international journal, university doctoral programs, and an international academy that meets regularly—it has been slower to gain a foothold in some Catholic contexts. In short, this book advances an important conversation between practical theology and Catholic theology.

Still, there is far more at stake than an academic guild or method. We are drawn to this work because it stands to make a difference in how we think about our common life, how we learn to speak about God and our human callings, how we bring a critical perspective to church and culture, how we cultivate a faithful way of life, and how we form and sustain religious leaders. Faith communities, including and perhaps, especially, the Catholic Church, have faced enormous challenges in recent years. Polarization and scandal within the church; failures of leadership; and complex issues of politics, religious liberty, poverty, and housing—these are but a few of the challenges before us. In such a time, it is more important than ever to marshal the best resources of scholarship to think critically about practice.

In practice, faith is embodied, lived, enacted in the particularities of contexts and cultures. Practice can open up theological knowing; as Craig Dykstra writes, through participation in practices "we may come to awareness of certain realities that outside of these practices are beyond our ken."[3] There are things we come to know only through practice, just as the disciples on the road to Emmaus knew Christ finally "in the breaking of the bread" (Luke 24:13–32). Yet, practice is not only a way of coming to know something of God. Practice also is the site of theological wars and power struggles. Practices are contested—and can be practiced wrongly, even in ways that distort and manipulate faith. Miroslav Volf aptly notes: "'wrong doing'—especially if deeply patterned and long lived—leads to twisted understanding...right practices well practiced are likely to open persons for insights into beliefs to which they would otherwise be closed."[4] Clear-minded, critical theological analysis of practice, then, is a central task of theology. How to practice faithfully and well? How to live with intellectual and spiritual honesty and vitality in changing, diverse contexts? How to form lay and ordained leaders for the church who are adept at "reading the signs of the times," knowledgeable about church tradition, skilled in critical theological reflection, and visionary in shaping a faithful community in and for the world? Practical theology brings all the critical resources of scholarship to bear on such timely questions.

Invitation to Practical Theology claims needed space for practical theology as an integral dimension of Catholic theological scholarship, method, education, and community life. Central features of practical theology are presented through an exploration of practices significant in Catholic tradition and communal life. Throughout, the authors address implications for research, teaching, pastoral formation, religious leadership, and everyday practices of faith.

Indeed, this book argues for the importance of cultivating what M. Shawn Copeland describes as "practical theological agency" (ch. 6) within cultures and faith communities (and particularly among marginalized groups).

In many ways, these aims assume the four working uses of the term *practical theology* that Bonnie J. Miller-McLemore, a leading figure in practical theology today, describes. Miller-McLemore notes that practical theology is a "multivalent" term that is used to refer to at least four distinct, though not unrelated, things: (1) an "activity of faith among believers"; (2) a "method for studying theology in practice"; (3) a curricular area within theological education; and (4) a scholarly discipline.[5] She rightly notes that practical theology understood in each way can imply distinct objectives and audiences. Still, there is merit in juxtaposing and interrelating (without collapsing) these four understandings of practical theology. Authors in this volume may attend to one more than another; put together, their work shows that these four arenas of practical theology are not mutually exclusive but inform one another.

In making practices the central organizing principle of this volume, we highlight the relevance of practical theology in and for the sake of the everyday life of believers. We also look to the everyday practice of believers as a central focus of practical theological scholarship. Here this book follows the work of practical theologians such as Dorothy C. Bass, whose extensive work on "practices of faith" has provided enormous resources for faith communities and theological education.[6] Still, much of the work by Bass and her collaborators reflects a Protestant theological orientation. This book gratefully acknowledges these contributions as it seeks to offer a parallel resource that draws deeply from the well of Catholic communities, traditions, and practices. Like Bass, we see this work as a contribution to ecumenical and interfaith reflection on religious practices.

The focus on practices of faith of the whole church in and for the world also indicates that this book eschews what has been called a "clerical paradigm" in practical theology. The term *clerical paradigm* generally refers to the fact that practical theology as it developed in Protestant European and American contexts—influenced strongly by Friedrich Schleiermacher—was primarily oriented to the tasks of church leadership. In his influential book *Theologia: The Fragmentation and Unity of Theological Education,* Edward Farley sharply critiqued the dominance of the clerical paradigm as leading to a functionalist understanding of the tasks of theology and the loss of theology as *habitus*.[7] Practical theology in recent decades has moved beyond a "clerical paradigm" to embrace a more "public paradigm" for practical theology—with strong focus on ethics and social transformation. At the same time, Miller-McLemore argues that practical theology is now captivated by an "academic paradigm" that belittles the importance of "technical know-how" and the significance of pastoral leadership.[8] Thus, debate continues about the orienting tasks and location of practical theology. *Invitation to Practical Theology* sees no necessary dichotomy between pastoral formation, public engagement, and academic scholarship. While the three certainly can entail distinct tasks and audiences, as David Tracy argued,[9] they are deeply interconnected. The range of topics we address will bring readers into, for example, concrete issues of politics and liturgy, mission history and social action, ecclesial dilemmas of authority and leadership, family ethics, philosophical discussions of theories of practice, and theological anthropology. The interconnections of all such issues are significant—and need greater attention in the formation of scholars and pastoral leaders for the church. We intend this book to be useful in shaping lay and ordained leaders for the church; indeed, lay leadership is particularly critical in this time. On theological grounds (a conviction that the laity share in the mission and ministry of the church by virtue of their baptism) and pragmatic grounds (ordained clergy are a shrinking group, with lay ecclesial ministers assuming increasingly important roles), we do not limit our focus to a clerical paradigm but rather address issues of pastoral leadership within the wider context of practices of faith.

While the practice of everyday believers is a leading interest here, it must be noted that the authors bring extraordinary scholarly expertise in particular disciplines to their analysis of practice. Thus, each chapter on practice also reflects a kind of dialogue of disciplines—showing how everyday faith practices are fruitfully illumined in dialogue with, for example, liturgical theology, philosophical theology, ecclesiology, moral theology, missiology, sociology, spirituality studies, cultural studies, education, and ministry studies. The authors draw on diverse methods and discuss the normative issues that are integral to methodological questions.

Practical theology attends closely to context and culture. In keeping with this attention to the particular, many of the chapters include specific "on the ground" examples and thick descriptions of practices, illustrating how theology arises in practice in the particularities of local contexts, communities, and cultures. The authors in this volume work in a variety of institutional settings, and the chapters point to a range of contexts for the doing of practical theology, including university-based departments of theology; centers of theology and ministerial formation such as the Catholic Theological Union in Chicago, Boston College's School of Theology and Ministry, the Instituto Fe y Vida in Los Angeles, and the Institute of Black Catholic Studies at Xavier University in New Orleans; parishes such as Our Lady of Angels in the Bronx; bishops' conferences and pastoral planning processes such as the *Encuentro*; faith-based community organizations; hospitals; families; lay apostolic movements; and centers of spiritual direction and training.

We anticipate that this volume will be of interest to theologians broadly and particularly to scholars in practical theology and Catholic theology. It is critical to bring this scholarship into theological education. Until now there has not yet been a graduate-level practical theology text that attends specifically to Catholic approaches, issues, questions, and contexts. *Invitation to Practical Theology* fills that void, providing a much-needed resource for teaching and learning. It is well suited for use in Catholic graduate theology and ministry programs, many of which are looking to practical theological methods but lack resources with a Catholic framework. This book expands the range of practical theology, and so brings a needed text for use in doctoral programs in theology and ecumenical ministry formation programs to expand the conversation beyond the predominantly Protestant practical theology texts available. This volume can also serve as a text for graduate and advanced undergraduate theology and ethics courses as it opens critical issues of practice/praxis for students in systematic and moral theology. Students can be engaged robustly—indeed are most likely to be engaged—with theology that takes up practice as a leading concern. The focus on practices makes this book relevant and accessible for parish-based adult education programs. For example, it could form the basis for a series of parish-wide workshops on practices or the focus for a small faith-sharing group.

This volume builds on some important building blocks, including an earlier series of discussions among Catholic practical theologians and the resulting articles published in the *International Journal of Practical Theology*.[10] We acknowledge also the contribution of an edited volume with authors primarily from the British context, *Keeping Faith in Practice: Aspects of Catholic Pastoral Theology*.[11] *Invitation to Practical Theology* expands on those earlier works to advance conversation and scholarship about Catholic work in practical theology. In no way is this book comprehensive or inclusive of all the Catholic voices who have made contributions to practical theology in recent decades. However, this volume does include very significant Catholic theologians who are prominent within the academy and who bring a real critical love for the church.

This volume is intentionally primarily focused on American Catholic authors and contexts; the Catholic conversation and scholarship in practical theology on a global scale is even more variegated. Exploring Catholic work in practical theology on an international scale is a very significant project, for the future, beyond the scope of this book although we offer a glimpse into it. *Invitation to Practical Theology* should be seen as a particular contribution that aims to introduce the reader to practices and practical theology primarily from an American Catholic perspective. We gratefully recognize the many who have helped to give shape to Catholic practical and pastoral theologies as we aim now to further that conversation.

INVITATIONAL PERSPECTIVE AND THE DISCIPLINE OF PRACTICAL THEOLOGY

Invitation to Practical Theology takes a wide and invitational perspective on what constitutes practical theology in Catholic approaches. We invite a broad dialogue—not seeking to encompass everything under the rubric of "practical theology" but opening a vigorous discussion about our shared work in theological thinking about matters of practice. Today, Catholic scholars are active leaders in the growing academic discipline of practical theology—seen, for example, in leadership of the International Academy of Practical Theology, the North American–based Association of Practical Theology, and the French-speaking Société Internationale de Théologie Pratique. Many other Catholic theologians do not assume "practical theology" as their primary scholarly identity; they work in disciplines such as systematic, philosophical, and moral theology with their own distinct histories, methods, and identities. And yet, they do research that is closely related and deeply complementary to the work of practical theologians. Their work intersects with or moves around the edges of practical theology. This book is a collaborative venture among both kinds of scholars. The dialogue with systematic and moral theologians is vital for the flourishing of practical theology in Catholic contexts—and also reveals the deep theological strength and contribution of Catholic practical theologies.

At the same time, practical theology as a scholarly discipline has emerged with a robust literature and sophisticated research methods. The challenge is to open the conversation across disciplines without either imperialistically calling everything practical theology or underselling the hard-won work of the distinct scholarly discipline of practical theology. As it is vital to learn from the work of philosophical and systematic theologians, so too practical theology scholarship stands to inform these other disciplines and has much to contribute to theological education broadly. In short, we seek a serious engagement that flows in multiple directions.

The field of practical theology encompasses multiple approaches, methods, and definitions—shaped by diverse faith traditions; geographic/cultural contexts; race, gender, ethnicity, and class; disciplinary trainings; and theological commitments. Don S. Browning, an influential leader in the field, describes practical theology as "critical reflection on the church's dialogue with Christian sources and other communities of experience and interpretation with the aim of guiding its action toward social and individual transformation."[12] Some thinkers characterize practical theology primarily as what Norbert Mette calls "a theological theory of action."[13] In this vein, Gerben Heitink defines practical theology as "the empirically oriented theological theory of the mediation of the Christian faith in the praxis of modern society."[14] Others critique a focus on human *action* as too narrow a descriptor of the object of practical theological study, calling for a broader attention to "lived religion" or "lived experience." For R. Ruard Ganzevoort from the Netherlands, practical theology is the "hermeneutics of lived religion," a "tracing of the sacred."[15] Emerging work brings practical theology into conversation with aesthetic theory, poetics, and mystical traditions as they open practical theology more to imagination, symbol, metaphor, and the creative power of language to express the "unspeakable."[16] Liberationist approaches insist that theology cannot be understood apart from a praxis commitment to liberation; Rebecca Chopp, for example, critiques practical theology's overemphasis on theory and urges a heightened focus on liberative transformation.[17] With a focus specifically on liberative praxis for women, feminist and womanist practical theological approaches lift up marginalized voices, texts, and practices as they contest a male-dominated theological discourse.[18] Postmodern approaches in practical theology, such as the work of Elaine Graham and Tom Beaudoin, examine the tasks of practical theology in a postmodern context of pluralism, fragmentation, hybrid identities, and the loss of "metanarratives."[19] The multiplicity of approaches and methodological commitments makes practical theology a wide-ranging discipline. I concur with authors such as Ganzevoort in seeing the multiplicity of self-understandings both as common to many academic disciplines and as a source of rich creativity and spaciousness in the field. The diversity of approaches in practical theology should coexist in fruitful tension and critical dialogue.[20] Here too, then, this book invites and aims to stimulate dialogue among diverse approaches, methods, and orientations in practical theology.

CATHOLIC COMMUNITIES, TRADITIONS, AND IMAGINATION

Invitation to Practical Theology aims to demonstrate that Catholic theology, tradition, and imagination are especially well suited to the creative work of practical theology. Indeed, forms of practical theology have long been central to Catholic theology and to the life of the Catholic community. We see it in the Catholic "sacramental imagination" and the centrality of the liturgy, the *opus dei*, as the primary means of expressing and shaping the theology of the community. We see it in ancient spiritual traditions—in their attention to practices (from reading scripture to prayer to silent contemplation) as a way of coming to theological understanding. We see it in the art of moral casuistry that long shaped the training of clergy, particularly from the early modern period up until the Second Vatican Council. Practical theology has been lived in vibrant Catholic lay movements, many of which followed Joseph Cardijn's see-judge-act method. Practical theology lives in Catholic social teaching, which, since the publication of *Rerum novarum* ("On Capital and Labor") in 1891, has brought a critical faith perspective to contemporary economic, political, social, and cultural issues. Practical theology flourishes in the turn to the world, to pastoral concerns, in the Second Vatican Council (1962–65); the *Pastoral Constitution on the Church in the Modern World* (*Gaudium et spes*) can be seen as a preeminent work of practical theology. As Kathleen A. Cahalan writes: "The Council was pivotal in claiming 'pastoral' as an ecclesial discourse pertaining to the church's relationship to the world, most notably in *Gaudium et spes*, the only constitution given the title 'pastoral.'"[21]

Latin American liberation theologies, with their turn to the praxis of the base communities, clearly are a form of practical theology. Brazilian practical theologian Valburga Schmiedt Streck writes:

> Even if the term *practical theology* is not commonly used in the Catholic Church, this does not mean that it has no practical theology. Suffice it to recall the ecclesial base communities, where lay people are the protagonists, as well as the great number of pastoral works (pastoral land work, pastoral work with children, pastoral work with the unemployed, pastoral youth work, to mention just a few) that engage both the urban and the rural context.[22]

So too we see strong resonances, implicit forms of practical theology, in the theologies arising from diverse ethnic groups within Catholicism. In delineating a Vietnamese Catholic theology that can reflect and inform the faith of the roughly 300,000 Vietnamese American Catholics, Peter C. Phan writes that a Vietnamese theology dynamically incorporates sociocultural analysis, critical interpretation, and critical practice (praxis):

> It must show how these reflections should lead to a more faithful practice of the Christian faith, in conformity with God's preferential love for the poor and the marginalized, and to a more authentic worship of God....And this critical practice will in turn bring new materials and resources to the theological mill to generate another cycle of critical analysis and interpretation and praxis.[23]

This book highlights and examines distinctive Catholic accents, issues, contexts, and theological commitments. Practical theology as a discipline offers a significant scholarly resource that can draw on the promise and particularity of these movements in Catholic theology and life. Of course, identities are hybrid, plural, and fluid; this volume illustrates both unity and diversity within Catholicism. We are interested in a discussion that explores a variety of Catholic approaches in practical theology; we are not interested in presenting a monolithic picture, ghettoizing Catholic thought, or claiming exclusive rights to shared traditions of wisdom. These contributions are highly relevant to the larger field of practical theology. Thus, we expect that this book will generate interest across denominational and faith traditions. We invite all readers into this conversation as significant voices in Catholic theology explore the import of practice in diverse ways and, in so doing, open up reflection about lived faith and the doing of theology.

OVERVIEW OF THIS BOOK

Invitation to Practical Theology is structured in three parts. Part 1 provides a historical overview of Catholic developments in practical and pastoral theologies as well as conceptual framing intended to help readers gain an initial understanding of key terms and issues. In chapter 2, Kathleen A. Cahalan and Bryan Froehle describe how the Catholic voice in practical theology can be found in specific movements and developments in theology and ecclesial life from the Middle Ages to the present—with roots in a medieval sacramental and moral framework, to a more marginalized position for practical theology with the growing embrace of abstract speculative reason, to the new Catholic engagement with the practical marked by the Second Vatican Council, to the contemporary situation, in which a distinctively Catholic practical theological synthesis has emerged, spurred by intercultural engagement with voices from Latin America, Asia, and Africa. Colleen M. Griffith then opens up the notion of "practice" as embodied knowing in chapter 3, exploring the theological and epistemological dimensions of practice, which is far more than the application of theory. Her analysis draws upon a breadth of philosophical and theological sources, providing a key introduction to the category of practice. David Tracy's argument in chapter 4 for a mystical-prophetic practical theology that draws on spiritual traditions and aesthetics offers a deeply Catholic vision of practical theology, calling for the discipline to retain but expand its strong emphasis on ethics. This chapter, originally penned as an address to the International Academy of Practical Theology during its 2009 Chicago meeting, is placed early in the volume because it sounds several key notes that will resound in other chapters—including the importance and interrelationship of spirituality, prophetic work for justice, and aesthetics in a Catholic vision of practical theology.

Part 2 is the largest section of the book, for here we explore concrete practices of faith. In inviting readers into the work of practical theology, it is natural that practices, understood as "theory-laden"[24] and as opening "epistemological horizons,"[25] should be the leading point of entry. The practices explored in this section are not comprehensive of all Catholic Christian practices, by any means, but the chapters do analyze highly significant faith practices, and, in so doing, open up diverse perspectives on practical theology. Through the lens of exploring practices, authors name and wrestle with contested issues of practice and illustrate the deep interrelationship of theology and practice. They also approach these practices through particular academic disciplines—and so the variety of chapters indicates a range of disciplinary pathways into practical theology and the importance of interdisciplinary study of practice.

Systematic and philosophical theologian Terrence W. Tilley leads off this section in chapter 5 by framing tradition—of course, a key concept in Catholic theology—as an "enduring, complex communal" practice or set of practices. Undercutting the idea that tradition is simply a collection of unchanging beliefs (*tradita*), Tilley focuses on *traditio*, the dynamic *practice* of handing on the faith, without which traditions have no life. By way of example, Tilley discusses the ritual celebration of the Eucharist and practices of reconciliation. As practices are the context in which theory arises, argues Tilley, so "practical theology is construed as the context in which systematic theology arises." Indeed, the Eucharist is a central practice of Catholic Christian faith. Liturgical scholar Edward Foley picks up this point in chapter 6 as he describes the Eucharist as a "foundational practice" and "enacted theology." Rooting eucharistic practices in Jesus' own subversive table ministry and not shying away from discussing deeply contested aspects of contemporary eucharistic practice (note the term *liturgy wars*), Foley explores shifting historical emphases on three interrelated "bodies of Christ"—the historical body of Christ, the ecclesial body of Christ, and the sacramental body of Christ. He concludes by naming the practice of celebrating the Eucharist as a form of "public theology."

Ritual is a key practice of *traditio*—and of course the handing on of the faith does not happen in the abstract but rather in the particularities of specific contexts, particular bodies. In chapter 7, M. Shawn Copeland turns to the ritual practices, symbols, and narratives of African American popular religion, providing a deep theological analysis of the practice of commemorating the ancestors, specifically as enacted at one center of theological education and ministerial formation, the Institute of Black Catholic Studies at Xavier University in New Orleans. She sees this ritual practice—

what she describes as a "critical cultural intervention"—as "creative practical theological response to the ongoing need for ebonization in the Catholic Church in the United States." Moreover, she argues that a goal of theological education is the "formation of practical theological agency," that indeed the formation of practical theological agency among black Catholic laity—an intellectual, ethical, aesthetic, and worshipful process—is a key component of the legacy of black Catholic *traditio*, handing on the faith.

Popular religious practice, or "lived religion," is rightly a very important focus for practical theology. In chapter 8, Roberto S. Goizueta emphasizes the aesthetic character of praxis through an analysis of the liberative narrative and ritual celebration of Our Lady of Guadalupe, a powerful dimension of Latino/a popular religion/spirituality. Following the lead of Latin American liberation theologians, Goizueta situates praxis as a key theological source, or *locus theologicus*, and argues that Christian praxis is "at the very heart of the theological task." Naming and developing Latino/a contributions to practical theology is a highly salient task—particularly in a U.S. Catholic Church that is nearly 40 percent Latino/a, with a Latino/a majority among its youth and young adults. In chapter 9, Carmen María Cervantes, Allan Figueroa Deck, and Ken Johnson-Mondragón note the "performative" nature of Latino/a Catholicism, the importance of practice and experience, and the fact that Latinos/as live and hand on the faith (*traditio*) foremost "in an aesthetic, corporal, intuitive, and affective way." As they address five practical theological areas of Latino/a influence—liturgy, spirituality, ecclesial movements, faith and justice, and ecclesial revitalization—the authors pay particular attention to the practical wisdom and pastoral imagination of *pastoral juvenil hispana*, ministry with youth and young adults in Latino/a contexts.

Janet K. Ruffing is well known as a leader in the field of spirituality studies. In chapter 10, she explores the practice of spiritual direction as a form of lay practical theology, in which director and directee collaboratively seek to discern and tell the story of God's presence in human experience. Spiritual direction is, then, she asserts, a process of discernment and dialogical narrative theologizing that is "one of the oldest recommended spiritual practices in our tradition for those who desire to practice their faith in a deep and reflective way" and one that is particularly important in contexts of ministerial formation. Ruffing illustrates her points through engagement with early monastic practices of spiritual guidance; a contemporary model of direction and training developed at the Center for Religious Development in Cambridge, Massachusetts; and two concrete case studies drawn from her own practice of spiritual direction.

Julie Hanlon Rubio brings a voice from moral theology/ Christian social ethics as she explores everyday practices in the context of family life in chapter 11. This is an important context and concern in Catholic theology; Catholic teaching describes families as "domestic churches" charged with primary responsibility for humanization and handing on the faith. Rubio examines five practices—eating, tithing, sex, serving, and praying— bringing Catholic social teaching, social analysis, and sacramental theology into the discussion. Family practices are not privatized matters but rather integrally connected to social justice and critical engagement with culture. Rubio sees these five practices as "essential practices of resistance embedded in the ordinary life of a Christian household committed to love and solidarity." While Rubio is not directly involved in practical theology as an academic discipline, her practice-oriented approach to ethics stands to make a highly relevant contribution to practical theology. Her essay also illustrates the value of increasing dialogue between practical theologians and ethicists. Protestant practical theologians have worked closely with ethics, particularly as practical theology made a more "public" turn in the 1980s. Yet, the possibilities of dialogue and cross-fertilization between Catholic moral theology and practical theology are just beginning to be addressed.[26]

Systematic theologian Bradford Hinze makes the case in chapter 12 for dialogue as a key ecclesial practice and a significant area of study for practical theology. Hinze offers a detailed picture of dialogue in action in the involvement of Our Lady of Angels Parish in a collaborative community organizing movement for better housing in the Bronx, New York. He connects this story with a theology of dialogue rooted in a Vatican II dialogical ecclesiology and an understanding of the "self-communicative and dialogical character of God's identity and mission." Following a practical theological interest in the formation and transformation of practice, Hinze includes reflections on learning dialogical skills, an acute need both within ecclesial life and in situations of injustice and conflict worldwide.

In chapter 13, Stephen Bevans frames missiology as a form of practical theology—specifically, one aimed at "understanding and embodying mission rightly as trinitarian practice." This is a task at the heart of Christian theology, according to Bevans's argument. Like Hinze, Bevans emphasizes the prophetic character of Christian practice—here Bevans frames mission as prophetic dialogue that is specifically enacted in witness and proclamation; liturgy, prayer, and contemplation; justice, peace, and care of creation; interreligious and secular dialogue; inculturation; and reconciliation.

The final section of this book most explicitly addresses practical theological teaching and research. In chapter 14, Thomas Groome, religious educator and a longtime member of the International Academy of Practical Theology, develops his most explicit essay to date on practical theology, "Practices of Teaching: A Pedagogy for Practical Theology." Following educational literature, Groome seeks to articulate the learning outcomes of practical theology in terms of *knowledge* and *competency*. According to Groome, the knowledge aims of practical theology distinguish it as a theological discipline; practical theology seeks as threefold learning outcome "reliable knowledge, spiritual wisdom for life, and the arts needed to render the services that enact Christian faith in the world." The competency intended by practical theological teaching then follows on its epistemology: "practical theologians intend to inform and form people in the habitus of 'doing' theology while deliberately taking account of their historical circumstances." Groome develops his "shared praxis" teaching method in relationship to these insights as he also addresses diversity within the discipline of practical theology and roots his pedagogical principles firmly in Catholic theological convictions.

By way of strengthening conversation between American Catholic theologians and the wider community of scholars in practical theology, in chapter 15, two Catholic scholars from European and French Canadian contexts present an important discussion of research methods. Annemie Dillen of Katholieke Universiteit in Leuven, Belgium, specializes in pastoral care, ethics, childhood studies, and practical theology. Robert Mager is professor of systematic theology and practical theology at Université Laval in Quebec, Canada; he also directs a doctoral program in practical theology there. Their chapter helpfully outlines diverse research methods current in practical theological scholarship—including qualitative empirical research, action research, content analysis, phenomenological research, and grounded theory. Yet, this chapter does not simply present these various models; it frames the normative theological issues that bear on method in practical theology, naming the normative issues that arise in any methodological option. Thus, Dillen and Mager connect theology and methodology in ways both distinctive to Catholic concerns and also highly relevant to the broader discipline.

Finally, chapter 16 offers my concluding reflections as it articulates key Catholic contributions and names future directions for advancing this work.

WORKING CREATIVELY WITH THIS BOOK IN THE CLASSROOM OR SMALL GROUPS

Invitation to Practical Theology has a flow and so can profitably be read from start to finish. It can also be used flexibly in educational settings. Chapters may be assigned in order, one or two per week. The volume can also be used as a course textbook or adult education text. It is best not to neatly segment chapters into discrete topics such as "ministry," "theology," or "popular religion"—these topics intersect within individual chapters in fluid and fruitful ways. Readers could miss these important intersections if chapters are too rigidly characterized as applying to one of those areas and not others. Noting this caveat, the chapters could be paired thematically in creative ways, depending on the course topic and the interests of students. For example, Copeland and Goizueta both open up issues of popular religious practice and culture that could be put in conversation fruitfully with Tilley's argument about the practiced nature of tradition. To explore the embodied nature of practice, readers would do well to juxtapose Griffith's chapter on practice with Foley's discussion of eucharistic practice and the three bodies of Christ. A course on ministerial formation could include a particular focus on Cervantes, Deck, and Johnson-Mondragón's analysis of the *pastoral juvenil hispana*; Ruffing's chapter on spiritual direction; Copeland's analysis of the Institute of Black Catholic Studies model of formation; and Groome's reflections on Christian religious education. Those interested in spirituality, aesthetics, and practical theology could bring Tracy, Goizueta, Ruffing, and Wolfteich into conversation. To address ethics, social justice, and the prophetic character of practical theology, readers could work closely with Rubio, Hinze, and Bevans. To gain a clear understanding of practical theology as an academic discipline, readers may want to look particularly to Cahalan and Froehle, Dillen and Mager, Groome, Griffith, Tracy, and the introduction and conclusion.

The possibilities are wide-ranging. We invite readers into this rich conversation and, more important, into the practical life that is its focus. Following in the ancient tradition of *lectio divina*, this book hopes to be not simply information but perhaps also a transforming intellectual, spiritual word. We invite you into this shared work of intellect, spirit, and imagination.

Notes

1. *Gaudium et spes*, no. 4.

2. Note, for example, the International Academy of Practical Theology, the *International Journal of Practical Theology*, the French-speaking Société Internationale de Théologie Pratique, and the American-based Association of Practical Theology. Note also the Practical Theology group at the American Academy of Religion Annual Meeting.

3. Craig Dykstra, "Reconceiving Practice," in *Shifting Boundaries: Contextual Approaches to the Structure of Theological Education*, ed. Barbara G. Wheeler and Edward Farley (Louisville, KY: Westminster John Knox Press, 1991), 45.

4. Miroslav Volf, "Theology for a Way of Life," in *Practicing Theology: Beliefs and Practices in Christian Life*, ed. Miroslav Volf and Dorothy C. Bass (Grand Rapids, MI: William B. Eerdmans Publishing Company, 2002), 257.

5. Bonnie J. Miller-McLemore, "The Contributions of Practical Theology," in *The Wiley-Blackwell Companion to Practical Theology*, ed. Bonnie J. Miller-McLemore (Oxford, UK: Wiley-Blackwell, 2012), 5.

6. See, for example, Dorothy C. Bass, ed., *Practicing Our Faith* (San Francisco, CA: Jossey Bass, 2010 [1997]), and the related Practices of Faith book series; Dorothy C. Bass and Craig Dykstra, eds., *For Life Abundant: Practical Theology, Theological Education, and Christian Ministry* (Grand Rapids, MI: William B. Eerdmans Publishing Company, 2008); Miroslav Volf and Dorothy C. Bass, eds., *Practicing Theology: Beliefs and Practices in Christian Life* (Grand Rapids, MI: William B. Eerdmans Publishing Company, 2002).

7. See Edward Farley, *Theologia: The Fragmentation and Unity of Theological Education* (Eugene, OR: Wipf & Stock, 2001; 1st ed.: Philadelphia, PA: Fortress Press, 1983).

8. Bonnie J. Miller-McLemore, "The 'Clerical Paradigm': A Fallacy of Misplaced Concreteness?" *International Journal of Practical Theology* 11, no. 2 (2007): 19–38.

9. David Tracy, *The Analogical Imagination: Christian Theology and the Culture of Pluralism* (New York: Crossroad Publishing, 1981).

10. In addition to Cahalan's article cited above, see also articles by Tom Beaudoin, Lynn Bridgers, Edward Foley, and Bryan Froehle in the *International Journal of Practical Theology* 15, no. 1 (2011). See also Lynn Bridgers, "Roman Catholicism," in *The Wiley-Blackwell Companion to Practical Theology*, ed. Bonnie J. Miller-McLemore (Oxford, UK: Wiley-Blackwell, 2012), 567–76.

11. James Sweeney, Gemma Simmonds, and David Lonsdale, eds., *Keeping Faith in Practice: Aspects of Catholic Pastoral Theology* (London, UK: SCM Press, 2010).

12. Don S. Browning, *A Fundamental Practical Theology: Descriptive and Strategic Proposals* (Minneapolis, MN: Fortress Press, 1991), 36.

13. Norbert Mette, *Theorie der Praxis* (Dusseldorf, Germany: Patmos, 1978), cited in Robert Mager, "Action Theories," in *The Wiley-Blackwell Companion to Practical Theology*, ed. Bonnie J. Miller-McLemore (Oxford, UK: Wiley-Blackwell, 2012), 256.

14. Gerben Heitink, *Practical Theology: History, Theory, Action Domains*, Studies in Practical Theology (Grand Rapids, MI: William B. Eerdmans Publishing Company, 1999), 6.

15. R. Ruard Ganzevoort, "Forks in the Road When Tracing the Sacred: Practical Theology as the Hermeneutics of Lived Religion," presidential address to the International Academy of Practical Theology, Chicago, IL, March 8, 2009, R. Ruard Ganzevoort Web site, accessed September 30, 2013, http://www.ruardganzevoort.nl/pdf/2009_Presidential.pdf.

16. See, for example, Heather Walton, "Practical Theology and Poetics," in *The Wiley-Blackwell Companion to Practical Theology*, ed. Bonnie J. Miller-McLemore (Oxford, UK: Wiley-Blackwell, 2012), 173–82; Paul Ballard and Pamela D. Couture, eds., *Creativity, Imagination, and Criticism: The Expressive Dimension in Practical Theology* (Cardiff, UK: Cardiff Academic Press, 2001); Terry A. Veiling, *Practical Theology: On Earth As It Is in Heaven* (Maryknoll, NY: Orbis Books, 2005); and Claire E. Wolfteich, "'Practices of Unsaying': Michel de Certeau, SJ, Spirituality

Studies, and Practical Theology," *Spiritus: A Journal of Christian Spirituality* (Fall 2012): 161–71.

17. Rebecca S. Chopp, "Practical Theology and Liberation," in *Formation and Reflection: The Promise of Practical Theology*, ed. Lewis S. Mudge and James N. Poling (Minneapolis, MN: Fortress Press, 1987), 120–38. For a useful overview of the influence of liberation theologies on practical theology, see Nancy J. Ramsay, "Emancipatory Theory and Method," in *The Wiley-Blackwell Companion to Practical Theology*, ed. Bonnie J. Miller-McLemore (Oxford, UK: Wiley-Blackwell, 2012), 183–92.

18. See, for example, Phillis Sheppard, *Self, Culture, and Others in Womanist Practical Theology* (New York: Palgrave Macmillan, 2011); Denise M. Ackermann and Riet Bons-Storm, eds., *Liberating Faith Practices: Feminist Practical Theologies in Context* (Leuven, Belgium: Peeters, 1998); Mary Elizabeth Moore, "Feminist Practical Theology and the Future of the Church," in *Practical Theology—International Perspectives*, ed. Friedrich Schweitzer and Johannes A. van der Ven (Frankfurt am Main, Germany: Peter Lang, 1999), 189–209.

19. See Elaine L. Graham, *Transforming Practice: Pastoral Theology in an Age of Uncertainty* (Eugene, OR: Wipf & Stock, 2002; 1st ed.: London, UK: Mowbray, 1996), and Tom Beaudoin, *Witness to Dispossession: The Vocation of a Postmodern Theologian* (Maryknoll, NY: Orbis Books, 2008).

20. I concur with Jaco S. Dreyer's argument for a "dialogical pluralist" approach to "intradisciplinary plurality"—that is, various approaches engage with one another, locate themselves in relationship to one another. See Jaco S. Dreyer, "Practical Theology and Intradisciplinary Diversity: A Response to Miller-McLemore's 'Five Misunderstandings about Practical Theology.'" *International Journal of Practical Theology* 16, no. 1 (2012): 34–54.

21. Kathleen A. Cahalan, "Locating Practical Theology in Catholic Theological Discourse and Practice," *International Journal of Practical Theology* 15, no. 1 (2011): 4.

22. Valburga Schmiedt Streck, "Brazil," in *The Wiley-Blackwell Companion to Practical Theology*, ed. Bonnie J. Miller-McLemore (Oxford, UK: Wiley-Blackwell, 2012), 530.

23. Peter C. Phan, *Vietnamese-American Catholics* (New York: Paulist Press, 2005), 102–3.

24. On this point see, for example, Browning, *A Fundamental Practical Theology*, 6.

25. On the embodied knowing that arises from participation in practices, see, for example, Craig Dykstra and Dorothy C. Bass, "A Theological Understanding of Christian Practices," in *Practicing Theology: Beliefs and Practices in Christian Life*, ed. Miroslav Volf and Dorothy C. Bass (Grand Rapids, MI: William B. Eerdmans Publishing Company, 2002), 13–32.

26. For some further discussion about dialogue between Catholic moral theology and practical theology, see Claire E. Wolfteich, "Time Poverty, Women's Labor, and Catholic Social Teaching: A Practical Theological Exploration," *Journal of Moral Theology* 2, no. 2 (June 2013): 40–59.

PART I

INVITATION TO PRACTICAL THEOLOGY

CHAPTER 2

A DEVELOPING DISCIPLINE

The Catholic Voice in Practical Theology

KATHLEEN A. CAHALAN AND BRYAN FROEHLE

INTRODUCTION

The intersection of practice and theology has always been integral to Catholic self-understanding, though not always in a formal academic way. The way in which practice has been situated in theology has shifted through Catholic history and theological developments. The Catholic voice in practical theology springs specifically from the profoundly Catholic concern with the intelligibility of practice and the ways in which beliefs, sacred narratives, ritual enactments, canons, and authorities cohere into a vital community of faith. Today, this voice is both concentrated in a discipline of "practical theology" and simultaneously diffused throughout the theological disciplines, grounded in a sacramental imagination of a world transformed by divine action.

The Catholic voice in practical theology springs specifically from the profoundly Catholic concern with the intelligibility of practice and the ways in which beliefs, sacred narratives, ritual enactments, canons, and authorities

cohere into a vital community of faith. Today, this voice is both concentrated in a discipline of "practical theology" and simultaneously diffused throughout the theological disciplines, grounded in a sacramental imagination of a world transformed by divine action.

The riches of the Catholic practical theological voice stem from a sensitivity to history, the multiple and intersecting lines of tradition, and the unique creative tension that sustains the distinctive configuration of Catholic communities and institutions. Specific theological resources account for such distinctiveness, including a highly robust structured ecclesiology, a deeply grounded pneumatology (including newly articulated accounts of the movement of the Spirit as well as sensitivity to God's grace from the beginning of the life of the church), a theological anthropology based on a keen sense of human goodness, and a christological and incarnational focus on the sacramentality of all creation.[1] At various points, Catholic theology has tended toward the theoretical and speculative, with the practical largely subsumed or sidelined. In the present moment, reflecting the New Evangelization and focus on the integration between faith and life, the question has returned with a new vigor.[2] The practical theological voice offers concrete insights and methods to address the challenges of pluralism, secularism, and globalization, issues definitively opened at the Second Vatican Council (1962–65).

One cannot adequately consider the Catholic voice in practical theology without seeing both these new developments and underlying deep continuities. This essay explores these questions in terms of the emergence of academic theology at the birth of the university, the Catholic engagement with modernity, the emergence of practical theological concerns during and after the Second Vatican Council, and the contemporary postmodern and postcolonial contexts that shape theology today. Throughout this history, diverse forms of Catholic spirituality, religious life, and lived practice have blossomed, sometimes connected to theological developments in academic theology and sometimes not.

ROOTS OF THE CATHOLIC VOICE IN PRACTICAL THEOLOGY

The Rise of the Universities and the Formalization of Theology

Practice has always been integral to lived Christian faith, and theology developed precisely to define an understanding of faith in which practice takes place. In the first centuries, bishop-theologians such as Athanasius, Augustine, and Gregory the Great explicated the truths of the Christian faith in light of practical realities, including widespread heterodox beliefs (Arianism), new practices (infant baptism), and changing cultural contexts (the decline of the Roman Empire). The influence of the bishop-theologians established the principle that practice was pastor directed and oriented to the salvation of souls.[3]

By the eleventh century, the diversity of practice and theology characteristic of the patristic period gave way to new codification and systematization, in part due to the reframing of theological discourse after the Great Schism of 1054, which effectively lost the diversity of Eastern theological developments to Western discourse. Catholic theological thought and sacramental praxis became increasingly aligned into a precise whole through the twin systematizing forces of Scholastic reason and canon law. Developments within the sacramental practice of penance illustrate this well.[4] The emergence of ecclesial and juridical norms for the practice of confession was closely related to the evolving approach to theology developing within the newly emerging universities. Flowing from the recently discovered works of Aristotle, these school-based, or "Scholastic," theologians systematized theological understanding through an intellectual apparatus built on rigorous philosophical constructs. They gathered the writings of patristic thinkers and pastoral sources, including the widely varying available *penitentials*, as part of a project of bringing unity to practice. The location of theological production thus shifted from the patristic model of the bishop serving the people to that of university scholars in service to the church universal. Lived faith shifted from being a subject of theology to being its object.[5]

The new speculative emphasis was not universally accepted, and Catholic tradition has always respected other understandings as no less orthodox. The great Franciscan thinkers Alexander of Hales, Bonaventure, and Duns Scotus, for example, countered the analytic approach by emphasizing the practical side of theology, which understood the practice of awakening fear and love of God, rather than intellectual encounter with the knowledge of God, as the highest good.[6] Their approach was rooted in the tradition of theology as *sapientia*, wisdom that sought to hold in union the theoretical and practical sides of life striving toward the good, which is God. The theological debates between the Franciscans and the Dominicans continued even as the Dominican-led Scholastic approach became the dominant and official approach to theology into the modern period.[7]

These developments meant that medieval and modern expressions of formal Catholic theology did not—could not—directly attend to the variety and multiplicity of the lived spiritual tradition expressed over the centuries in monastic, mendicant, and apostolic communities of vowed religious as well as in lay movements such as the Beguines.[8] The profuse blossoming of Catholic devotional, mystical, and charitable practice was possible precisely because it was not as regulated as formal theological work. In the medieval period, this might include practices such as the Franciscan crèche, Julian of Norwich's writings, and the *ars moriendi* practices of care for the dying, and in the early modern period, the devotion of the Sacred Heart, the mysticism of Theresa of Avila, and the rise of the apostolic (meaning "sent forth") religious orders. These modern, entrepreneurial forms of practical theological life underwrote the great Catholic missionary enterprises and its institutions of social work, health care, and education. The vitality of such practices and ways of life grew from multiple contexts, both the encounter with the "other" in colonization and trade and in religio-political absolutism, political economic oppression, and dislocation. Such vital and creative aspects of practice remained on the edges, less systematized into rules and rubrics, yet nonetheless profoundly significant to the Catholic practice of the faith.

Systematizing Practice: Catholic Modernity from Trent to Neo-Scholasticism

If the medieval theological move was toward the practice of systemization through Scholastic and legal reasoning, Catholic modernity was about the systematization of practice, first through the manualists and then through the neo-Scholastics. The impulse toward the formalization of theology gained a heightened place and importance at the Council of Trent (1545–63), a principal concern of which was to form priests in right teaching and practice.[9] The council decreed the creation of diocesan seminaries, which in turn stimulated the development of curricula and manuals ("handbooks"), which now became the repository of pastoral practice. Theology marked by the rise of university life in the medieval period now became about seminary-based priestly formation. The term *pastoral theology* emerged at this time, in the work of Peter Canisius, SJ (1521–97), author of many manuals and catechisms.[10] Pastoral practice was learned through the art of casuistry, the case-based application of church norms (canon law), designed to help determine the acceptable pastoral decision.[11]

Within the Protestant world, the move was similar: theological education became education to produce Protestant clergy, and the disciplines and specializations that developed within theology reflected the areas of training deemed critical for clergy.[12] Reflective of developments at the time among both Catholics and Protestants, a professorship in pastoral theology was established for seminarians at Vienna in 1774,[13] preceding similar moves within Protestantism by a generation.[14] In the eighteenth century, the Benedictine Franz Rautenstrauch argued that pastoral theology should be required in all German Catholic faculties of theology. Johann Michael Sailer (1751–1832) took this further, arguing that all theology must be understood as pastoral and that pastoral wisdom depends on practical experience and the ability to critically theorize from praxis.[15]

Catholicism's sacramental and analogical orientation demands consideration of the arts as well as the academy. A review of Catholic practical theological understanding must surely also consider the eruption of the baroque. This unique style of art and architecture embodied the Catholic experience of grace and sacramentality in the Tridentine period, engaging Catholic spiritual sensibilities well after other secular styles developed. Such representational art (paintings, sculpture, and especially architecture) narrated God's grace-filled spatial presence in the world to all, literate and illiterate alike, suggesting a world transfused with grace. It engaged both the interior, psychological dimension of the person and the exterior identity and action of the community. Such a practical theology of grace was inevitably in contradiction to the modern project founded on a rationalism that secularized Christian eschatology into a myth of scientific progress.[16]

Catholicism was just as modernist, however, in the sense that it had an equally univocal project. It offered a complete and separate intellectual and social universe, one that found its fullest synthesis in the "long nineteenth century."[17] Such oppositional practices that emerged as part of the Catholic restorationist project were intended to resist and even undo the inroads of the hostile forces threatening the church. Catholic intellectual life became particularly marked by a common agenda when Leo XIII, pope from 1878 to 1903, formally named Thomism as the official philosophical and theological system of the Catholic Church. The resulting neo-Scholasticism quickly became the reigning form of Catholic intellectual life, remaining so through the Second Vatican Council.

The most significant school of thought to engage Thomas and his sources in turn was the mid-twentieth-century French movement of the *nouvelle théologie.* Its leaders, the Dominicans Yves Congar and Marie-Dominique Chenu and the Jesuits Henri de Lubac and Jean Danielou, were distinguished for exploring the relationship between theory and practice.[18] They and others identified with a *ressourcement* that first retrieved Aquinas from simplistic accounts in the manuals, engaged other critical figures in the tradition,[19] and ultimately gestured toward a recovery of the Christian experience of the first centuries and the Gospels. They offer an approach that was less systematizing, more grace-focused, and deeply engaged with context and the ordinary challenges of human existence.[20]

These moves reflected and were nourished by the liturgical movement. Beginning around 1830 in a French Benedictine monastery, liturgists engaged the religious imagination of new generations of Catholic thinkers in parishes, universities, seminaries, and religious orders. Their primary aim was to bring to light the liturgical practices of the past so as to renew contemporary Catholic practice. By the early twentieth century, liturgical experiments were taking place in Germany and France in the form of dialogue Masses. New forms of practice and insight developed as people began to say parts of the Mass rather than simply listen to those on the altar, as had been the case for centuries.[21]

In a similar and related way, catechetical renewal began to blossom, nourished by a deep practical concern that the long-established question-and-answer method was no longer adequate to helping people learn and live the faith. The first phase focused on better methods, leading to the Munich method that developed after World War I. The second phase turned to concerns about content. In the 1930s and 1940s, "catechesis" itself became increasingly seen as the "pastoral mission" of the whole church rather than schooling for children.[22]

By the mid-twentieth century, the Catholic intellectual world was exceptionally vibrant, though its most dynamic bits tended to be outside mainstream, formal theological work. Catholic vitality was fueled by intellectuals and pastoral agents inspired by practically rooted conversations in liturgical practice, religious education, and social action. Such ferment decisively shaped the contemporary Catholic voice in practical theology. One such example of vitality that informed practical theological thinking is Catholic Action.[23] Initiated and led largely by the hierarchy as a project of the popes, particularly in its Italian form, Catholic Action took form as a cluster of movements that fostered Catholic praxis in a remarkably vital, coordinated way. In Northern Europe, Catholic Action developed and enshrined the praxis-oriented method of see-judge-act.[24] The method itself has its origins in Aristotle and represented another fruit of the Catholic concentration on Thomas and his engagement with classic Greek philosophy.[25] Popularized in the mid-twentieth century by the Belgian priest, later cardinal, Joseph Cardijn for the Young Christian Workers,[26] praxis-based methods moved from the heart of Catholic theological reflection, decisively synthesizing with academic theology to foster a more context-oriented approach.

As always, the two poles of Catholicism, the vertical (the community's relationship to the transcendent through incarnational expression and sacrament, including dimensions of hierarchical and magisterial authority) and the horizontal (the community's relationship to its members, expressed through family, culture, and a lively religious imagination), made up the warp and woof of Catholic praxis, shaping its symbolic universe.[27] While formal theology became knowing about God more than knowing God, spirituality and mysticism naturally remained central to Catholic life and practice, but simply shifted location. This integrated, dialogical reality explains the continuing focus within the Catholic practical theological voice on ecclesiology, liturgy, spirituality, pastoral care, and ethics.

The Second Vatican Council as a Practical Theological "Revolution"

In the era preceding the Second Vatican Council, the ancient practical, creative tension between the horizontality of faith life and the verticality of hierarchical power fueled a particularly dynamic quality. The energy for reform during the postwar decades was real, as was its remarkable retrieval-oriented, "backward" mentality. This countermodern "looking back"-ness suggests a largely premodern communal instinct, one relatively stronger than that found in many other Christian traditions. These dynamics fueled a back-and-forth relationship between reform and preservation, one that would continue its course through the Council and after.

This contrasts with forms of U.S. Protestant practical theology in the 1950s through 1980s, a largely modernist and individualist engagement between pastoral care and psychology, as represented by the work of Anton Boisen, Seward Hiltner, and Charles Gerkin.[28] Even the term *living human document* suggests something natural for mid-twentieth-century Protestant Christianity, particularly in the United States—a text-oriented, individualist approach. Catholic resources for the practical theological conversation came from different sources, arguably pre-text and less individualist, if at times quite absolutist.

These distinctive sources provided strong roots for the Catholic practical theological flowering of the early post–Vatican II period.[29] Such developments did not happen out of thin air or from simple absorption within a larger ecumenical framework, but were grounded from within the Catholic tradition. The intellectual energy behind the movement toward praxis in Catholic theological thinking allowed it to offer major contributions to the new ecumenical conversation in practical theology taking place in the 1970s and 1980s. The long-established focus on the individual turned toward a deeper engagement with theories of action, along with wider social and communal dimensions due in part to the effects of new social movements in church life.

What John XXIII had convened as a distinctively "pastoral" Council[30] could not but be about the relationship between "theory" and "practice." As a result, practical theological concerns, including spirituality, came to be repositioned within the theological enterprise itself.[31] New methods arose out of the turn to the subject and the focus on human experience. Theological reflection and praxis-based reflection entered theological education and became a legitimate direct source for theological development. Shortly after the Council, Karl Rahner, SJ, turned his attention to producing a massive work on "pastoral theology" and concluded that the best term would be *practical* and not *pastoral* theology, precisely to emphasize its praxis-based origins.[32] Nonetheless, many continued to use the term *pastoral* even as they moved beyond the clerical paradigm.

The result was a new focus on the "call to holiness" of all the baptized, along with renewed exploration of the proper relationship between the church and the world. This was not a planned topic but rather emerged on the floor of the council and resulted in the final document of the Council, *Gaudium et spes*, the only constitution given the title "pastoral." This final conciliar document meant to broaden the idea of "pastoral" beyond its traditional association with ordained ministers, thus embracing the call of the entire people of God to witness and so transform the world. All theology was charged with becoming more open and directed to social and cultural realities, and thus more pastoral, turning away from patterns of essentialist, non-historical discourse.[33] Theology embraced biblical, historical, and especially patristic studies, but also contemporary philosophy and the social sciences. Moral theology shifted its attention to a more biblical, dynamic approach, taking up social issues, new medical technologies, and the fundamental question of what it means to practice Christian virtue. Inspired by the Council, newly established bishops' conferences began to engage major cultural, social, and political questions, reflecting the great practical theological energy released by the Council.[34]

DIRECTIONS FOR THE CATHOLIC VOICE IN PRACTICAL THEOLOGY

Praxis in Theological Education

Very little in Catholicism is entirely new, and any attempt to see future directions thus rests on the ability to clearly see roots in the past. This is the case with the praxis methods now solidly established in theological education. Catholic Action's see-judge-act method and liberation theology's social analysis–theological reflection–pastoral planning model, sometimes called the hermeneutic or pastoral circle, was extended by Joe Holland and Peter Henriot, SJ, as "observation, interpretation, and response."[35] Theological reflection was developed for a theological education context by Evelyn and James Whitehead in the late 1970s and later expanded by Patricia Killen and Robert Kinast in the 1980s. Though its sources are far more ancient, this turn in Catholic thinking is reflected in Karl Rahner's turn to experience and Bernard Lonergan's "theological empirical method," as well as David Tracy's revised correlation method.[36] Though they emerged from somewhat separate streams, these developments have an analogue in Paul Tillich's correlation model, which strongly influenced the conversation in Protestant practical theology.

Parallels in these more general theological developments may be drawn with ones in religious education, such as Thomas H. Groome's "shared praxis approach."[37] Building from the heart of the Catholic tradition, including Council documents and the *General Directory of Catechesis*,[38] Groome's method is based on five critical steps: naming present experience, critically reflecting on experience, engaging scripture and tradition, appropriating the faith through dialectical hermeneutics, and deciding how to live. These praxis-based approaches rely heavily on bringing the interpretation of texts to the interpretation of experience, in turn producing insights that renew and guide action. Such methods made a significant contribution to the understanding of theology as a "practical" endeavor in which all the baptized participate.[39] The net effect is to shift the practice of ministry toward enabling and empowering the people of God to claim the faith as their own and let it become a true leaven for change.[40]

By the mid-1960s, many seminary educators were eager to embrace aggiornamento (a "bringing up to date"). Some freestanding seminaries sought affiliations with other academic institutions or merged. They opened curricula and faculty to new areas of study following the lead of the Council, tilting in directions that were practical theological, though this term was not frequently used. By this time, the liturgical and religious education movements were well on their way to producing fully formed disciplines in the wake of the Council. These and other new fields and approaches often found their way into seminary education in one way or another.

The greatest expansion in Catholic theological education at the time, however, was within Catholic universities. Initially geared primarily toward women religious, university summer and other programs expanded, as did diocesan-based ministry training efforts. In such settings,[41] the connection between practice and theory clearly emerged, often initially more as a theology of application, privileging experience in a fresh but naïve sort of way, in part due to the typical institutional separation of these programs from the doctoral degree–granting Departments of Theology that also emerged during this time. The neo-Scholastic underpinnings of Catholic intellectual life readily accommodated the emerging engagement of philosophy and social science.

The first major points of development in practical theology within Catholic circles after the Council occurred in the German-speaking lands and the Netherlands, where conversations were far advanced well before the Council. The first Catholic handbook of practical theology was published in German, by Karl Rahner,[42] followed by various related works, including those of Norbert Mette, Hans-Georg Ziebertz, and Ottmar Fuchs. A chair in pastoral theology was established in 1964 at Nijmegen, and in 1967, thirty smaller Catholic seminaries were fused into five and moved to university campuses, with the Catholic University of Nijmegen (renamed Radboud University Nijmegen in 2004) as one of the privileged locations of Catholic theology in the Netherlands. The Belgian Dominican Edward Schillebeeckx joined the faculty in 1958 and increasingly addressed practical theological–type questions in his writings. The Dutch priest and empirical theological pioneer Johannes A. van der Ven joined the faculty in 1968.[43]

In the United States, new, ecumenical forms of practical theology emerged at the University of Chicago after David Tracy joined the divinity school in 1968. His connection to the European scene and with other international colleagues at the Divinity School influenced many other Catholic practical theologians, most notably the Protestant scholars Don Browning and Rebecca Chopp.

Since the Council, an explosion of information in these areas of ministry has taken place, including the development of professional organizations, conferences, journals, and continuing education for ministers.[44] The Catholic voice in practical theology can also be consciously self-identified within seminaries and universities at undergraduate as well as graduate levels. Within an undergraduate context, the postmodern condition for practicing Catholic faith is explored, contested, and engaged with young adults. Within graduate theology training at Catholic universities, practical questions reside primarily in research on liturgy, spirituality, and ethics. There the work of practical theology goes on, though often without any explicit identification. While relatively few programs explicitly use practical theology as a discipline or curricular heading, increasing numbers identify as practical theologians or actively pursue research agendas with attention to lived religious experience, practice, embodied knowing, and performance. The Catholic voice in practical theology can also be found in the ecumenical conversations that have characterized the field since the 1980s.[45]

Context and Culture

Developments in Catholic practical theology during and immediately after the Council happened quickly. Rahner's student Johann Baptist Metz argued for a starting point other than a theoretical reflection on grace, beginning instead with direct experience: the fact of suffering. This approach can be closely correlated with the beginnings of liberation theology.[46] Such a turn was deeply rooted in the hermeneutic circle and pastoral engagement characteristic of the time. It has further informed much of missiology and the wider intercultural or contextual emphasis, including the theological study of the world church.[47] The rich tradition of the missionary orders and intercultural experiences of all sorts fed this emerging new conversation, culminating in the renewed discussion of evangelization, followed by the New Evangelization.[48]

Catholic theological thinking on cultural and contextual questions developed at a dramatic pace during the immediate post–Vatican II period as a result of major social and cultural shifts globally, including those impelled or opened by the Council itself.[49] In the mid-twentieth century, the twin factors of global depression and world war had led to pent-up religious and institutional energies. Catholic religious life and vocations enjoyed a vertiginous increase from 1945 to 1965, at which point a rapid decline set in, particularly within religious life in the global North. The related growth in missions led to increased intercultural studies, along with practical theological dialogue with missiology in inculturation, language work, anthropology, and other fields.[50]

This led to renewed focus on the lived religiosity of ordinary people, encouraging theologians to drink from their own cultural wells.[51] This changed the purpose of theology, as Gustavo Gutiérrez famously put it, from a concern with engaging the nonbeliever toward addressing the nonperson. The practical implications of a shift from a Catholicism grounded in the North Atlantic to one truly globalized began to be seen, and practical theology grew to reflect this reality.

The face of Catholic ministry rapidly changed in ways consistent with the Council but yet largely unforeseen by it. Diminishing numbers of women religious as well as religious priests and brothers became obvious in many contexts worldwide. Yet such a change reflected the logic of the Council, where a major emphasis was on the universal call to holiness. No longer could anyone misconceive religious life as a superior way to respond to the call to holiness or to ministry. Consecrated life remained critically important within the Catholic tradition, but the Council called attention also to the role of catechists, lay ecclesial ministers, and others.

Such a turn naturally feeds into "ordinary theology,"[52] or the work of Francesco Zaccaria, who explores popular religiosity within the Italian context.[53] The field of empirical theology may be understood as an extended meditation on the intersection of ordinary believers with church, formation, human rights, and related topics tied to ordinary experience.

These developments reflect a deeper claim. Ultimately, revelation and scripture itself fundamentally transcend the text and point toward an event, rather than a parsed relationship between encoded theory and unencoded act. This signifies "interruption," best interpreted in the light of a hermeneutic of space-time engagement rather than a circular set of pure analytical reasoning. Perhaps this is why missiological language is and has been so helpful—it is about a "sending," an "encountering" in time-space—not to mention context and culture, interculturality and interconfessionality. Rather than a linguistic turn or philosophical theology, the most helpful approach might be a hermeneutic of narrative or meme,[54] understood as action or "event." Such missiological concerns, including interest in theologizing from the standpoint of the world church and interculturality, are very much part of Catholic self-reflection today, in part simply because the nature of Catholic demographics has changed so profoundly.

Yet another reality must be addressed. At the precise moment when Catholicism in all its richness and diversity becomes truly global, the practice of the faith seems to be declining and identity splintering. If neo-Scholasticism provided a coherent worldview in modernity, developments in the late twentieth century opened theology and practice up to multiple sources. Theology responds to realities in the world; it cannot create a fortress world to shelter believers.

Case Study: Latino/a Theology in the United States

The practical theological turn within Catholicism today both engages the "mystical-political dimension of the Christian faith" and has reintegrated spirituality into the theological enterprise.[55] One of the best illustrations of this is Latino/a theology in the United States. Its emphasis on popular religiosity is reminiscent of broader shifts within contemporary missiology as is its interdisciplinary focus on cultural and contextual dimensions. Such insights deeply influence the work of U.S. Latino/a theologians who often have relatively more connections to developments in Latin America and the European scene than other U.S. theologians, and who work to theologically engage the reality of a people experiencing poverty, migration, and profound questions of identity.[56]

Their approach has nourished a major body of work engaging questions of popular religious practice as legitimate areas of theological inquiry, starting with Virgilio Elizondo,[57] but also including Orlando Espin,[58] Ada Maria Isasi Diaz, and others.[59] Their work has renewed focus on the *sensus fidei,* the sense the individual believer has of the faith, and the *sensus fidelium,* the community's sense of the faith,[60] which in turn correlates with divergent understandings of change, between those who focus on the dynamic nature of tradition[61] and those who focus on its stability.

Such practical theological concerns are at the heart of U.S. Hispanic/Latino(a) theology, though most who work in this area self-identify as systematic theologians—thus reflecting the identity in which most were formed as well as the power of the discipline at the heart of Catholic theological life.[62] Engaging various forms of embodied and emplaced theologies, seeing material religion as theological expression,[63] points to a critical opportunity for practical theology today.

It also suggests a resource the Catholic voice in practical theology has to offer: bringing the messy, everyday lived spirituality of ordinary people into dialogue with theological theory such as ecclesiology, pneumatology, Christology, ethics, and sacramental theology.[64] As Latino/a theology illustrates, what makes it open rather than closed, able to engage fragment and paradox, is its move from text to event.

CONCLUSION

Given that Catholicism is so intensely practice-laden, practical theology may have sometimes been relatively subterranean or sidelined but it has always been present in some form. Catholic reflection on practice has become readily taken for granted today in part because it has always been part of the tradition. Consistent with the call of the Council and the nature of the times, practical theology has simply been relocated, not created *ex nihilo*. The task of practical theology is not to clarify or systematize doctrine. The question is instead how doctrine and belief are embodied and enacted in a lived faith rather than in the realization of a neat and coherent fit with systematic categories.

Whether or not one begins with experience, the Catholic voice in practical theology insists that knowing God and knowing about God are intrinsically connected functions. The goal is to engage concrete lived realities and the theories embedded in them, as well as theories outside them, to help understand what faith is and how it is lived, in and through practice. Such lived religious practice does not derive ultimately from a logically coherent set of ideas, but rather flows from practice that is always embedded within a varied, complex, and fragmented set of constructions.

Rather than proceeding one "living human document" at a time, the distinctive Catholic voice in practical theology is about entering into an event. As a practice such as *lectio divina* teaches, it is ultimately not about the text but rather the act, the doing, the encounter of God's life and human life intertwined. This raises critical questions for our time, ones very appropriate for the contemporary practical theological conversation. The Catholic voice in practical theology is both more modest and more expansive, not only about examining practices but also offering an approach to the entire theological enterprise, whether the term *practical theology* is used or not. Done well, it offers something to the social sciences as well as other disciplines. The force and configuration of this voice derives from rich and deep traditions of Catholic practice, offering a rich vantage point for other traditions and theological disciplines.

Notes

1. See Aloysius Pieris, SJ, "Vatican II: Glimpses into Six Centuries of Its Prehistory," *East Asian Pastoral Review* 44 (2007): 4.

2. See the *Instrumentum laboris* for the 2012 Synod of Bishops, dedicated to the New Evangelization for the Transmission of Christian Faith.

3. Jose Ignacio Gonzalez Faus, SJ, *Builders of Community: Rethinking Ecclesiastical Ministry* (Miami, FL: Convivium, 2012), 97–125.

4. Regis A. Duffy, OFM, *A Roman Catholic Theology of Pastoral Care* (St. Paul, MN: Fortress Press, 1983), 31–40.

5. See Pieris, "Vatican II," 4. For a Protestant practical theological perspective, see Edward Farley, *Theologia: The Fragmentation and Unity of Theological Education* (Eugene, OR: Wipf & Stock, 2001; 1st ed.: Philadelphia, PA: Fortress Press, 1983).

6. Wolfhart Pannenberg, *Theology and the Philosophy of Science* (Philadelphia, PA: Westminster Press, 1976), 231.

7. Mary Beth Ingham, CSJ, *Rejoicing in the Works of the Lord: Beauty in the Franciscan Tradition* (St. Bonaventure, NY: Franciscan Institute Publications, St. Bonaventure University, 2009), 71. See Gerben Heitink, *Practical Theology: History, Theory, Action Domains*, Studies in Practical Theology (Grand Rapids, MI: William B. Eerdmans Publishing Company, 1999), 107, for a discussion contrasting Thomas Aquinas (*scientia* tradition) and Duns Scotus (*sapientia* tradition).

8. Massimo Faggioli, *Vatican II: The Battle for Meaning* (Mahwah, NJ: Paulist Press, 2012), 76.

9. Gonzalez Faus, *Builders of Community*, 136–39.

10. Heitink puts it as follows: "The term pastoral theology was probably first employed by Peter Canisius. As early as 1591, a book entitled *Enchiridion Theologiae Pastoralis* (Handbook on Pastoral Theology) appeared, written by Peter Binsfeld, the suffragan bishop of Trier." Heitink, *Practical Theology*, 98.

11. Kathleen A. Cahalan, *Formed in the Image of Christ: The Sacramental-Moral Theology of Bernard Häring* (Collegeville, MN: Liturgical Press, 2004), 33–60.

12. See Farley, *Theologia*, 56–57.

13. Heitink, *Practical Theology*, 98.

14. *Pastoral theology* is a term used by Catholics to refer to a curricular category having to do with courses and topics related to pastoral ministry, which is distinct from Protestant usage of *pastoral theology*, which refers to pastoral care. *Practical theology* in the Protestant context generally refers to all ministry studies, following Schleiermacher's encyclopedia.

15. Duffy, *A Roman Catholic Theology of Pastoral Care*, 60–61, based on Norbert Mette, *Theorie der Praxis* (Dusseldorf, Germany: Patmos, 1978), 26–65. See also Rolf Zerfass, "Praktische Theologie als Handlungswissenschraft," in *Praktische Theologie heute*, ed. Ferdinand Klostermann and Rolf Zerfass (Grunewald, Germany: Kaiser, 1974), 164–77; and Norbert Mette, "Praktische Theologie als Handlungswissenschraft," *Diakonia* 10 (1979): 190–203.

16. John Milbank, *Theology and Social Theology: Beyond Secular Reason* (London, UK: Wiley-Blackwell, 2006).

17. Eric Hobsbawm, *The Age of Revolution: Europe, 1789–1848* (New York: Vintage Books, 1962), and *The Age of Extremes: The Short Twentieth Century, 1914–1991* (New York: Pantheon, 1994); John W. O'Malley, SJ, *What Happened at Vatican II?* (Cambridge, MA: Belknap Press of Harvard University Press, 2008); and John W. O'Malley, Joseph A. Komonchak, Stephen Schloesser, and Neil J. Ormerod, *Vatican II: Did Anything Happen?* (Mahwah, NJ: Paulist Press, 2007).

18. Maurice Blondel, *Action: A Critical Essay of Life and the Science of Practice* (Notre Dame, IN: University of Notre Dame Press, 1984 [1893]).

19. For example, in the series Sources Chretiennes in France, as described in Etienne Foulilloux, La Collection "Sources Chretiennes," *Editer les Peres de l'Eglise au XXe siècle* (Paris: Cerf, 1995). See Massimo Faggioli, *True Reform: Liturgy and Ecclesiology in Sacrosanctum Concilium* (Collegeville, MN: Liturgical Press, 2012), 25.

20. See Hans Boersma, *Nouvelle Theologie and Sacramental Ontology: A Return to Mystery* (Oxford, UK: Oxford University Press, 2009).

21. Faggioli, *True Reform*, 19–45.

22. The third phase in the catechetical movement began in the 1960s and 1970s, with an interest in both new methods from new educational sources and the content flowing from Vatican II. It was reflected in new textbooks; the Rite of Christian Initiation of Adults (RCIA) in 1972; and national catechetical directories, such as the U.S. bishops' *Sharing the Light of Faith* in 1977.

23. The Italian expression seems to be the oldest, traced back to a Catholic youth movement in 1867. In 1886 the Association Catholique de la Jeunesse Francaise was founded in France. Ana Maria Bidegain, "From Catholic Action to Liberation Theology: The Historical Process of the Laity in Latin America in the Twentieth Century," *Kellogg Institute Working Paper* 48 (Notre Dame, IN: Kellogg Institute for International Studies, University of Notre Dame, 1985), 3–4, accessed on July 8, 2013, http://kellogg.nd.edu/publications/workingpapers/WPS/048.pdf. Bidegain raises the critical importance of Pius XI's encyclical *Ubi arcano Dei consilio* (1922) and Pius X's earlier *Il fermo proposito* (1905). See Gianfranco Poggi, *Catholic Action in Italy: The Sociology of a Sponsored Organization* (Stanford, CA: Stanford University Press, 1967).

24. It fed Liberation Theology and allied hermeneutical approaches. See Joe Holland and Peter Henriot, *Social Analysis: Linking Faith and Justice* (Maryknoll, NY: Orbis Books, 1983). John XXIII's 1961 encyclical, *Mater et magistra*, enshrined the see-judge-act model at the heart of Catholic social teaching. See also

Bradford E. Hinze, *Practices of Dialogue in the Roman Catholic Church: Aims and Obstacles, Lessons and Laments* (New York: Continuum, 2006), and Helen Cameron et al., *Studying Local Churches: A Handbook* (London, UK: SCM Press, 2005), 23.

25. Joe Holland, "Roots of the Pastoral Circle of Praxis in a Much Older Catholic Social Tradition," in *The Pastoral Circle Revisited: A Critical Quest for Truth and Transformation*, ed. Frans Jozef Servaas Wijsen, Peter Henriot, SJ, and Rodrigo Mejía (New York: Orbis Books, 2005), 1–12.

26. Joe Holland, *Postmodern Catholic Social Teaching* (Washington, DC: The Warwick Institute, 2010), 132.

27. See Lynn Bridgers, "Roman Catholicism," in *The Wiley-Blackwell Companion to Practical Theology*, ed. Bonnie J. Miller McLemore (Oxford, UK: Wiley-Blackwell, 2012), 568.

28. See Anton Boisen, *Religion in Crisis and Custom: A Sociological and Psychological Study* (New York: Harper, 1955); Charles Gerkin, *An Introduction to Pastoral Care* (Nashville, TN: Abingdon Press, 1997); and Seward Hiltner, *Preface to Pastoral Theology* (Nashville, TN: Abingdon Press, 1979).

29. Heinz Schuster's practical theological work and that of his teacher, Karl Rahner, quickly moved beyond a clerical paradigm under the influence of "people of God" theologies.

30. John XXIII issued the apostolic constitution *Humanae salutis*, calling for the council, on December 25, 1961.

31. See James Keenan, *Goodness and Rightness in Thomas Aquinas's Summa Theologiae* (Washington, DC: Georgetown University Press, 1992); Stephen Pope, *The Ethics of Aquinas* (Washington, DC: Georgetown University Press, 2002); Alasdair MacIntyre, *After Virtue: A Study in Moral Theory* (Notre Dame, IN: University of Notre Dame Press, 1984); Alasdair MacIntyre, *Whose Justice? Which Rationality* (Notre Dame, IN: University of Notre Dame Press, 1988).

32. Rahner's student Heinz Schuster may have been the one to introduce the word *practical* in place of *pastoral* theology as early as 1965, the year the Council concluded, in a *Concilium* article.

33. Kathleen A. Cahalan, "Locating Practical Theology in Catholic Theological Discourse and Practice," *International Journal of Practical Theology* 15, no. 1 (2011): 1–21.

34. National Conference of Catholic Bishops, *The Challenge of Peace: God's Promise and Our Response* (Washington, DC: USCC Office of Publishing and Promotion Services, 1983), and National Conference of Catholic Bishops, *Economic Justice for All: Pastoral Letter on Catholic Social Teaching and the U.S. Economy* (Washington, DC: USCC Office of Publishing and Promotion Services, 1986).

35. Holland, "Roots of the Pastoral Circle," 1–12.

36. James D. Whitehead and Evelyn Eaton Whitehead, *Method in Ministry: Theological Reflection and Christian Ministry* (New York: Seabury Press, 1980); Patricia O'Connell Killen, *The Art of Theological Reflection* (New York: Crossroad Publishing, 1994); Robert Kinast, *Let Ministry Teach: A Guide to Theological Reflection* (Collegeville, MN: Liturgical Press, 1996); David Tracy, *Blessed Rage for Order* (New York: Seabury Press, 1975).

37. Thomas H. Groome, *Sharing Faith: A Comprehensive Approach to Religious Education and Pastoral Ministry* (San Francisco, CA: HarperSanFrancisco, 1991).

38. See the Vatican Web site, accessed July 8, 2013, http://www.vatican.va/archive/hist_councils/ii_vatican_council/ for documents of Vatican II; and see the document, accessed July 8, 2013, http://www.vatican.va/roman_curia/congregations/cclergy/documents/rc_con_ccatheduc_doc_17041998_directory-for-catechesis_en.html for the *General Directory for Catechesis*.

39. Paul S. Fiddes, *Participating in God: A Pastoral Doctrine of the Trinity* (Louisville, KY: Westminster John Knox Press, 2000).

40. The Center for Applied Research in the Apostolate (CARA) studies Catholic ministry formation programs that prepare men and women for ministry as priests, deacons, and lay ecclesial ministers. In 2009 CARA reported 46 theologates in the United States that had a combined enrollment of 3,357; 167 dioceses with formation programs for deacons, with a total enrollment of 2,319; 17,538 lay ecclesial ministry candidates were enrolled in 273 lay ecclesial ministry formation programs. Candidates for the priesthood generally receive the Masters of

Divinity degree; deacons enrolled in diocesan formation programs receive a certificate; two-thirds (69 percent) of lay ecclesial ministers are enrolled in certificate programs, about 30 percent in degree programs. Mary L. Gautier, *Catholic Ministry Formation Enrollments: Statistical Overview for 2008–2009* (Washington, DC: Center for Applied Research in the Apostolate, April 2009), 1, 19–20, 25.

41. Especially those schools that were part of the Association of Graduate Programs in Ministry (AGPIM), where the notion of "practical theology" became central to self-understanding and collective definition.

42. See, for example, Karl Rahner's "Practical Theology within the Totality of Theological Disciplines," in *Theological Investigations*, vol. 9 (New York: Herder and Herder, 1972), 101–17.

43. For the history of Nijmegen, consolidation of Catholic seminaries, and the development of a chair in pastoral theology, see Heitink, *Practical Theology*, 74.

44. See Cahalan, "Locating Practical Theology," 9–10.

45. Dana Wright, "The Contemporary Renaissance of Practical Theology in the United States: The Past, Present, and Future of a Discipline in Creative Ferment," *International Journal of Practical Theology* 6, no. 2 (2002): 288–319.

46. "Metz himself has said that he finds in liberation theology the most forceful and thoroughly going application of the insights and intentions of his own 'post-idealist' paradigm." James Matthew Ashley, *Interruptions: Mysticism, Politics, and Theology in the Work of Johann Baptist Metz* (Notre Dame, IN: University of Notre Dame Press, 1998), 189.

47. Massimo Faggioli, *True Reform: Liturgy and Ecclesiology in Sacrosanctum Concilium* (Collegeville, MN: Liturgical Press, 2012), 54. See also Walbert Buhlman, OFM Cap, *The Coming of the Third Church: An Analysis of the Present and Future of the Church* (Maryknoll, NY: Orbis Books, 1977).

48. See Paul VI, *Evangelii nuntiandi* (1975), and John Paul II, *Address to Latin American Bishops' Conference* (1983), respectively. See also United States Conference of Catholic Bishops *Disciples Called to Witness: The New Evangelization*, 2012, http://www.usccb

.org/beliefs-and-teachings/how-we-teach/new-evangelization/upload/Disciples-Called-To-Witness-The-New-Evangelization.pdf.

49. See Melissa Wilde, *Vatican II: A Sociological Analysis of Religious Change* (Princeton, NJ: Princeton University Press, 2007). See especially 126–28.

50. Clemens Sedmak, *Doing Local Theology: A Guide for Artisans of a New Humanity* (Maryknoll, NY: Orbis Books, 2002).

51. Gustavo Gutiérrez, *We Drink from Our Own Wells: The Spiritual Journey of a People* (Maryknoll, NY: Orbis Books, 1984).

52. Jeff Astley, *Ordinary Theology: Looking, Listening, and Learning in Theology*, Explorations in Pastoral, Practical, and Empirical Theology (Aldergate, UK: Ashgate, 2003).

53. Francesco Zaccaria, *Participation and Beliefs in Popular Religiosity* (Leiden, Netherlands: Brill, 2009).

54. Jack Balkin, *Cultural Software: A Theory of Ideology* (New Haven, CT: Yale University Press, 1998).

55. Claude Geffré and Gustavo Gutiérrez, *The Mystical and Political Dimension of the Christian Faith* (New York: Herder and Herder, 1974), 15–16.

56. This represents the turn to *lo cotidiano*, the everyday. For the importance of this insight from Latino theology for practical theology, Bryan Froehle is grateful to the work of Claudia Herrera, a doctoral student in the PhD program in practical theology at St. Thomas University, Miami.

57. For example, see Virgilio Elizondo, *Galilean Journey: The Mexican-American Promise* (Maryknoll, NY: Orbis Books, 2000).

58. Orlando O. Espin, *The Faith of the People: Theological Reflections on Popular Catholicism* (Maryknoll, NY: Orbis Books, 1997); Orlando O. Espin, *Grace and Humanness: Theological Reflections Because of Culture* (Maryknoll, NY: Orbis Books, 2007).

59. Miguel A. De La Torre and Edwin David Aponte, *Introducing Latino/a Theologies* (Maryknoll, NY: Orbis Books, 2001), 118.

60. See Ormond Rush, "*Sensus Fidei*: Faith 'Making Sense' of Revelation," *Theological Studies* 62 (2001): 232.

61. Terrence W. Tilley, *Inventing Catholic Tradition* (Eugene, OR: Wipf & Stock, 2011; 1st ed.: Maryknoll, NY: Orbis Books,

2000); John Thiel, *Senses of Tradition: Continuity and Development in Catholic Faith* (Oxford, UK: Oxford University Press, 2000); and Orlando O. Espin, ed., *Futuring Our Past: Explorations in the Theology of Tradition* (Maryknoll, NY: Orbis Books, 2006).

62. Arguably works like Terrence W. Tilley's *The Disciples' Jesus: Christology as Reconciling Practice* (Maryknoll, NY: Orbis Books, 2008), or Bradford E. Hinze's *Practices of Dialogue in the Roman Catholic Church: Aims and Obstacles, Lessons and Laments* (New York: Continuum, 2006), can be seen as practical theological, even though the authors do not identify their work as such.

63. See Manuel A. Vasquez, *More Than Belief: A Materialist Theory of Religion* (New York: Oxford University Press, 2011).

64. Tom Bamat and Jean-Paul Wiest, *Popular Catholicism in a World Church: Seven Case Studies in Inculturation* (Maryknoll, NY: Orbis Books, 1999).

CHAPTER 3

PRACTICE AS EMBODIED KNOWING

Epistemological and Theological Considerations

COLLEEN M. GRIFFITH

In the absence of paints, a watercolorist cannot work. Minus a bow, a violinist cannot make music. Divorced from the realm of practice, one cannot speak as a practical theologian.

Amid evolution and growth in the discipline of practical theology, a core commitment has emerged that remains constant across divergent methodological lines. It is a commitment to the study and promotion of *practice*. This commitment serves as the melody line that governs all other elements of practical theology. It is a distinguishing hallmark, one that makes rich contributions to theology as a whole. Those who study practice enable us all to reflect more critically on what it is that can be known in practice. Those who view practice as a constitutive dimension of the *content* of Christian faith invite us to look more carefully at how faith is bodily incorporated and enacted in the lives of people.

Despite their formative power, *practices*, like the physical bodies from which they spring, have held a less pronounced role within Christian theology, tending to appear in the shadows and margins of what "counts" formally as theology "properly understood." The origins of this oversight lie in a Western tradition that has tended to hierarchically order mind and body, reason and emotion, and theory and practice. Practices—those intentionally chosen embodied modes of action that engage the culture, religious tradition, community, and self of the practitioner—have too often been relegated to the realm of application, referenced primarily as illustrations and examples of theological or doctrinal principles at work. As a result, the distinctive knowing *in* practice itself has been overlooked. And the access that spiritual practices in particular provide both to a *sensus fidei*, a sense for the faith, embodied in people, and the *sensus fidelium*, the sense of the faithful as a whole, has been insufficiently recognized as well, reflecting shortsightedness as to what practices can reveal that is of benefit to all theologians.

> Practices—those intentionally chosen embodied modes of action that engage the immediate world, culture, religious tradition, community, and self of the practitioner—have too often been relegated to the realm of application, referenced primarily as illustrations and examples of theological or doctrinal principles at work. As a result, the distinctive knowing *in* practice itself has been overlooked.

This essay focuses on the significance of practice and its knowing, and it underscores epistemological and theological contributions that the study of practice yields. It does so from a Catholic Christian standpoint with an eye turned toward spiritual practices in particular. While this is but one corner of the realm of practice explored by practical theologians, it is the realm with which this author is most familiar.

Christian spiritual practices are intentional activities engaged in by Christians who seek a more meaningful and faith-filled way of living in their concrete circumstances. The path of life sought is reflective of God as known in Jesus Christ, and the practices chosen are ones that practitioners sense have the ability to address existential concerns. The whole area of "Christian spiritual practice" is vast,[1] displaying both depth and breadth. Christian practices arise from an array of dominant and less dominant strands of the historic Christian tradition, and possibilities for practice are continually expanding. As "performative expressions,"[2] or bodily enactments that both reflect and construct spiritual identity, Christian spiritual practices provide access to the living faith of persons.

MAKING A CASE FOR PRACTICE

Spiritual practices have long historical roots. Christians have always engaged in practices, the pursuit of which has served to enliven their faith and stimulate more meaningful action in the world. In their ways of living their faith, historic Christians never waited until they had a full set of clear and certain theological ideas or a complete grasp of doctrines before engaging in faith-based practices. They frequently engaged in such practices without any high degree of accompanying theological articulation.[3] Christian faith, as operative in their lives, found bodily lodging and expression through spiritual practices, and their practices stimulated new commitments and knowledge of faith.

In our own time, especially in contemporary modes of theological education, there has been a privileging of intellectual understanding of the faith that has led many to assume that practice follows insight. But for the earliest of Christians, it was the integration of the two, thought *and* practice, that defined the spiritual self.[4] The cumulative effect of certain practices created a certain consciousness. Practice was never understood to be solely the result of theological or doctrinal insight. It was seen as something that itself gave rise to insight and to heightened consciousness.

When studying spiritual practices, one is able to observe palpable human desires and needs. Persons who engage in spiritual practices, traditional and nontraditional, seek cooperation with the movement of God's creative Spirit in addressing specific concerns that they have pertaining to self, the Other, one's community, and the world. They bring their lives to their practices eager to find embodied ways of underscoring hopes, yearnings, and commitments.

Examining practices, one finds not only observable hopes and desires but sociocultural-religious presumptions apparent as well, lively assumptions regarding what faithful response to specific circumstances in particular historical times and places involves, according to the best lights of a particular community of faith. Taking notice of spiritual practices makes it possible to see if, where, and how the needs and capacities of persons are being oriented by a religious community's sacred stories and visions, and to observe what specific aspects of a religious tradition and community life are proving more or less helpful for people. One is able to detect transformational elements emerging in persons too, as a result of the knowing embedded in and born of practice. Practitioners so often come to see their worlds and their potential for agency differently as a result of their practice. The best of practices manages to turn people not only to their present in light of their faith community's past, but also toward a hoped-for future approached with a fresh set of eyes.

Spiritual practices are never static entities and therefore prove particularly rich to study over time. There is dynamic energy in intentional enactments of faith. Modulations in these enactments can occur, even in established practices that have deep roots. As practices are repeated in different periods and places, new words, gestures, images, and accents emerge. Thus practices, like the religious traditions of which they are so often a part, become negotiated and reconstructed over time.[5] Thus, a rich practice like Sabbath-keeping that has traditionally been associated with a day of rest, worship of God, and festivity can begin, in a more ecologically conscious era, to connote and carry the possibility of being a day of simplicity as well, one of voluntary restraint.

One cannot assume that spiritual practices are always and everywhere positive and growth-fostering activities. Perfectly sound practices in one era can become stultifying and oppressive in another. Even practices once deemed "dead sound" may begin to emerge as problematic over time. Craig Dykstra and Dorothy C. Bass observe: "When the concern of practitioners does not reach beyond the self or the cares of a self-absorbed community, Christian practices lose touch with the larger realities within which they are normatively embedded."[6] Thus, the study of practice necessarily involves critical thinking and adjudicating eyes. Practical theologians have to consider the conceptual and moral adequacy of practices and be able to do their thinking about them in dialogue with major tenets of Christian faith.

Christian communities play an essential role in discerning both the life-filled possibilities of practices and the problematic features of them as well. Practices of faith, like core beliefs, stand as essential aspects of the content of faith and deserve wise handling as such. Sadly, the theological enterprise and the magisterial teaching office of the church have paid proportionally more attention to beliefs than to practices. Yet there is a commonly held hope for a "creative and faithful integrity between our beliefs and our practices."[7] As coexisting partners, beliefs and practices serve to shape, fashion, push, and question one another in fruitful ways. Practices and beliefs stand as benchmarks of the spiritual wisdom of the Christian community over time. It is true that ever since the Enlightenment divided theoretical and practical reason, we have leaned toward a hierarchical ordering of these two. But the epistemic privileging of faith claims over faith practices is being questioned today and will be all the less likely to continue if we gain better grasp of the substantive *knowing* that *exists in practice.*

EPISTEMOLOGICAL EXPLORATION OF PRACTICE

The knowing that exists in practice arises from embodied actions, and it is sometimes referred to as "performative knowing."[8] It is a mode of knowing affixed to doing. Donald Schön, author of *Educating the Reflective Practitioner,* describes this knowing as "ordinarily tacit, implicit in our patterns of action and in our feel for that with which we are dealing."[9] This knowing is squarely located *in* intentionally chosen activities.

Participants engaged in practice always "know" more than they can say about what they are doing. The "knowing how" of practice spills wider than any "knowing that." The British philosopher Gilbert Ryle (1900–76), who made the language of "knowing how" and "knowing that" a common currency, describes "knowing how" as "a disposition, but not a single-track disposition like a reflex or a habit." For Ryle, the exercises of "knowing how" are "observances of rules or canons or the application of criteria, but they are not tandem operations of theoretically avowing maxims and then putting them into practice."[10]

In his classic text *The Concept of Mind*, Ryle takes on the intellectualist myth that assumes that "knowing how" is a mere offshoot of "knowing that." He attributes this way of thinking to Cartesian dualism. Standing in strong opposition to any argument rising from a "ghost in the machine" mentality, Ryle makes a case for the "knowing how" of practice in its own right, as its own species of knowing. He refuses to see the knowing in practice as a mere application of considered truths. He writes emphatically: "Intelligent practice is not the step-child of theory. On the contrary, theorizing is one practice amongst others and is intelligently or stupidly conducted."[11] As for any reconstructive work needed with respect to the rules and grammar of a tradition's practices, *engagement in practice*, for Ryle, remains key. He observes: "Efficient practice precedes the theory of it; methodologies presuppose the application of the methods, of the critical investigation of which they are the products."[12] Thus people can engage in religious practices without being able to consider all of the propositions enjoining how they should practice. There are indeed principles inherent in practices, but meaningful practice is not determined by the completeness of one's grasp of these principles. The notion that intelligent practices have to be prefaced by consideration of all pertinent propositions inherent in the practice, in the words of Ryle, simply "rings implausibly."[13] The intelligence of practice cannot be determined by anterior recognition of the full conceptual underpinnings of the practice. This is neither a requirement for practice being formative nor one for practice giving rise to new knowing.

A person who knows very little about Christian traditions and theologies of prayer will probably not be great at the practice of leading prayer. Knowing various traditions of prayer can heighten one's sensitivities and abilities as a leader. But excellence in leading others in prayer is not the same thing as having knowledge of schools and traditions of prayer; nor is it simply the product of this. In the actual practice of leading prayer, a ministerial leader will draw on and learn an array of aptitudes. Her or his "knowing how" is not the same as her or his "knowing that."[14]

A person practicing a preferential option for the poor through a weekly commitment involving the preparing and serving of a meal in a Catholic Worker House may have come into that commitment, at least in part, through exposure to Catholic social teaching. But she or he does not need a full grasp of the principles of Catholic social teaching in order to engage intelligently and meaningfully in this spiritual practice. The practice itself generates a deep bodily knowing of more than the principles found in Catholic social teaching. Such a practice is not a mere illustration of the principles of a religious tradition's social teaching. It stands as a working of this tradition of social justice, an element *of* the tradition.

In addition to encompassing a "knowing how" and a "knowing that," practices are contextually placed and positional. One can expect to find analyzable inscriptions of concrete specific sociocultural commitments and those of one's religious tradition in the actions of practice. These inscriptions are frequently part of the content of spiritual practices, yet the agency of practitioners may resist, outpace, or reconfigure them. One of the most fascinating dimensions of practice is that despite all the inevitable influences of sociocultural-religious inscription, practices frequently move in very fresh directions. They "respond improvisationally to a *situation*" and often with great grace "say or do something well *for a circumstance*."[15]

In his book *Outline of a Theory of Practice*, Pierre Bourdieu (1930–2002), the French sociologist, anthropologist, and philosopher, opts to transcend both an "objectivism" and a "subjectivism" with respect to the knowing in practice. For him, an objectivist stance views practice as the enactment of sociocultural (religious tradition included here) scripts alone; he believes this to be an error. A subjectivist stance, on the other hand, fails to grasp and wrestle sufficiently with the socially constructed dimension of practice and its knowing. Bourdieu steers a middle ground, highlighting strong sociocultural influence on the knowing of practice and making room for the possibility of unpredictability and originality through human agency as well.

A celebrated element in Bourdieu's thought is the notion of *habitus*, which he describes as "systems of durable, transposable *dispositions*, structured structures predisposed to functions as structuring structures."[16] *Habitus* is a referent for acquired ways of thinking and acting that individuals and groups develop in response to absorbed conditions of social structures. Socialization ensues at a bodily level in what is often a preconscious or at least pre-reflexive way. *Habitus* functions as "the residuum of past actions, a deposit of past knowledge and practice, but which is always available as the raw material for creative agency, or 'regulated improvisation.'"[17] While avoiding any suggestion of sociocultural determination of the knowing in practice, Bourdieu acknowledges the very real sociocultural influence on it. At the same time, he grants human agency the ability to know and to create otherwise in relation to sociocultural-religious influence. In his own words, "It is necessary to abandon all theories which explicitly or implicitly treat practice as a mechanical reaction, directly determined by the antecedent conditions and entirely reducible to the mechanical functioning of pre-established assemblies, 'models' or 'roles.'"[18] Thinking further about Bourdieu's *habitus*, the theologian Elaine L. Graham observes: "the conventions of the habitus are often transformed in the very process of its reproduction."[19] Practices can and do give rise to new realms of understanding. And the knowing in practice, which is both socioculturally *and* agentially constituted is, in both respects, a markedly bodily phenomenon.

PRACTICE AS EMBODIED KNOWING

To catch sight of the materiality of religious life, one has to look to practice and to the bodies that make the sensing, knowing, feeling, and doing in practice possible.[20] Is a person's grasp of the Christian religious tradition ever whole without engagement in concrete practices of prayer, asceticism, communal worship and ritual, engagement with the sacraments, works of justice and service, and contemplative awareness of the created order? It is difficult to imagine a faith without religious practices. Yet theologies and institutions do fall prey to what Manuel Vasquez identifies as "a suffocating textualism that approaches religions as symbols, essentially systems of beliefs, narratives, and cosmologies."[21] In so doing, other material dimensions of faith get overlooked, as does the significance of embodied knowing in practice.

One may ably profess the creedal formula "I believe in the forgiveness of sins," but until one participates in something akin to the practice of a communally celebrated sacrament of reconciliation, one is unable to give bodily testimony to the experience of being forgiven. Practices involve bodies and depend on bodily knowing. As Kathleen A. Cahalan asserts, practices are never just "concepts in our minds but rather enacted and inscribed actions that take place in relationship in the world."[22] The body with its physical senses and its felt social sense[23] is the "subject" in practice. As "subject/agent," the body then moves out into the world the far side of practice, potentially transformed by it. In religious practices, one comes face to face with the bodily status of knowing that becomes manifest in situated physicality, engaged senses, expressive postures, gestures, and actions that emanate from and give rise to thought, something that itself remains biologically grounded.[24] Consider, for a moment, the bodily dimensions apparent in the practice of eucharistic liturgy. There is the spatial location of the liturgy, something perceived bodily, and there is the felt sense of the assembled community. There is word, song, lighting, and movement; recitation of common prayers; and a host of bodily postures signaling different moments of the communal celebration. There are processions and exchanges of peace, offerings of cherished elements of bread and wine, and a magnificent invitation to "taste and see" as a community commemorates the givenness of God in bodily form. The body experiences all of this and still there is a surplus to its knowing.

At times, the knowing body can provoke what is an all too static theology. Regarding this provocation of theology, M. Shawn Copeland observes, "The body contests its hypotheses, resists its conclusions, escapes its textual margins."[25] Meanwhile, the body in practice continues to affectively incarnate personal and communal values, and looks beyond the immediate to fuller engagement with others, the world, and God through incorporative grasps of the intentionally enacted actions at hand.

Exploration of the body in practice requires attention to the many dimensions of human bodiliness itself. Such exploration must be able to take into account conscious experiences of physicality in the actions of practice *and* less conscious bodily aspects of practice that operate beneath the level of immediate consciousness. It must consider sociocultural-religious commitments impinging on the actions of participating bodies *and* think too about the sociocultural inscriptions on the bodies performing these actions. Furthermore, it must acknowledge the degrees of choice and agency operative in the differing bodily iterations in practice, noting also the many levels of bodily appropriation that remain options for participants in practice.

In previous writing on a theology of human bodiliness, I have suggested a three-pronged construct of bodiliness that honors these various elements and proves suggestive when thinking about the embodied knowing of practice. The threefold construal of bodiliness I offer is that of body as *vital organism*, as *sociocultural site*, and as the *enactment of consciousness and will*.[26] This trifold description corresponds with what physiologically makes bodily knowing possible, what is socially constructed about it, and what is personally chosen regarding it. These three facets of bodiliness braid together and there is overlap between the strands. Yet each component of this description points in the direction of a significant aspect of the body and its knowing.

The body as *vital organism* includes all of the physiological aspects of being bodily that make practice and the knowing that emerges there possible. Bodies are able to actualize themselves in specific times and spaces because of the living matter of the humanly animate organism. As living matter, the body in practice has a particular situatedness and a spatiality that is preconceptual. Its material presence or standpoint becomes a perspective from which persons engage the world. It forms a live context of self that participates in practice.

The bodily knowing of practice depends on dialectical exchanges with the elements of practice, other bodies, the community, the world, and God. The body's power of perception makes this kind of dialectical exchange possible. Perceptual selves find themselves located in the environments of religious practices in highly tactile, olfactory, auditory, and visual ways.[27] What persons think, feel, or do as they participate in a practice happens as a result of an array of interrelated senses found in the body as animate organism.

A fascinating competency of the body as vital organism is tacit knowing, something clearly operative in religious practice. The structure of tacit knowing, according to Michael Polanyi (1891–1976), the European polymath who first wrote about it, is based on two categories of awareness: focal awareness and subsidiary awareness. When lighting a candle as part of a shared ritual practice, a person is not only aware of the candle but also of the match and of the feeling of one's fingers holding the match and striking it. One's awareness of the candle is focal awareness and the feeling of the match in one's hand is subsidiary awareness. "Tacit knowing"[28] appears in the lively process of attending from subsidiary awareness to focal awareness. It has a "from-to" structure that shows intentionality. Both awarenesses are apparent as one participates in practice, with the body being the crucial element here.[29] Polanyi writes: "Every time that we make sense of the world, we rely on our tacit knowledge of impacts made by the world on our body and the complex responses of our body to these impacts."[30] The knowing in practice presupposes a subsidiary awareness of our bodies.

Examination, then, of the knowing in practice that emanates from the sense of the body as *sociocultural site* begins by looking at specific ways in which religious traditions, societies, and cultures exert influence on the knowing of practice and impinge on the bodies of participants who soak in distinct sociohistorical contexts. Religious institutions, societies, and cultures advise codes for practices and set the boundaries of bodily participation. The intentions brought to the embodied actions of practice get learned largely (though not exclusively) through sociocultural-religious environments. Recall here Pierre Bourdieu, who in describing *habitus* spoke of ways in which "the body ingests and digests and assimilates, physiologically and psychologically,"[31] sociocultural ideals, and does so pre-reflexively. One can expect to find disclosive manifestations of sociocultural-religious commitments in practices themselves and in participants' ways of being bodily engaged. At the same time, transgression of sociocultural-religious norms and commitments will also be seen because the knowing of practice is never entirely socioculturally constituted.

Turning next to the body as the *enactment of consciousness and will*, the third strand of the construct of bodiliness proposed, one observes that persons who engage in spiritual practices hold on to a high degree of freedom with respect to the incarnate identities they present in their chosen practices and the somatic patterns of attention they choose to assume as participants. I may decide to participate in a regular practice of shared scriptural reflection with women inmates at a local prison. I can embrace this practice wholeheartedly or go through the motions of it in a more guarded way. I may bring a listening heart to my participation in this group practice or opt for a less demanding level of focus, one more removed from my immediate life concerns.

Persons also retain right of choice when interpreting the movements and actions of practice. Engaged in scriptural reflection with the inmates, I may view the *lectio divina* approach that we are bringing to our shared scriptural reading as nothing more than one acceptable method for keeping us all on task. Alternatively, I may interpret this element of our practice to be a very evocative set of dynamics that serve to draw so much out of the group. There are choices apparent regarding my appropriation of the knowing in practice as well. I may decide that the insights emerging from our scriptural reflection practice are fine to consider on an intellectual level alone, or I may opt for much fuller appropriation that engages my intellect, emotions, and full self.

Spiritual practices can serve as powerful bodily iterations of deep commitments and hopes of persons and communities, and they can give rise to new knowing that can better orient existential lives. But the agents of practice, the ones with the concrete histories and distinct abilities to incorporate the knowing in practice, must choose to bring consciousness and will to their participation. For the knowing *in* practice to become appropriated in a fuller bodily way, participants have to opt for and will the ways of being that a specific practice highlights. Conscious decision to participate in spiritual practice is a first step toward embodying one's faith more fully. Willed response to the unexpected invitations in practice that point in the direction of wider ways of thinking, loving, and relating can follow, serving to fashion a greater *sensus fidei* in those assembled.

PRACTICES OF FAITH AND THE *SENSUS FIDELIUM*

One catches glimpses of *sensus fidei,* the sense for the faith embodied in people's participation in spiritual practices. Those who practice are predominantly nonelites. The utter numbers and diversity of practices alone render it impossible for practice to be the exclusive sphere of those in ministerial leadership. Persons involved in spiritual practices are, as Dolores Leckey points out, "those at work in the banks and studios, the offices and classrooms and homes."[32] For the vast majority, spiritual practices support the living out of their faith in the world. These are people with the ability to stir up the present in Spirit-led ways, by bringing fresh theological observations and questions to the Christian tradition, observations that have been shaped by spiritual practices.

Catholic tradition gives an honored place to the notion of the *sensus fidelium,* the sense of the faithful as a whole. Orlando Espin describes *sensus fidelium* as "the 'faith-full' *intuition* of Christian people, moved by the Spirit, that senses, adheres to, and interprets the Word of God."[33] For Espin, the living testimony and faith of Christian people as reflected especially in spiritual practices is "as important as the written texts of Tradition."[34] Practice witnesses to what people know and choose to live out regarding their faith. Thus, practices stand as a true *locus theologicus*[35]and are an evocative dimension of the *sensus fidelium.*

> Practices stand as a true *locus theologicus* and are an evocative dimension of the *sensus fidelium.*

The origins of the Catholic claim for *sensus fidelium* lie in the earliest Christians' Easter experience of being accompanied and aided in their understanding of the event by the Spirit of God. Historic Christian writers attest to "a faith endowed with eyes"[36] as the gift of this Spirit, living in the midst of God's people. In the words of the Johannine community, the Spirit is sent in Christ's name to teach, to remind, and to speak anew (John 14:25–26). Addressing the work of the Spirit in the *sensus fidelium*, Ormond Rush writes: "The Holy Spirit is the principle which enables reception of revelation, who animates the church, and who gifts baptized individuals and the whole community with a *sensus fidei*, a sense for the faith enabling them to make sense of the faith."[37] The sense of the faithful in practical terms gets expressed in "the commitment, witness, and worship of Christian individuals and communities as they daily attempt to incarnate the Gospel of Jesus Christ through the power of the Spirit."[38] In embodied practices of faith, the perceptive skills of the organon of *sensus fidelium* thrive.

The study of practice, something previously pushed to the margins, looks forward to firmer footing on theology's research agenda. Debates will undoubtedly continue about how practices should be approached and what adjudicating principles need to be brought to this task. But increased regard for the significance of practice and its epistemological and theological contributions is becoming only the more apparent. "Faith has its eyes." And it has its ears, hands, feet, and heart as well, as evident in the rich practices of contemporary disciples who seek to live the grace of the Spirit who rouses and sustains them.

Notes

1. Throughout this essay, I use the term Christian *spiritual practices* to refer to plural practices of prayer and discernment, practices of justice and care, practices of spiritual growth and ministry. I intend the word *practice* to be conceived by the reader in broad terms, keeping both traditional and nontraditional expressions of it in mind. For a sampling of practices from the Catholic Christian tradition, see Thomas H. Groome and Colleen M. Griffith, eds., *Catholic Spiritual Practices: A Treasury of Old and New* (Brewster, MA: Paraclete Press, 2012).

2. In my use of this specific expression, I am indebted to the work of Elaine L. Graham. See Elaine L. Graham, *Transforming Practice: Pastoral Theology in an Age of Uncertainty* (Eugene, OR: Wipf & Stock, 2002; 1st ed.: London, UK: Mowbray, 1996).

Performativity is an interdisciplinary term, frequently used to describe the ways in which words, gestures, and actions serve to construct identity. It is a term often associated with the work of Judith Butler, a poststructuralist philosopher who considers the construction of gender identity. See Judith Butler, *Gender Trouble* (New York: Routledge, 1990).

3. See Margaret R. Miles, *Practicing Christianity: Critical Perspectives for an Embodied Spirituality* (New York: Crossroad Publishing, 1988).

4. See Miles, *Practicing Christianity*. See also Edward Farley, *Theologia: The Fragmentation and Unity of Theological Education* (Eugene, OR: Wipf & Stock, 2001; 1st ed.: Philadelphia, PA: Fortress Press, 1983).

5. For an excellent discussion of how traditions of thought and practice come to shift over time, see Terrence W. Tilley, *Inventing Catholic Tradition* (Eugene, OR: Wipf & Stock, 2011; 1st ed.: Maryknoll, NY: Orbis Books, 2001).

6. Craig Dykstra and Dorothy C. Bass, "A Theological Understanding of Christian Practices," in *Practicing Theology: Beliefs and Practices in Christian Life*, ed. Miroslav Volf and Dorothy C. Bass (Grand Rapids, MI: William B. Eerdmans Publishing Company, 2001), 29.

7. Amy Plantinga Pauw underscores that this is what we pray for. See Amy Plantinga Pauw, "Attending to the Gaps Between Beliefs and Practices," in *Practicing Theology: Beliefs and Practices in Christian Life*, ed. Miroslav Volf and Dorothy C. Bass (Grand Rapids, MI: William B. Eerdmans Publishing Company, 2001), 45.

8. See Elaine L. Graham, Heather Walton, and Frances Ward, *Theological Reflection: Methods* (London, UK: SCM Press, 2005), 170.

9. Donald A. Schön, *Educating the Reflective Practitioner: Toward a New Design for Teaching and Learning in the Professions* (San Francisco, CA: Jossey-Bass, 1990), 49.

10. Gilbert Ryle, *The Concept of Mind* (Chicago, IL: University of Chicago Press, 2000), 46.

11. Ibid., 26.

12. Ibid., 30.

13. Ibid., 29.

14. Here I am influenced by a parallel example of a surgeon practicing offered by Ryle. See Ryle, *The Concept of Mind*, 49.

15. See here Mary McClintock Fulkerson as she speaks about the "everyday knowledge" of *habitus*. Mary McClintock Fulkerson, *Places of Redemption: Theology for a Worldly Church* (New York: Oxford University Press, 2010 [2007]), 47–48.

16. Pierre Bourdieu, *Outline of a Theory of Practice*, trans. Richard Nice (Cambridge, UK: Cambridge University Press, 1977), 72.

17. Graham, *Transforming Practices*, 102–3.

18. Bourdieu, *Outline of a Theory of Practice*, 73.

19. Graham, *Transforming Practice*, 102.

20. See here Manuel A. Vasquez's materialist theory of religion as articulated in his book *More Than Belief: A Materialist Theory of Religion* (New York: Oxford University Press, 2011).

21. Ibid., 49.

22. Kathleen A. Cahalan, *Introducing the Practice of Ministry* (Collegeville, MN: Liturgical Press, 2010), 108.

23. See Meredith B. McGuire, "Why Bodies Matter: A Sociological Reflection on Spirituality and Materiality," in *Minding the Spirit: The Study of Christian Spirituality*, ed. Elizabeth A. Dreyer and Mark S. Burrows (Baltimore, MD: Johns Hopkins University Press, 2005), 118–34.

24. For a discussion of the bodily basis of thought, see Mark Johnson, *The Body in the Mind* (Chicago, IL: University of Chicago Press, 1990).

25. M. Shawn Copeland, *Enfleshing Freedom: Body, Race, and Being* (Minneapolis, MN: Fortress Press, 2010), 7.

26. See Colleen M. Griffith, "Spirituality and the Body," in *Bodies of Worship: Explorations in Theory and Practice*, ed. Bruce T. Morrill (Collegeville, MN: Liturgical Press, 1999), 67–83.

27. For an in-depth discussion of the role of the body in perception, see Maurice Merleau-Ponty's classic text *Phenomenology of Perception*, trans. Colin Smith (London, UK: Routledge & Kegan Paul, 1962).

28. See Michael Polanyi, *The Tacit Dimension* (Gloucester, MA: Peter Smith, 1983).

29. In my discussion of Polanyi's understanding of tacit knowing, I am indebted to Yu Zhenhua. See Yu Zhenhua, "Embodiment in Polanyi's Theory of Tacit Knowing," *Philosophy Today* 52 (Summer 2008): 126–35.

30. Michael Polanyi, *Knowing and Being* (London, UK: Routledge, 1969), 147–48.

31. This reference gets highlighted in Bonnie J. Miller-McLemore, "Embodied Knowing, Embodied Theology: What Happened to the Body?" *Pastoral Psychology* (January 13, 2013): 1–16, accessed May 1, 2013, http://link.springer.com/article/10.1007/s11089-013-0510-3, DOI 10.1007/s11089-013-0510-3.

32. Dolores R. Leckey, *Laity Stirring the Church: Prophetic Questions* (Philadelphia, PA: Fortress Press, 1987), 13.

33. Orlando O. Espin, *The Faith of the People: Theological Reflections on Popular Catholicism* (Maryknoll, NY: Orbis Books, 1997), 80.

34. Ibid., 65.

35. Ibid., 2.

36. For historical Christian treatment of the existence of an organ for perceiving the faith, see Ormond Rush, *The Eyes of Faith: The Sense of the Faithful and the Church's Reception of Revelation* (Washington, DC: Catholic University of America Press, 2009), 1–4.

37. Ibid., 11.

38. Ibid., 291.

CHAPTER 4

A CORRELATIONAL MODEL OF PRACTICAL THEOLOGY REVISITED

DAVID TRACY

In memory of Don S. Browning

[Originally published in *Religion, Diversity, and Conflict,* ed. Edward Foley (Berlin, Germany: LIT Verlag, 2011)].

INTRODUCTION

At the request of my longtime friend, colleague, and—in matters of practical theology—mentor, Don Browning, I reread my essay on practical theology of some years ago to see where I might stand now in relationship to what I wrote then. I came away with mixed reactions. On the one hand, I affirm now as then the basic correlational model for practical theology, namely,

> Theology is the discipline that articulates mutually critical correlations between the meaning and truth of an interpretation of the contemporary situation. This general notion of theology, moreover, can be further distinguished into three subdisciplines: fundamental theology, systematic theology, and practical theology. The logical spectrum for these subdisciplines is the

> spectrum from the relatively abstract (fundamental theology) to the concrete (practical theology). Each subdiscipline develops public criteria for its claims to meaning and truth. Those criteria also range from the necessary and abstract (transcendental or metaphysical) criteria of fundamental theology through the hermeneutical criteria of truth as disclosure and concealment in systematic theologies to the concrete praxis criteria of truth as personal, social, political, historical and natural transformation and ethical reflection in practical theology. All three subdisciplines are needed to assure the presence of the public character of theology's claims to meaning and truth.[1]

I found my earlier argument sound but, at the same time, too narrow. As emphasized then, practical theology must correlate the Christian tradition and ethics (including the ethical-political and social scientific). If anything, further instructed by liberation, political, and feminist theologies and other theologies focused on justice especially for the oppressed, I hold even more strongly that this ethical-political correlation partner for practical theology is necessary. The horrors of the twentieth century as well as the massive global suffering still overwhelming us in this century make the focus on the ethical-political still central.

The emphasis on the ethical-political in contemporary practical theology continues the prophetic center of Judaism, Christianity, and Islam. At the same time, however, I now wish I had also emphasized in that early article a further need for correlational practical theology: a theological correlation with the aesthetic, the contemplative metaphysical, and the several spiritual traditions of Christianity.

I now wish I had also emphasized in that early article a further need for correlational practical theology: a theological correlation with the aesthetic, the contemplative

metaphysical, and the several spiritual traditions of Christianity.

The principal tasks—complementary to the correlation of practical theology correlated with ethics, politics, and the social sciences—are the correlation of practical theology to art and to explicitly spiritual traditions: both prophetic traditions (akin to ethics and politics) and wisdom and mystical traditions (akin to aesthetics and metaphysics). Indeed, for the ancients as well as for such modern metaphysicians as Alfred North Whitehead, aesthetics and ethics (i.e., the beautiful and the good) are intrinsically related. Ethics, in this ancient and modern reading, is more a teleological ethics of appreciation rather than—as in Immanuel Kant and most moderns—an ethics of obligation.

Whichever way (appreciation or obligation) a particular practical theologian construes ethics, the theologian should also add the correlation with art (thus, aesthetics) to the ethical-political emphasis first encompassed by practical theology as a method of mutual critical correlation. The addition of art, moreover, makes the further addition of wisdom and even mystical traditions of spirituality a natural move to complement the prophetic spiritualities of any practical theological correlation with ethics and politics, therefore emphasizing justice, especially for the downtrodden, marginal, and oppressed throughout the world and within every society.

All ethically and politically focused practical theologies (e.g., liberation, feminist, postcolonial, gay, and political theologies) will emphasize justice, as did many of the major justice-demanding prophets, including Jesus (especially the Lukan Jesus). All aesthetic, metaphysical, wisdom, and mystical theologies will ordinarily emphasize love, more exactly contemplative loving wisdom-in-action as in most Eastern Orthodox theologies. Western Christians, Protestant and Catholic, still have much to learn about the roles of contemplation and of aesthetics in theology, for example, the theology of icons and the theology of liturgy as the Christian practice. Gustavo Gutiérrez is correct: all serious theology should be practical (praxis-determined) as both ethical-political (prophetic) and aesthetic meditative, even mystical. All theology—especially all practical theologies designed for liberation in all forms (personal, social, economic, political, ecclesial)—should be mystical-prophetic or, in terms of correlation partners, ethical-aesthetic. To summarize, in my 1983 article on practical theology, I wrote of the need to correlate practical theology with ethics. Here I wish to add the aesthetic. An aesthetic-ethical correlation should, in turn, aid the further development of mystical-prophetic practical theologies.

ART, AESTHETICS, AND PRACTICAL THEOLOGY

Consider such exemplary modern poets as William Butler Yeats and T. S. Eliot.[2] Yeats wanted to be a William Blake, that is, a modern, deeply spiritual poet driven to express in his poetry an original and singular spiritual vision that could help to heal modern alienation. Yeats respected and learned from Blake's great poetic Christian vision but could not finally share it. Blake's Christianity—even in its strangeness and Gnosticism, which Yeats appreciated far more than many of Blake's fellow Christians did—was not a live spiritual option for Yeats, whose relationship to Christianity was always a distant and troubled, but not antagonistic, one. Yeats learned French symbolism (especially from Stéphane Mallarmé) in Paris. He still remained unsatisfied. He returned to the Ireland he loved and with his great mentor, Lady Gregory, learned the ancient Irish myths and symbols still alive among the rural peoples of Ireland. In the great poetry of his first phase, Yeats articulated a modern version of the ancient Celtic mythic world (as had Arthur Rimbaud with his pride in being a non-Parisian barbarian Celtic "pagan" of northern rural France). Yeats produced great diverse poetry in every era of his life—a rare accomplishment for any poet. Eventually, after the early fine poetry articulating the Celtic traditions, Yeats became spiritually and poetically uneasy anew. He next turned to spiritualism, especially that of the redoubtable Madame Helena Petrovna Blavatsky. He joined the Theosophical Society for eleven years. Thus, the second great stage of Yeats's search for a Blake-like vision occurred in his second great period: poems on the cycles of life, cosmic religion, and hermetic symbols. We can hear Yeats finding himself anew, "turning and turning in the widening gyre," where the falcon cannot hear the falconer. We sense his spiritual power: "what rough beast, its hour come round at last, slouches toward Bethlehem to be born?"

Unlike so many other poets (William Wordsworth or Walt Whitman, for example), Yeats's final poetry is just as strong, though very different from his earlier Celtic and middle hermetic periods. His final vision was a highly personal summation of his lifelong spiritual and poetic journey: amazing poems on Byzantium, on "Crazy Jane among the Bishops," and his "The Tower" poems. At last Yeats finally could rest content and die. Yeats knew that he never reached a Blakean single overwhelming vision, but he discovered that, for his troubled age, perhaps it was more helpful not to be a Blake of a singular, oft-repeated vision but to be the ever-searching Yeats. His final vision was a stunning poetic vision of the spiritual Real as worked out over many years and detours. Most of us are probably more Yeatsian searchers than Blakean or Rimbaudian visionaries. We all rethink, revise, and reformulate. Theologians in modernity also attempt (over a lifetime) ever new forms for articulating what we have learned of the multiform Christian vision and the diverse ways of living both genuinely Christian and authentically modern. Like Augustine before us, we are never fully healed but convalescents trying ever new methods, practices, and theories to forge ever revised practical theology.

There are, of course, many other examples of modern poets restlessly searching as there are modern philosophers and theologians continuously searching for a fuller vision of the Christian vision irretrievably united to a way of life. Most modern poets, like most thinkers and most of us, are not given a single vision of the Real that lasts a lifetime. Rather, we spend a lifetime searching, trying experiment after experiment, always restless, never satisfied, but longing for some aesthetic and spiritual vision of the God as manifested through Jesus Christ in the Spirit as the ultimately Real.

Intellectual historians find that they must, for clarity's sake, speak of the early and late Friedrich Wilhelm Joseph Schelling, the early and late Martin Heidegger, the early and late Karl Barth or Karl Rahner, the early and late T. S. Eliot or William Butler Yeats. Perhaps these restless Yeatsian spiritual types will prove ultimately more helpful to our longings than even the great Blakes and the Rimbauds. One cannot but admire the great visionaries of a single vision: one need not envy them, however, as both Yeats and Eliot discovered. For eminently practical reasons, it is better for all theologians, especially practical theologians, to keep experimenting and enriching the theological vision as well as the modern Christian personal and communal way of life.

As Søren Kierkegaard justly said, all authentic thinking has become in modernity a series of thought-experiments. Indeed, Kierkegaard once observed that if only G.W.F. Hegel had written at the beginning of all his great works "A Thought Experiment" then Kierkegaard too would admit that Hegel was the greatest of modern philosophers. But Hegel, a thinker of totality, could never write such a line. Most of us now find in Hegel fragments of a former totality system. Hegel's vision of totality now seems more like a Giovanni Battista Piranesi–like vision of multiple fragments of stunning beauty and power: the totality is no more. Whoever enters Hegel's *Phenomenology* begins to fear, as Michel Foucault nicely observed, that a smiling Hegel may be waiting for us at the end of our particular journey. For Hegel's extraordinary mind may have already thought our "new" way out. He may have closed that escape-route too in his system—the greatest and most tempting totality-system of modern thought.

As Karl Barth said, Hegel is the greatest attempt and the greatest temptation. Karl Rahner wrote, almost enviously, of the "mad and secret dream of Hegel." We are now all thinkers of infinity, not totality (Emmanuel Levinas). We are now all holders of the fragments of all our traditions trying to discern which fragments can be burst open to the vision of the Infinite God we moderns yearn for.

All thought-experiments help us because they remind us that even the great religious visions responsive to our longings are, for most of us, now aesthetic, metaphysical, and contemplative-mystical fragments. All these artistic and spiritual fragments from the highly rich and pluralistic Christian tradition as well as other cultural and religious traditions (Zen *haiku,* Noh theater, African masks, Native American rituals, ancient temples, etc.) may, in fact, burst open as frag events manifesting healing, artistic, religious, metaphysical, and mystical visions of the Real to correlate with a Christian vision and way of life.

Practical theologians are best placed in theology to recover and help others recover the great artistic, metaphysical, and mystical fragments: above all, in the diverse Christian traditions (icons, Michelangelo, Rembrandt, Johann Sebastian Bach, Antonio Vivaldi, Dante Alighieri, John Milton, slave narratives, gospel songs, folk tales, Federico Fellini, Ingmar Bergman, Robert Bresson, Martin Scorcese). Practical theologians are best trained to help people discern the significant moments that occur in each human life that manifest the directions of our lives.

All of us have experienced in everyday life our own revelatory events, our own happenings, our own manifestations, visions, and gifts. Most human beings, at one time or another, are engifted to fall in love with another person. Notice the language we are driven to use here: we "fall" in love, we do not achieve it; we "are" in love, we do not "have" a person's love. When we are in love, reality seems clearer, cleaner, and more hopeful.

At the very same time that love empowers an ever increasing and disclosive clarity, the beloved seems ever more mysterious. Love, like theology, is both cataphatic and apophatic—ever greater understanding, ever greater mystery. Dante needed the particular person Beatrice to learn how human love also discloses Christian love. In *Paradiso,* Dante—ever more aware of Beatrice's person—knew that she remained a mystery in herself and as manifesting God as "the ever-greater" mystery to all mystics, the ever-greater God. The famous last line of *Paradiso* speaks the Christian truth: *L'amor che muove il sole e l'altre stelle.*[3]

We non-prophets, non-mystics, and non-saints can learn from the texts and lives of these exceptional ones: the prophets, witnesses, saints, and mystics. As William James observed, the mystics cognitively suggest to the rest of us (i.e., those who do not share their overwhelming visions of God) this much: "something more" may well be more the case than what we presently think possible. James, who insisted that he never experienced the kinds of positive experiences that he read in the texts of the mystics (including those of his Swedenborgian father), nevertheless found mystical texts illuminating that "something more" available to any open, sensitive seeker. James, as a psychologist and philosopher of consciousness, found that most of us are in touch, through our great gift of reason, with only a part (perhaps even only a minor part) of the full range and depth of consciousness. Perhaps the mystics and prophets were in touch with and expressed in thought and action that "something more." Their texts and the stories of their actions are fully practical resources for practical theologians to read and employ.

The excessive realities of desire and love, the wonder of a seemingly impossible "forgiveness" or reconciliation (South Africa), the reality of such "saturated" phenomena as the gift that breaks through the usual economy of return: all these often forgotten or even repressed phenomena—forgiveness, gift, frag event, love, excess of the good in many lives (not only those officially called "saints" or "witnesses" or the "elect" or the "just")—are the phenomena needing close study in practical theology. There are good, even "godly," persons who exist in every congregation, every particular setting of practical theology: "attention must be paid" to such persons (*Death of a Salesman*). The practical theologian is the one to whom we rightly turn to help us discern these phenomena: ethically-politically, psychologically, aesthetically, and spiritually. The more practical theologians learn to reverence and love art, to discern the spiritual realities still alive in our traditions, cultures, and ordinary lives, the more concretely practical will theology prove to be.

In some scientists, the same sense of the manifestation of the Real emerges. Albert Einstein was alienated from the revelation of the personal God of his Jewish tradition. Yet it was Einstein who articulated two spiritual realities for the modern scientific mind: first, the fact that the universe is comprehensible is the most incomprehensible thing about it; second, that in the tradition of his spiritual and metaphysical mentor (Baruch Spinoza), this comprehensibility cannot but suggest an impersonal God. For Einstein, like James, intelligible reality itself suggests "something more." Perhaps all these frag events in our traditions as in our lives and thinking suggest not only "something more" but what Eliot brilliantly named "hints and guesses."

What for the Eliot of *The Waste Land* was only "fragments I have shored against my ruins" became for the later Eliot of the *Four Quartets* frag events of "Hints followed by guesses....The hint half guessed, the gift half understood, is Incarnation" (Third Quartet).

Like Yeats, Eliot too longed for an overwhelming singular poetic-spiritual vision: not one like Blake's, but one more like Dante's more catholic and Catholic vision. In his own life, Eliot had experienced—in the terrible history of the twentieth century and in his own tortured personal life—his *Inferno* and his *Purgatorio*. As some Eliot scholars suggest, Eliot waited after completing the Third Quartet in hopes that he too, like his mentor Dante, might now experience some glimpse of *Paradiso*. He knew, as Dante did, that he could not merit such a glimpse. It must be pure grace. Eliot hoped, however, that perhaps God would grant his prayer for a glimpse of *Paradiso*. It was not to be. Eliot realized that Dante's manifestation of the Real as love would not come to him save as the healing, manifesting realities available in a pluralistic and secular age so different from Dante's more unified Christian culture. At the end, Eliot admitted this and contented himself, as do so many of us, with "hints followed by guesses." He found his own post-Dante gifts and manifestations—perhaps the only ones available to us moderns; they were and are enough. Indeed, for Eliot, these "hints and guesses" even led him to "the hint half-guessed, the gift half-understood...Incarnation" (Third Quartet).

All these fragments give hope: the hope, above all, that if we learn to listen to these hints and use our best reason to understand them (as in all good practical theology) we may yet sense a way to help ourselves and our contemporaries to name God again in our everyday lives aided by the concrete "hints and guesses" all around us and present with great clarity in the great works of art.

THE RETURN OF SPIRITUAL EXERCISES IN PRACTICAL THEOLOGY

A major difficulty for modern Westerners in reading the texts of the ancient and medieval philosophers and theologians in Western cultures as well as the texts of other great cultures—for example, not only classical but also contemporary Buddhist texts in East Asian, South Asian, and now Western forms—is the habitual belief of modern Western philosophers and even some theologians that theory should be separate from practices, especially practices as specific as what an ancient thinker meant by the phrase "spiritual exercises." The ancients and the monastic medieval schools as well as the great Reformed theologians would have found a separation of theory and practical exercises not merely strange but self-destructive for true philosophy or theology. For the ancients, philosophy was, above all, a love of wisdom, a unity of thought, and a way of life. Philosophy and theology were eminently practical: theory in the practical service of helping one discern the good life and to live it. For the ancients, the philosopher-theologian was unclassifiable in ordinary life. The unclassifiable character of the philosopher-theologian determined, as Pierre Hadot maintains, all the major schools (Aristotelianism, Stoicism, Epicureanism, Platonism) and the two major philosophic movements (skepticism and cynicism) of the entire Hellenistic period from the third century BCE (when the "sorting out" of the schools as schools occurred) to the third century CE (when the classic neo-Platonist synthesis of Aristotelian and Stoic schools with Platonism was achieved).

Each school maintained itself (and its fidelity to its founding sage) by a specific training in intellectual and spiritual exercises. Each school possessed its ideal of wisdom and corresponding fundamental attitude or orientation. These orientations, of course, differed depending on the ideal itself: for example, a tensive attentiveness for the Stoics or a relaxation or letting-go for the Epicureans. Above all, every school employed exercises to aid the progressive development of its philosophical proponents to the ideal state of wisdom. At that ideal state, the transcendent norm of reason ultimately coincides with what functions as God or the Good or the One. Christian theologians of the period also directed their theologies to the theoretical practical task of living a good Christian life (e.g., Augustine as well as all great Cappadocians—Basil, Macrina, Gregory of Nyssa, and Gregory of Nazianzen).

Such practical spiritual "exercises" were understood by all the ancient schools as analogous to the exercises employed by an athlete for the body, as well as analogous to the application of a medical cure. In contemporary post-Freudian culture, one could expand the analogy to the exercises needed to appropriate one's feelings in therapy and pastoral counseling. Among the ancients, such exercises included intellectual exercises: recall the use of mathematics to help the exercitant to move from the realm of the sensible to the realm of intelligible in Pythagoras and Plato. These exercises also encompassed more obviously spiritual exercises, including the use of images, memory training, and reflection on the basic doctrines or beliefs of the school, as well as exercises of increasing one's attentiveness to the implications of those beliefs for life and thought. Through all such exercises, the exercitant can clarify her or his relationship to the ultimate norm, for example, a Stoic's exercise of attention to one's personal relationship in one's own *logos* to the *Logos* pervading the entire cosmos. The Christian theologian's efforts are in the same direction: to understand God and all other realities, theoretical and practical, as they relate to God. In sum, all reflection among the ancients on the relationship between theory and practice must be understood from the perspective of such practical spiritual exercises, especially but not solely meditation. Even on the very limited basis of this summary of Hadot's analysis of ancient "spiritual exercises" and ancient theory, it is clear that contemporary practical theology explicitly and brilliantly corresponds to the ancient insistence on the role of practical exercises for personal and communal living.

In practical theology, we may also recall the ethical, metaphysical, and spiritual import of our most quotidian practices. For example, our ordinary human interactions are often our best opportunity both for self-delusion and for spotting those self-delusions as we feel—through the very attractions and confusions of our interaction with others—the magnetic pull of God. A second example: erotic love can wrench us from our usual self-interest to face some other reality as authentically other. A third example, as we argued above in the second section: art can, at times, free us to consider the possibility, as Iris Murdoch nicely says, of

> a pure transcendent value, a steady visible enduring higher good, [that] perhaps provides for many people, in an unreligious age without prayer or sacraments, their clearest *experience* of something grasped as separate and precious and beneficial and held quietly and unpossessively in the attention. Good art which we love can seem holy, and attending to it can be like praying. Our relation to such art though "probably never" entirely pure is markedly unselfish.[4]

As the ancients insisted, many intellectual practices are also spiritual practices. Mathematics and dialectics direct our attention out of ourselves by their demand that we acknowledge, by intellectually entering a world of pure intelligibility. Indeed, learning anything really well—any genuine painstaking work of scholarship, any careful attention to learning another language well, any organization of a group project—takes us immediately out of ourselves to a different kind of call and demand.[5] That call is to a sense of objectivity as our paying virtuous attention to particular realities outside ourselves: a call to the Other as other. Moreover, as Simone Weil suggests, explicitly spiritual exercises are available to anyone, not only to intellectual elites. Above all, practical theologians can help persons to cultivate moments of tact, silence, and attentiveness to the world outside ourselves as ways of decreasing our natural egoism. We can learn to pay attention to nature. Such careful attentiveness to nature can help exhibit the futility of selfish purposes—one of the noble purposes of practical theology.

My hope here for the reunion of thought and spiritual exercises is not focused on a Kantian abrupt call for the will to abide by duty nor on a Kierkegaardian leap of faith as a sudden radical transformation or conversion of the self from evil to good. Instead, my hope is more modest and more practical: a slow shift of our attachments, a painstaking education of desire—education in theory and practical spiritual exercises like that which Plato foresaw as our best hope for both living and thinking well. Metaphysics and aesthetics serve not only an intellectual but also a spiritual purpose: another great barrier against our natural egoism.

The spiritual exercises now available to practical theologies, therefore, include not only the diverse traditions of Christian spirituality but also the great works of art and the many practices of the good in the ordinary lives of Christians. The very ordinariness of spiritual practices shows that such practices already active (if often too little reflected on as spiritual practices) can free practical theologians to continue to be in the vanguard of the many attempts by Christians to reconnect theology with spirituality.

SPIRITUALITY AND PRACTICAL THEOLOGY

The spiritual situation of our age is marked by an increasingly globalized acknowledgment of double spiritual pluralism: first, the diverse kinds of spirituality at work in both explicitly religious and secular forms; second, the intensely pluralistic character of each major religious tradition. Let me offer some examples. First, the academic work of Gershom Scholem has greatly enhanced the acknowledgment of the mystical-kabbalistic aspect of the "ethical monotheism" of rabbinic Judaism. Second, a profound commitment across Christianity has recovered the many forms of spirituality and theology, especially those forms highlighted by feminist and liberation theologians as prophetic-mystical. Finally, the most developed religious case of uniting spirituality and public, practical theology is neo-Confucianism—an outstanding example of an explicit, systematic, and even institutionalized attempt to integrate the three classical religious traditions of China: the practical, ethical-political tradition of classical Confucianism integrated with the more mystical and metaphysical-meditative traditions of Taoism and Chan Buddhism. The large number of interreligious dialogues suggests the reemergence of a call for each religious tradition as well as each theological tradition to recover the full range of the rich classical traditions of spirituality.

More and more secular persons in Western societies can be heard repeating the refrain (almost by now a cliché) "I am not religious" (shorthand for I am not a practicing member of any institutionalized form of religion), "but I am spiritual." Such declarations should be honored by all theologians and churches as, among other matters, a clear call from the hearts of "secular" seekers for guidance for some vision and way of life beyond secularity. There is, to be sure, always a danger in our consumerist and individualistic modern Western societies that "spiritualities" can become new consumer-goods, new divertissements without ethical and religious demands toward others and the Other.

That is a danger but not a necessity. Sometimes the great works of art are not allowed to challenge one (recall Rainer Maria Rilke on his first viewing the *Apollo Belvedere*: "I must change my life") but only provide a new frisson of purely private experience. So too the plethora of "spiritualities" may not challenge but only fascinate for a moment: some rather thin, at times even trivializing spiritualities (e.g., the hollow domesticated "angels" of recent vintage) or vulgarizing uses of some great religious ways. Sometimes, with all the "spiritualities" and third-rate works of art crowding contemporary consciousness, Eliot's *cri de coeur* begins to seem prophetic: art has become today an *ersatz* religion—and so has religion.

A more judicious view would say that sometimes Eliot's words are disturbingly true, at other times, however, profoundly false. In fact, the rediscovery of the classical traditions of spirituality by theologians, especially practical theologians, is liberating. Through the rich and exponentially expanding scholarship of the history of Christian spiritualities, each theologian now has the possibility to learn more deeply the depth and plurality of her own Christian spiritual tradition. For example, Martin Luther's spirituality, thanks to Finnish scholarship, now includes Luther's spirituality of *unio Christi* and even several (thirty-seven to be exact) references to deification in his sermons. A second example: John Calvin's own profound spirituality is related to early modern Christian humanist spiritualities as well as to Bernard of Clairvaux and several patristic writers. A third example: medieval Christian theology is no longer considered by scholars as concentrated only in the Scholastics—wherein theology moved to the universities and began to distinguish between academic theology and personal spirituality but not separate them (Thomas Aquinas and Bonaventure)—as different from the late medieval nominalist theology wherein a separation of theology and spirituality occurred with deeply unfortunate consequences. Besides Scholastic theologies there are two forms of medieval theology wherein theology and spirituality are integrated: twelfth-century monastic theology and mystical theologies, especially of many forgotten (or repressed) medieval and early modern women mystics. As all these contemporary scholarly retrievals testify, theology without spirituality becomes increasingly empty of spiritual substance; without strong fundamental, systematic, and practical theology, spirituality can drift off into sentimental and unfocused individualistic piety.

Even after the reunion of theology and spirituality by the Reformers, new orthodox confessional theologies largely divorced from spirituality returned in rationalist neo-Scholastic theologies. These led inevitably to the usually marginalized Pietist revolts in Protestant cultures and the similar marginalization of those named "mystics" in Catholic culture. Michel de Certeau has argued how in seventeenth-century France the word *mystique* ceased being a normal adjective for traditional spiritual readings of the scriptures and became a noun for those persons and groups (e.g., Quietists) considered excessively spiritual.

As the scholarship of our own day has made clear (e.g., Bernard McGinn's five-volume work in the history of Western Christian mysticism), mysticism is simply a depth awareness of the presence of God to one's consciousness: mysticism is not about "visions," "hallucinations," or "stigmata," although such may occur. Mystics like Meister Eckhart and John of the Cross were, in fact, deeply suspicious of such "visions." The mystical texts and lives are resources for all Christians, especially practical theologians. All Christians can possess some mystical consciousness. Through "prayer, observance, discipline, thought and action" (Third Quartet), every Christian can become more aware of the presence of God in daily life. All observant Muslims (not only Sufi mystics), for example, call God's presence to mind by their disciplined prayers to Allah five times a day, methodically recalling God's presence through daily prayer. This common Muslim practice is a spiritual practice eminently worthy of becoming incorporated in Christian forms for every practicing Christian.

The deeply practical and contextual nature of contemporary

theologies like liberation, feminist, and contextual theologies is enriching the attempted reunion of spirituality and theology in our day. Feminist theologies, among other contributions, have helped Christians understand how gendered all Christian spiritual practice is. At times even central Christian spiritual ideals (e.g., love as self-sacrifice) can become, unless reflected on critically, a gendered unloving and unjust (and therefore unChristian) ideological imposition trying to reinforce stereotypical female roles of "self-sacrifice" as a cruel caricature of the common, noble Christian call to authentic Christian love. Moreover, liberation theologies have aided us all (including the elites of academic theology) by enacting liberationist theologies throughout the world. Indeed, more and more formerly marginalized Christian communities (especially communities of the poor) now discover, describe, and live new Christian practical theologies and spiritualities. These theologies should find mutually critical correlation with the classical traditions of Christian spirituality.

Art and spirituality should join ethics, politics, and social science as conversation partners for all forms of theology, especially for the apex of all theology: contemporary practical theologies.

Notes

1. Don S. Browning, ed., *Practical Theology: The Emerging Field in Theology, Church, and World* (San Francisco, CA: Harper & Row, 1983), 62–63.

2. See T. S. Eliot, *The Complete Poems and Plays* (New York: Harcourt, Brace and Company, 1950); and William Butler Yeats, *The Poems: A New Edition*, ed. Richard J. Finneran (New York: Macmillan, 1983).

3. English translation: "The love that moves the sun and the other stars."

4. Iris Murdoch, *The Fire and the Sun: Why Plato Banished the Artists* (Oxford, UK: Clarendon Press, 1977), 76–77.

5. See Iris Murdoch, *Metaphysics as a Guide to Morals: Writings on Philosophy and Literature* (New York: Viking Press, 1992).

PART II

PRACTICES, CONTEXTS, AND CONVERSATIONS

CHAPTER 5

PRACTICING THE FAITH

Tradition in a Practical Theology

TERRENCE W. TILLEY

What is the place of tradition in practical theology? How are practices important for understanding tradition? Theologians from diverse contexts and religious communities must address these sorts of questions. Such questions are highly significant for Catholic practical theology because of the centrality of tradition in Catholic faith.

> This essay construes a "tradition" as a practice or set of practices. As this approach assumes that *practices* are seen as the context in which theory arises, so practical theology is construed as the context in which systematic theology arises.

This essay summarizes and extends a line of investigation articulated in *Inventing Catholic Tradition* (2000). It construes a "tradition" as a practice or set of practices. As this approach assumes that *practices* are seen as the context in which theory arises, so practical theology is construed as the context in which systematic theology arises. This reversal of most modern approaches, characteristic of American post-liberal theology, practical theology, and some liberation theology, opens up a new way to think of tradition.[1] While this approach is indebted to postliberal theology, it is more rooted in practical theology. Robert J. Schreiter, CPPS, describes practical theology as follows: "Rather than moving from faith to life (theory to practice), it moves from life to faith and then back to life....Practical theology begins, therefore, by describing the situation of the congregation and then correlates that situation with the faith and the beliefs of the congregation. From there, practical theology moves back to the life of the congregation to a refocused practice."[2]

We practice our faith; faith is lived. Traditions, then, are enduring, complex, communal practices with rules that shape the participants' practice of the faith. Traditions shape persons, and persons reshape traditions in the way they receive and enact them. Faith traditions are thus neither fixed nor given, but invented and reinvented by those who practice their faith from generation to generation. "Invention" does not imply that we build traditions *ex nihilo*, but that we creatively use in the present the materials we mine from the past.[3]

The concept of tradition is what philosopher W. B. Gallie has identified as an essentially contested concept. It means that there is substantial, longstanding, ineradicable disagreement about what constitutes a tradition. Clearly, since the Reformation of the sixteenth century, Protestants and Catholics have not only disagreed about the use and the normativity of tradition, but have also disagreed about what tradition is.[4] The Orthodox and the Western churches also have different concepts of tradition, with theologians of the former often writing of "Holy Tradition" and using tradition as a norm in a way significantly different from the Western churches.

Many Catholics conceptualize their faith-tradition as an unchangeable body of beliefs. The magisterium, for example, often seems to take the Catholic tradition as the set of beliefs explicated in the *Catechism of the Catholic Church*. Tradition is imagined as a weighty tome that is passed unchanged from one generation to the next or a folded cloak that the magisterium unfolds over time.[5] This common belief preserves the centrality of the *tradita*, the contents of tradition. But it so seriously underplays the practice of *traditio*—handing on the faith—that many problems, both historical and theoretical, arise. To treat tradition as merely *tradita* reveals a lack of understanding of the history of Christianity, the teaching of the Catholic Church in the Second Vatican Council, and communication theory.[6]

Traditio is the practice of handing on "how to" practice the faith. The *tradita* communicated may change in the processes of *traditio*, of "transmission" and "reception."[7] A living tradition is not static. In order to live it must change. As Blessed John Henry Cardinal Newman wrote in the *Essay on the Development of Christian Doctrine*, "In a higher world it is otherwise, but here below to live is to change, and to be perfect is to have changed often."[8] A tradition lives in practitioners living in and living out—practicing—the faith in different times and places.

PRACTICES

The term *practice* has become a technical term in contemporary philosophy and theology. Contemporary theories of practice differ on what practices are and what is significant about them.[9] This essay develops an account influenced by Alasdair MacIntyre and James Wm. McClendon Jr., which effectively illumines the role of practices in practical theology. Here a practice is understood as a pattern of activity that employs specific *means* to reach an *end* or *goal* and requires participants' intentional participation following the *rules* of the practice. Practitioners typically have a *shared vision* about the point of the practice and *dispositions* (both beliefs and attitudes) appropriate for participants in that practice. A religious tradition, then, is an enduring practice or set of linked practices that constitutes practicing the faith.[10] One terminological problem needs to be addressed. Some theologians disdain the term *practice* and instead use *praxis*. Some think *practice* just means following a rule blindly. Some think *practice* merely means repetition (and not all practices require repetition). As we will see below, following a rule is a complex component of a practice—at least as *practice* is understood here. As Roberto S. Goizueta notes in his contribution to this volume (p. 149), *praxis* may not have a clear goal, but *practice* as defined here usually does. So *practice* as used here is a kind of *praxis* or a variant form of *praxis*—a pattern of activity with an envisioned goal internal to the practice.

To begin understanding practices, consider a ritual practice. In participating in the celebration of the Eucharist, for instance, participants have a shared vision of the means and goals of practice (worshiping God), engage in prescribed patterns of action guided by rubrics, and have dispositions to believe (in the Real Presence, for example) and to feel (gratitude, trust) appropriate for the practice. The elements of such practices are so woven together that they can be distinguished analytically but not separated practically.

Specific beliefs can function as presumptions of or rules for practices. One example is Catholic belief in the Real Presence. Such a belief shapes the properly devout Catholic's attitudes and behavior not only toward the Eucharist and the way the eucharistic elements are to be handled in a ritual setting, but also toward oneself as a participant in the ritual. The ritual behavior shapes beliefs and attitudes, as when during the Mass the presider engages in gestures highlighting the consecration of the bread and wine. These actions shape a reverential attitude and reinforce belief in the Real Presence. The participants' attitudes reflect their beliefs. Proper beliefs, attitudes, and actions are necessary for proper participation in a ritual practice.[11]

Practices are conditioned by their history and their context. For example, practitioners' status functions may change over time. After the deaths of the apostles, no one could have that status—a hierarchical leadership of successors of the apostles eventually emerged. After the declaration of papal infallibility, the pope acquired a certain status when performing specific acts in the practice of promulgating doctrine.[12] After the invention of oral contraceptives, a practice of resistance to so-called traditional teaching on birth control became widespread among faithful Catholics—a new status of "faithful dissenters" emerged. And the argument about women's ordination to the priesthood is finally about whether only men can have the status function of presider in the ritual practice we call the Eucharist.

Behaviors may change over time. One behaves differently as one approaches the eucharistic table today from the ways one approached the altar rail a century ago. Behaviors alone do not constitute practices.[13] Religious traditions have been helpfully understood as "cultural-symbolic systems,"[14] "discourse practices,"[15] and "semiotic systems"[16] in which semantic, syntactic, and pragmatic components are interrelated. These approaches to religious traditions have in common the claim that religious traditions are a nexus of practices; they focus on the ways religious beliefs acquire meaning in the context of shared religious practices. What these analyses show in various ways is that because there are such tight connections between actions, beliefs, and attitudes in a tradition, one cannot understand beliefs without understanding the actions and attitudes with which they are linked in a practice.[17]

The expressions of belief change as well. Our everyday language provides the vocabulary for articulating our beliefs. Our ambient cultures condition our religious practices as well. We cannot engage in a religious practice in a way that is "free from contemporary signifying practices" of our culture.[18] This means that no verbal formula, no *tradita,* no matter how cherished, can either guarantee identity of belief from one time and place to another or exclude confusion about the meaning of a belief when it is proclaimed in a new context.[19] For example, after 1700, the term *natura* and its cognates, such as *nature,* changed meaning substantially. What had been ordinarily understood as a normative philosophical universal term (*nature,* as in *animal nature*) became understood as a descriptive indicator of what science investigates (*nature*). The Baconian revolution changed the common meaning of the term.[20] Hence, the meaning of the christological formula that Jesus Christ was "one person with two natures" is an expression that no longer clearly communicates in the modern era what it had communicated in patristic times. Linguistic identity over time does not guarantee identity of meaning over time.

I may know *what* the "goal" of participating in a practice is, but if I do not know *how to* engage in the practice, then I cannot really understand the point of the practice. It may be hard for Christians, for instance, to hope for heaven in a culture wherein immediate gratification is the norm. To "believe in" heaven and "hope for" eternal life requires participating in a practice or practices that are *not* immediately gratifying, but that will shape one into a person worthy of heaven.[21] The "means" are knowing how to engage in those patterns of actions and attitudes that carry the vision. Mere "knowing that" or mere notional belief will not do; we must learn how to believe, sometimes despite our cultural mores, or our practices that have a heavenly goal will die.

If we understand that practicing the faith is living in and living out a tradition, what do we gain? First, we can understand the meaning of a belief by understanding how it is used, how it fits within a practice. As beliefs can fit in multiple ways in multiple practices, disagreement about what beliefs mean may be resolved by seeing how they fit in our practices. Second, we can see how one becomes a Christian. Practices shape persons and reshape them, their beliefs, and their attitudes. To become a Christian (or an architect) requires learning the disciplines or practices that constitute Christianity (or architecture) and becoming, in certain ways, a new person. Of course, the practice of Christianity and the practice of architecture in the twenty-first century are radically different from those in the first century. The problem is not to notice their diversity, but to find their practical constancies.[22] Third, a practical theology of tradition can account for change. As contexts change practices change. When people carry old practices into new places, the practices are changed in the process of transmission. As new skills are developed, the education of a practitioner may also well change, as surgeons had a lot to learn (and unlearn) after the introduction of asepsis and anesthesia. Changes in practices are often necessary if traditions are to thrive. Fourth, we can account for diversity in the formulation of beliefs. As practices change, whether intentionally or unintentionally, the significance of the concepts and beliefs they carry changes. To mean "the same thing" in a different context may require one to say something different from the "old" formula. Fifth, we can understand how faith is communicated. Since traditions cannot be reduced to bare *tradita*, traditions must live and be communicated in and through practices. The point is not to memorize propositions; the point is to live and practice a faith. Hence, the communication of the "how to" live is as important as, or more important than, much of the "what" that is communicated. So learning a faith-tradition is learning how to practice the faith, typically by participating in local communities that teach one how to live in and live out a faith-tradition.[23]

RULES

Rules are the grammar of a practice. A grammar is a set of rules for speaking or writing a language, derived from our practices of speaking and writing and made normative for our linguistic practices. So practicing the faith has analogous "grammatical" rules.

Rules show how the elements of a practice are linked. The formation of a constitution for a nation is an example of rules being derived from practices. Given a set of actual or desired practices that have structured or should structure a form of life, constitutions attempt to formulate the basic rules implicit in such practices. For instance, the right to vote given to property-owning males in our own constitution at its origins reflects the practice of power at the time. The movements toward universal adult suffrage over the past two centuries are successful attempts to change the practice of voting by changing that rule. The practice of suffrage is instituted in a certain context and as either the context changes or a widespread desire to amend the practice occurs, the shape of the practice is altered by a change in the rule. But the basic point remains: practices come first; rules second.[24]

But what is often forgotten in the discussion of rules is an insight expressed in various ways, but put most pithily by James C. Edwards: "A formula doesn't apply itself."[25] Rules don't apply themselves. Practitioners apply rules; good practitioners understand how and when to apply the rules. The ability to understand and to follow a rule is not demonstrated by being able to state the rule, but by someone's knowing how to put it into practice. One doesn't test accounting students' understanding of the rules of accounting by giving them a test on the content of a rule. One tests them by giving them a new problem or situation and seeing if they have the know-how to apply the rule. A state does not license physicians only on the basis of their being able to pass written tests about the rules for good diagnosis and treatment. The state requires the completion of an internship and/or residency in which the newly minted doctor with "book knowledge" is supervised as an apprentice in learning how to apply that knowledge in order to become a physician, a participant in the practice of medicine. In general, one has a concept or knows a rule if and only if that person can apply it well, can put it into practice.

A curious thing about rules is this: Ultimately, there is no rule for applying a rule. Of course, we can formulate a rule for applying a rule, a "second-order rule." But how do we know when that second-order rule applies? Well, then we can formulate a "third-order rule." But this cannot go on to infinity. Rules must come to a halt. Eventually we say, "That is just what we do." Some may want to say that we differ because we *interpret* rules differently. However, if we want to ask, "Which 'interpretation' is correct?" how could we decide without recourse to our own practice as a norm? And how could we appeal to our own practice when the normativity of the two different practices for following this rule is what is in dispute? That doesn't solve the problem either because "interpretation" is an appeal to another rule: "Interpret this sign this way." Again, we cannot avoid an infinite regress if we invoke "differing interpretations."

Moreover, the problem is even more complex. Consider now the wide variety of circumstances in which you might be standing in front of a pedestrian traffic signal that reads "Don't Walk." Must you follow that rule? With a bursting bladder and a bathroom across the street? With a bus across the street closing its doors? With no motor vehicle traffic in sight in the middle of the night? Carrying a baby? With a toddler at your side? Is there some set of rules that one might teach one's children to capture the appropriate responses in different circumstances? Since circumstances vary indefinitely and unpredictably, no rule can cover them all.

Whether crossing a street or making the Sign of the Cross, participating in a practice is not and cannot be a "blind" and "repetitive" following of rules. Practitioners develop good judgment as they learn the practice. They learn when to cross the street or Cross themselves. This ability is "practical wisdom" or "phronesis."[26] Following the practical theologian Richard R. Osmer, we can describe *phronesis* as

> the capacity to interpret episodes, situations, and contexts in three interrelated ways: (1) recognition of the relevant particulars of specific events and circumstances; (2) discernment of the...ends at stake; (3) determination of the most effective means to achieve these ends in light of the constraints and possibilites of a particular time and place...it [*phronesis*] allows us to see the relationship between interpretation,...character, and wise judgment.[27]

In short, the practice of applying a rule is not essentially an exercise in interpretation or repetition, but in judgment, and describing someone having good judgment cannot be done by listing rules. This is not to say that we do not often engage in merely repetitive rule-following behavior. We do—but this is not the same as participating in a practice, especially the practice of the faith. Just as knowing or following grammar alone is not sufficient to produce excellent speaking or writing, so knowing or listening to or following blindly rules or beliefs alone is sufficient neither to participate in a practice nor to show what good judgment is.[28]

But then a further problem arises: "How do we learn good judgment?" We learn from exemplary practitioners. To discern good judgment in a practice, we imitate those who engage in good judgment in crossing streets, in good writing or speaking, in knowing when to stop burrowing in archives and come to judgment, in discerning when surgery is indicated, or in good performance in any other practice. That imitation is necessarily *not* slavish imitation or mere repetition, but creative imitation, what philosopher Paul Ricoeur calls *mimesis*. *Rules don't apply themselves, but exemplars show how they are to be applied, extended, and even ignored.*

Exemplars are recognized, not cognized. As we become good practitioners, the rules seem less important because we have learned how to engage in the practice. If one must slavishly follow rules, one may be engaging in a sort of practice, but not the sort of practice characteristic of practical theology.

We generate rules from our practices so we can teach others the "basic" way to engage in a practice. As language teachers know, teaching rules is not sufficient for teaching a language; but ignoring rules completely would make teaching practically impossible.

CHRISTIAN PRACTICE AS CHRISTIAN TRADITION

If the argument above is on target, then learning how to engage in the practices laid out in the chapters later in this book is learning how to live in and live out the Catholic Christian tradition. But these are not sufficient to produce disciples. I have argued in *The Disciples' Jesus* that disciples are the ones who embody in practice the ways that Jesus taught.[29] To pass on the tradition that began with Jesus, we must teach children, converts, and the lapsed how to practice the faith by carrying on the practices of reconciliation that characterize the tradition that began with the Jesus movement.

We believe that in Jesus, God was reconciling humans to God, to each other, and to themselves. If sin is separation from who one is and ought to be in front of God and with each other, then the saving work of Christ is reconciliation, at-one-ment. A doctrine of the atonement may be practically impossible to formulate—indeed, the absence of any definitive soteriological doctrine in the tradition (as opposed to the definitive christological doctrine) suggests that no formulation captures the reconciling work of Christ.[30] Jesus healed the sick and troubled, taught the ignorant, engaged in table fellowship even with outcasts, and forgave sinners. How are we to engage in those reconciling practices in his name today? We may not exorcise as he did, but may nurse the sick in hospitals and comfort the dying in hospices—practices quite different from his in appearance, but the same practices that have evolved through time. We may not use parables or sermons, but we run schools to serve the poor and to re-educate the rich. We may not invite prostitutes and tax-gatherers to our table, but we give alms, shelter the homeless, feed the hungry, and work to ensure that all have access to clean water. And we pray that our trespasses be forgiven, even as we forgive those who trespass against us.

How do we learn how to do this? Our exemplars are saints—all God's people—the body of Christ in the world today, carrying out Christ's work in the world today.[31] The saints show us how to engage in the practices of reconciliation. They show the extravagance of what it means to love God and exhibit the ways—sometimes radical ways—to carry on the tradition. Some are canonized, some not; some timely, some timeless in their exemplarity. But we can look to the saints—"friends of God and prophets"[32]—to see how to keep a tradition alive in graceful practice. Saints witness to those who will follow us and those who live in and live out other traditions what it means to be a Christian.

To live in and live out the Catholic tradition is to engage in these reconciling practices "in Jesus' name" in communion with others who practice this faith. The means of our reconciling practices are quite similar to others who heal, teach, work for justice, and pray. But our goal is not just to do these things, but to do them so that we are God's agents in this world at this time who are commissioned to make the reign of God as real as it can be here and now.

To practice the Christian faith is to live under God's rule, in God's house, in communion with God's other disciples. This vision of the reign of God welds our various practices into a tradition. This vision marks our differences from and similarities to others who work for reconciliation. And it is this vision that is the ultimate goal of practicing our faith, living in and living out a tradition that shows how human flourishing just is living in and under the freedom of God's rule, a freedom that is realized when we engage in the practices of reconciliation and teach others how to live in and live out that tradition well.

Notes

1. For further argument on points made in the text, see my *Inventing Catholic Tradition* (Eugene, OR: Wipf & Stock, 2011; 1st ed.: Maryknoll, NY: Orbis Books, 2000).While I am indebted to post-liberal theology, I also am very critical of its presumption of intratextuality and its tendency toward a postmodern form of fideism. See Terrence W. Tilley, *The Wisdom of Religious Commitment* (Washington, DC: Georgetown University Press, 1995), chap. 3.

2. Robert J. Schreiter, CPPS, *The Ministry of Reconciliation: Spirituality and Strategies* (Maryknoll, NY: Orbis Books, 1998), 25.

3. Some would prefer to say that we discover or uncover our traditions. However, John Thiel, *Senses of Tradition: Continuity and Development of Catholic Faith* (Oxford, UK: Oxford University Press, 2000), argues persuasively that "tradition" is itself a retro-

jective category, that each "present" builds its own tradition out of its perceived "past."

4. For evidence for this claim, see the brief but useful overview of modern Protestant understandings of tradition written by a Catholic theologian before the Second Vatican Council (wherein the concept of tradition evolved again), in James P. Mackey, *The Modern Theology of Tradition* (London, UK: Darton, Longman & Todd, 1962), chap. 6. Moreover, social historians have weighed in with important writing about traditions. Their descriptive definitions of what constitutes tradition seem both adequately descriptive and to be inscribed in a totally different conceptual universe from that of the theologians. See, for example, Eric Hobsbawm and Terence Ranger, eds., *The Invention of Tradition* (Cambridge, UK: Cambridge University Press, 1983), 1–6. I thank Margaret Steinfels for this reference.

5. In one way, this seems remarkable insofar as the Second Vatican Council has a much more flexible and nuanced view of tradition, apparently based in large part on the work of Yves Congar. For a brief summary, see Joseph Komonchak, Mary Collins, and Dermot Lane, eds., *The New Dictionary of Theology* (Wilmington, DE: Michael Glazier, 1987), especially 1040–41.

6. In Tilley, *The Wisdom of Religious Commitment*, 27, 55, 58, I describe a "presumption of substitutability" for philosophers of religion who substitute debate over the rationality of holding religious propositions for the wisdom of being a member of a religious tradition. Similarly, reducing *traditio* to *tradita* is useful for some purposes, but such reduction ought not to blind one to the other components of tradition.

7. Robert J. Schreiter, CPPS, *The New Catholicity: Theology Between the Global and the Local* (Maryknoll, NY: Orbis Books, 1997), 110–12, claims that an insider ordinarily does not have to be aware of the process of *traditio*, but is normally only aware of the *tradita*, that which is passed on. In his view, it is the outsider who raises claims about the process. However, in some sense, insofar as a person is constituted not within one tradition alone, but in several, a person comes to take this "outsider" perspective while remaining an "insider." Schreiter recognizes this for times of crisis, but this has become practically normative in Western

society. Moreover, it is surely arguable that people have never been formed solely in "the Christian tradition," but necessarily in an inculturated version of that tradition with the admixture of political, social, and economic patterns that are distinguishable from the Christian tradition. Writing from a radically different perspective, Presbyterian feminist theologian Mary McClintock Fulkerson has persuasively argued that there cannot be a theological discourse free from any "contemporary signifying practices," in *Changing the Subject: Women's Discourses and Feminist Theology* (Minneapolis, MN: Fortress Press, 1994), 368.

8. John Henry Cardinal Newman, *Essay on the Development of Christian Doctrine* (London, UK: Basil, Montague, Pickering, 1878), 40, accessed September 24, 2013, http://archive.org/stream/a599872600newmuoft#page/n5/mode/2up.

9. For a useful survey of recent theories of practice and their use in practical theology, see Ted A. Smith, "Theories of Practice," in *The Wiley-Blackwell Companion to Practical Theology*, ed. Bonnie J. Miller-McLemore (Oxford, UK: Wiley-Blackwell, 2012), 244–54.

10. This analysis is based on James Wm. McClendon Jr., *Systematic Theology*, vol. 2, *Doctrine* (Nashville, TN: Abingdon Press, 1994), 28; see also Alasdair MacIntyre, *After Virtue: A Study in Moral Theory* (Notre Dame, IN: University of Notre Dame Press, 1984). Some material in the first part of this section is based, in part, on material first published in Tilley, *Wisdom of Religious Commitment*, chap. 2. The distinction between *praxis* and *practice* also neglects the fact that this use of *practice* derives primarily from the work of Ludwig Wittgenstein, especially in *Philosophical Investigations*. Wittgenstein wrote in German and used the term *praxis*, as in "Darum ist 'der regel folgen' eine Praxis." Ludwig Wittgenstein, *Philosophical Investigations*, 3rd ed., trans. G.E.M. Anscombe (New York: Macmillan, 1958), 202.

11. Yves Congar, OP, *Tradition and Traditions: An Historical and a Theological Essay*, trans. Michael Naseby and Thomas Rainborough (New York: Macmillan, 1967), lists the liturgy as the first principal monument or witness to tradition (427–31). Congar tends to rely on ritual as a "fixed thing" (428), yet notices how rituals have shifted (428–30). The present essay focuses on

the shifts visible to all; to see the constancies requires a trained eye, a point Congar undervalues.

12. For the concept of status functions, see John Searle, *Making the Social World: The Structure of Human Civilization* (New York: Oxford University Press, 2010), esp. 7–24, 38.

13. Of course, it is possible for people to engage in practices, especially ritual practices, "mindlessly" or "by rote." This is the truth in the rejection of "ritualism." But my point is that the folk who participate in practices mindlessly are *not* participating in practices, but merely going through the motions. That sort of behavior is not participation in a practice.

14. For example, see Clifford Geertz, "Religion as a Cultural System," in *The Interpretation of Cultures* (New York: Basic Books, 1973), 87–125.

15. For example, see Kathleen Boone, *The Bible Tells Them So: The Discourse of Protestant Fundamentalism* (Albany: State University of New York Press, 1989).

16. See Robert J. Schreiter, CPPS, *Constructing Local Theologies* (Maryknoll, NY: Orbis Books, 1985).

17. This is one of the points made in the scathing satire, Harold Miner, "Body Ritual Among the Nacirema," *The American Anthropologist* 58 (1956): 503–7. Nacirema ritual behaviors, as observed by the fictional anthropologist writing the essay, are absurd and senseless until the reader connects them with familiar activities, beliefs, and attitudes that the reader knows and that make the behaviors comprehensible and the descriptions the fictional writer gives of them hilarious.

18. Fulkerson, *Changing the Subject*, 368, makes the even stronger claim that "'theological' or faith discourses and those of 'culture' come into being at the same time." In this she is arguing that neither the traditions passed on nor the already realized cultural and social locations of those receiving the traditions have a priority over each other. Descriptively, this is indeed correct as an analysis of the emergence of local theologies (and *all* theologies are local!). Normatively, however, for theologians like Schreiter, there is a need to give some form of priority to the tradition and some criteria for discerning appropriate from inappropriate inculturations; see Schreiter, *Constructing Local Theologies*, 117–21.

Nonetheless, the tradition cannot be a sufficient ground or warrant for such judgments: both Schreiter and Fulkerson would agree on this point.

19. A classic dilemma here is whether a missionary can and ought to use the proposition that Christ is really present in the eucharistic elements to evangelize a tribe that has a tradition of practicing ritual cannibalism. For our purposes, the point is not how to resolve the problem, but that the problem arises. The dilemma such a missionary faces illustrates the point that an item of tradition like a doctrine may have significantly different religious meanings, determined by the different places it takes in (religious and nonreligious) practices, especially when these practices vary widely between the initiating culture (French Catholicism) and the target culture (Iroquois and Huron tribes); see Tilley, *Inventing Catholic Tradition*, 73–74, 168.

20. See Terrence W. Tilley, *History, Theology, and Faith: Dissolving the Modern Problematic* (Maryknoll, NY: Orbis Books, 2006), 71–75, and the literature cited therein. I also note that in this same process, the realm of the preternatural disappeared from discourse traditions in which it had been at home.

21. Lest someone think otherwise, I do not mean by this that people "earn" heaven. However one interprets the parable of the vineyard (Matt 20), I think it shows that "worthiness" or "desert" is not necessarily connected with "earning."

22. As William A. Clebsch, in his discussion of the wild diversity of the ways Christ appears to people and the lack of any single constant (save a bare and practically meaningless referent to Jesus of Nazareth), put it this way: "The point is not that there have been no Christophanic constancies, but that constancies have been unimportant in Christophanies." William A. Clebsch, *Christianity in European History* (New York: Oxford University Press, 1979), 19.

23. Two objections to this account from different directions are (1) that this approach underemphasizes the role of elites, and (2) that it gives short shrift to the truth of tradition. For responses, see Tilley, *Inventing Catholic Tradition*, 80–86; and Terrence W. Tilley, *Faith: What It Is and What It Isn't* (Maryknoll, NY: Orbis Books, 2010), 102–38.

24. This position seems to create severe problems as it is formulated for natural law theory, at least in some of its strong constitutive forms. It can be overcome by recognizing that our rules are recognized as made by us and warranted in use, but which reflect, more or less well, the natural law. Of course, this move reduces "correspondence with the natural law" to no use in the process of *justifying* moral or other claims since such correspondence functions as *a condition of* but not *a criterion for* the rightness of our views. But doesn't that actually reflect the shape of the arguments anyway—that appeals to "natural law" fail to help us discern which actions are moral?

25. James C. Edwards, *The Authority of Language: Heidegger, Wittgenstein and the Threat of Philosophical Nihilism* (Tampa: University of South Florida Press, 1990), 162.

26. For a discussion of this virtue, see Tilley, *The Wisdom of Religious Commitment.*

27. Richard R. Osmer, *Practical Theology: An Introduction* (Grand Rapids, MI: William B. Eerdmans Publishing Company, 2008), 84–86.

28. It is the argument of *The Wisdom of Religious Commitment* that the issue of the rationality of religious belief is not finally an epistemic issue in the technical sense (e.g., whether person *p* at time *t* is warranted in believing proposition *p*, "God exists," given circumstances *q, r, s*) but an issue of prudential judgment.

29. *The Disciples' Jesus: Christology as Reconciling Practice* (Maryknoll, NY: Orbis Books, 2008).

30. For a brief account of the problems of atonement theology, see Ian T. Ramsey, *Christian Discourse: Some Logical Explorations* (London, UK: Oxford University Press, 1965), 28–60; also see Lisa Sowle Cahill, "The Atonement Paradigm: Does It Still Have Explanatory Value?" *Theological Studies* 68, no. 2 (2007): 418–32.

31. See my earlier books: *Story Theology* (Wilmington, DE: Michael Glazier, 1985), 147–78, 60–64, and *The Disciples' Jesus*, chap. 19. A similar approach can be found in Robert Barron, *The Priority of Christ: Toward a Postliberal Catholicism* (Grand Rapids, MI: Brazos Press, 2007), 298–342. Barron uses Edith Stein as a model of courage, Thérèse of Lisieux as a model of prudence,

Katherine Drexel as a model of justice, and Mother Teresa as a model of temperance—all exemplars not of merely natural cardinal virtues, but of virtues elevated by divine grace. These virtues are developed by their engagement in virtuous practices. The similarities in our approach are likely due in part to the fact that both of us are North Americans who have been influenced in different ways by the work of Baptist theologian James Wm. McClendon Jr., *Systematic Theology*, vol. 1, *Ethics* (Nashville, TN: Abingdon Press, 2002 [1986]) as well as by our Roman Catholic heritage.

32. See Elizabeth A. Johnson, *Friends of God and Prophets* (New York: Continuum, 1999).

Chapter 6

EUCHARISTIC PRACTICE—EUCHARISTIC THEOLOGY

The Fount and Summit of Ecclesial Life

Edward Foley

In 1939, as rumors of war rumbled across France, the visionary Jesuit theologian Henri de Lubac (d. 1991) penned these stunning words: "the Eucharist makes the Church."[1] It was not baptism or priesthood, Rome or the episcopacy, infallibility or some Marian dogma that made the church for de Lubac, but the Eucharist. While it is true that de Lubac's theology was officially criticized and he was silenced by his superiors during the 1950s, his work quickly rebounded to influence significantly the Second Vatican Council. The *Constitution on the Sacred Liturgy*—the first document of Vatican II that addressed the theology and reform of the liturgy—seems to echo de Lubac's eucharistic insight when it states that "the liturgy is the summit toward which the activity of the church is directed; it is also the source from which all its power flows" (no. 10).[2] Later Pope John Paul II (d. 2005) not only made de Lubac a cardinal, but also drew on his writings for his last papal encyclical, "The Church from the Eucharist" (*Ecclesia de Eucharistia*, 2003).

Though revolutionary at the time, de Lubac's contention that the Eucharist makes the church is not surprising to anyone who reads the New Testament. That point was precisely, however, one of the contributions of de Lubac and other French and German Catholic theologians of the mid-twentieth century who were part of the *réssourcement* ("return to the sources") movement. Also known as the proponents of *nouvelle théologie* ("new theology"), they showed a renewed interest in primary sources of the Christian faith such as scripture and patristic writings. This approach contradicted the prevailing theological trends of the day, which were often more concerned with defending current church teaching than with theological inquiry and reliant on secondary commentaries, or "manuals," rather than the primary sources of the faith. Starting points do make a difference, and by shifting the terrain from neo-Scholastic manuals to the New Testament, one not only discovers that the Eucharist makes the church, but it does so through what could be considered a surprising, even subversive practice.

THE JESUS TABLE: A SUBVERSIVE PRACTICE

Even when turning to the New Testament, there are still multiple possible starting points for exploring the nature of the Eucharist. There are, for example, what could be considered more "theological" passages on the Eucharist, such as the "Bread of Life" discourse in John 6. Predominant in the New Testament, however, are not words about the meaning of the Eucharist as much as descriptions of it as a foundational practice. The Eucharist in the New Testament is an enacted theology more than a discourse, a verb more than a noun as symbolized by the Greek word *eucharistein*, itself a verb that means "to give thanks."

Making the New Testament turn to practice when pondering the nature of the Eucharist requires further decision-making: for example, which eucharistic practices take priority? Many people gravitate to the "Last Supper" stories as pivotal. It seems ironic if not problematic, however, to begin examination of this "practice" by looking at the last stories and not at the many and diverse others that led up to that climactic, nonrepeatable event. Predominant in the New Testament, however, are not words about the meaning of the Eucharist as much as descriptions of it as a foundational practice. Furthermore, some scholars would contend that Last Supper narratives were not the primary source from which early Christians drew for shaping eucharistic practice or belief.[3]

Predominant in the New Testament, however, are not words about the meaning of Eucharist as much as descriptions of it as a foundational practice.

What might be broadly termed the *table ministry* of Jesus seems a much more potent starting point for examining the foundations of eucharistic practice.[4] As one scriptural scholar noted, in the meal-laden Gospel of Luke "Jesus is either going to a meal, at a meal, or coming from a meal." This is not simply a matter of geography, however, for as that same scholar asserts, "Jesus got himself crucified by the way he ate."[5] This bold assertion is affirmed by the textual data that demonstrate that the one consistent charge leveled at Jesus throughout the various strata of the Gospel is not that he blasphemes or that he speaks against the government or that he challenges Jewish authorities: rather, it is that he "eats and drinks with sinners."[6]

While Jesus is often remembered as a great teacher, there is not agreement, even among the Evangelists, about what Jesus said. His central message certainly announced the in-breaking of God's reign,[7] and parable was unquestionably a privileged speech pattern for Jesus' teaching about God's reign.[8] Beyond that, however, scholars are sharply divided about what gospel texts reflect the actual words or sayings of Jesus.[9] On the other hand, tradition seems to be on surer footing when it comes to his table praxis, which can be characterized as Jesus' enacted parable about the in-breaking of God's reign.

Employing the categories of ritual theorist Catherine Bell (d. 2008), it is possible to conceive of Jesus' table praxis as a kind of "technology" for reshaping thinking about God and God's reign. Bell defined ritualization as a "strategic way of acting" that shapes social agents and aligns them with relationships linked to an ultimate power.[10] The table technology of Jesus invited a raft of the unexpected to the banquet: not just sinners, but the ritually impure, Samaritans, social outcasts, and the unwashed *illiterati*. Sometimes, these folk mingled with the A-list of the rich and influential. All were welcomed as long as they were willing to be reshaped as a community of spiritual and social agents aware of their sinfulness and open to being aligned with a God who actually seemed to relish contact with the socially and spiritually contaminated. This table technology was a direct challenge to the prevailing technology of Palestinian Jews of the time that shaped social agents around the temple, where God's holiness was thought to abide.

Bruce Chilton argues that Jesus' overturning of the money changers' tables (Mark 11:15) signaled a turning point in Jesus' ritualizing strategies. In Chilton's opinion, this dramatic act was the culmination of a ritual program that stressed the forgiveness of sin. It further announced that the meals shaping Jesus' "unholy" social agents (i.e., the disciples) were a more acceptable form of worship than temple sacrifice, which Jesus came to regard as impure. The scandal of this table reversal was its strategy not only to align the outcast as disciples with God but, in the process, to redefine that ultimate power as One that preferred the "contaminated" table of the Jesus gathering to temple sacrifice.[11] This technology of reversals not only shaped disciples around a newly defined "body of Christ" but shaped them into the same.

THE "THREE BODIES"

While it might sound odd to the contemporary hearer, there is a long tradition within Christianity for both speaking about and believing in three *distinctive* though not *separate* "bodies of

Christ." St. Ambrose (d. 397), in his commentary on the Gospel of Luke, wrote: "we remember that Joseph received the body from Pilate....There is also a body of which it is said 'My flesh is truly food'....There is also the body that is the Church."[12] These "three bodies" are commonly identified as (1) the historical body of Christ, (2) the ecclesial body of Christ, and (3) the sacramental, or eucharistic, body of Christ. One of the dynamics of evolving eucharistic theology and practice that catches the attention of the practical theologian is the interplay of these three "bodies" and especially the pendulum swings between emphasis on the ecclesial body and emphasis on the sacramental body. Employing the language of Catherine Bell, one might ask: What are the alignment strategies or the eucharistic technologies that shape the community in their belief about these distinctive bodies of Christ, and what is the alternating import of these different bodies through Christian history? Given our New Testament reading of the Jesus table whose flawed participants seemed to be of more ritual importance than the food that was consumed at that table, it is interesting how the eucharistic technology will adjust in succeeding centuries to value the sacramental body, sometimes at the expense of the ecclesial body.

Through his textual analysis of patristic and medieval texts, de Lubac has demonstrated that for the emerging Christian community the "true body" (*corpus verum*) was the assembly of believers, in all of its sinfulness. This is clearly the image in Paul's First Letter to the Corinthians, in which he waxes eloquently about the followers of Christ as one body (12:12–31). Reminiscent of Jesus' own table ministry, this emphasis has unavoidable ethical implications for the way the followers of Jesus treat one another, and Paul sharply criticizes the Corinthians for their unacceptable behavior in a eucharistic gathering that threatens to bring judgment on them (11:27–31). St. Augustine (d. 430) offers one of the richest reflections on this ecclesial and ethical mystery when he preaches, "If you, therefore, are Christ's body and members, it is your own mystery that is placed on the Lord's table. It is your own mystery that you are receiving. You are saying Amen to what you are.... Be a member of Christ's body, then, so that your Amen may ring true!"[13]

According to de Lubac, when the term *mystical body* (*corpus mysticum*) of Christ emerged in the fifth century of the Common Era it ordinarily referred to the consecrated host, or "sacramental body."[14] The church, on the other hand, was the "body of Christ," or the *corpus verum* ("true body"). The medieval period, especially from the ninth century forward, was a time of renewed debate about eucharistic theology. In particular, theologians for the first time tried to explain in a systematic way how Christ was present in the Eucharist. The challenge was to affirm that Christ was truly present in the Eucharist, even though that presence does not appear to be the same as his physical presence manifested in his historical body. A key figure in this debate was Paschasius Radbertus (d. ca. 860), who attempted to clarify the nature of Christ's sacramental presence by distinguishing between the visible "figure" (bread and wine) and the underlying truth (Christ's presence). This allowed him to argue that the relationship between Jesus' historical body and the sacramental body was one of identity.

While theologians in succeeding generations rejected Paschasius's somewhat crude formulation, this strategy of explaining the eucharistic presence of Christ by linking it with the historical body contributed to a rethinking and ultimate reversal of the definition of the "mystical body." While originally the eucharistic species was considered to be the "mystical body," by the mid-twelfth century it became common to refer to the consecrated host as the "true body" (*corpus verum*) while, in a telling reversal, the church became the "mystical body" (*corpus mysticum*).[15] According to de Lubac, this change both symbolized and contributed to a widening gap between the sacramental body and the ecclesial body, between reverence for the host and reverence for the baptized.

The movement from the teachings of the New Testament to that of the twelfth century could be considered a pendulum swing from giving pride of place to the ecclesial body to ceding priority to the sacramental body. For example, Jesus freely welcomed sinners to his table; by the twelfth century, the church had many rules in place to keep sinners from the Eucharist in order to protect the dignity of the sacrament. Ironically, Paul's community had no tabernacles for a reserved sacrament; twelfth-century tabernacles were centerpieces of medieval churches. Multiple other examples could be given of this theological pendulum swing that had enormous implications for eucharistic practice in Western Christianity. Already in late antiquity bishops such as John Chrysostom (d. 427) were complaining about the infrequent reception of the Eucharist by some, a result of Christianity's growing social acceptability and then prominence in the empire. Waning baptismal fervor, increased infant initiation, and the social acceptability of this religion sanctioned by Roman emperors spawned a form of Christianity far different from its origins. Mix in the widespread belief in the doctrine of original sin, and one arrives at a stage in medieval Western Christianity in which the faithful understood themselves fundamentally as sinners who expected to spend a significant time in purgatory after the particular judgment. Ironically, however, this sinfulness that was the passport to the Jesus table became a roadblock to the medieval eucharistic table. The cup began to be withdrawn from the laity by the ninth century, a process complete by the thirteenth century. So few people were receiving communion that the Fourth Lateran Council (1215) decreed that people had to go to at least once a year, but only after they had confessed their sins.

A determinative practice that was both a result of and impetus for developments in eucharistic theology was that of "ocular communion," or watching the consecrated host. The origins of this devotion are related to the introduction of the elevation in the twelfth century as a definitive marker for when the consecration of the bread occurred. Once the elevation was introduced, there is evidence that people would move from side altar to side altar in some large cathedrals waiting to see the elevation before moving on to the next altar for their next eucharistic sighting. Ocular communion became such an important spiritual exercise for the faithful that it achieved the status of a "second sacrament" alongside receiving.[16] Eventually this eucharistic devotion inside of the Mass moved outside of the Mass, and adoration of the consecrated bread displayed in a monstrance—sometimes performed as "Benediction of the Blessed Sacrament"—became a widespread and thoroughly Roman Catholic devotion.

LEX ORANDI, LEX CREDENDI: CORRELATION IN LITURGY

The pendulum swings throughout the centuries from emphasizing the ecclesial body of Christ to emphasizing the sacramental body of Christ can be understood, in practical theological terms, as an ongoing correlation between what the church practices and what it teaches or believes. The liturgical equivalent to a formula of correlation between theory and practices is a celebrated maxim from Prosper of Aquitaine (d. 475): *legem credendi lex statuat supplicandi* ("the law of praying established the law of believing"),[17] sometimes abbreviated *lex orandi, lex credendi* ("law of praying, law of believing").

In some ways, our previous visiting of the Jesus table suggests that the early community was more concerned with practice than theory, more about *orandi* than *credendi*. This is not to suggest that the early community was devoid of what we would call "eucharistic theology," but their theologies were often more implicit than explicit, and usually arose in response to a very particular pastoral issue. Like some forms of contemporary practical theology—for example, the many forms of theological reflection that place the experiences of the community front and center in this process[18]—this could be understood as ceding priority to communal experience. Paul's eucharistic reflection for the Corinthians, for example, could be understood as the response of a practical theologian to a thorny contemporary issue faced by this local community. Paul does not really tell us much about Jesus throughout his letters—no parables, not the Our Father or Beatitudes, and virtually no events from his public ministry except his death: a fact that captivated Paul's theology. Given that pattern, it is unlikely that Paul would have reported anything about Jesus' action at the Last Supper (1 Cor 11:23–26) unless the Corinthian community had raised a question about eating meat left over from pagan sacrifices that he addressed in the previous chapter.

Throughout the so-called patristic period of the church, the teaching about the Eucharist was often from bishops like Ambrose and Augustine, who were deeply engaged in the pastoral care of their flocks and whose eucharistic reflections were ordinarily in clear dialogue with their local contexts. For example, Augustine's continual emphasis on the Eucharist as a sacrament of unity was precisely because of his struggles with the Donatists, who were so concerned about safeguarding their own holiness that they isolated themselves from anyone whom they did not judge as worthy.[19] Thus, in a sermon delivered to those preparing for Christian initiation, Augustine teaches, "The Eucharist is our daily bread and the power belonging to this divine food renders it as a bond of union. Its effect is understood as unity, so that, gathered into his Body and made one with him, we may become what we receive."[20]

Increasingly, however, this correlation between the experience of a local community and the teaching of a bishop or theologian weakened. Paschasius, for example, while writing to instruct monks, did so in a somewhat rarified pastoral context. As the innovator in attempting to explain how Christ is present in the Eucharist, Paschasius no longer dealt with the Eucharist as a stage in the process of Christian initiation as did, for example, someone like Augustine. Rather, he took a more abstract approach in an attempt to make a soteriological rather than a pastoral argument—in other words, we are saved because we eat the body of

Christ.[21] In the centuries following Paschasius, as eucharistic theologies in the West increasingly engaged philosophy as a primary dialogue partner (e.g., Thomas Aquinas [d. 1274] and Aristotle [d. 322 BCE]), the discourse became even more pastorally remote and largely disconnected from the lives of ordinary believers.

One way to characterize this pendulum swing from the ecclesial body to the sacramental body, away from pastoral practice to abstract theories about the Eucharist, from emphasis on *orandi* to that of *credenda*, is a move from what could be considered "liturgical theology" to "sacramental theology." Liturgical theology, as it emerged in the twentieth century, is a style of theologizing that takes the ritual practice and the experience of communities in that practice seriously. So conceived, liturgical theology resonates with many forms of practical theology that evolved at the end of the twentieth century that similarly take communal experience as a theological source.[22] Sacramental theology, on the other hand, could be characterized as a more theory-preoccupied form of theologizing that seldom resources, much less seriously honors, the ritual experiences of the faithful. It gives priority to the theory, or *credenda*, abstracted from its actual context that is often distilled into rules or rubrics that need to be followed in the particularities of public worship. Such theologizing could be considered a form of applied theology or sacramental theology in Schleiermacherian mode.[23]

CONTEMPORARY PENDULUM SWINGS

The mid-twentieth century witnessed a renaissance in eucharistic theologizing that the Roman Catholic Church had not witnessed since the twelfth century. Much of this was achieved by European theologians who were either part of or influenced by the previously noted *réssourcement* movement. While there were many vectors of thinking in this vast theological arena, one dominant flow or pendulum swing was certainly toward emphasizing and revaluing the ecclesial body. This is apparent in the writings of the famed Belgium theologian Edward Schillebeeckx (d. 2009), who spent most of his career as a professor at the University of Nijmegen in the Netherlands. Rather than theologizing about the Eucharist from the viewpoint of the philosophy of nature, as Aquinas did through Aristotle, Schillebeeckx makes the turn to the social sciences, especially anthropology.[24] Part of this move was an embrace of interpersonal categories for explaining sacramental and eucharistic theology, that is, that sacraments are an interpersonal "encounter" with God in Christ.[25]

The noted German theologian Karl Rahner (d. 1984), who served with Schillebeeckx as an expert at Vatican II, made parallel moves toward embracing anthropology as a key dialogue partner for twentieth-century theology.[26] Similar to the language of "encounter," Rahner held that grace was not some "thing" that comes from God, but God's very own self-communication.[27] Sacraments, according to Rahner, require the free response of a human being to God's self-communication; they are a divine word in which God self-communicates to us, and that self-communication liberates us in our freedom to accept God.[28] Consequently, sacraments are not only acts of God, and certainly not simply human acts, but the encounter of the two through the power of God's own graciousness.

In many respects the *Constitution on the Sacred Liturgy* reflects this shift toward anthropology, encounter, and human subjectivity—that is, a pendulum swing toward the ecclesial body—when it stresses that the liturgy is an action of "the Head [Christ] and His members" (no. 7) and by emphasizing that "in the restoration and development of the sacred liturgy the full and active participation by all the people is the paramount concern" (no. 14). This renewal in theology and *credenda* was anticipated and prepared for by almost a half century of a renewal in *orandi*. Throughout the twentieth century "liturgical movement," the beginning of which is sometimes dated to the 1909 National Congress of Catholic Works in Belgium,[29] monasteries and parishes in Europe and then in the United States were experimenting with new worship forms that more actively engaged the faithful. At the German monastery of Maria Laach in the 1920s, for example, monks and laity celebrated the *Missa recitata* ("dialogue Mass") in which people recited the *Gloria, Sanctus,* and other Latin texts in common, and sang hymns in the vernacular. In Germany, this practice became "normative in as many as seventy-five percent of the parishes."[30] The practice quickly migrated to the United States, where it took hold in several dioceses. In Chicago, for example, 65 of its 250 city parishes had introduced the practice by 1939.[31] Such a dialogic praxis of the Eucharist, along with the growing trend of local hymnody and popular "daily missals" with their side-by-side translations of the Latin and vernacular texts, could be understood as a kind of ritual technology that shaped believers toward a belief in an immanent God akin to that revealed in the table ministry of Jesus.

While it appeared to many that this pendulum swing toward the ecclesial body aligned with a more immanent God was to be an enduring trajectory, such was not to be. Criticisms of the new Order of Mass (1969) and its implied eucharistic theologies were early and sometimes virulent. Five months after the new Mass was approved, two retired cardinals sent a letter to Pope Paul VI (d. 1978) along with "A Brief Critical Study of the *Novus Ordo Missae,*" which opined that in many ways the new Mass would satisfy "the most modernistic of Protestants."[32] Under the leadership of Pope John Paul II, in 1984 the bishops of the world were given broadened authority to allow the celebration of the Tridentine Mass that had been suppressed by Pope Paul VI. The same pope, after having excommunicated Archbishop Marcel Lefebvre—who rejected the liturgical changes of Vatican II and without authorization consecrated bishops who held similar views—wrote that "respect must everywhere be shown for the feelings of all those who are attached to the Latin liturgical tradition."[33]

One primary focus of the growing "liturgy wars" at the end of the twentieth century was the English retranslation of the Roman Missal for celebrating the Eucharist. A 1998 translation, approved by eleven English-speaking conferences of bishops and sent to Rome for approval, continued the pendulum swing toward immanence. It was never approved. In 2001 new rules for translating liturgical texts were promulgated that seemed to value the Latin text and language of transcendence over the accessibility and engagement of the faithful.[34] The end result was the 2011 publication of the newly translated Roman Missal, whose sometimes turgid sentence structure and arcane language suggest a continuing pendulum swing away from the ecclesial body toward the sacramental body in a technology of transcendence.

THE PENDULUM SWINGS: COMMUNION AS PRACTICAL-PUBLIC THEOLOGY

Some scholars consider practical theology a form of public theology;[35] similarly, one could consider the celebration of the Eucharist a form of public theology.[36] Few ritual moments in the eucharistic liturgy are as potentially revealing and contentious in that act of public theology as that of receiving communion. One of the ways in which the interplay of *lex orandi* and *lex credendi* and the pendulum swings between emphasizing the ecclesial body and the sacramental body have recently been manifest is in the relationship between the act of receiving communion and perceived compliance with aspects of church teaching on the part of the communicant—for example, regarding abortion, which the Roman Catholic Church strongly opposes.

During the 2004 presidential election, various prelates and theologians debated about politicians who supported abortion or supported legislation that implicitly or explicitly recognized abortion as a legal act and whether they should be allowed to receive communion. The topic was discussed by the U.S. Catholic bishops at their June 2004 meeting in Denver. Their statement "Catholics in Political Life"[37] addressed the issue and concluded that the decision to withhold communion from any Catholic politician rested with the local bishop. At least one bishop issued a public ban on "pro-abortion" politicians from receiving communion.[38] The vast majority of U.S. bishops, however, have not denied or threatened to deny communion to such politicians. More common is the 2009 response of Archbishop Wuerl of Washington, DC, who in a published interview disagrees with using communion as a "weapon." In the interview, referencing the section of canon law that some have cited as justification for denying communion to such politicians, he comments, "I stand with the great majority of American bishops and bishops around the world in saying this canon was never intended to be used this way." He further believes that "there are two different approaches [here]. One is the pastoral teaching mode, and the other is the canonical approach." Clearly affirming the former he remarks, "I have yet to see where the canonical approach has changed anyone's heart."[39]

Some scholars consider practical theology a form of public theology; similarly, one could consider the celebration of Eucharist a form of public theology.

Eucharistic practice is a powerful, even explosive ritual event. It makes the church but also, as a theological and ecclesial technology, it has the potential to polarize, even divide the church. Practical theologians have particular insights and methods in service of this practice, especially so that it truly builds rather than divides the church.

Notes

1. The 1949 revision of that work is translated as Henri de Lubac, *Corpus Mysticum: The Eucharist and the Church in the Middle Ages*, ed. Laurence Paul Hemming and Susan Frank Parsons, trans. Gemma Simmonds (Notre Dame, IN: University of Notre Dame Press, 2006), 88.

2. Translations of this document are from Austin Flannery, ed., *Vatican Council II: The Basic Sixteen Documents* (Northport,

NY: Costello Publishing Company; Dublin, Ireland: Dominican Publications, 1996).

3. Paul Bradshaw, "Did Jesus Institute the Eucharist at the Last Supper?" in *Issues in Eucharistic Praying in East and West*, ed. Maxwell E. Johnson (Collegeville, MN: Liturgical Press, 2010), 1–19.

4. Edward Foley, "Which Jesus Table? Reflections on Eucharistic Starting Points," *Worship* 82, no. 1 (2008): 41–52.

5. Robert Karris, *Luke: Artist and Theologian* (New York: Paulist Press, 1985), 47; this perspective is reiterated by many other authors; see Arthur A. Just, *The Ongoing Feast: Table Fellowship and Eschatology at Emmaus* (Collegeville, MN: Liturgical Press, 1993), 193.

6. Explicitly: Matt 9:11; Mark 2:16; Luke 5:30; 15:2 (from the Q source); implicitly: Luke 7:36–47; 15:11–32; 19:1–10; John 4:4–42; see the discussion in Edward Schillebeeckx, *Jesus: An Experiment in Christology*, trans. Hubert Hoskins (New York: Vintage Books, 1981), 206–13.

7. E.g., Matt 12:28; 19:24; 21:31; 21:43; Mark 1:15; 4:30; 9:1; 9:47; 10:14; 10:15; 10:23–25; 14:25; Luke 4:43; 6:20; 7:28; 8:1; 8:10; 9:2; 9:11; 9:27; 9:60; 9:62; 10:9; 10:11; 11:20; 13:18; 13:20; 13:28–29; 14:15; 16:16; 17:20–21; 18:16–18; 18:24–25; 18:29; 19:11; 21:31; 22:16–18; 23:51; John 3:3–5.

8. A classic work on the topic is C. H. Dodd, *The Parables of the Kingdom* (New York: Scribner, 1961); more recently, Klyne Snodgrass, *Stories with Intent: A Comprehensive Guide to the Parables of Jesus* (Grand Rapids, MI: William B. Eerdmans Publishing Company, 2008).

9. The members of the Jesus Seminar, for example concluded that only about 18 percent of the Jesus sayings in the New Testament had a high probability of having been said by him. See R. W. Funk, Roy Hoover, and the Jesus Seminar, *The Five Gospels: The Search for the Authentic Words of Jesus* (New York: Macmillan, 1993).

10. Catherine Bell, *Ritual Theory, Ritual Practice* (New York: Oxford University Press, 1992), 141.

11. Bruce Chilton, *A Feast of Meanings: Eucharistic Theologies from Jesus through Johannine Circles*, Supplements to *Novum Testamentum* 72 (Leiden, Netherlands: Brill, 1994), 70n28.

12. *In Lucam*, 8 (*Patrologia Latina* 15:1781–82), as translated in De Lubac, *Corpus Mysticum*, 127.

13. Sermon 272 (*Patrologia Latina* 38:1247), trans. Nathan Mitchell, *Assembly* 23 (1997): 14.

14. De Lubac, *Corpus Mysticum*, esp. chap. 1, 1–36.

15. Ibid., 106.

16. Caroline Walker Bynum, *Holy Feast and Holy Fast: The Religious Significance of Food to Medieval Women* (Berkeley: University of California Press, 1987), 55.

17. *Patrologia Latina* 51:209.

18. See, for example, the groundbreaking work of James D. Whitehead and Evelyn Eaton Whitehead, *Method in Ministry*, rev. ed. (Kansas City, MO: Sheed & Ward, 1995), esp. 10–11, 46.

19. See, for example, J. Patout Burns, "The Eucharist as the Foundation of Christian Unity in North African Theology," *Augustinian Studies* 32, no. 1 (2001): 1–23.

20. Sermon 57:7, *Patrologia Latina* 38:389.

21. "Letter to Fredugard" as cited in Gary Macy, *Theologies of the Eucharist in the Early Scholastic Period* (Cambridge, UK: Cambridge University Press, 1984), 28.

22. One significant example is Margaret Mary Kelleher, "Liturgical Theology: A Task and a Method," *Worship* 61, no. 2 (1988): 2–25. In this work, Kelleher pays tribute to other leading voices in this movement, including Alexander Schmemann, Aidan Kavanagh, and David Power.

23. On the practical theology of Friedrich Schleiermacher (d. 1834) as a form of applied theology, see Gerben Heitink, *Practical Theology: History, Theory, Action Domains*, Studies in Practical Theology (Grand Rapids, MI: William B. Eerdmans Publishing Company, 1999), 27.

24. Edward Schillebeeckx, *The Eucharist*, trans. N. D. Smith (New York: Sheed & Ward, 1968), 93 *et passim*.

25. Schillebeeckx already explored this approach in his 1952 doctoral work published in Dutch. A nontechnical summary of

that work is accessible in English as *Christ the Sacrament of the Encounter with God* (New York: Sheed & Ward, 1963).

26. Rahner unfolded many of his ideas in articles that were eventually published as collections, known in English as the *Theological Investigations.* Late in his life he wrote *Foundations of Christian Faith,* trans. William Dych (New York: Seabury Press, 1978 [1976]), which draws together many of his previously stated positions in a more systematic treatise. On the anthropological turn, for example, see 24–43.

27. Rahner, *Foundations of Christian Faith,* 116–37.

28. Ibid., 415.

29. See the discussion in Keith Pecklers, *The Unread Vision* (Collegeville, MN: Liturgical Press, 1998), 12.

30. Ibid., 55.

31. Ibid., 61.

32. See the letter and "Brief Critical Study," accessed May 18, 2012, http://www.sspx.org/sspx_faqs/brief_critical_study_of_the_new_order_of_mass-ottaviani-intervention.pdf.

33. *Ecclesia Dei,* no. 6c, accessed May 18, 2012, http://www.vatican.va/holy_father/john_paul_ii/motu_proprio/documents/hf_jp-ii_motu-proprio_02071988_ecclesia-dei_en.html.

34. *Liturgiam authenticam,* no. 27: "Thus it may happen that a certain manner of speech which has come to be considered somewhat obsolete in daily usage may continue to be maintained in the liturgical context. In translating biblical passages where seemingly inelegant words or expressions are used, a hasty tendency to sanitize this characteristic is likewise to be avoided. These principles, in fact, should free the Liturgy from the necessity of frequent revisions when modes of expression may have passed out of popular usage." Accessed May 18, 2012, http://www.vatican.va/roman_curia/congregations/ccdds/documents/rc_con_ccdds_doc_20010507_liturgiam-authenticam _en.html.

35. See, for example, Elaine L. Graham, "Why Practical Theology Must Go Public," *Practical Theology* 1, no. 1 (2008): 1–17.

36. See Edward Foley, "Engaging the Liturgy of the World: Worship as Public Theology," *Studia Liturgica* 38, no. 1 (2008): 31–52.

37. Approved by a vote of 183 to 6, accessed May 18, 2012, http://old.usccb.org/bishops/catholicsinpoliticallife.shtml.

38. This was the position of Raymond Burke, then bishop of LaCrosse, Wisconsin. Subsequently, as archbishop of St. Louis, he published his arguments in a canonical journal in which he also challenged his brother bishops who had not spoken out on the issue. Raymond Burke, "The Discipline Regarding the Denial of Holy Communion to Those Obstinately Persevering in Manifest Grave Sin," *Periodica De Re Canonica* 96 (2007): 3–58.

39. Melinda Hennenberger, "Wuerl: Why I Won't Deny Pelosi Communion," *Politics Daily* (May 6, 2009), http://www.politicsdaily.com/2009/05/06/archbishop-wuerl-why-i-won-t-deny-pelosi-communion/.

CHAPTER 7

WEAVING MEMORY, STRUCTURING RITUAL, EVOKING *MYTHOS*

Commemoration of the Ancestors

M. SHAWN COPELAND

"We are surrounded by so great a cloud of witnesses."

Hebrews 12:1

The phrase "popular religion" or "popular religious expression" refers to particular devotions or rituals or practices that originate from within a people's religious response to their particular historical and social circumstances and needs.[1] Such practices or devotions emerge from the *sensus fidelium,* that is, the faith-filled sense of the people's relationship with God and their desire to express that relationship concretely and publicly in an embodied way. These practices in no way oppose "official" devotions of the church, but complement and enrich them through the creative audacity and assumptive authority of socially and/or religiously marginalized groups. These peoples adapt or revise or reconfigure certain devotions or rituals to ongoing and, sometimes, new ends. Thus, the "popular" in popular religion adverts "to the sociohistorical fact that [its] religious symbols, practices, and narratives are *of the people*."[2]

Several symbols, narratives, and practices compose African American (or black) Catholic popular religion.[3] These include the iconography of the cross, Marian iconography (Our Mother of Africa), veneration of saints, pouring libation, rites of passage, the *kujenga* youth retreat, ancestor commemoration, ritualized Vespers, celebrations of Kwanzaa, the installation of elders, humming or moaning, and spontaneous utterances affirming parts or the whole of a sermon or a testimony (e.g., "Watch out, now!" or "Amen!" or "Yes, Lord!"). These practices reflect African American Catholic spiritual pragmatism[4] and practical theological agency. By the term *practice,* I mean the performance of certain words or actions through which something is realized. Religious or spiritual practices are complex integrative practices: linked behaviors and sayings joined through cognitive, prescriptive, and affective structures that seek to bring about certain inner dispositions (e.g., peace or patience) or ends (e.g., stillness or transcendence).[5] Ritual practices insinuate ambiguity: even though they are not rigid, they are fixed; even though they evolve, they are circumscribed. African American Catholic religious practices are demarcated by a thick psychic and spiritual force field woven together from (1) desire for union with Divine Mystery, (2) fragile cultural memories, (3) personal relationships, (4) critical mindfulness, (5) convergences of intention, (6) meaningful signification, and (7) theological intelligibility of purpose and action.

In this essay, I want to deepen an earlier treatment of the Commemoration of the Ancestors as conducted annually by the Institute for Black Catholic Studies (IBCS) of Xavier University of Louisiana, New Orleans.[6] In this discussion, I want to reflect on this ritual practice as a creative and practical theological response to the ongoing need for ebonization in the Catholic Church in the United States. Further, I want to underscore the commemoration as an *African diasporic practice* by attending to its theological educational and geographic-aesthetic setting, the significance and fragility of collective cultural memories, and the recrudescent power of African aesthetic principles. Finally, I want to draw attention to the ontological and moral effect of this ritual practice on African American Catholics and its capacity to sustain them in an affirming and nurturing *mythos* of belonging.

THE SETTING: THEOLOGICAL EDUCATIONAL AND GEOGRAPHIC-AESTHETIC

The Institute for Black Catholic Studies is the first and primary laboratory for research, study, and practical theological analysis and reflection on African American Catholic experience. The curricula of its constituent programs (graduate studies in pastoral theology and continuing education in youth ministry, catechist formation, and leadership in the faith community) are developed from "an interdisciplinary and participative vantage point, shaped around solid theological core courses, and focused on critical reflection regarding pastoral work."[7] Since its inception in 1980, the Institute has committed itself to the formation and nurturance of a black Catholic religious praxis, that is, conscious affective, moral, aesthetic, and cognitive responsiveness to Divine Mystery expressed through sensibilities, styles, and practices rooted in an African heritage recognized as diverse and plural. This praxis aims for critical and practical theological engagement with the black life-world. To this end, the Institute appropriates and transmits Roman Catholic doctrinal and theological traditions and steeps its faculty and students in serious historical, theological, cultural, and sociological research, teaching, study, and action for *critical cultural interventions* in local parishes. Thus, the comprehensive theological orientation of the Institute is critical and praxial, providing "a black articulation of Catholic faith and a Christian interpretation of black experience."[8]

New Orleans provides more than a mere geographic setting for the Institute. The city has been the site of and witness to profound spiritual, cultural, and aesthetic agony and power. As the leading city of the lower South in the nineteenth century, New Orleans rivaled New York, Philadelphia, Baltimore, and Charleston in commercial activity and prosperity; but, in large measure, its success rested on trade in black bodies. The first ship carrying captured Africans for sale arrived in Louisiana in 1719, and "over the next dozen years roughly 6,000 bound men, women, and children entered the colony through the slave trade."[9] Nearly a century later, New Orleans hosted the largest slave market in the United States.

Historian Gwendolyn Midlo Hall contends that, like other colonial cities in the Americas, New Orleans was the site of vivid, "intense and often violent contacts among people of varied nations, races, classes, languages, and traditions." But in New Orleans, she concludes, "the African imprint was formidable."[10] Indeed, traces of Bakongo, Mandé, and Yoruba cultures reverberate throughout the city: in Congo Square, where enslaved Africans drummed and danced well into the nineteenth century; in the Tremé district, where St. Augustine's Catholic Church holds the tomb of the Unknown Slave; in the French Quarter's Royal Orleans Hotel and Café Maspero, where slave traders and slave holders conducted the sale and purchase of black human flesh; in the "cities of the dead," the eighteenth- and nineteenth-century cemeteries St. Louis I and II, where Mandé blacksmiths and their descendants left coded symbols wrought in iron on grave vaults; in the dance movements of second-line parades; in the spices and peppers, greens and roux, that flavor the cuisine; in the polyphony and polyrhythm, dissonances and synchronicities, grotesque and beauty, of daily life.

These signs along with the practices of masking and music, drumming and dance, storytelling and speech, vivid vesture and vivacious gesture, coalesce as a fertile, variegated, and dense religious-aesthetic-cultural ground. In African American cultural consciousness, New Orleans radiates power and liminality: here the dead and the living vie for space; here spirit and flesh bare themselves, couple and uncouple, heal and astonish; here love supreme subverts culture and race to sculpt new identities and possibilities; here blues fugues a transcendental aesthetic that welds mourning and joy. In the "highly energized interaction of history and memory," New Orleans forms a *lieu de mémoire*, a "material, symbolic, and functional"[11] site of iconic religiosity, sensuous imagination, and historical consciousness.

FORMATION OF PRACTICAL THEOLOGICAL AGENCY

The Institute for Black Catholic Studies assumes responsibility for the pastoral formation of African American Catholic laity and those who minister in predominantly African American Catholic parishes. While black Catholics may and do matriculate in other pastoral programs of study, *as far as I know, only* the Institute carries out a comprehensive pedagogical and practical pastoral program of study through which African American Catholic cultural specialists, historians, liturgists, musicians, experts in ministry and spirituality, and theologians collaborate to hand on the faith and to discern and instantiate gifts of African American culture within the Roman Catholic Church.[12] On the one hand, this collaboration meets a longstanding and continuing deficiency in the national ministerial priorities of the American Catholic Church. For too long a time now, African American Catholics have been perceived as numerically insignificant and presumed to be a religious Other (*read*: Protestant). As Dominican theologian Jamie T. Phelps states: "African American Catholics experience a double invisibility, and devaluation. In the Black world we are marginalized because of our religious identity as Catholics, and in the Catholic world we are marginalized because of our racial identity as African Americans."[13] Under these circumstances this collaborative mode unveils the moral fortitude and *uncommon faithfulness* of African American Catholics.

On the other hand, that most of those involved in this collaboration are laypeople should come as no surprise. Cyprian

Davis in *The History of Black Catholics in the United States* shows the historic indispensability of educated, dedicated, and proactive lay leadership in handing on and sustaining the faith. The Black Catholic Lay Congresses of the nineteenth century represent a conspicuous example of laity taking responsibility for the care of black souls. Between 1889 and 1894, black Catholic lay delegates from across the nation[14] met in assembly to read and hear papers, conducted surveys of the treatment of black Catholics in parishes and dioceses, proposed recommendations for the education of black Catholic youth as well as for sound catechesis, called for the recruitment of blacks to the priesthood and vowed religious life, and pledged to take responsibility for evangelization among the larger black community.[15]

The Institute is heir to this legacy of black Catholic *traditio*, of handing on of the faith. It does so through the formation of practical theological agency among black Catholic laity. At the same time, the Institute's programs of study and formation welcome and nurture clergy and vowed religious of *all* races and cultures, *all* ages, and *all* geographic locales, who minister to and/or seek to understand and to affirm the *religious praxis* of African American Catholics for the good of the whole church.

The Institute is heir to this legacy of black Catholic *traditio*, of handing on of the faith. It does so through the formation of practical theological agency among black Catholic laity.

The Institute provides an intellectual, worshipful, and aesthetic experimental laboratory in which black Catholic laity are "educated in ways of knowing, perceiving, relating, and acting that enable" effective leadership in service to the mission of Jesus.[16] The Institute accords primacy to daily Eucharist and daily communal prayer and is imbued with an active commitment to the liberation of the Christian message in order to bring about a way of living that nurtures reconciliation between human persons and God, among human persons of *all* races and cultures, and between humankind and all creation. To this end, the Institute takes up the formation of black Catholic practical theological agents. This entails (1) instruction in critical and theological, historical and cultural, studies necessary for ministry in local parishes; (2) sound training in doctrine; (3) competence in theological reflection; and (4) development of a practicum project, a *critical cultural intervention* that concretely and practically demonstrates the integration of interdisciplinary pastoral study and theology and that contributes to local parish life or to a diocesan program.[17] A sample of more than three decades of such *critical cultural interventions* includes a program for training catechists in pedagogies drawing on African American culture, a plan for reviving spirituality among inactive black Catholics, cultural strategies to enhance self-esteem among black Catholic female adolescents, approaches to the use of African American literature to enhance faith witnessing and sharing within families, a program to introduce African American culture to a religious order of men, correlations between African American practices of discernment and the Spiritual Exercises of St. Ignatius of Loyola, constructing an oral history of a black Catholic parish, and formulation of models of communal parish theological reflection.[18] These and many other *critical cultural interventions* in parishes in Baltimore; Brooklyn; Chicago; Houston; Lake Charles, Louisiana; St. Louis; and Washington, DC, have enabled African American Catholics (and their collaborators) to live out practical theological agency in handing on the faith. As agents of practical theology, African American Catholics enrich parish intellectual life with the goods of passionate and rigorous research and saturate parish liturgical life with the Spirit's gifts of embodied prayer, spontaneous responsorality, dance, chant, and song.

As agents of practical theology, African American Catholics enrich parish intellectual life with the goods of passionate and rigorous research and saturate parish liturgical life with the Spirit's gifts of embodied prayer, spontaneous responsorality, dance, chant, and song.

THE RITUAL PRACTICE: COMMEMORATION OF THE ANCESTORS

The Annual Commemoration of the Ancestors forms the primary public popular religious practice of the Institute.[19] This event is held on or close to the U.S. Day of Independence, the Fourth of July. The choice of date directly contests any simplistic celebration and interpretation of freedom in the United States and raises the memory of chattel slavery, which the nation so slyly obscures. For several years, the Institute has partnered with the Ashé Cultural Center of New Orleans in commemorating *Maafa*. The word *maafa* is of Kiswahili origin, means "great" or "horrific" tragedy, and refers to the trauma of the Middle Passage. Commemoration of *Maafa* takes place on the Saturday closest to the Fourth of July.[20] This event begins at Congo Square with drumming, libation, intercession, and prayer, and, perhaps, one or two brief speeches are made. Accompanied by drumming, participants process in relative silence through the French Quarter and pause at sites historically associated with the slave trade. The procession concludes at the banks of the Mississippi River, although on some occasions the group has ferried across the river to pay homage at Algiers Point, the site of an

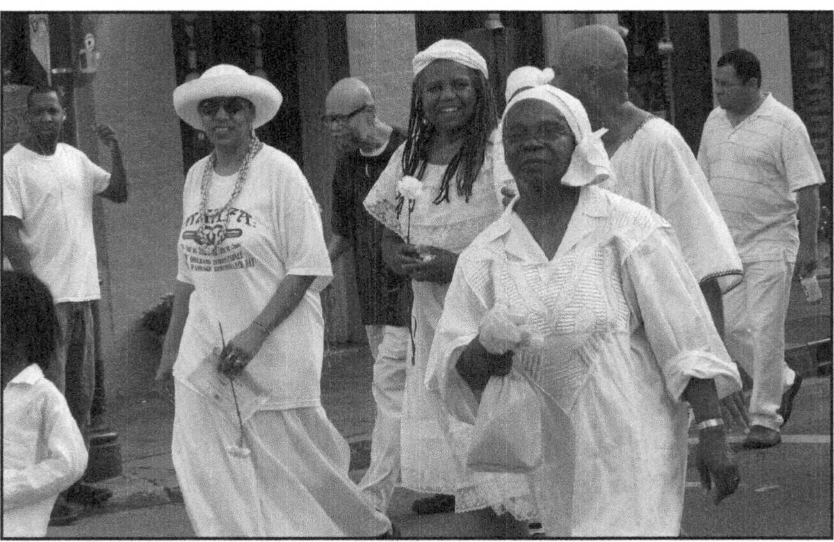

African village during the period of enslavement. Finally, participants are welcome to feasting at the Cultural Center.

An established, if flexible, rubric orders the Commemoration of the Ancestors, even as improvisation and adaptation to circumstance contribute energy and acknowledge particularity. Nonetheless, several more or less common features and a general structure of the ceremony may be outlined as follows: summons of the drum to gather the community and guests; libation and prayer; processional; readings; singing; storytelling; "walking" the circle; and feasting with the ancestors, guests, and members of the Institute community.

The drum calls participants to the appointed place of gathering and holds their waiting. Ordinarily, the director of the Institute presides over the ritual, but a female or male member of the Institute faculty (ordained or nonordained) also may assume this role. Male and female dancers and drummers—some professionals, others students—all take part. Institute community elders, female and male, pour libation (most often water) onto the ground as an offering of respect to the One Holy Triune God and to the ancestors. Libation enables the symbolic and ritual participation of the ancestors and is accompanied by a litany addressing them and those canonized as saints of the church. Among those who are petitioned for guidance and protection and invited to be present are Our Mother of Africa (Mary), Daniel Rudd, Harriet Thompson, Booker Ashe, Dolores Harrall, Joseph Davis, Lucy Williams, Beatrice Jeffries, Leon Roberts, St. Katharine Drexel, St. Josephine Bakhita, Venerable Pierre Toussaint, Servant of God Elizabeth Lange, and Venerable Henriette Delille.

When the recitation of the litany has been completed, the gathered assembly moves in silent procession to the site of commemoration, swaying and dancing, led by an incense bearer and dancers, the drums setting the pace and rhythm. Once participants reach the site of the ceremony, singing follows, the music chosen from the spirituals. Next, a person or persons (male and female) serving as the *griot*, the keeper and teller of the story,

recites the origin of the Institute, placing it in the context of black and black Catholic history. Since the ancestors "are not mental concepts, but historical people,"[21] the *griot* identifies, names, and calls on the local or familial ancestors of the Institute. The gifts and achievements of these beloved dead are publicly recited, received, affirmed, and reincorporated into the black Catholic story.[22] When the prayers to and for the dead and the living are completed, when meditation, drumming, and singing cease, the ceremony flows into dancing and tears, joy and sorrow, and feasting with the ancestors, guests, and the Institute community.

The Commemoration of Ancestors poses a correspondence with the communion of saints, for the unity of the dead and living forms an ancient and treasured part of the faith. On Catholic doctrinal teaching, the very term *communion of saints* intimates communion in holy things (*sancta*) and communion among holy persons (*sancti*) who, brought together by the Lord to his own table, feed from his own hand on his own flesh and blood that they might grow in the communion (*koinonia*) of the Holy Spirit and communicate the gospel's message to a broken and hurting world. The notion of organic solidarity provides the interpretative key that unlocks theological resonances between these two memorials. The ancestors are a "source of solidarity, communication, and reciprocity among the living."[23] Not only do they command reverence and remembrance, but the ancestors also bind *a people* one to another in acts of mutual love and compassion, respect and shared responsibility for the present. Thus, the dead *mission* the living to *all* those whom the dominant society excludes, consigns to the prison-industrial complex, and criminalizes by homelessness, substance abuse, and poverty; and the living resolve to respond and participate with greater determination in Christ's redemption of the future.

COLLECTIVE CULTURAL MEMORY

Heuristically, as Bernard Lonergan suggests, culture denotes a set of meanings and values that inform a way of life.[24] In the articulation, depiction, performance, and handing on (*traditio*) of those meanings and value, memory performs a vital task: it opens access to a past, makes a future possible, and renders the present functional. Collective cultural memory emerges from a field of common and complementary experience and is enriched by diverse expressions of those experiences. Collective cultural memories constitute *a people as who they are*. Collective cultural memory socializes; most of what human beings learn about how to operate in the world, they learn from others. It selects, retains, preserves, "distinguishes significant events and people from the mundane, and so infuses the past with moral meaning."[25] But when loss and indifference, absence and evasion, also inflect collective cultural memories, their ontological and moral potential may be fragmented or damaged. Sometimes whole peoples forget or choose not to remember, sometimes they will themselves not to forget, and sometimes they are coerced not to remember. Still memory not only is not disinterested, it is also fallible and malleable.

Chattel slavery problematizes African American collective cultural memory. The violent tearing of *embodied* gestures, behaviors, languages, styles, dispositions, rhythms, taboos, and norms from their original matrices has unmoored their expressions from their original meanings and value and left them fragmented and scattered throughout the Americas. Centuries of bondage, physical and sexual abuse, lynching, segregation, and discrimination have not eradicated *completely* cultural memories within African American communities. But these events, Anthony Pinn contends, have left those memories "fragile and cultural artifacts decontextualized."[26] At the same time, detached from their contexts, these memories and cultural artifacts, as Franz Fanon declares, have been disfigured and distorted by the dominant culture.[27] The artifacts of African American culture have been made to vanish, rendered invisible, considered as belonging to no one. Thus, even African Americans wonder whether African Americans have a culture.[28] But "fragile memory," Pinn remarks, "is [not] worthless; rather simply fragile."[29]

In structuring ritual practices, the fragility of memory demands patience, persistence, rigorous research, critical scholarship, and creativity. Moreover, practices require time and practice; complex practices require more time and more practice. For at least twenty years now, members of the Institute for Black Catholic Studies have collaborated to develop, evolve, review, refine, and adapt the ritual practice of commemoration of ancestors. Their active communal work demonstrates practical theology's commitment to research, to "reflective conversation,"[30] to critical interpretation, and to pragmatic revision and refinement. More specifically, their work depended (and depends) on critical attunement of mind and eye, heart and ear, to rhythms that permeate the black life-world; passionate and rigorous research of signs and significations of Bakongo and Yoruba cultures; vigorous and delicate, subtle and adamant, negotiations of fragile cultural memories; improvisations of thought and word (theology), tension and nuance; and active contemplative presence, silence, and prayer.

COMMEMORATION OF ANCESTORS AS AN AFRICAN DIASPORIC PRACTICE

The term *African diasporic practice* denotes the religio-cultural and aesthetic sayings and doings of people of African descent in the Americas. Diasporic practices reflect the influence of certain African aesthetic principles, including "dominance of a percussive performance; call and response; battles of aesthetic virtuosity between two singers, or two dance groups, and so forth."[31] These principles are best recognized, understood, and appreciated when we know what Robert Farris Thompson calls their "atomic weight," which I take to mean the quality of resonance of a particular practice or performance relative to an indigenous standard. In the case of the complex practice of Commemoration of Ancestors, those standards "lie embedded in the aesthetic vocabularies of the Yoruba of Nigeria and Benin, and the Bakongo of Congo, Bas-Zaire, and Angola."[32]

African diasporic practices figure as "utopian eruptions of space into the linear temporal order" of modernity.[33] Whereas casual onlookers or the uninitiated or inattentive might see in diasporic practices only the exotic or outlandish, prepared participants or those informed by African cultures recognize processioneering or solemnized walking as the rerouting of habitual geographic circuits, forming a circle for ritual action as claiming and commanding and marking sacred a space and place—all in the mediation of dense religio-cultural significations. Most important, these practices make present those living memories that cannot be erased: the very bodies of the descendants of the Africans who survived the Middle Passage and enslavement provoke the dangerous memory of a past that is only obscured and must be confronted.

In structuring the ritual practice of Commemoration of the Ancestors, the Institute draws on properties of Bakongo culture.[34] This ritual practice brings together Roman Catholic and Bakongo regard for the dead: the African American Catholic community embraces and addresses the Many Thousand Gone of the Middle Passage, intercedes for African and African American ancestors as well as the Church Suffering, and remembers those African American Catholic dead who are the very seed of our faith. Moreover, this ritual practice represents more than an annual and solemn necrology, although it *is* this; Bakongo and Roman Catholic regard for the dead compenetrate one another. The honored dead, both those who died long ago and the deceased of more recent memory, remain, even in death, most intimately connected to the living—involved in daily affairs, bestowing blessing, or meting out punishment.

Great care is taken with the environment of the ritual space. No liturgical or ritual activity is "simply an activity of the spirit," writes Nwaka Egbulem; "the eyes, the nose, the ears, the hands, the feet, the mouth all have to be involved in one way or another [to realize] a unifying experience."[35] Pattern and color caress the eye: a crucifix draped in kente cloth commands prominence, baskets and gourds filled with flowers and fruits are artfully arranged, material imprinted with Adinkra symbols from Ghana's Akan culture covers tables and pedestals. Finally always, photographs of those recognized as founders of the Institute, Thaddeus J. Posey, OFM, Cap, PhD; Reverend Joseph Nearon, SSS, STD; Sister Thea Bowman, FSPA, PhD; and Brother Bede Abrams, OFM, Conv, STL—all now deceased—are displayed along with those of two recently deceased elders of the community, Mother Elencia Shynes and Mother Vivian Rouson.[36]

A circular "social geometry"[37] features in this ritual. The visual and physical arrangements of chairs and/or stools and, often, pebbles on the floor of the room literally replicate the Bakongo cosmogram. This figural rendition offers a way of stating in ideograph or picture writing the vitality and significance of the connection of the community of the living to the visions and hopes of the dead. Participants, ordinarily dressed in white traditional West African attire, enter the site moving in a counterclockwise direction and take their seats. This counterclockwise movement accords with Bakongo belief that the rhythm of human life (ontology) follows the rhythm of nature (cosmology). Bakongo hold that human life has no end, that it constitutes a cycle.[38] That cycle signifies the four moments of the sun: (1) rising—meaning birth or beginning, (2) ascendency—indicating maturity and responsibility (e.g., initiation, taking of titles, marriage, and so on), (3) setting—meaning death as a transition or transformation, and (4) midnight—inferring existence in the other and ancestral world and reincarnating birth. Moreover, counterclockwise movement echoes the four winds and four corners of the earth. For the men and women and children who underwent the trauma of the Middle Passage, this ocean journey physically charted the *kalunga line,* the boundary line that reckoned the unity of the living and the dead; but the Middle Passage would have disoriented the captive Africans' sense and experience of time, life, death, and life in death.

Members of the Institute community may be invited to "walk" the circle for or on behalf of the dead. Each person moves counterclockwise around the space. This ritual walk honors the Many Thousand Gone, the ancestors of the Middle Passage, and the honored and beloved black and black Catholic dead. Moreover, as Estella Conwill Majozo points out, this ritual walk makes present "the pilgrimage path upon grounds made holy by the tears, sweat, and blood of our people."[39] With regard to the local or familial ancestors of the Institute, it allows for their *personification,* and, in this way, the memory of a particular man or woman is vivified in the body of another. Often, Institute elders, administrators or faculty, or visiting national or diocesan or local parish leaders are invited to walk the circle as their contributions to church, community, and society are publicly recited, received, affirmed, and incorporated into the African American Catholic story. The walk *marks, performs,* and *resonates*. The walk *marks* a point of contact between the worlds of the living and the dead. It *performs* the duty of attending the pilgrimage of the dead to their place of rest. Finally, the walk *resonates* with parading in Yoruba and Bakongo cultures. As Thompson observes: "[T]o parade, with or without masks, was a serious matter in Kongo. Bakongo believe the ritual processioners ideally carry fortune and spiritual rebirth to a village that they circle [and] that processioneering around a village can mystically heal its hidden problems, can 'cool' the entire settlement with circling gestures of felicity and good faith."[40]

The Commemoration of Ancestors as an African diasporic practice insinuates a continual return of the past in order to revivify and reconstitute *both* the Institute as a community *and* each member who forms and is formed within that community. Thus, the ritual strengthens communal and personal faith, reinvigorates purpose, enfolds participants in black and black Catholic history, and energizes weary spirits. At the same time, the ritual evokes and performs mourning and loss. Mourning for the dead of the Middle Passage, mourning for the unnamed and unknown enslaved women and men who survived on whispers, hopes, and prayers of freedom for their children's children's children can never be completed. Always, weight must be and is given to ambiguity, opacity, and incalculability of loss. Finally, as an African diasporic practice, Commemoration of the Ancestors *choreographs* movements of nature, of being, and of history. Respectfully and delicately appropriating Bakongo belief regarding the unity of nature and human being, tensively holding a history at once terrifying and terrifyingly beautiful, the ritual practice of commemoration of ancestors reiterates the ethical responsibility of memory and the "ethical impossibility of forgetting."[41]

EVOKING *MYTHOS*, MAKING MEANING

"But, where is home? In a fragmented state, home is a mythic place to which there is no return."[42] G. M. James Gonzalez asks and answers a poignant longing, one that fragile cultural memories yearn to answer, yet will never do so fully. Popular religious practices and, in particular, ritual practices gesture toward home, evoke myth, make meaning—make home. For a people whose black bodies are despised, whose faith praxis comes under suspicion, whose culture is dismissed as nonexistent or pathological or deprived,[43] popular religious ritual practices provide a crucial mediation for human subjectivity. These practices evoke *mythos* through which meaning is made and sustained, even if only for a few minutes, as flashes of consciousness of home erupt and "heaven's glamour"[44] embraces those in longing.

The ceremony of Commemoration of the Ancestors functions in at least five ways. *First,* as a *critical cultural intervention* in devotional practices in the U.S. church, the ceremony advances recognition of this regional church as a diverse and plural community of differing races, cultures, ethnicities, and nationalities, with differing gifts and needs, differing challenges and difficulties, yet drawn together for the mission of Jesus. *Second,* the ritual illustrates the practical theological competence of trained African American Catholics—women and men, lay and ordained—and their desire and willingness for collaboration. *Third,* for African American Catholics, the ritual practice promotes the remembrance of the dead who have lived and worked for, among, alongside, and on behalf of this community. The ritual practice lifts up their lives, for example, and allows those lives to influence and shape the lives and ministries of members of the black Catholic community. *Fourth,* the ritual allows the living cocreators of black Catholic thought and praxis to be seen by the Institute community. Through their public presentation to the ancestors and to the whole African American Catholic community as represented by the Institute, this cadre of leaders and teachers, vowed religious and priests and laity, are challenged and strengthened to live a life worthy of their calling. Moreover, the leadership these women and men exercise is recognized publicly *as African American Catholic* and acknowledged as rooted in baptismal charism and in educational and cultural competence, as self-initiating and attentive to the signs of the times, as committed to social justice in the concrete, as collaborative, and as prayerful. And, the entire community is invited to personal and communal self-examination.

Fifth, the ceremony teaches the African American Catholic story as one of uncommon faithfulness and love, perseverance and service, courage and integrity. Telling and performing the story nurtures an intimate bond with the ancestors and between and among the Institute and its new members, both students and faculty, and reaffirms that bond between returning members. Finally, as members of a church in which all too often they have been denied the joys, challenges, and possibilities of intersubjective community, the very elemental meaning of belonging, African American Catholics seek and find communion, belonging, and home with the ancestors and the beloved black Catholic dead. To pour out libation to them signifies conscious and willing acceptance of the wisdom, comfort, and courage of that great cloud of witnesses whose visitation descends in accord with the Spirit.

Notes

1. As a theological category through which to apprehend *traditioning* and traditions (*traditiones*), popular religion has been associated with the work of Latino/a theologians Orlando O. Espín, *The Faith of the People: Theological Reflections on Popular Catholicism* (Maryknoll, NY: Orbis Books, 1997); Roberto S. Goizueta, *Caminemos, Con Jesús: Toward a Hispanic/ Latino Theology of Accompaniment* (Maryknoll, NY: Orbis Books, 1995); Alejandro García-Rivera, *St. Martin de Porres: The "Little Stories" and the Semiotics of Culture* (Maryknoll, NY: Orbis Books, 1995); and Jeanette Rodríguez-Holguín, *Our Lady of Guadalupe: Faith and Empowerment Among Mexican-American Women* (Austin: University of Texas Press, 1994).

2. Goizueta, *Caminemos, Con Jesús*, 21.

3. The designations "African American" and "black" are used interchangeably here to refer to the descendants of the enslaved Africans in the United States; however, I am aware that not all black Catholics are African Americans. Moreover, the descriptor "African American" may be applied as well to descendants of enslaved Africans in Latin America (e.g., Brazil, Colombia, Ecuador) and the Caribbean (e.g., Haiti, Cuba,

Jamaica, Trinidad and Tobago). Within the United States, this appellation has been problematized by contemporary immigration from Africa and the Caribbean. Kobina Aidoo popularized this issue in his documentary film *The Neo-African-Americans: Black Immigrant Identities* (2008).

4. Africans have often been described as spiritual pragmatists; in other words, they are comfortable in selectively incorporating or utilizing multiple religious traditions in the resolution of difficulties or the pursuit of wisdom. Spiritual pragmatism is an African and African diasporic cultural characteristic.

5. Theodore R. Schatzki, *Social Practices: A Wittgensteinian Approach to Human Activity and the Social* (Cambridge, UK: Cambridge University Press, 1996), 89–90, 99–101.

6. See my "Tradition and the Traditions of African American Catholicism," *Theological Studies* 61, no. 4 (December 2000): 632–55. From 1991 through 2005, I served as a member of the faculty at the Institute, a member of the Policy Committee and associate director for the Degree Program, and had the privilege of collaborating in development of the Commemoration of the Ancestors. I am *not* suggesting in any way that no other racial, cultural-ethnic group honors its dead; nor am I implying that this practice happens *only* in New Orleans, since many students and faculty from the Institute have spread the ritual practice of Commemoration of Ancestors to many other cities and parishes. I am lifting up a ritual practice that has become a significant event with ongoing meaning in the life of a practical theological community.

7. "Educational Philosophy," on the Web site for the Institute for Black Catholic Studies, Xavier University of Louisiana, New Orleans, accessed September 7, 2013, http://www.xula.edu/ibcs/index.php.

8. Joseph Nearon, "Introduction," in *Theology: A Portrait in Black, Proceedings of the 1978 Black Catholic Theological Symposium*, ed. Thaddeus J. Posey (Pittsburgh, PA: The Capuchin Press, 1980), 5.

9. Emily Clark and Virginia Meacham Gould, "The Feminine Face of Afro-Catholicism in New Orleans, 1727–1852," *The William and Mary Quarterly* (April 2002): para. 9, accessed September 7, 2013, http://www.historycooperative.org/cgi-bin

/justtop.cgi?act=justtop&;url=http://www.historycooperative.org/journals/wm/59.2/clark.html.

10. Gwendolyn Midlo Hall, "The Formation of Afro-Creole Culture," in *Creole New Orleans: Race and Americanization*, ed. Arnold R. Hirsch and Joseph Logsdon (Baton Rouge: Louisiana State University Press, 1992), 58.

11. Pierre Nora, "Between Memory and History: *Les Lieux de Mémoire*," in *History and Memory in African-American Culture*, ed. Geneviève Fabre and Robert O'Meally (New York: Oxford University Press, 1994), 295.

12. I mention here the names of a few *Roman Catholics* who teach or have taught at the Institute: *cultural specialists*: Eva Regina Martin and Sue Houchins; *historians*: Cyprian Davis, Cecilia Moore, Thaddeus Posey; *liturgists/musicians*: Rawn Harbour, Veronica Downs-Dorsey, Luther Grey; *experts in ministry and spirituality*: Kathleen Dorsey Bellow, C. Vanessa White; *theologians*: M. Shawn Copeland, Shawnee-Marie Daniels-Sykes, Diana Hayes, Bryan Massingale, Paulinus Odozor, Jamie T. Phelps, Elochukwu Uzukwu. For reasons of space, I have not named Protestant scholars who have taught at the Institute for many years.

13. Jamie T. Phelps, "Introduction: Theology from an African American Catholic Perspective," in *Black and Catholic: The Challenge and Gift of Black Folk, Contributions of African American Experience and Thought to Catholic Theology*, ed. Jamie T. Phelps, 2nd ed. (Milwaukee, WI: Marquette University Press, 2002), 21.

14. Women were not among delegates to the first Congress in 1889 and, in his address to the assembly, Robert L. Ruffin of Boston commented on their absence. "I should liked to have seen delegates from the females," he said, "for I recognize the work which women are doing in bringing men to a higher civilization," cited in *Three Catholic Afro-American Congresses* (Cincinnati: The American Catholic Tribune, 1893; reprint ed.: New York: Arno Press, 1978), 17. It is not clear if women were delegates to other meetings, but close inspection of a photograph of some of the participants attending the 1892 Congress reveals the faces of at least four laywomen and one religious sister (*Three Afro-American Congresses*, 1).

15. Cyprian Davis, *The History of Black Catholics in the United States* (New York: Crossroad Publishing, 1990), 163–94. Daniel Rudd, born a slave in Bardstown, Kentucky, in 1854, was the chief inspiration and organizer of these congresses; in 1886 he founded and published the *American Catholic Tribune*, a weekly black newspaper through which he introduced black Catholics and their needs to the church.

16. Dorothy C. Bass and Craig Dykstra, "Introduction," in *For Life Abundant: Practical Theology, Theological Education, and Christian Ministry*, ed. Dorothy C. Bass and Craig Dykstra, Kindle Edition (Grand Rapids, MI: William B. Eerdmans Publishing Company, 2008), Loc. 20/4865.

17. The Institute for Black Catholic Studies, Xavier University of Louisiana, The Master of Theology, Handbook (2013), 24, accessed September 7, 2013, http://www.xula.edu/ibcs/documents/degreeHandbook.pdf.

18. These topics of *critical cultural interventions* were proposed and carried out by Juanita Blackshear, LaReine-Marie Mosley, Willa Ellis Golden, Richard M. Potts, J. Timothy Hipskind, Thomas Clark, and Donald Chambers.

19. The Institute also has adapted the recitation of Vespers as an African American Catholic practice. In the format devised by the Institute, this evening prayer of the church includes a processional, singing (ordinarily from among spirituals), readings from the Bible and other culturally pertinent text(s), antiphonal recitation of prayers, periods of silence, a sermon, and a spirited recessional. Ordinarily, a laywoman or layman presides and preaches at Vespers.

20. Developed by Dr. Marimba Ani, the concept of *Maafa* denotes the experience of the Middle Passage. The Ashé Cultural Center notes, "the Maafa Commemoration offers an opportunity for the whole community to pause and reflect on this great transgression against humanity and to personally, as a community, agree to distance ourselves institutionally in word and deed from that transgression, its legacy and the evolved practice of racism in our civic, social, spiritual and personal lives." "What is the Maafa?" on the Web site for the Ashé Cultural Center, accessed on

September 7, 2013, http://www.ashecac.org/main/index.php/news-a-events/what-is-the-maafa.

21. Nwaka Chris Egbulem, *The Power of Afrocentric Celebrations: Inspirations from the Zairean Liturgy* (New York: Crossroad Publishing, 1996), 91.

22. The reader should note that, among most African cultures, *not every deceased person becomes a true ancestor*. According to Egbulem, "Moral excellence, bravery, successful social and family life, and other qualities are important criteria in establishing who is truly an ancestor. In some tribes it is still true that people who do not have offspring may never be regarded as ancestors, since they have no descendants to perpetuate their names" (Egbulem, *The Power of Africentric Celebrations*, 60). The Institute addresses the ancestors without name, yet infers that certain beloved black Catholic dead may be counted among their company.

23. F. Eboussi Boulaga, *Christianity without Fetishes: An African Critique and Recapture of Christianity*, trans. Robert Barr (Maryknoll, NY: Orbis Books, 1984), 82.

24. Bernard Lonergan, "Response of the Jesuit as Priest and Apostle in the Modern World," in *A Second Collection by Bernard J. F. Lonergan*, ed. William F. J. Ryan and Bernard J. Tyrrell (Philadelphia, PA: Westminster Press, 1974), 183.

25. Barry Schwartz, "Iconography and Collective Memory: Lincoln's Image in the American Mind," *The Sociological Quarterly* 32, no. 3 (Autumn 1991): 301–19, at 302, http://www.jstor.org/stable/4120910.

26. Anthony Pinn, *Varieties of African American Religious Experience* (Minneapolis, MN: Fortress Press, 1998), 190, 192. In this section, I am following his argument closely.

27. Franz Fanon, "On National Culture," in *The Wretched of the Earth*, Kindle Edition, trans. Richard Philcox (New York: Grove Press, 2004 [1963]), 149.

28. A few years ago, an African American undergraduate at Boston College told me some of her Caribbean friends insisted that African Americans had no culture. "Do we have culture?" she asked. I assured her that African Americans do have culture, naming our music, inventions, cuisine, style, and so forth. But, I also pointed out that most of the time those contributions are over-

looked as distinctively our contributions and are appropriated as "universal" by the dominant culture.

29. Pinn, *Varieties of African American Religious Experience*, 190, 192.

30. Richard Osmer, *Practical Theology: An Introduction* (Grand Rapids, MI: William B. Eerdmans Publishing Company, 2008), 4.

31. Robert Farris Thompson, "Recapturing Heaven's Glamour: Afro-Caribbean Festivalizing Arts," in *Caribbean Festival Arts: Every Little Piece of Difference*, ed. John W. Nunley and Barbara A. Bettelheim (Seattle: University of Washington Press, 1988), 19.

32. Ibid.

33. Paul Gilroy, *The Black Atlantic: Modernity and Double Consciousness* (Cambridge, MA: Harvard University Press, 1993), 198.

34. Philip Curtin, *The Atlantic Slave Trade, A Census* (Madison, WI: University of Wisconsin Press, 1969); see also Robert Farris Thompson and Joseph Cornet, *The Four Moments of the Sun: Kongo Art in Two Worlds* (Washington, DC: National Gallery of Art, 1981), 32, 27.

35. Egbulem, *The Power of Afrocentric Celebrations*, 129.

36. Thaddeus J. Posey died August 7, 2013, as this essay was being written; Mother Shynes was a native of Philadelphia, Pennsylvania, and Mother Vivian Rouson most recently of Washington, DC.

37. Thompson, "Recapturing Heaven's Glamour," 20.

38. Robert Farris Thompson, *Flash of the Spirit: African and Afro-American Art and Philosophy* (New York: Random House/Vintage Books, 1984), 108.

39. Estella Conwill Majozo, *Libation: A Literary Pilgrimage through the African-American Soul* (New York: Harlem River Press, 1995), 11.

40. Thompson, "Recapturing Heaven's Glamour," 20.

41. I take the term *choreograph* from an article by Sara Kaplan, "Souls at the Crossroads, Africans on the Water: The Politics of Diasporic Melancholia," *Callaloo* 30, no. 2 (Spring 2007): 511–526, at 518 and 522.

42. G. M. James Gonzalez, "Of Property: On 'Captive' 'Bodies,' Hidden 'Flesh,' and Colonization," in *Existence in Black: An Anthology of Black Existential Philosophy*, ed. Lewis R. Gordon (New York: Routledge, 1997), 133.

43. See Jamie T. Phelps, "African American Culture: Source and Context of Black Catholic Theology and Church Mission," *Journal of Hispanic/Latino Theology* 3, no. 3 (February 1996): 43–58.

44. Thompson, "Recapturing Heaven's Glamour," 17.

CHAPTER 8

PRACTICING BEAUTY

Aesthetic Praxis, Justice, and U.S. Latino/a Popular Religion

ROBERTO S. GOIZUETA

Over the course of four decades, U.S. Latino/a theologians have helped retrieve several important dimensions of Christian tradition as sources for theological reflection. Perhaps the most significant such theological source has been popular religion. Latino/a theologians have mined key dimensions of Latino/a Christian life for their theological and spiritual riches. In so doing, Latino/a scholars have been inspired and informed by the ground-breaking insights of Latin American colleagues who have argued for the foundational methodological import of a "preferential option for the poor," thereby locating Christian praxis at the very heart of the theological task—not as this latter's consequence but as its very source. Latin American and U.S. Latino/a theologies are thus intrinsically "practical" theologies, even if the term itself is not often found in the literature of either. While retrieving the methodology of Latin American liberation theology, however, U.S. Latino/a theology has also made its own contribution to the understanding of the preferential option for the poor—and, thus, practical theology—by foregrounding dimensions of that practical option that become particularly salient when praxis is mediated by popular religion.

The understanding of praxis rooted in popular religion in turn reflects a particular theological anthropology, a particular understanding of not only what it means to *be* human but, even more important, what it means to *act* as a human. This way of acting, of "doing," is what one might call "aesthetic praxis."

In this essay, I examine the notion of aesthetic praxis and the underlying theological anthropology as embodied in the fiesta and narrative of Our Lady of Guadalupe. I suggest that the people's participation in the fiesta and recounting of the Guadalupan narrative reinforce a way of acting, a praxis that subverts the way of acting, or praxis of the dominant, post-Enlightenment U.S. culture. As sources for practical *theology*, moreover, such practices reveal not just a different understanding of *human* acting but a different understanding of *divine* acting, divine praxis, which represents an American resurrection-Pentecost.

To understand the significance of Our Lady of Guadalupe as embodying a particular, liberating understanding of praxis we should examine not only the ritual celebration, or fiesta, which takes place every year on December 12, but especially the narrative itself. As the story of an *encounter* between the Virgin and Juan Diego, this account is unlike other Marian apparitions in that the "recipient" of the apparition is an active participant and as much a protagonist as the Virgin herself; indeed, Juan Diego's emergence as a human subject is the mode in which he receives the Virgin's self-revelation and message. This uniqueness is neither coincidental nor irrelevant, for it is precisely what makes Our Lady of Guadalupe a liberating symbol and ritual; together, Guadalupe and Juan Diego reveal not only who God is and who we are but also how God *acts* and how we are thus called to act. Consequently, the narrative itself is central to the fiesta, providing the rationale for the latter and incorporating the community itself as its members reenact the story. Through such reenactments, the people themselves enter into and become actively identified with the indigenous man whose own identity is transformed by his encounter with *La Morenita* (the dark-skinned Lady).

GUADALUPE

The narrative enacted in the fiesta of Our Lady of Guadalupe is based on the *Nican Mopohua*, a text dating from the 1560s and written in Náhuatl, the language of the indigenous Nahua people. The events relayed in the text are said to have taken place in 1531, that is, "ten years after the conquest of Mexico City."[1] The first character that appears in the story is an Indian named Juan Diego Cuauhtlatoatzin. The terms used to describe him suggest that he is quite poor, though honorable and dignified.[2] As an indigenous man under Spanish colonial rule, Juan Diego is on his way to the bishop's palace in Mexico/Tlatelolco to receive instruction in the Christian faith. While traversing the hilly countryside, he hears the sound of many birds singing. So beautiful is the music that he imagines he must be in paradise. At this point, he cannot help himself; he must go find the source of such beautiful music, even if it means his trip to the bishop's palace is delayed. As he reaches a hill called Tepeyac, he hears another beautiful sound, this one a soft human voice calling out to him in his native tongue: "*Quihuia; Iuantzin Iuan Diegotzin*" (roughly, "my dearest, most beloved and dignified Juan Diego"). Knowing that Tepeyac was a sacred mountain, "the site where the goddess virgin-mother of the gods [*Tonantzín*] was venerated,"[3] Juan Diego proceeds to the top of the hill, where he comes face to face with a woman clothed in raiment of blinding beauty: "He marveled at her perfect beauty. Her clothing appeared like the sun, and it gave forth rays."[4] The woman identifies herself as the Virgin Mary: "Know and rest assured in your heart, my dearest child, that I am the Ever Virgin Mary, Mother of the God of Great Truth, *Téotl*, of Him by Whom we live, of the Creator of Persons, of the Master of what is Close and Together, of the Lord of Heaven and Earth."[5] She is the Mother of both the Christian God and the Nahua *Téotl*. After Juan Diego informs her that he is on the road to the bishop's palace (in Juan Diego's words, "her house") to receive religious instruction, the Virgin commands him to tell the bishop to construct a temple on Tepeyac, from where she can extend her love and protection to all her people. *This*, she insists, would be "her house" (i.e., not the bishop's palace).

Upon arriving at the episcopal seat of Tlatelolco, Juan Diego delivers his message to the bishop, Juan de Zumárraga, but is summarily turned away. Since he is a mere Indian, Juan Diego is not surprised by the bishop's rejection; he thereupon gives his report to the Virgin, entreating her to please send someone else on the important mission, someone more worthy of the bishop's attention: "Because, for sure, I am a meager peasant, a cord, a little ladder, the people's excrement, I am a leaf."[6] The Virgin not only spurns his request and self-deprecating language but, even more insistently, commands him to make a second attempt at delivering her message to the bishop. Finally acquiescing, Juan Diego returns to the bishop's palace, whereupon he is granted an audience but, once again, is turned away. This time, however, the bishop extends a fig leaf: bring me a sign that what you are saying is true, he tells Juan Diego, and I will believe you. Again making his report to the Virgin, she now tells Juan Diego to go home for the evening and return to Tepeyac the next morning, at which time she will give him a sign to take to the bishop.

The next morning, however, Juan Diego decides not to go to Tepeyac to see the Virgin, as his uncle, Juan Bernardino, has become extremely ill and is dying. The nephew will indeed now go to Tlatelolco, but on a quite different mission, for he is in search of a priest who can come and minister to his dying uncle. On the way, however, Juan Diego is intercepted by the Virgin, who asks him why he skipped their appointment on Tepeyac. Sheepishly, he gives his explanation. Telling him not to worry, the Virgin chides Juan Diego for not trusting in her love and protection, and assures him that Juan Bernardino will indeed recover from his illness.

Now confident and at peace, Juan Diego asks the Virgin for a sign to take to the bishop. She directs him to climb to the top of a nearby hill and bring her the roses he finds growing there. Juan

Diego is rather incredulous since that particular hill is known for its barren, rocky topography. Moreover, roses do not bloom during this time of the year. Nevertheless, he does as she asks and, indeed, finds beautiful roses, which he cuts, carefully places in his *tilma* (cloak), and brings to her. These flowers will be the sign that Juan Diego is to take to the bishop to convince him to build a temple on Tepeyac. Yet again, then, Juan Diego returns to the bishop's palace, though this time with the new "evidence." When he arrives at the bishop's residence, is ushered in, and opens his *tilma*, the flowers cascade to the floor. And on the *tilma* itself appears a detailed, brightly colored image of the Virgin. The bishop is converted and orders the construction of the temple on Tepeyac.

Throughout the Americas, this story is reenacted annually (often during a Mass) on December 12, the Feast of Our Lady of Guadalupe. These celebrations, usually beginning the evening before, involve plenty of music and dancing, with the community (usually led by mariachis) serenading the Virgin with the traditional song "Las Mañanitas." Also sung traditionally at birthdays, the lyrics of "Las Mañanitas" celebrate the birth of a new day:

> This is the morning song that King David sang.
> Because today is your feast day, we sing it to you.
> Wake up my dear, wake up, look, it's already dawn!
> The birds are already singing and the moon has set.
> How lovely is the morning in which I come to greet you.
> We all come with joy and pleasure to congratulate you.
> The day you were born all the flowers were born
> and in the baptismal font sang the nightingales.
> Already the dawn is coming, light of day is here.
> Awake in the morning and see that it has dawned.

LIBERATING PRAXIS

In the remainder of this essay I suggest that the narrative and celebrations of Our Lady of Guadalupe reflect and give expression to a particular understanding of the nature of divine action in the world, as well as the nature of human action—theopraxis and human praxis. This divine action is defined by at least five characteristics: (1) a divine "preferential option for the poor," (2) the consequent inversion of the relationship between evangelizer and evangelized, (3) the affirmation of an intrinsically relational theological anthropology, (4) the subversion of instrumentalist notions of human praxis, and (5) an affirmation of "aesthetic praxis" as revelatory, normative, and liberative.

It is no coincidence that the narrative is set in 1531, at the moment of greatest despair for the indigenous peoples of Mexico, shortly after they had been decimated by the conquering Spaniards. In the first part of the Guadalupan drama, Juan Diego's words reflect the self-deprecation of a downtrodden, vanquished people: "Because, for sure, I am a meager peasant, a cord, a little ladder, the people's excrement, I am a leaf."[7] As an indigenous man, Juan Diego internalized the belittling, dehumanizing image of the Amerindians promulgated by the Spaniards; like so many oppressed persons, he had learned self-hatred. He saw himself as literally a no-body: "a rope" and "a little ladder," mere tools with no intrinsic value beyond their usefulness to others.[8] Juan Diego had come to see himself as merely the object or instrument of someone else's actions. The contemporary community enacting the drama is well aware of that history, for they themselves have relived it repeatedly over the subsequent five centuries—whether in the nineteenth century, when the United States annexed almost half of Mexico, or in more recent decades, when the Mexican border has become an instrument of exclusion, violence, and death.

Into that despair erupts an utterly unanticipated figure, the Lady of Tepeyac. The Indian who is nothing but "the people's excrement" is confronted by the Lady who identifies herself as the Virgin, the Mother of God, and calls Juan Diego her "dearest." The tables have now been turned; the Indian who had been vanquished by the Spanish and left for dead is singled out as the most beloved child of the Virgin and, hence, of God. Moreover, the

Virgin orders Juan Diego to tell the bishop to build a chapel to her on Tepeyac, that is, not in the capital city, where the bishop and the Spaniards reside, but on the hill outside the city, where the mother goddess of the Nahuas lives. The Virgin reveals a God whose preferred residence is among the vanquished, on the outskirts or margins of the centers of power and influence.

The drama of Guadalupe thus establishes God's preferential solidarity with the poor as the very source of Mexican identity, for it was the encounter between the Virgin and Juan Diego that made possible the emergence of the Mexican nation from out of the very depths of defeat and despair. And the God who, through the Lady of Tepeyac, transforms Juan Diego from a mere "leaf" into a "dearest child" continues to do so for all those communities that today continue to retell and reenact this sacred drama. Through such recounting and reenactment the narrative makes credible and palpable for the Mexican people—and all Latin Americans—the Christian narrative of the resurrection, in which the crucified Innocent Victim is justified and raised from the dead at the very moment when he seemed abandoned by God. As God's justification of the unjustly violated Juan Diego, Guadalupe confirms God's loving presence in the midst of despair and thus makes the resurrection believable; this is no longer merely a dogma or doctrine learned from the Spanish bishop and his successors, but a reality at the very heart of the Mexican experience itself. Reverend David García, rector of San Fernando Cathedral in San Antonio, Texas, explains the identification between Juan Diego and the Mexican people:

> Juan Diego's story is our story. His hesitancy is ours in the face of being called to share the Good News and change our world. His feelings of nothingness are reflected in our sense of inadequacy against a society that puts us down at every turn. His call to take the message is our call to tell others that God wants things different, that God loves those who are poor and

> powerless, that God does not forget the sufferings of God's people, and that God is with us on our pilgrimage through a hostile world.[9]

In Juan Diego, "the people's excrement" becomes the locus of God's self-revelation (certainly no more shocking than the possibility that God could be revealed in the person of a tortured, condemned criminal hanging from a cross).

What is particularly significant—and subversive—about God's special love for and presence among the residents of Tepeyac, on the city's margins, is the expressly *theological* significance of that preference. That is, the Virgin does not merely declare her love for Juan Diego (a noteworthy action in any case); she "deputizes" him as her messenger—and not just any messenger, but her messenger to the Spanish *bishop*. It is not the Indian but the bishop who is in need of conversion. The Virgin's action thus has not only ethical but, especially, *soteriological* import; Juan Diego is chosen, not only as a passive recipient of God's love, but as the agent of God's self-revelation to the religious authorities in Mexico City: "This is quite a reversal of what had been happening. Juan Diego is told to go to the palace of the bishop. He is not to go there, however, to learn about the things of God; rather, he is to go to tell the chief spokesperson of God what to do."[10] Initially on his way to the bishop's palace to *receive* instruction in the faith, Juan Diego will now go to the bishop to *give* him the Virgin's instruction; the evangelizer will become the evangelized, and vice versa. The poor Indian man will become, literally, the bearer of the sacred image. Juan Diego will bring the "good news" to the bishop—that God's self-revelation is taking place among the poor, on Tepeyac, and that, therefore, Tepeyac is where the bishop must go and where the church must be built. "At Tepeyac," notes Virgilio Elizondo, "Juan Diego functions as the priest. He responds to the divine call and climbs the hill to be the mediator between the Mother of God and the bishop, between his people and the powerful people from Europe....The call of Juan Diego is a divine protest against the elitist policies of a church that refuses to recognize the giftedness of the poor and lowly, especially the non-Western ones."[11]

What is truly subversive about the drama, then, is that it does not presuppose belief and *then* command action based on that belief; rather, the encounter between Guadalupe and Juan Diego reveals praxis as *itself* the precondition and foundation of belief. More specifically, it is the relationship or *inter*action between the Lady and Juan Diego that drives the drama forward and makes possible the bishop's conversion.

The encounter between Guadalupe and Juan Diego reveals praxis as *itself* the precondition and foundation of belief.

That interaction results in the gradual transformation of Juan Diego from an object of other's actions ("a cord, a ladder") into an empowered agent able not only to engage and, indeed, command the Spanish bishop but even to disobey the Lady herself (by opting to stay with his uncle and skip his appointment with her). Initially agreeing to the Virgin's request only out of deference to her, by the time of the third trip to Tlatelolco, Juan Diego was eager to try again, to confront the bishop: he "pleaded very much with her to send him immediately to see the Lord of the priests to take him her sign"[12] Once again, we see Juan Diego gradually becoming the agent of historical action rather than the instrument of another's activity.

As the contemporary participants in the Guadalupan fiesta are drawn into this drama they are introduced to the liberating power of this praxis, through which they themselves are invited to interact with the Virgin, the bishop, and, ultimately, the God who is being made present here. It is the interaction between the Lady and Juan Diego that ultimately makes possible the conversion of the bishop as Juan Diego becomes gradually empowered to take on his task as evangelizer. What the community is invited to participate in is the birth of a person as subject, as some*one*. In turn, the contemporary participants experience themselves as empowered and constituted by their relationship with *La Morenita*. In the words of Socorro Durán, director of Hispanic ministry at Saint Leander's parish in northern California:

> The hope of the Christmas season we are approaching shows itself on your faces, on the faces of your parents and children when you see the story of Tepeyac reenacted every year. People just like you play the parts of Juan Diego, the bishop and his attendants, the Virgin, and all the others who appear in the drama. The story is about how the underdog is finally heard. We Latinos are "underdogs," and so we can feel close to Juan Diego, his sick uncle Juan Bernardino, and all his people. The drama of Tepeyac makes you laugh and imagine. You laugh because you see how Juan Diego tries to *dar vueltas*, to avoid the Virgin, but she catches him. You laugh because he becomes so familiar with the Lady that he nicely talks back to her. He becomes like us, a little *rezongón* (grumbler). And you also imagine how it is that God speaks *to you* through this beautiful woman and mother, how God leads *you* forward toward something much better. We want to hear this. We need to hear it. The story of Guadalupe, like the story of Christmas, renews hope in our wilting spirits.[13]

What is thus implied in the Guadalupan narrative and fiesta is an inherently relational theological anthropology, one that grounds human freedom not in the autonomous ego but in the bonds of love and companionship. Juan Diego becomes a free human agent, capable of confronting authority (the bishop) and even disobeying authority (the Virgin), not by relinquishing relational bonds but by being drawn into a relationship with the Lady and, through her, with God. In her interviews with Mexican American women, Jeanette Rodriguez repeatedly encountered this understanding of human subjectivity and agency:

> Again and again, the women in my study found that in encountering and being in the presence of Our Lady of Guadalupe they regained their sense of self in an accepting and empowering relationship. Our Lady of Guadalupe images power *with*, in a dynamism centered around mutuality, trust, participation, and regard.[14]

And the relationship itself was not born of a "rational" choice on his part (after all, it interrupted his original trip to Tlatelolco to attend to his responsibilities as catechumen); he was *compelled* to enter into the relationship by the beauty of the birds' singing, which originally signaled the Virgin's presence, the beauty of the flowers that the Lady offered as the sign of her love for him, and the beauty of the Lady herself. The birth of Juan Diego as a human subject thus takes place utterly unexpectedly, not through his own rational agency but through his openness and receptivity to a divine presence that approaches him in the form of beauty, that of music, flowers, and the Lady. Guadalupe thus confirms the ancient Aztec belief in *flor y canto* ("flower and song") as privileged mediators of the sacred.

The relationship between Juan Diego and the Virgin thus implies a notion of human agency and subjectivity that subverts the Cartesian *cogito ergo sum*. That is, the ground of that subjectivity is not the autonomous, rational ego that "relates" to its environment only as subject to object, utilizing its environment (whether natural or human) as an instrument to achieve its own self-conceived ends. Rather, the ground of subjectivity lies "outside" the ego or, more precisely, in the subject-to-subject relationship that is intrinsic to the ego but whose origins are not egocentric but other-centric. "Juan Diego is converted from the pain of social nonbeing to become a full, confident, and joyful human person. He is transformed from his debasement and shame to a new, confident self-image....He is now a full man; he is now an integral human being!"[15]

This theological anthropology implies a radically different

understanding of human action. The human subject's mode of interacting with his or her environment can no longer be conceived in instrumentalist terms. Because he is an "actor," Juan Diego's identity is not constructed on the basis of an autonomously self-directed activity; indeed, it is not "constructed" at all. That identity is a byproduct of a relationship that Juan Diego did not seek, initiate, desire, or intend; it sought, compelled, and seduced him. Virgilio Elizondo describes the conflicting theological anthropologies:

> For the Europeans, the true, the good, and beautiful human being was a rational individual who could conquer whatever he or she set out to obtain and control. According to this view, anyone who did not seek to conquer was an inferior and weak human being who should be dominated by the "superior" peoples of the earth. In contrast, the indigenous world of knowledge saw the human as a creature whose very existence depended on interconnectedness within the self, nation, earth, creation, and beyond. Two anthropologies clashed: the European anthropology of rationality and the native anthropology of creatureliness. For the Europeans, conquest—of self and of others—was the measure of the human, while for the Amerindians, harmony within the self and all of creation was the measure of the human. The former view emphasized argumentation and linear discourse; the latter view emphasized cosmic signs and rituals. One was a world of reason, logic, and argumentation while the other was a world of omens, dreams, myths, and rituals.[16]

It is no coincidence, therefore, that such a relationship is mediated, above all, by *beauty*; the subject's interaction with beauty is always fundamentally one in which he or she is not in control (as is necessarily the case in any instrumental activity). Beauty compels, attracts, and seduces unexpectedly; we are "caught up" in something greater than and beyond our selves. Yet, paradoxically, this experience that we do not control nevertheless is ultimately energizing, inspiring, and empowering. "The ultimate proof," observes Elizondo, "was not the military might of God, as had been claimed by the missioners, but the attractive power of beauty, respect, and compassion."[17]

What the narrative as well as the fiesta of Guadalupe demonstrate, therefore, is the foundational importance of human praxis as distinct from *poiesis*—human action as an end in itself rather than as a means to an extrinsic end. What defines the human is its relationship to beauty, whose only "purpose" is simply to be enjoyed. As beautiful, human action has no fundamental purpose beyond the action itself. This in no way suggests that usefulness or purpose is irrelevant, simply that they do not define the human subject; the goals of human action are always *by*products of a praxis which, by definition, cannot have a goal since the praxis is not ultimately self-directed (at least not a goal that the human subject conceives and intends). Juan Diego never dreamed that he could possibly order or command the bishop to do anything; such a goal was, for the indigenous man, literally inconceivable. Only as he is gradually drawn into the relationship with the Virgin does he eventually discover (to his own surprise!) that he is able to confront the bishop and, indeed, to compel the bishop's own obedience.

The narrative and fiesta of Guadalupe thus reveal and affirm a new way of *being* human, a new way of acting that privileges beauty as the mediation of divine presence and human subjectivity:

> The *flor y canto* of God's revelation today shine through brightly in the colorful and joyful fiestas of God's poor that invite all to join in without distinction—all are attracted, as Juan Diego was, to the beautiful music, to the spontaneous joy of these religious fiestas. Many of our modern programs give a lot of information but little or no experience of the divine.[18]

Human action is not fundamentally physical or instrumental; it is *aesthetic*. At the same time, however, this fundamentally aesthetic character of praxis is mediated by particular, concrete, shared, and goal-oriented human practices.

Praxis is not simply the physical action of an autonomous subject on an external object that is used to achieve a preconceived end. *Fundamentally*, praxis is the subject's participation in a relationship with another subject, whose own self-expression compels that participation. While including these, human action is not fundamentally physical or instrumental; it is *aesthetic*. At the same time, however, this fundamentally aesthetic character of praxis is mediated by particular, concrete, shared, and goal-oriented human practices; relationships do not exist in a vacuum but are born and nurtured in common activities with intrinsic goals that generate particular forms of knowledge (see Terrence W. Tilley's discussion of *phronesis* in this volume). The ground of all rational or instrumental knowledge (insofar as that is knowledge of the human) is participatory or aesthetic praxis:

> Guadalupe is not an isolated, abstract, doctrinal truth; neither is it a legal or moralistic truth. According to the Guadalupan vision, truth exists in the relational, the interconnected, the beautiful, and the melodic.... Ultimate truth cannot be corralled by definition; it can only be approximated through *flor y canto*....Guadalupe is the truth about truth itself....In the epistemology of Guadalupe, truth cannot be obtained or arrived at through observation, rational analysis, and argumentation alone, but can only be grasped through the beauty of sight and sound followed by critical questioning and analysis....Truth will be known through the synthesis of image, beauty, and words. The synthesis constitutes what Christians call the "word of God." It is neither the sensual and gut knowledge of *flor y canto* alone, nor

> intellectual knowledge alone, but knowledge of the whole person involving all the avenues of knowing: the senses, the mind, and the heart.[19]

The word of God is thus much more than information about God; it is the inconceivable invitation to participate in God's own praxis, God's own ongoing self-disclosure in history.

AN AMERICAN GOSPEL: BETWEEN EASTER AND PENTECOST

Ultimately, then, what the narrative and fiesta of Guadalupe embody and express is the unfolding of God's self-communication in the world; what is revealed is the *theo*logy mediated by a *theo*praxis. In an Amerindian society and culture where the divine word could only be received and perceived in the form of the beautiful, *flor y canto,* Guadalupe is the revelation of who God is because it is the revelation of how God acts. Above all, God is one who accompanies and liberates, one who liberates *because* God accompanies. The fiesta of Guadalupe is the Mexican celebration of both Easter and Pentecost; it is the celebration of the victory of life over death, of justice over injustice, and of communion over estrangement.

Our ability to appreciate the theological significance of Guadalupe is dependent, therefore, on our appreciation of the aesthetic praxis at the heart of both the narrative and the fiesta; Guadalupe liberates because Guadalupe *stays* when others have abandoned us. Timothy Matovina recounts that one Guadalupan devotee defined her simply as the one who stayed: *se quedó*:

> Devotees' fundamental conviction about their celestial mother is that she never abandons them. As contemporary parish leader Mary Esther Bernal put it, "She is love, but first and foremost she is hope in all that we face." The most certain statement about Guadalupe's

> future is that she will continue to abide amidst the evolving web of relationships, communal structures, needs, and desires that her devotees create and inhabit, serving as a mirror that simultaneously reinforces and transforms their attitudes, actions, and aspirations.[20]

In a society and culture with an intrinsically relational theological anthropology, where life itself is defined by the relationships that give birth to and sustain it, death will likewise be defined by the destruction of those relationships, by ostracism, exclusion, and abandonment. Conversely, what engenders hope (and belief) is *presence,* that is, the refusal to abandon.

As an American inculturation of the gospel, Guadalupe thus makes possible a retrieval of an aspect of the Christian kerygma too often overlooked in our modern individualistic society, namely, the Christian belief in the intrinsic connection between the victory of life over death (resurrection) and the victory of communion over estrangement (Pentecost). While giving birth to a new people, a "new creation," Guadalupe also, "like the biblical Pentecost itself,...provides a symbol of unity and coherence in which distinctive cultures could be fused together respectfully to form something new."[21] Virgilio Elizondo notes how Guadalupe unites Easter and Pentecost:

> On the feast of Our Lady of Guadalupe the people come together early in the morning to celebrate the irruption of new life—the dawn of a new humanity. This is the Easter sunrise service of the people. Before the first rays of the sun, they come together to sing *Las Mañanitas,* which is our proclamation of new life. It is the roses of Tepeyac that take the place of the Easter lilies of Western Christianity. Guadalupe was also a *pentecost* event: it opened the way to true dialogue between Europeans and Mexican Indians. It was a symbol of unity over and above their many and serious diversities. It marked the beginning of the fusion of two mother

> cultures—the Spanish and the Mexican Indian—which in turn gave birth to a *mestizo* culture.[22]

As we follow and identify with Juan Diego in this extraordinary sacred drama, we participate in a divine praxis in which what had been ruptured is reunited, what had been estranged is reconciled. This "dawn of a new humanity" will now be represented not merely by the singular figure of Our Lady of Guadalupe but by the new, inseparable companions, *La Morenita* and Juan Diego.[23]

Notes

1. Clodomiro L. Siller Acuña, *Para comprender el mensaje de María de Guadalupe* (Buenos Aires, Argentina: Editorial Guadalupe, 1989), 58. The historical authenticity (more specifically "facticity") of the Guadalupan narrative has been questioned by some scholars, for example, Stafford Poole, *Our Lady of Guadalupe: The Origins and Sources of a Mexican National Symbol, 1531–1797* (Tucson: University of Arizona Press, 1995). Conversely, other scholars have challenged Poole's own methodological assumptions, for example, Richard Nebel, *Santa María Tonantzín, Virgen de Guadalupe: Continuidad y transformación religiosa en México* (Mexico City, Mexico: Fondo de Cultura Económica, 1995). Likewise, the ideological manipulation of the Guadalupan narrative has been critiqued insofar as, for example, the identification of Guadalupe with women exclusively can serve to legitimate certain oppressive constructions of gender roles. See, for example, Sandra Cisneros, "Guadalupe the Sex Goddess," in *Goddess of the Americas: Writings on the Virgin of Guadalupe*, ed. Ana Castillo (New York: Riverhead Books, 1996). This short essay cannot hope to address these and other very important, indeed crucial debates surrounding the origins, prehistory, and history of Guadalupan devotion. What I hope to do is provide a *theological* analysis that, as such, does not depend on the facticity of events narrated or on later ideological distortions but, indeed, *subverts* interpretations that would legitimate such oppressive distortions precisely as distortions of the God revealed in the narrative and the fiesta and, more specifically, distortions of that God's praxis in

history. Precisely *as* lived narrative, Guadalupe cuts against the grain of the ideological manipulations, just as the Gospel itself ultimately undermines attempts to place it in the service of domination and empire. Thus, for example, I would assume and understand the Guadalupan narrative's identification of *La Morenita* with Mary-Tonantzín precisely as an overturning of the dominant identification of Mary with the conquering and colonizing Spanish Church. For an analogous explanation of the distinction between the historical-critical work of scholars like Poole and expressly theological analyses of Guadalupe, see Maxwell E. Johnson, *The Virgin of Guadalupe: Theological Reflections of an Anglo-Lutheran Liturgist* (Lanham, MD: Rowman & Littlefield, 2002), 80–81.

2. Virgilio Elizondo, *Guadalupe: Mother of the New Creation* (Maryknoll, NY: Orbis Books, 1997), 40.

3. *Nican Mopohua,* quoted in Virgilio Elizondo, *La Morenita: Evangelizer of the Americas* (San Antonio, TX: Mexican American Cultural Center Press, 1980), 72.

4. *Nican Mopohua,* quoted in Elizondo, *Guadalupe,* 62.

5. *Nican Mopohua,* quoted in Siller Acuña, *Para comprender el mensaje de María de Guadalupe,* 68.

6. Ibid., 74.

7. Ibid.

8. Ibid.

9. David Garcia, "You Can Do It," in *The Treasure of Guadalupe,* ed. Virgilio Elizondo, Allan Figueroa Deck, and Timothy Matovina (Lanham, MD: Rowman & Littlefield, 2006), 22.

10. Elizondo, *Guadalupe,* 53.

11. Ibid., 46.

12. Ibid., 84–85; Elizondo, *La Morenita,* 78.

13. Socorro Durán, "A Great Sign Appeared in the Sky," in *The Treasure of Guadalupe,* ed. Virgilio Elizondo, Allan Figueroa Deck, and Timothy Matovina (Lanham, MD: Rowman & Littlefield, 2006), 98.

14. Jeanette Rodriguez-Holguin, *Our Lady of Guadalupe: Faith and Empowerment Among Mexican-American Women* (Austin: University of Texas Press, 1994), 156.

15. Elizondo, *Guadalupe,* 88.

16. Ibid., xiv–xv.
17. Ibid., 75.
18. Ibid., 77.
19. Ibid., 117–18.
20. Timothy Matovina, *Guadalupe and Her Faithful: Latino Catholics in San Antonio, From Colonial Origins to the Present* (Baltimore, MD: Johns Hopkins University Press, 2005), vii, 177.
21. Johnson, *The Virgin of Guadalupe*, 78.
22. Virgilio Elizondo, "Living Faith: Resistance and Survival," in *Mestizo Worship: A Pastoral Approach to Liturgical Ministry*, ed. Virgilio Elizondo and Timothy Matovina (Collegeville, MN: Liturgical Press, 1998), 19.
23. A powerful symbol of this inseparability is the image of Juan Diego that even today can be seen reflected in the eyes of Our Lady of Guadalupe on the *tilma*. The centrality of Juan Diego to the narrative is also exemplified by his recent canonization.

CHAPTER 9

PASTORAL MINISTRY AND VISION

Latino/a Contributions to the Transformation of Practical Theology in the United States

CARMEN MARÍA CERVANTES,
ALLAN FIGUEROA DECK, SJ, AND
KEN JOHNSON-MONDRAGÓN

In a 2009 memorandum to the United States Conference of Catholic Bishops, researchers Robert D. Putnam and David E. Campbell declared that "Latinos are the leading indicators of the Catholic Church's future in the United States."[1] As widely reported, the decisive role played by Latinos/as in the reelection of President Barack Obama demonstrated the rising importance of Latinos/as in the social and political arenas nationally. Even more, the election of Argentine Cardinal Jorge Mario Bergoglio to the papacy highlights the distinctive role of Latin America in what appears to be a new period of reform and renewal for global Catholicism. U.S. Latinos/as, as this chapter argues, have made significant contributions to the U.S. Catholic Church, contributions that are unthinkable without their moorings in the post–Vatican II pastoral theological vision of Latin America in which Pope Francis has been steeped.[2] This chapter seeks to provide an overview of the Latino/a presence as it impacts the life of the church in the United States from a practical theological point of view with emphasis on *pastoral juvenil hispana,* the Spanish phrase used to refer to youth and young adult ministry in the Latino/a context. The fact that six out of every ten U.S. Catholics under the age of thirty-five are Latino/a adds more than a touch of relevance and even urgency to this topic.[3]

This chapter seeks to provide an overview of the Latino/a presence as it impacts the life of the church in the United States from a practical theological point of view with emphasis on *pastoral juvenil hispana,* the Spanish phrase used to refer to youth and young adult ministry in the Latino/a context.

While *pastoral theology* and *practical theology* have been seen in some contexts as synonymous in terms of a theological discipline because both refer to the theological reflection that comes out of and gives light to the praxis of the church in a particular context, this chapter favors *pastoral theology* as a term that better captures and embraces the reflection on the pastoral action of the people of God, active in their own sociocultural and historical context. We use the term *pastoral theology* here to convey a specific, rich meaning: a practical theology applied to a theology of a liberating pastoral action of the community of faith.

We use the term *pastoral theology* here to convey a specific, rich meaning: a practical theology applied to a theology of a liberating pastoral action of the community of faith.

The Latino/a contributions to the church's life have often gone unrecognized by U.S. Catholics, who have tended to minimize the strong Hispanic underpinnings of U.S. Catholic Church history in the movement northward of missionaries, people, and commerce from Mexico and the Caribbean over centuries.[4] The Latinoization of the Catholic Church, nevertheless, is more pronounced than ever and affects virtually every region of the nation. In his ground-breaking study *Latino Catholics*, Timothy Matovina describes the growing impact of Latino/a Catholicism.[5] In this chapter we describe this influence and identify major pastoral opportunities and challenges that arise today in light of today's contextual sea change.

DISTINCTIVE LATINO/A CONTRIBUTIONS TO THE PASTORAL LIFE OF THE CHURCH

It has often been remarked that Latino/a culture and Catholicism are characterized by performativity.[6] This refers to the fact that whatever is meant by culture and "Catholicism" in the case of Latinos/as at the grassroots level is more experienced, put into practice, than analyzed or reflected on by them. On the other hand, Latino/a theologians and pastoral leaders have produced a substantial body of literature that undergirds this practice of the faith and guides pastoral care among Latinos/as. Even so, Latino/a families and communities continue to live and transmit the faith foremost in an aesthetic, corporal, intuitive, and affective way. This circumstance, however, does not make that culture and that type of Catholicism any less real. In fact, it enjoys a remarkable vitality that transforms aging Euro-American faith communities into vibrant centers of ecclesial life, as documented by the Center for Applied Research in the Apostolate (CARA) studies and supported by findings of the Pew Research Center.[7] This vitality has to do with a deep-seated spirituality, popular religion, practices inspired by Vatican II, and pastoral-theological approaches originating in Latin America—strong characteristics of U.S. Latino/a Catholicism. Here we consider Latino/a influence in the areas of liturgy, ecclesial movements, faith and justice, and ecclesial revitalization, noting how this influence is grounded in a rich spirituality.

Liturgy

In the area of liturgy one notes a distinctive Latino/a liturgical ethos: in more than 4,800 parishes throughout the United States that celebrate the Mass in Spanish, worship often reflects the influence of the homegrown and heart-felt popular religion of immigrant communities. In this context, the liturgy honors official orientations while providing its own flavor, one that contrasts with both the traditionalist and progressive approaches of Euro-American liturgies. Indeed, pastors have often observed that this widespread combination of elements has enriched and reinforced the Second Vatican Council's mandate that, above all else, the liturgy should promote "fully conscious and active participation" (*Sacrosanctum concilium* 14). Despite the frequent commotion of restless children and crying babies, Latino/a congregations are often engaged and prayerful—including many youth and young adults who bring energy and contemporary musical styles through youth choirs or participation in intergenerational music ministries.

Latino/a liturgies are infused with an ethnic vitality that flourishes when pastoral leaders support the distinctive nature of Latino/a Catholicism; its devotion; the centrality of the extended family; and the power of its religious rituals, symbols, and narratives. Spanish-language liturgies, moreover, have not been affected by the perceived formalism of the latest edition of the Roman Missal in English. Rather, the liveliness of the popular religious practices, spontaneity, and the community's music continue to blend with the official liturgy, adding both devotion and spark to worship in Spanish. Indeed, that vitality has sometimes been integrated into the style and content of English-language liturgies on feast days and liturgical seasons, at bilingual celebrations of the *posadas* before Christmas and the *via crucis* on Good Friday. Rocco Palmo has reported that the Feast of Our Lady of

Guadalupe, even though not a holy day of obligation, has surpassed all other Marian feasts in the United States in terms of the participation of the faithful.[8] In many places, the ritual and devotional tendencies of Latinos/as have begun to resonate with the liturgical prayer life of U.S. Catholics bilingually or in English in the form of music, style, processions, and imagery.[9]

Ecclesial Movements

Latinos/as have significantly contributed to the pastoral life of the church in the United States by means of their agency in the origins, development, and expansion of several highly influential ecclesial apostolic movements—among them the Cursillo, Marriage Encounter, the Christian Family Movement, and, most of all, the Charismatic Renewal. Unlike the movements that arise in middle-class, Euro-American contexts, these movements possess a distinct communal and ecclesial character and stress a collective experience open to the contexts of family, community, parish, and diocese, rather than the more individual spiritual journey consistent with the contemporary lifestyles of the urban middle class. The Cursillo, for example, which originated in Spain, offers an affective approach to foundational faith formation that resonates with people in powerful weekend experiences of faith sharing, prayer, and community building. Going by many different names, the Cursillo methodology creates the conditions for a profound conversion experience, as countless *cursillistas* have experienced over several decades.[10]

Most notable of all is the positive response of Latinos/as to the lively, affective approach of Pentecostalism in its Catholic charismatic form. The embrace of charismatic/Pentecostal spirituality has caught on among many Latinos/as in large part due to its affinity with the spiritual worldview and practices of Latin American popular piety. It comes as no surprise, then, that people of Latin American origin account for a significant percentage of worldwide charismatic/Pentecostal movements.[11] An underreported story, however, is that the majority of these Latinos/as are Roman Catholics, not Protestants.[12]

The large number of today's Latino/a seminarians, young priests, permanent deacons and their wives, and lay ecclesial leaders with experiences in the Charismatic Renewal attests to the strength of the ecclesial movements rooted in a charismatic spirituality, especially among immigrant Latino/a young adults. Moreover, all the movements taken together constitute a very meaningful development for the life of the church in the United States because they provide a context for leadership formation of the laity that may equal—or arguably surpass—what the laity experience in standard parish or diocesan ministries and in university-based programs alone.[13]

Linking Faith and Justice

Given the upward mobility of Euro-American Catholics in the second half of the twentieth century, the contemporary presence of at least 32 million U.S. Latino/a Catholics of whom a sizable proportion are working class, living below the poverty line, and sometimes undocumented has created a significant *social class bifurcation* in U.S. Catholicism. This means that the working-class credentials of U.S. Catholicism have been reinforced to create a church with footholds in three distinct and sometimes competing worlds: the working poor, the middle, and the upper classes. Consequently, bishops, pastors, and other leaders have felt the need to reassert the strong prophetic current of the Second Vatican Council and the prior period of social struggle that characterized U.S. Catholicism in the late nineteenth and the first half of the twentieth centuries with its energetic defense of workers, union organizing, and human rights.[14]

For the past forty years in connection with a huge Latino/a migration, and inspired by the teachings of Vatican II, Catholic social doctrine, and liberation theologies, the church has become a voice in U.S. society defending a consistent life ethic, one that goes beyond concern about abortion. This point was brought home emphatically by the first Latino archbishop of Los Angeles, José H. Gomez, who has insisted that immigration is also a pro-life issue.[15] The United States Conference of Catholic Bishops (USCCB), moreover, has played a major role in both advocacy on behalf of Latino/a rights and human dignity and, perhaps more important, in the empowerment of Latinos/as within civil society itself. Nowhere has this been more the case than in the work of the bishops' Catholic Campaign for Human Development (CCHD), which has provided significant seed monies for community organizations such as the Pacific Institute for Community Organizations (PICO) and the Industrial Areas Foundation (IAF). Thousands of Latinos/as in virtually every region of the country have been formed in ecumenical, faith-based community organizing in the style of Saul Alinsky (see also the chapter by Bradford Hinze in this volume).[16]

This development parallels the global identification of the institutional Catholic Church with the poor and marginalized in Africa, Asia, and Latin America, where the vast majority of its members are found today.[17] Pastorally, this means that the local church is being recalled to a real rather than theoretical concern for those on the margins of mainstream society. Hence, teaching and preaching must seek to link faith with justice in response to the reality of people's lives.[18] The church's pastoral activities are informed by the need for works of charity and advocacy that respond to immediate human needs and provide a voice to those who are denied it by oppression or marginalization, not just across the oceans but next door. This puts a premium on advocacy and empowerment in addition to the church's traditional commitment to charity, understood as a response to the symptoms of poverty rather than to its underlying, structural causes. Beyond that, however, U.S. Hispanic ministry emphasizes empowering Latinos/as of all ages and situations to become subjects of their own history rather than objects of the good will of others. The ubiquitous Latino/a presence in U.S. Catholicism contributes a distinctive pastoral orientation and social mindfulness, even a palpable urgency, to parishes, dioceses, and schools throughout the United States as they realize that they stand in solidarity with their fellow Latinos/as and other marginalized groups in their struggles for human rights, dignity, education, and holistic development. This trend can only increase, as events in Rome suggest. The largely unexpected election of Pope Francis and events surrounding his first moves as Supreme Pontiff suggest that the option for the poor and the essential connection between Christian faith and the struggle for socioeconomic justice are becoming signature practical theological orientations of worldwide Catholicism.

Ecclesial Revitalization

Latinos/as bring life and energy to the church in virtually every area—parish, ecclesial movements, vocations, lay ministries, and leadership in general. Of note, however, is the substantial impact that Latinos/as have made on the U.S. church in terms of pastoral orientations originating in Latin America that have made significant contributions to the life of all Catholics, not just Latinos/as. The U.S. bishops, particularly the growing cohort of Latinos/as among them, have presided over a remarkable period of visioning and planning that is arguably unprecedented in the history of U.S. Catholicism. This process, or *encuentro* vision, embodies a holistic pastoral theological approach that creates an "encounter" between the people's lived experience, their spiritual yearnings, and their pastoral needs, with scriptural and Vatican II orientations. The vision began to take shape in 1972 under the aegis of the USCCB with the First National Hispanic Pastoral Encuentro, which was followed by two more Encuentros—one in 1977 and another in 1985—and culminated in Encuentro 2000 in Los Angeles, an unprecedented, national gathering of more than five thousand pastoral leaders from all ethnicities, not just the Latino/a.[19] The *encuentro* process has grafted a distinctly Latin American pastoral vision onto the larger Catholic reality of the United States, and it is here to stay.

Among the first features of this Latino/a pastoral vision is an ecclesiology of the people of God imbued with the spirit of *Gaudium et spes* and of the Second and Third General Conferences of Latin American Bishops at Medellín (1968) and Puebla (1979). These episcopal conferences emphasized an *inductive* pastoral methodology, one that proposes the socioeconomic, religious, and cultural reality of the community as *the* starting place for theological reflection and pastoral planning. A second signature feature of this practical ecclesiology is the nurturing of small ecclesial communities and apostolic movements as especially effective instruments for carrying out the church's evangelizing mission. A third outstanding feature of Latin American Catholicism that inspires Hispanic ministry in the United States is the above-mentioned preferential option for the poor, a pastoral priority that Pope John Paul II was quick to embrace and enshrine in Catholic social doctrine.[20]

It is undeniable, moreover, that a Latin American theology of liberation left a permanent mark in the thinking and attitudes of the Catholic Church in the United States through U.S. Latinos/as and others, of course, who enthusiastically accepted its prophetic vision, many of its premises, and its method.[21] Indeed, Latino/a leaders, including bishops, have integrated this vision in the institutional histories and practices in the field of Hispanic ministry over the past four decades in virtually every region of the United States. Even a casual reading of the U.S. bishops' documents *The Hispanic Presence: Challenge and Commitment* (1983), the *National Pastoral Plan for Hispanic Ministry* (1987), and *Encuentro and Mission* (2002) reveals the extent to which the theological vision and pastoral methodologies first proposed in Latin America have resonated with Hispanic ministry in the United States.

By means of the *encuentro* vision Latinos/as have become a conduit for an enriching ecclesial ethos that has gradually defined an approach to pastoral planning and care at both the grassroots and leadership levels. Of singular importance here is the pastoral circle, the see-judge-act methodology rooted in the Young Christian Workers movement of the early decades of the twentieth century. In Latin American and in U.S. Hispanic ministry contexts the pastoral circle became—and continues to be—a change-inducing tool by which Latino/a ministry has taken root over the past forty years and now flourishes in parishes and dioceses across the nation. Timothy Matovina succinctly captures the significance of the Latino/a pastoral vision thus: "Underscoring the church as a community charged to embody Christ's presence in the concrete circumstances of human life, the *encuentro* vision encapsulates the theological foundation that animated Hispanic ministry leaders in their collective efforts to transform U.S. Catholicism through their pastoral planning and action during the Vatican II era."[22]

Roberto Treviño illuminates the context of the *encuentro* vision with his historical study of Latino/a "ethno-Catholicism" as it unfolded over many decades in Houston, Texas. Treviño explains how Latinos/as have been able to engage the dominant Anglo-American culture of both society and the U.S. Catholic Church with a dual consciousness that has produced a distinctive Catholicism that complements the more standardizing and intellectualizing tendencies of Euro-American culture.[23] Richard A. García in his review of Treviño's book notes that "Treviño is providing a new theoretical framework based on the theological tensions between the American churches' (Enlightenment's) 'reason' and the barrio's (Medieval) 'mystical spiritualism,' which centered on the culture core principle of ethno-Catholicism."[24] Curiously, U.S. Latino/a Catholics are agents of a forward-looking Vatican II pastoral vision that originated in Latin America while, at the same time, they also remain grounded in the Spanish medieval ethos of their initial evangelization along with significant additions from both their Native American and African ancestors.

THE CASE OF *PASTORAL JUVENIL HISPANA*

How has the *encuentro* vision taken shape in ministry with Latino/a youth and young adults? A brief overview of the evolving reality of U.S. Latino/a ministries with these populations will serve as background for this exploration. The umbrella term for these ministries in Spanish is *pastoral juvenil hispana* (*PJH*). It includes the pastoral and evangelizing work of parish *grupos juveniles* (youth and young adult ministry groups) and the various ecclesial apostolic movements with outreach to *jóvenes* (single youth and young adults, ages sixteen to thirty), both of which may gather young people together across a broad spectrum of ages. Also included are the ministries targeting Hispanic adolescents (usually in a bilingual setting) or young adults separately. The field has taken to preserving these Spanish terms even when writing in English because the concepts are not equivalent to either "youth," "young adult," or their respective ministries.[25]

The pastoral practice of *PJH* arose in a distinct historical and conceptual context and manifests influences from both its Latin American roots and the U.S. social and ecclesial environment. Its Latin American roots go back to Acción Católica Juvenil (Young Catholic Action) of the 1950s. After the Second Vatican Council, the bishops in Latin America were among the first to embrace the vision of the Council, especially through their landmark general meetings in Medellín (1968), Puebla (1979), Santo Domingo (1992), and Aparecida (2007).[26] The bishops have consistently pursued an agenda of renewal that responds with Gospel-based teachings, updated to address the contemporary context in this epoch of continuous and dramatic social change. Over decades their pastoral directives have continued to reflect a strong *encuentro* vision and insist on the need for "pastoral conversion" in line with the teaching of Vatican II.[27]

The word *joven* in Spanish, often mistranslated as "youth," refers to a sociological category of young people that does not exist in U.S. culture. In Latin American countries, young people begin to take their place in the adult world at the end of adolescence, which begins around age fifteen or sixteen and is completed for most when they enter marriage or start raising a family. The developmental goals of *PJH* therefore relate to accompanying young people as they begin to engage in the world of adults—

socially, politically, economically, and spiritually—as protagonists. This task is grounded in a profound understanding of Vatican II's teaching regarding the baptismal vocation to be leaven for the reign of God by means of an active participation in the life and mission of the Christian community *in the world.*[28] In contrast, the mainstream culture in the United States sees adolescence as an extended period of protected development (extending into the late twenties for some) during which young people are free to focus on increasing their personal potential through schooling, without having to deal with the pressures of the adult world, such as work, political participation, and providing for a family. Consequently, mainstream youth, campus, and young adult ministries tend to focus on forming the personal spiritual practices and theological understanding of young people, taking on some of the methods of the academic formation system around which they revolve.

Over the past five to six decades immigrant priests and lay ministers from Latin America, former U.S. missionaries (men and women) to Latin America, and *jóvenes* formed in Latin America, all of whom work within a pastoral framework gained in Latin America, have brought forth their pastoral vision and developed *PJH* in the United States. In the 1970s several archdioceses and dioceses opened offices to coordinate this ministry and offer formation programs. The First (1977) and Second (1979) National Hispanic Pastoral Encuentros officially recognized *PJH,* which was declared a priority in the U.S. bishops' *National Pastoral Plan for Hispanic Ministry* (1987). Moreover, the First National Encuentro for Hispanic Youth and Young Adult Ministry took place from 2004 to 2006. It entailed an analysis of the pastoral reality by more than 40,000 young Latino/as at the parish level, and included a pastoral theological reflection by young adult leaders who were delegates at the diocesan, regional, and national levels of the *encuentro*. This process served to define the principles, goals, and models of *PJH* in the United States. It also documented the pastoral needs, aspirations, and contributions of young

Latino/a Catholics as they relate to their Christian faith and to their participation in the life and mission of the church. The *Conclusions* were published in 2008 by the National Catholic Network de Pastoral Juvenil Hispana—La RED, the national *PJH* ministry organization that convoked the Encuentro.[29]

The majority of U.S. Catholic youth and young adults today are Latinos/as, and for most of the past twenty years the majority of young Hispanic Catholics have been immigrants. A recent study by Robert Putnam and David Campbell found that 67 percent of Catholic young adults who regularly attend Mass are Latino/a.[30] Population surveys indicate that the next Latino/a generation will be larger than the current one. However, it will consist of more people born in the United States than in Latin America.[31] Based on this trend, the proportion of young Latino/a Catholics will continue to grow, but these young people will be more acculturated. From 2004 to 2012, the raw number of Latino/a immigrants between the ages of fifteen and twenty-nine decreased by nearly 900,000 (17 percent), while the number of second-generation Latinos/as in the same age group grew by 2.2 million (70 percent), and the third generation increased by 1.3 million (51 percent).[32] This implies the need to address linguistic and cultural differences that place Latino/a *jóvenes* somewhere in between the worlds of working-class Latin Americans and that of the highly influential U.S. middle class. Without neglecting the needs of roughly 3 million Latino/a immigrant youth, we must learn how to provide pastoral accompaniment to a broader, culturally diverse population on the rise.

One of the lessons to be learned in the ever changing context of Latino/a youth in which the pastoral reality is a swiftly "moving target" is that effective pastoral care demands the ability not only to *adapt* but also to *differentiate* by developing ministries that incarnate the gospel in diverse pastoral settings. A practical theological mindset that puts a premium on the tried and true, on univocal approaches, on stability and continuity is often off the mark, ineffective, and irrelevant for this dynamic situation. In this context it is very significant that the USCCB Committee on Certification and Accreditation approved the certification norms and procedures of the Alliance for the Certification of Lay Ecclesial Ministers in 2011. The five major partners in the various fields of lay ecclesial ministry that make up the alliance wisely integrated *pastoral juvenil hispana* into the revised norms in order to recognize the distinctive Latino/a perspective and approach to the understanding and formation of *jóvenes*.[33] The justifications for doing so were many, but the most obvious was that in insisting on integration rather than assimilation of Latinos/as into society and the church's life and mission as the goal of Hispanic ministry, the U.S. bishops recognized the need for *differentiated* pastoral methods rather than a one-size-fits-all, univocal approach.[34] The work of Instituto Fe y Vida has contributed to the development, recognition, and validation of *pastoral juvenil hispana* as a necessary alternative to either a forced assimilation of young Latinos/as into the structures and methods of Euro-American Catholic youth ministries or their de facto marginalization from the church's pastoral care. In this context, *PJH* provides a sharp, cogent example of how the Latino/a presence is shaping pastoral practice and theology in the United States today.

Profiling Pastoral Juvenil Hispana: From Objects to Subjects of Action

How might the vision of *pastoral juvenil hispana* be characterized? One of its most notable features is its insistence on encouraging young people to become protagonists in the evangelization of their peers by assuming their baptismal call to continue the threefold mission of Jesus as priest, prophet, and servant-king. As noted, the origins of Latin American *pastoral juvenil* go back to Catholic Action and contrast markedly with the origins of U.S. Catholic youth ministry in the Protestant Sunday school and the social/sport activities of the Catholic Youth Organization (CYO). The fact that historically Latin American youth entered the workforce and got married at an early age imbued *pastoral juvenil* with a strong orientation to responsible participation and even leadership in church and society. This was evidenced in the historic role played by Catholic *jóvenes* in the period leading up to the Second Vatican Council. Catholic young people became serious protagonists of Catholic Action in defense of workers and *campesinos* in Mexico and other nations of Latin America in the first half of the twentieth century. Mexican Catholic *jóvenes*, for example, were galvanized around the values of faith as combatants in both the Mexican Revolution and the Cristero War of 1924–29, in which tens of thousands of them gave their lives in pursuit of religious freedom and other human rights. In the 1980s Central American *jóvenes* had to take sides, fight, and die in bloody civil wars in El Salvador and Nicaragua and insurgencies in Guatemala and southern Mexico. Consequently, *pastoral juvenil hispana* evinces fewer *in loco parentis* concerns and tends to challenge the *jóvenes* rather than comfort or entertain them. Whether in the United States or Latin America, *pastoral juvenil* emphasizes the *jóvenes'* own commitment to and willingness to participate in a peer-led ministry marked by shared responsibility, with the support and guidance from pastoral "advisers," rather than depending on professional leadership within the group. This is demonstrated in the remarkable histories of parish *grupos juveniles* that have existed for more than thirty-five years and by ecclesial movements like Jóvenes para Cristo in Southern California, which was created more than thirty years ago as a de facto "association of the faithful" led by young adult working-class Latinos/as, in communion with the church but without any direct financial support up to the present from the several dioceses and parishes it serves.

Years ago Michael Warren observed the need for "replacing the nineteenth century legacy of programs limited to trivial concerns—programs which offered youth a largely privatized view of their own lives and extended their dependence on adults. So persistent and taken-for-granted is this legacy that many have difficulty seeing it."[35] *Pastoral juvenil hispana* is a good example of a vision for youth and young adult ministries in the United States that responds to Warren's concern by emphasizing Latin American Catholicism's insistence on a see-judge-act methodology that stresses both the cultural and social awareness (conscientization) and the moral and religious agency of youth. Arguably, as one explores the U.S. ecclesial landscape one may see this methodology taking shape in Latino/a pastoral ministry contexts more than in standard Euro-American ones. The Latino/a presence is making a profound difference in pastoral practice as a result of its inductive methodology and linkage to the pastoral vision of Latin American Catholicism.[36]

The Latino/a presence is making a profound difference in pastoral practice as a result of its inductive methodology and linkage to the pastoral vision of Latin American Catholicism.

The Prophets of Hope Model for Pastoral Juvenil

The social class context and currents from Latin America have added distinctive elements to the tone and shape of ministry with young people in the United States. Nothing illustrates this point better than the Prophets of Hope model for *pastoral juvenil hispana* designed and developed by Instituto Fe y Vida for the purpose of providing a vision, direction, and consistency to a communitarian evangelization process for young Latino/a Catholics. The model integrates several essential elements in a deeply engaging, experiential, and dynamic process that can be carried out partially or in its entirety at both the grassroots and the professional levels.[37]

At the heart of this model lies a biblically based, christocentric spirituality that animates and guides all pastoral and formative actions. Following the pastoral circle methodology, this model insists on *formation-in-action* rather than taking a "when-are-we-going-to-grow-up?" schooling approach that induces passivity in young people. The focus, moreover, is on forming small ecclesial communities and making the parish a community of communities, an emphasis reinforced by both the U.S. bishops and the bishops at Aparecida.[38] The 2012 Synod on the New Evangelization likewise put a premium on small ecclesial communities.[39] In the Prophets of Hope model, each community reflects on its journey in light of five dimensions in the lives of the *jóvenes*: (1) personal, human development; (2) interpersonal relationships; (3) the local and global cultural context in which they live; (4) their integration into the larger society; and (5) the life of faith in relation to the previous four dimensions.

Another aspect integral to the model is what is called in Spanish *pastoral de conjunto*, and an emphasis on missionary discipleship as shared leadership and responsibility. *Pastoral de conjunto* (coordinated pastoral action) was repeatedly endorsed in the U.S. Latino/a *encuentro* process and is understood as "the harmonious coordination of all the elements of the pastoral ministry with the actions of the pastoral ministers and structures in view of a common goal: the Kingdom of God. It is not only a methodology but the expression of the essence and mission of the church, which is to be and to make communion."[40]

Acutely aware of the need for pastoral harmony, the Prophets of Hope model encourages a broad range of collaborative initiatives by insisting on the concept of *pastoral de conjunto* that shows itself in close communication and collaboration with the Euro-American youth and young adult ministries. This is especially important when a growing number of Latino/a youth are U.S.-born and prefer English while retaining several characteristics of Latino/a ethno-Catholicism, notably a strong sacramental sense and the centrality of community. Today, the cultural diversity of the church and society demands a greater ability to serve distinct segments of the young Catholic population and calls for a continuous pastoral conversion or adaptation on the part of the pastoral leadership.

With respect to the Latino/a community, this means Catholic parishes and schools must learn how to build on and enhance the faith life of the domestic church—that is, the family and home environments that are so crucial to religious identity—

in order to avoid confusing young Latino/a Catholics, in some cases to the point of rejection of the faith. Latino/a youth too often experience the faith and religious practices of their parents as being dismissed, neglected, or even ridiculed by well-intentioned but uninformed teachers and ecclesial leaders. Effective ministry has to be cross-cultural and intercultural if it is to adequately *bridge* the multiple worlds that youth and young adults must navigate today. The "community of communities" approach to ministry fostered in the Prophets of Hope model provides pastoral accompaniment to a broad and diverse parish youth population by creating an accepting, inviting context that stresses mutual support and recognition of culture, first steps in ecclesial integration. The Prophets of Hope model has been implemented in many areas of the United States and continues to be evaluated and improved. Tens of thousands of Latino/a *jóvenes* have been touched one way or another by it in some area of ecclesial life—in parishes, dioceses, and ecclesial apostolic movements.[41]

CONCLUSION

For several decades the nature of the church's demographic shift from primarily a Euro-American institution to one massively influenced by a distinctive Latino/a presence has been dawning on U.S. ecclesial leadership. This chapter has been an attempt to flesh out some of the pastoral implications of the shift in the areas of liturgy, social justice, ecclesial communities and movements, and youth and young adult ministries. Latino/a Catholicism, rooted in the original evangelization of the Americas five centuries ago, yet youthful and hybrid in nature, has a major role to play as a bridge between the faith and the mounting pluralism and secularism of the twenty-first century. Whatever the prevailing theoretical and theological orientations of the post–Vatican II period, Latinos/as and their pastoral ministers have been at work quietly transforming practice from within. The productive energy of Latino/a Catholicism is rooted in the legacy of the Latin American Church;

enriched by lively popular religion; endowed with the methods and prophetic theological vision of the Second Vatican Council; and gifted by the contributions of the Latin American Bishops' Conference (CELAM), liberation theology, and Catholic social doctrine. Recognition must also be given to the U.S. bishops, particularly the Latino/a bishops, who authorized and supported the *encuentro* vision and process discussed above in the course of four decades.

In addition, the vitality of Latino/a Catholicism, what some might call its evangelical fervor, has much to do with the remarkable revivalist ethos of charismatic Christianity that many Latinos/as have embraced with enthusiasm. That vitality also owes much to a well-grounded *pastoral juvenil* that accompanies *jóvenes* in their maturation process as Christians. All of this represents a great opportunity that needs to be recognized, pondered, and made accessible to pastoral ministers as the Catholic Church in the United States faces crucial pastoral challenges ahead that require more pastoral imagination and zeal than ever.

Notes

1. Robert D. Putnam and David E. Campbell, "The Changing Face of American Catholicism," memo to the U.S. Conference of Catholic Bishops (Washington, DC, May 22, 2008).

2. Cardinal Bergoglio served as chair of the redaction committee that oversaw the final document of the 2007 Aparecida Conference titled *Concluding Document: Fifth General Conference of the Bishops of Latin America and the Caribbean* (Washington, DC: USCCB Publications, 2008). The document is a remarkable affirmation of the main pastoral theological directions pursued in Latin America from Vatican II onward, consistent with the groundbreaking orientations of the previous episcopal conferences of Medellín and Puebla, with Catholic social teaching, and even with the theology of liberation, in its insistence on the option for the poor, the importance of base ecclesial communities, and popular religiosity as key instruments for inculturation. Now that one of its principal redactors has become pope, maybe

more attention will be given to it. See Jorge Mario Bergoglio, "Religiosidad Popular como Inculturación de la Fe," in *Testigos de Aparecida*, vol. 2 (Bogota, Colombia: CELAM, 2008), 281–325.

3. Robert D. Putnam and David E. Campbell, *American Grace: How Religion Divides and Unites Us* (New York: Simon and Schuster, 2010), 300.

4. Timothy Matovina, *Latino Catholicism: Transformation in America's Largest Church* (Princeton, NJ: Princeton University Press, 2012). Matovina provides a detailed analysis of Latino/a contributions to U.S. Catholicism. See also Timothy Matovina, "Latino Contributions to Vatican II Renewal," *Origins* 42, no. 29 (December 20, 2012): 465–71, and Allan Figueroa Deck, "Toward a New Narrative for the Latino Presence in U.S. Society and the Church," *Origins* 42, no. 29 (December 20, 2012): 458–64.

5. Matovina, "Remapping American Catholicism," in *Latino Catholicism*, 1–41.

6. See Shane T. Moreman, *Performativity and the Latino/a-White Hybrid Identity: Performing the Textual Self* (PhD diss., University of South Florida, 2005), 1–25.

7. *Changing Faiths: Latinos and the Transformation of American Religion* (Washington, DC: Pew Hispanic Center, 2007), 1–5.

8. Rocco Palmo, "The 'Super Bowl' Begins; In L.A., A Morenita Mass (and) Procession," December 4, 2011, accessed February 15, 2013, http://whispersintheloggia.blogspot.com/2011/12/big-week-begins-in-la-mass-and.html.

9. Matovina, "Latino Contributions," 466.

10. Kristy Nabhan-Warren, "Blooming Where We're Planted: Mexican-Descent Catholics Living Out Cursillo de Cristiandad," *U.S. Catholic Historian* 28 (Fall 2010): 99–125.

11. Gastón Espinosa, "The Pentecostalization of Latin American and U.S. Latino Christianity," *Pneuma: The Journal of the Society for Pentecostal Studies* 26, no. 2 (2004): 266.

12. Gastón Espinosa, "The Impact of Pluralism on Trends in Latin American and U.S. Latino Religions and Society," *Perspectivas* (Fall 2003): 13–21.

13. Edmundo Rodriguez, SJ, "The Hispanic Community and Church Movements: Schools of Leadership," in *Hispanic Catholic*

Culture in the United States, ed. Jay Dolan and Allan Figueroa Deck, SJ (Notre Dame, IN: University of Notre Dame Press, 1994), 206–39.

14. An example of this is the Justice for Immigrants Campaign of the United States Conference of Catholic Bishops, which pursues advocacy throughout the country in the U.S. Congress and state legislatures on the issue of comprehensive immigration reform.

15. José H. Gomez, "Immigration Reform After the Election," *Origins* 38 (November 13, 2008): 363–66.

16. Stephen C. Kokx and Nicholas C. Lund-Molfese, "An Analysis of the Formative Years of the Catholic Campaign for Human Development" (Washington, DC: USCCB, Secretariat of Justice and Peace, 2010), 1–20.

17. Michael L. Budde, *The Two Churches: Catholicism and Capitalism in the World System* (Durham, NC: Duke University Press, 1992), 1–22, 38–73.

18. *Preaching the Mystery of Faith: The Sunday Homily*, Pastoral Statement on Preaching at the Sunday Liturgy by the U.S. Bishops (Washington, DC: USCCB Publications, 2012), see 37–40 on adapting to the social and cultural reality of Latinos/as.

19. *Encuentro 2000: Many Faces in God's House* (Washington, DC: USCCB Publications, 2000).

20. *Compendium of the Social Doctrine of the Church* (Rome: Pontifical Council for Justice and Peace, 2004), nos. 189 and 448.

21. Peter C. Phan, "Method in Liberation Theologies," *Theological Studies* 61 (2000): 40–63.

22. Matovina, "Latino Contributions," 470.

23. Roberto Treviño, *The Church in the Barrio: Mexican American Ethno-Catholicism in Houston* (Chapel Hill: University of North Carolina Press, 2006).

24. Richard A. García, "Changing Chicano Historiography," *Reviews in American History* 34 (2006): 521–28.

25. Carmen M. Cervantes and Ken Johnson-Mondragón, "*Pastoral Juvenil Hispana*, Youth Ministry and Young Adult Ministry: An Updated Perspective on Three Different Pastoral Realities," *Perspectives on Hispanic Youth and Young Adult Ministry* 3 (2007).

26. See Massimo Faggioli, *Vatican II: The Battle for Meaning* (Mahwah, NJ: Paulist Press, 2012), 54.

27. *Concluding Document: Fifth General Conference of the Bishops of Latin America and the Caribbean*, 17–22; see also Oscar Rodríguez Madariaga, "Una Conversión Pastoral," in *Testigos de Aparecida*, vol. 1 (Bogota, Colombia: CELAM, 2008), 411–25.

28. National Catholic Network de Pastoral Juvenil Hispana—La Red, *Conclusions: First National Encounter for Hispanic Youth and Young Adult Ministry* (Washington, DC: USCCB Publishing, 2008).

29. *Conclusions: First National Encounter for Hispanic Youth and Young Adult Ministry* (Washington, DC: USCCB Publications, 2008).

30. Putnam and Campbell, *American Grace*, 300.

31. U.S. Census Bureau Current Population Survey, March 2012.

32. Ken Johnson-Mondragón, "Pastoral Care for the Second Generation," Instituto Fe y Vida Research and Resource Center for Hispanic Youth and Young Adult Ministry, *Fe y Vida Insights* (January 30, 2013), accessed February 5, 2013, http://www.feyvida.org/research/second-generation/.

33. The Alliance for the Certification of Lay Ecclesial Ministers, *Revised National Certification Standards for Lay Ecclesial Ministers and National Certification Procedures*, accessed March 5, 2013, http://www.lemcertification.org/standards.htm.

34. See USCCB Committee on Catholic Education, Subcommittee on Certification for Ecclesial Ministry and Service, accessed March 28, 2013, http://www.usccb.org/certification.

35. Michael Warren, *Youth, Gospel, Liberation* (San Francisco, CA: Harper and Row, 1987), 12.

36. Franz Josef Servaas Wijsen, Peter Henriot, SJ, and Rodrigo Mejía, eds., *The Pastoral Circle Revisited: A Critical Quest for Truth and Transformation* (Maryknoll, NY: Orbis Books, 2005), 1–15.

37. Instituto Fe y Vida, Stockton, CA, accessed February 16, 2013, http://www.feyvida.org/resources.html.

38. *Encuentro and Mission* (Washington, DC: USCCB Publications, 2002), no. 40; and *Concluding Document of the Fifth*

General Conference of the Bishops of Latin America and the Caribbean (Aparecida), nos. 99, 368, 369.

39. "Message to the People of God From the XIII Ordinary General Assembly of the Synod of Bishops," Synod of Bishops on the New Evangelization (Rome, October 26, 2012), Proposition 13, accessed February 15, 2013, http://www.zenit.org/en/articles/message-to-the-people-of-god-from-the-xiii-ordinary-general-assembly-of-the-synod-of-bishops.

40. *National Pastoral Plan for Hispanic Ministry* (Washington, DC: USCCB Publications, 1987), 28.

41. *Fact Sheet 2010* (Stockton, CA: Instituto Fe y Vida, 2010).

CHAPTER 10

THE PRACTICE OF SPIRITUAL DIRECTION

A Theologically Complex Process

JANET K. RUFFING, RSM

The practice of Christian spiritual direction is a complex process that is inherently, although not exclusively, theological. Spiritual directors also draw on insights from various psychological perspectives, the history of Christian spirituality, and tools such as the "Experience Cycle" adapted from the pastoral circle as well as models of supervision.[1] Spiritual direction supports the directee's graced discernment in recognizing God's self-communication and action in the whole of a believer's life and in responding to that grace in concrete and practical ways. It is one of the oldest recommended spiritual practices in the Catholic tradition for those who desire to practice their faith in a deep and reflective way. Spiritual direction also is particularly important in contexts of ministerial formation. Seminarians, candidates for diaconate and religious life, and those preparing for lay ecclesial ministry participate in a variety of spiritual practices that foster their spiritual life and their "personal appropriation, both intellectual and practical, of the tradition"[2] in such a way that it promotes their personal spiritual growth and informs their ministerial practice.

Spiritual direction is thus a significant practice to be studied and taught by practical theologians and pastoral leaders. I would argue that spiritual direction also is a form of practical theology enacted by both director and directee; in this sense, spiritual direction illustrates a kind of lay practical theology that follows an experience-theology-experience rhythm and is highly attentive to the grace of experience as theological source.

Spiritual direction illustrates a kind of lay practical theology that follows an experience-theology-experience rhythm and is highly attentive to the grace of experience as theological source.

In order to discuss spiritual direction, it is necessary first to offer a field definition of "spirituality." As a scholar-practitioner in the academic field of spirituality as it has developed since the 1970s, I situate my practice of spiritual direction within this recently defined discipline. David M. Perrin offers an apt description of the subject of the study of Christian spirituality:

> Christian spirituality is the experience of transformation in the Divine-human relationship as modeled by Jesus Christ and inspired by the Holy Spirit. Christian spirituality is appropriated as a lifestyle within all relationships in the broader Christian community as well as in society in general. While Christian spirituality embraces Christian traditions and beliefs, it exceeds the boundaries of established religions and their theologies. As such the way the Spirit of God is actively incarnated in human history, whether within the Christian traditions or from outside of them.[3]

As a spiritual director, I am attentive to the whole of directees' lives as they identify movements of the Spirit in all of life's complexity, whether or not these movements take place in Christian contexts or directees talk about them in explicitly Christian terms.

THE RELATIONSHIP OF THEOLOGY AND SPIRITUALITY

Debates within the field continue about how theology relates to Christian spirituality and its study as well as the role of practice in academic settings that prepare students for ministry. Regardless of the specific relationship between spirituality and theology, theology is always implicated.[4] Within Roman Catholicism, spirituality was studied through the disciplines of moral, ascetical, and mystical theology in the post-Tridentine period.[5] Themes or topics such as virtue, conversion, or mysticism were prescriptively elaborated and then applied to people. Spiritually transformative experiences of actual people exerted little influence on the received teaching; rather, the role of the confessor/spiritual director was to correct penitents and to bring both their behavior and theology into conformity with the received teaching. Nonclerical spiritual directors or mystical teachers usually needed clerical supporters in order to function as spiritual guides or belonged to a religious community in which some members were responsible for formation alongside clerics.

Perrin's definition of spirituality, however, suggests an understanding of spirituality in which experience also may shape theological understandings. Reflection on the transformative action of the Triune God in human experience draws on these major themes in systematic theology—theologies of God, Christologies, pneumatologies, revelation, grace, and theologies of the human person as well as scripture, liturgy, and ethics. When directees bring their unique experiences of God to spiritual direction, they also bring their practical theologies in an implicit and sometimes explicit form.[6] The directee, under the sway of the Spirit, embodies the received tradition, illuminates it, challenges it, adds to it, or diverges from it. There is often a reciprocal relationship between the lived experience of the believer and the tradition mediated through the directee's faith community in multiple contexts as well as through the spiritual director's responses. As Hans Georg Gadamer has argued, participants in a tradition not only receive a tradition, they also contribute to it through new experience.[7]

Sandra Schneiders comments that "one of the most interesting characteristics of Christian spirituality as lived experience is its capacity to be outside of or even ahead of theological developments and to introduce into the theological and/or religious purview of the Church insights and convictions which stretch the received theological categories and paradigms."[8] In my own experience, creative theologians and directees may be "ahead" of the received categories for a considerable period of time. All forms of liberation theology come to mind since they arose out of the experience of socially disadvantaged people. Practical theologians helped whole communities articulate theologies that led to action for social justice or internally supported the full humanity of each group.[9] These theological developments were deeply liberative for those who espoused them. In many instances they were based on scripture. These new readings of scripture not only illumined experience but also created conflicts within various communities and could be deeply threatening to those who embraced them and then found themselves at odds with their church leadership and some members. Others avoided these insights because they sensed that entertaining them might result in their abandoning or being excommunicated from their particular church tradition. Spiritual directors often provided a holding environment that allowed their directees to voice their insights, discern their responses in prayer, take prophetic action for social change, and entertain new ways of living the gospel while respecting their tradition's norms—all in God's company.

A SELF-REVEALING, LOVING GOD AT THE HEART OF THE PRACTICE OF SPIRITUAL DIRECTION

Contemporary spiritual direction takes place in this borderland of freedom where two Christians (who participate in and symbolize the larger community of faith) focus on how God is revealing God's self to the directee through every dimension of human existence. Together they interpret these movements and their claim on the directee to respond. How else can the Spirit change minds and hearts, inspire prophets, and bestow charismatic gifts for the good of the community? It is important for spiritual directors to be aware of their own theological assumptions in this ministry. Reflection on case work and supervision challenges spiritual directors to recognize when and how their espoused and operative theologies influence their work. This helps them notice and explore similar discrepancies in their directees' accounts of religious experience as well as wait for grace in their directees rather than impose their own theology on them.[10]

Thirty-year-old Sister Mary...is seeking greater intimacy with Jesus in her prayer. While on retreat, she discovers through the help of her director that although she believes Jesus is loving, compassionate, and interested in her (her espoused theology), she actually harbors a hidden fear that to get closer to Jesus will inevitably result in suffering (her operative theology). Her director suggests to her that her relationship with Jesus might feel different if she stopped approaching it as if she were going to the dentist.[11]

All Mary needed was this observation, which freed her to revise her embedded theology. She understood that suffering was a part of every human life and not necessarily a result of her deepening relationship with Jesus. She easily adopted a theology of the paschal mystery that was more open and hopeful; this theology was available in her tradition.

Most religious traditions develop some form of spiritual guidance among their most committed practitioners that places the practical wisdom accrued from the learning, personal experience, and practice of the more experienced at the service of both neophytes and peers. Wise spiritual teachers and elders developed the practice of consulting another of equal or greater spiritual development as a useful practice to counter their own blindness, ignorance, egocentricity, and internal obsessive preoccupations even as they served the neophytes who came to learn and share their specialized way of life. More important, such a teacher or elder provided essential encouragement on the spiritual path.

AN ANCIENT SPIRITUAL PRACTICE AMONG THE DESERT ASCETICS

Within Christianity, spiritual direction is an ancient practice that originated among the desert ascetics in the fourth century. In this form of spiritual guidance, newcomers placed themselves under the tutelage of a more experienced person, often living with or nearby the elder, learning this way of life from observation of the elder, practicing silence, reciting psalms, meditating on the word of God, regulating food and sleep, renouncing sexual relationships and the responsibilities entailed by them, and doing the mundane tasks required for sustaining life. Once martyrdom began to diminish, this austere life was embraced as a more intense form of Christian life. The practice led to growth in holiness not possible in ordinary, settled, agrarian or urban life.

In this model of spiritual direction, the one seeking direction was free to choose an elder of either gender and to ask for a "word" related to a concrete situation. If the elder responded with a charismatic word, which depended on the dispositions of the seeker, it was usually a brief response of direct advice, a parable, or an enigmatic statement that the neophyte pondered until its possible meanings opened. The Holy Spirit was considered to be the primary guide for the ascetic, along with the cell (solitude), meditating on the scriptures, and only then this "word" of the elder. Discernment as both discretion or moderation and discerning the spirits influencing the person seeking direction was the core of the practice of spiritual guidance, along with encouragement in the life itself. This form of spiritual direction was charismatic, freely embraced as a necessary practice for the neophyte, and recommended for the experienced.[12]

Elements of this original practice of spiritual direction continue today despite several intervening historical models. In its most institutionalized form following the Council of Trent, these earlier charismatic origins and the respect for each person's unique experience of God were minimized and the role of director merged with a clerical confessor to whom the penitent owed obedience.

THE PRACTICE OF CONTEMPORARY SPIRITUAL DIRECTION ROOTED IN VATICAN II THEOLOGY

In its contemporary form, restored and renewed as a result of theological developments before and after the Second Vatican Council, spiritual direction enjoyed a renaissance, rapidly extending to include all Christian lifestyles understood as participating in the universal call to holiness taught so eloquently in *Lumen gentium*[13] and influenced by the many renewal movements that followed the council.

Within Catholic life and practice, spiritual direction became one of the most important spiritual practices supporting the renewal movements inspired by Vatican II. Spiritual direction became a privileged place for individual exploration of the effects of new religious experiences, dramatic change in lifestyles, and theological understandings. Those who practiced spiritual direction appreciated growth in discernment of spirits through careful reflection on personal experience in conversation with an experienced guide. Thus, spiritual direction supported rapid adult spiritual development among those who participated. When Roman Catholic ecclesiology emphasized the rightful role of the entire people of God in the church, and explicitly taught the universal call to holiness as well as lay responsibility for Christian mission in the world, academic programs in the discipline of Christian spirituality began to develop. These academic programs built on the retrieval of individually directed Ignatian retreats within the retreat movement and renewal movements in religious life for both men and women that preceded them. The theological changes, both the return to ancient sources and the development of the new theology, directly influenced the retrieval and renewal of the practice of spiritual direction.

THE THEOLOGICAL GROUNDING OF THE DIRECTOR

I can think of a no more complex theological activity in a practical context than the ministry of spiritual direction, although describing this practice theologically may not be the most common approach. I consider first the theological grounding of the director since the experience and competency of accompanying another as a spiritual director is not identical with the experience of being a directee. Directees articulate a narrative of their experience of God, grace, challenge, conversion, and mystery before they might notice theological themes in their stories or the theology informing this practice. As I argue in *To Tell the Sacred Tale,* the director intimately influences the narrative a directee creates orally from session to session; this essentially collaborative narrative process is already a meaning-making activity in the directee's life. This is a form of grassroots narrative theology, focusing on the story of experienced grace, informed as it already is by the biblical narratives of theophanies, call, mission, sin and conversion, healing, suffering, death, and new life in both the Hebrew Scriptures and the New Testament. These stories are shaped by a relationship with Jesus through sacramental life, the story of Jesus as enacted in the liturgical year, and the Gospel narratives and teachings that form a privileged medium of prayer in individual *lectio divina* or Ignatian contemplation. Christians believe that God reveals God's self through scripture as well as within ordinary life. Frequently, these already biblically encoded theologies and spiritualities provide the first shared language for interpretation in spiritual direction.

There are many ways of describing the theology that both grounds this practice and that may surprisingly flow from it both as concrete action on the part of the directee and as a new word about God, an experience-based theological insight.[14] In practice, the director's espoused and operative theologies are constantly at play in dialogue with the directee's experience within this particular pastoral conversation.[15] The director brings a lifetime of experience of practicing the faith and the theology, beliefs, and convictions that inform it. This includes the director's espoused theology, how the director understands and has appropriated Catholic belief and the corresponding behaviors and spiritual practices that flow from that belief, and operative theologies that may or may not match the espoused version. Likewise, directees come to spiritual direction with similar theological perspectives, whether implicit or explicit, that may be similar to or different from those of their directors.

Most contemporary models of spiritual direction dramatically shifted away from a prescriptive model of spiritual direction that subordinated the spiritual longings and experience of directees to doctrinal formulations and their behavior to the dictates of moral theology. Instead, it took the religious experience of the directee as its starting point, trusting that God is a self-revealing, self-communicating God and exploring the directee's awareness of and reaction to these movements.

The first moment of interpretation robustly elicits this story of grace from the directee and then explores the directee's response to it, first in the initial moment of awareness of this communication or in prayer and then how it might lead to future action in response to this amplified understanding of this incident. This is a shared exercise of practical theology and discernment. Is this impulse consonant with who God is for us? Is it coming from some other source?

This exploration begins with the experience—what happened? What more might be there that wasn't noticed at first? Frequently, the directee notices the implicit theology within in this step. Second, the directee moves toward discerning a response or possible responses, and then over time, traces the pattern of events and responses in order to discern a deeper response or a decision guided by the pattern of grace over time.

RELIGIOUS EXPERIENCE MODEL OF SPIRITUAL DIRECTION

The Center for Religious Development (CRD) in Cambridge, Massachusetts, explicitly developed a religious experience model of spiritual direction in 1971; the model spread rapidly in Roman Catholic circles and beyond. It focused almost exclusively on the religious experience of the directee. The CRD contracted for a course on the theology of religious experience for the associates it trained. This course was based primarily on Karl Rahner's theology of grace and his essay "The Experience of the Spirit" as well as theologian Brian McDermott's treatment of the grace of Christ, which drew on both Karl Rahner and Edward Schillebeeckx's understanding of the grace of Christ as "an experience" of the disciples that is described in the scriptural narratives in a Christic pattern.[16]

In my own work influenced by these same sources, I tried to describe the narrative process that spiritual direction employs as its primary discourse, which always embeds this experience of grace in a story; thus both the director and the directee can easily notice themes from the Creeds and the Gospels as they emerge because these are essentially narrative forms of theology that interact in unpredictable ways with the directee's story. This faith narrative is learned and rehearsed over the liturgical year in and through the eucharistic community of believers who are already in communion with a trinitarian God. Directors need sufficient theological literacy in order to recognize when and how their directees' accounts disclose how they are living the gospel or enjoying an experience of shared belief of the community of faith that has been elaborated theologically so that they can reflect it back to their directees, enabling them to appropriate these themes as living mysteries. Spiritual direction is thus also a dialogical narrative form of practical theology.

I believe such theological grounding is essential to the practice of spiritual direction, which, since the 1970s, sometimes had a more psychological emphasis, helpfully informed by depth psychology, developmental psychology, and transpersonal psychology. While I, too, believe that these insights from another discipline are helpful and necessary to be able to engage in spiritual direction responsibly, spiritual direction as a practice is not psychotherapy but a pastoral ministry that is more focused on the mystery of God's relating to the human person and thus more informed by theological sources than psychological ones.

William Reiser, SJ, a systematic theologian who later provided a course on the theology of spiritual direction at CRD, notes that he expanded his reflections beyond the theological understandings of experience. Reiser came to see that embedded in the Christian practice of spiritual direction are particular theologies of revelation, the church, the gospel, and the human person. A theology of revelation presupposes that God continues to reveal God's self to individual believers and to communities of believers. As he wrote, "The divine mystery is first experienced and only then schematized" as theology.[17]

The ecclesial element of spiritual direction is increasingly problematic because of the number of people who were caught up in the conflict of interpretations over Vatican II and who find themselves on the margins of ecclesial life. These conflicts deeply affect the spiritual lives of those on the side of ongoing reform and renewal, many of whom continue to feel called to prophetic witness to the ecclesial community as well as to prophetic action in ministry to the underserved in society. The spiritual direction relationship can be a safe and grace-filled place of support and shared commitment between directors and directees on the prophetic margins. At the same time, the irregularity of participation in eucharistic community of many can undermine how directees and even their directors experience their ecclesial belonging.

Yet spiritual direction embodies an ecclesiology from below—two Christians who usually share a rather broad sense of coherent belief centered on Jesus, all of which is contextualized by a community of believers, however differently each may believe. The spiritual direction relationship is an intimate ecclesial community and is today exceedingly important, as are many other faith-based small Christian communities that represent the reality of church beyond officially constituted parish or diocesan structures. Many laity who have not had the advantage of theological education beyond their own sacramental formation at a much earlier time in their lives may struggle in their spiritual lives because they do not have an adult understanding (theology) of their faith. Spiritual direction cannot provide this education, but directors can recommend that they pursue some form of theological updating that enables them to become as adult in their faith understanding as they are in the rest of their lives.

Case Study #1: Spiritual Direction in the Wake of Hurricane Sandy

In order to exemplify some of these themes, I draw on a directee's account of a session that occurred shortly after Hurricane Sandy struck the Northeast.[18] Jane is a mature woman religious currently involved in a ministry serving trafficked women. She described our spiritual direction session as follows:

We spoke initially of the hurricane and the effects on so many in the NY area: flood damage, loss of power, no heat—so many were affected in this way and many others through the shortage of gas—lots of stress and anxiety flowing from the disruption of life in the city. I became aware of how this anxiety stirred up my own propensity to be anxious. We spoke about intercessory prayer—I was aware I was doing this—breathing deeply and holding individuals and situations in my heart. The breathing is healing and opens my heart to what is situational and what is my own anxiety.

In this first portion of the session, I was attentive to her particular experience of the hurricane and her community's housing a displaced family. Jane was simultaneously noticing that some of her anxiety was not related to the disaster.

Jane has long practiced a silent kind of contemplation, and I asked her about her intercessory prayer during this time. She was practicing a breathing prayer, but as a result of my question, she noticed that while she was praying for others, her own personal anxiety was also being healed. Jane then moved to a discussion of how a book on contemplative prayer I had recommended to her was affecting her.[19]

I begin to understand what he is saying—he is putting words on my experience—and yet at the same time he is opening up my experience for me. I am being drawn into knowing God in a deeper silence…it isn't an intellectual knowing…but a knowing in the silence.

This text gave her words that resonated with her and helped her make the connection between head and heart as well as opening into prayer. As a result of Martin Laird's "putting words" on her experience, she was able to notice and tell me more about her prayer than previously. As we lingered with her prayer experience, she noticed:

As we talked I was aware of a gratitude welling up. A gratitude for what I did not know! Janet offered the following observation—Gratitude is the deep response to the gift of life—God is all there is!—simple words that mean so much! I know this. It is not as if this is a gratitude for something, anything, a material good.

"God is all there is"—only—belief and trust in God—this is the foundation. Janet spoke of Liberation Theology and a sense of dependence on God. I experienced this on my trip to Peru—the people lack many of the daily necessities yet share the little they have and celebrate life amidst their poverty—they have a deep dependence on God. The gratitude stayed with me as we spoke—what I am becoming aware of, are the movements taking place—the profound gift that is life—the word "Emeth" speaks to me of this (a Hebrew word of mine from the past)—the paradox of those places/wounds in myself that cry out for healing are the gifts that actually bring healing—I am not sure I understand this...but I am knowing this on another level. The scripture, "by his wounds we are healed," is speaking to me. Is it the very wounds that bring us/me to know life in its fullness?

In this final part of Jane's account, simultaneous with experiencing her own gratitude that was present initially but not noticed, she begins to extend the very brief opening into theological reflection on her own. She first identifies with my mention of gratitude as a major theme in liberation theology by connecting it with a fairly recent experience in Peru. As gratitude continued to well up within her as she was speaking and reflecting, she describes and develops her own theological reflection about how she is being touched by God right within the session. She continues with a scripturally based theological insight that is part of her own religious history and that takes her deeper into the mystery of God healing her through her wounds, and through the wounds of Christ. And she arrives at her own conclusion about how she wants to learn this gratitude.

As a director, I can see in this account how I had offered this particular directee a contemplative text in the previous session, leaving her and God free to make use of it.[20] This was intuitive on my part, an act of discernment, recognizing without saying very many words the quality of her silent contemplative prayer despite anxiety states rooted in her personal psychological history. I inquired about what was happening in her intercessory prayer in the context of Hurricane Sandy, which led to an account of how God was healing her anxiety even as she was concerned about others. She was able to differentiate between her prayer for others and God's grace to her personally within this cycle of breathing prayer. In probably less than one short paragraph, I made a theological connection between the gratitude for the gift of life, for God's presence in the midst of suffering from liberation theology, holding together a first-world experience of a disaster affecting so many but each differently. By naming the gratitude she was feeling but had not yet named, she did her own practical theology, describing it in her own words and in relationship to her graced history and her own theological language. Spiritual direction can help directees do practical theological reflection on their own lives. Discrete experiences of God begin to accumulate meaning, and patterns emerge that connect directees to the larger faith community and help them to appropriate the mysteries of faith more deeply.

As directees grow and mature in the spiritual life, directors should begin to see in each one a unique and original appropriation of the mysteries of Christian faith. It is reasonable to expect that those whose spiritual lives take place within the context of Christian faith communities will change, personalize, and grow in their theological understandings and articulation of their faith. They will discover these mysteries coming alive within their own experience[21] and frequently turn to scriptural themes or theological language to express them.

Case Study #2: Recognizing the Mystery of Grace in the Practice of Forgiveness

William, a professor at a college of criminal justice, provides another example of reflecting theologically on his experience of receiving the grace of forgiveness as a result of a larger transformation from self-centeredness to God-centeredness. This first change in his character might be described as growth in virtue through awareness of his defects, practicing altruism, and focusing more on Jesus than himself.

> *There was a time when I had a terrible ego problem. I've learned that the me, the ego, is…something to be ignored, putting one's personality aside and thinking of the other's needs. Now I place my ego to the side, saying [to Jesus], "What do you need, what do you want, what would you do?"*

In describing this change in himself, he spontaneously began to engage in theological reflection. William recognized that he had gradually become less self-centered through the ongoing grace of Christ over fifteen years. He realized that this growth in altruism was not something entirely in his power but turned to Jesus in his prayer asking for guidance.

> *I've been able to go to people that really hurt one of my daughters. I went to my enemies and I knocked on the door and I said, look, I'm a Eucharistic Minister and I know your father is dying. Would you like me to bring communion? So I became a sacramental minister to people that injured my family. It was a beautiful gift, but if my old ego had been in place, my pride would have [gotten in the way], and I would have been unforgiving, I would have been condemning myself because we are going to be forgiven as…as we forgive.*

> *So when the whole thing was over, I said, "Oh my God, you gave me this gift to forgive people that were so injurious to my family. You helped me to forgive them. Now if terrible me can forgive, how much more will my God be able to forgive me.*[22]

When "his enemies" were suffering, he discovered the answer to those questions. Notice how he reflected theologically on his experience. He realized he could never have offered communion to his neighbors in his former ego-state. He expressed awe and gratitude at what God had done in him. He named it as the gift of forgiving his enemies. Even more than that, he discovered something about God. William's way of thinking about God had perhaps changed. He did not forgive his neighbors *because* that is the condition for God's forgiveness. He forgave his neighbors because God enabled that forgiveness, and as a result William appreciated God's goodness and willingness to forgive.

According to the storyteller-theologian John Shea, religious traditions provide believers with a common language, symbols, and rituals that help us interpret our experience.[23] William knew from the scriptures that Christians *ought* to forgive their enemies, but he was unable to do so. When he received the grace of forgiveness, it felt differently from what he had imagined. Yet he recognized that grace-empowered forgiveness had come alive in him.

It is important that directors pay attention to the theological interpretations of their directees when they emerge in their narratives and explanations. This noticing and theologizing is best done first within their directees' worldviews in order to foster their ongoing response to God and the mystery they are encountering. There are times when a director might gently offer an alternative perspective to a directee whose world is too limited, but this challenge can be done in a climate of empathy and acceptance of the other.

Such theological reflection is only one aspect of the conversation and may not be explicit in every session. Experiences that are not explicitly interpreted theologically, however briefly, can remain so inchoate that directees may not be able to make the connection between their experience and the faith of the community, and as a result they may fail to welcome its mystical deepening. William's interpretation of his experience led to a second theological insight about God's willingness and ability to forgive. Had William focused only on his empowered forgiving, his director might have asked what, if anything, his experience suggested about God. Such a theologically based prompt invites directees to express their changing understandings (theologies) of whatever mystery of faith is already present in the conversation, both in a single session and over time.

CONCLUSION: SPIRITUAL DIRECTION AS THEOLOGY IN A PRACTICAL MODE

In both accounts of these directees' religious experience and their reflection on them within a spiritual direction conversation, theology in a practical mode is already evident. Because spiritual direction encompasses the whole of directees' lives, they become increasingly skilled at discerning responses and next steps in response to grace. Jane moves more deeply into gratitude as she discovers it already present. She implicitly but not explicitly associates the distress wreaked by Hurricane Sandy to a kind of liberation theology, although her experience in Peru is more consciously linked to it.

William's insights into his self-centeredness led him to make serious efforts over time to center himself around Jesus instead of himself. His interior grace that impels him to make an overture to his "enemies" circles back to an awareness of God's transforming action in him. He discovers how he has become a Jesus-kind of person as he reflects on how grace moved him to respond to his enemies' losses in such a way that the gift of forgiveness was given. Gradually, the enmity fades between these two families.

William's response to the Spirit's prompting enables him to take the first step and gradually several subsequent ones.

Practices of spiritual direction thus display a form of practical theology. It is an ongoing process of recognizing Spirit-initiated actions felt in the life of believers. When they bring these impulses and situations to spiritual direction along with their often inchoate or partially formed insights and sort through additional responses, they engage in both practical theological reflection and discernment of spirits in conversation with a spiritual director. Ideally the spiritual director opens up greater theological insight, loving possibilities for action, and mystical deepening that is unique for each directee.

Notes

1. Elizabeth Liebert, "Supervision as Widening the Horizons," in *Supervision of Spiritual Directors: Engaging the Holy Mystery*, ed. Mary Rose Bumpus and Rebecca Bradburn Langer (Harrisburg, PA: Morehouse Publishing, 2005), 125–45; and Margaret Ellen Burke, "Social Sin and Social Grace," *The Way Supplement* 85 (Spring 1996): 40–54. Both offer a reflection on this tool adapted specifically to spiritual direction; see Frans Jozef Servaas Wiljsen, Peter Henriot, SJ, and Rodrigo Mejía, eds., *The Pastoral Circle Revisited: A Critical Quest for Truth and Transformation* (Maryknoll, NY: Orbis Books, 2005). It was published on the twenty-fifth anniversary of *Social Analysis: Linking Faith and Justice* by Joe Holland and Peter Henriot (Maryknoll, NY: Orbis Books, 1983), who describe the subsequent history and development of the pastoral circle; Janet K. Ruffing, "An Integrated Model of Supervision in Training Spiritual Directors," *Presence* 9, no. 1 (February 2003): 24–30, reprinted in *The Soul of Supervision: Integrating Practice and Theory*, ed. Margaret Benefiel and Geraldine Holton (Harrisburg: PA, Morehouse Publishing, 2010), 153–64. This work describes some aspects of spiritual direction supervision dependent on psychological understandings. See also Maureen Conroy, *Looking into the Well: Supervision of Spiritual Directors* (Chicago, IL: Loyola University Press, 1995), 25–26. Conroy includes moral, theological, and spiritual differences

between director and directee as important issues for directors to explore in supervision. Her model presumes that a theology of religious experience informs the practice of spiritual direction and encourages directors to process their theological differences with directees in supervision so that they remain free to support directees in being affected by God in ways that enable directees to expand these meaning-making assumptions through deeper reflection on their own actual graced experience rather than on espoused beliefs alone.

2. Sandra Schneiders, "A Hermeneutical Approach to the Study of Christian Spirituality," *Christian Spirituality Bulletin* 2, no. 1 (Spring 1994): 13.

3. David M. Perrin, *Studying Christian Spirituality* (New York: Routledge, 2007), 32.

4. See Sandra Schneiders, "The Study of Christian Spirituality: Contours and Dynamics of a Discipline," *Christian Spirituality Bulletin* 6, no. 1 (Spring 1998): 3–6. Schneiders offers a nuanced description of how theology is related to the academic study of spirituality. This argument asserts a variety of roles for theology but also insists on the interdisciplinarity of spirituality; see also Philip E. Sheldrake, "Spirituality and Theology" and "Trinity and Anthropology: The Self and Spiritual Transformation," in his *Explorations in Spirituality: History, Theology, and Social Practice* (New York: Paulist Press, 2010), 37–53, 54–74. Sheldrake argues for a more distinctive relationship between theology and spirituality than Schneiders espouses.

5. "Spirituality is that part of theology which deals with Christian perfection and the ways that lead to it. *Dogmatic Theology* teaches what we should believe, *Moral Theology* teaches what we should do to avoid sin, mortal and venial, and above them both, though based on them both, comes *Spirituality* or *Spiritual Theology*. This again, is divided into *Ascetic Theology* and *Mystical Theology*." Pierre Pourrat, cited by Sheldrake in "Trinity and Anthropology," 60.

6. This is a fine example of Don S. Browning's view that theology or theories are already embedded in practices so that they "are meaningful or theory-laden" and not simply the application of theology to a practice. *A Fundamental Practical Theology:*

Descriptive and Strategic Proposals (Minneapolis, MN: Fortress Press, 1991), 6.

7. Hans Georg Gadamer, *Truth and Method*, trans. and ed. Garrett Barden and John Cumming (New York: Crossroad Publishing, 1975), 248.

8. Schneiders, "A Hermeneutical Approach to the Study of Christian Spirituality," 11.

9. I think of the theologians who dismantled the theology that maintained apartheid in South Africa, black theology in the United States that resisted the effects of racism and supported the civil rights movement, the retrieval of the prophetic imagination among mainstream traditions that supported resistance to "royal consciousness" both in churches and in society, feminist theologies that supported the full personhood of women in church and society as well as contested exclusively male images of the Divine, and systematic theologies that spoke about God as mystery and love that diminished the hold of punitive and sadistic images that developed in popular imagination on the basis of theologies of atonement.

10. Janet K. Ruffing, "Panning for Gold: Attending to Theological Themes in Spiritual Direction," in *Spiritual Direction Beyond the Beginnings* (New York: Paulist Press, 2000), 57–94.

11. Ibid., 60.

12. See Janet K. Ruffing, RSM, *To Tell the Sacred Tale: Spiritual Direction and Narrative* (New York: Paulist Press, 2011), 3–6, for a brief account of this form of spiritual direction and the literature that describes it. See "The Sayings of the Fathers," in *Western Asceticism*, trans. Owen Chadwick (Philadelphia, PA: Westminster Press, 1958), for a topically arranged collection of sayings and stories that offer a window onto this original practice of spiritual direction.

13. Second Vatican Council, *Dogmatic Constitution on the Church* (1964), chap. 5, nos. 38–42.

14. See Janice Edwards, *Wild Dancing: Embraced by Untamed Love* (Sea Cliff, NY: Brookville Books, 2012). Edwards offers an account of such an experience-based theological insight of the God within that she acquired following brain surgery. She draws on themes in spirituality, theology, and cosmology explicitly as

well as certain mystics in order to subsequently articulate her mystical experience, which occurred before she recovered speech and other motor abilities after surgery. As an experienced spiritual director, she also uses case material from her directees that show these same themes at work in her directees, essentially a God who embraces us in untamed love; see also Brother Emmanuel of Taizé, *Love, Imperfectly Known: Beyond Spontaneous Representations of God*, trans. Dinah Livingston (New York: Crossroad Publishing, 2011). He draws on the Gospel of John and depth psychology in order to challenge the obstacles many people experience from God-representations that are essentially rooted in their own psyches that prevent belief in and experience of a God of love. In many instances these psychologically rooted, negative God-representations became embedded in theologies of God that become an obstacle to people's experience of God as unlimited love. In personal correspondence, Brother Emmanuel described the mystical experience that initiated his call to religious life and that led him to try to free others of God-representations that prevent the very love God offers all of us.

15. See Ruffing, "Panning for Gold," 57–94, as well as Ruffing, *To Tell the Sacred Tale*, 126–29. Sufficient theological competence is required in directors to help directees make connections between their own experiences and insights with the larger tradition. If directors are only narrowly or ideologically trained theologically, they will police their directees' unfolding life of grace and faith practice rather than welcome their theologically fresh insights. As a feminist, I am particularly attuned to the theologizing of my women directees as a liberative practice. At times, my directees have also been theologians, doctoral students, and divinity students. These individuals, of course, have the theological tools needed to relate their own experience to the tradition. But other directees benefit from the director's explicitly connecting their story to the lived tradition either through Scriptural themes, through the symbols of the Creed, or through a variety of contemporary theologians who are concerned with living or practicing the faith, such as Elizabeth Dreyer, *Manifestation of Grace* (Collegeville, MN: Michael Glazier, 1990). Dreyer offers rich, accessible vocabulary relating theologies of grace to lived experi-

ence. The current series she is editing, Called to Holiness: Spirituality for Catholic Women (St. Anthony Messenger Press, 2008–present), is a model for doing practical theology with adult women; Nicholas Lash, *Believing Three Ways in One God: A Reading of the Apostles Creed* (Notre Dame, IN: University of Notre Dame Press, 2010), offers theologically informed "meditations" on the clauses of the Creed related to the believer's life. These reflections would well serve Rite of Christian Initiation of Adults (RCIA) programs as well as help spiritual directors recognize these creedal themes as they arise in the conversation; Karl Rahner's published sermons, prayers, and *The Practice of Faith: A Handbook of Contemporary Spirituality* (New York: Crossroad Publishing, 1983) all relate directly to daily life.

16. See Denis Edwards, *The Human Experience of God* (New York: Paulist Press, 1983). Edwards offers an accessible presentation of Rahnerian themes in less technical language; see also Edwards's *Breath of Life: A Theology of the Creator Spirit* (Maryknoll, NY: Orbis Books, 2004). This more recent work is a pneumatology that shows the Spirit at work in the world from the beginning of creation that supports appropriation of the new cosmology and ecological themes so necessary today as well. See also Denis Edwards, *Ecology at the Heart of Faith: The Change of Heart that Leads to a New Way of Living on Earth* (Maryknoll, NY: Orbis Books, 2006); Karl Rahner, "Reflection on the Experience of Grace," in *Theological Investigations*, vol. 3, trans. Karl-H. Kruger and Boniface Kruger (Baltimore, MD: Helicon Press, 1967), 86–90. Excerpts of this essay along with some of his teachings on mysticism, prayer, and mission can be found in *The Practice of the Faith*, which is organized around the theological virtues of faith, hope, and love; see more recently, *Karl Rahner: Spiritual Writings*, ed. and intro. Philip Endean, Modern Spiritual Masters (Maryknoll, NY: Orbis Books, 2004). Also very accessible is Brian O. McDermott's *What Are They Saying about the Grace of Christ?* (New York: Paulist Press, 1984). Edward Schillebeeckx, *Christ: The Experience of Jesus as Lord*, trans. John Bowden (New York: Crossroad Publishing, 1981) is clearly more difficult.

17. William Reiser, SJ, *Seeking God in All Things: Theology and Spiritual Direction* (Collegeville, MN: Liturgical Press, 2004), 3.

18. Because this session had taken an explicitly theological turn, I asked Jane to write an account of the session and give me permission to use it.

19. Martin Laird, *A Sunlit Absence: Silence, Awareness, and Contemplation* (New York: Oxford University Press, 2011).

20. Spiritual reading of this nature is another time-honored spiritual practice. The spiritual direction conversation depends on the directee's other spiritual practices of prayer, reading, journaling, eucharistic life, and the ongoing noticing of how she is being affected by grace on a day-to-day basis. This directee is theologically literate and creates continuity between her previous spiritual history and this present moment through "Emeth." She had not yet made the connection for herself about how her immersion in anti-trafficking work might also be related to the experience she associates with Peru. When she returned for the next session life had moved on to completely different themes so I did not bring up this previous session.

21. Kathleen Norris, *Amazing Grace: A Vocabulary of Faith* (New York: Riverhead Books, 1998). Norris describes her struggles with the received vocabulary of Christian tradition and infuses these words with meanings to which she can relate from her own gradual experience of coming to belief in adulthood. These literary gems resemble the way directees articulate their experiences of faith in more fragmentary and less literary expressions of their lived theologies.

22. Ruffing, "Panning for Gold," 62.

23. See John Shea, *Stories of Faith* (Chicago, IL: Thomas More Press, 1980), 76–125; see also Shea's *Experiences of the Spirit* (Chicago, IL: Thomas More Press, 1983).

CHAPTER 11

PRACTICES OF LOVE AND SOLIDARITY

Family Ethics

JULIE HANLON RUBIO

WHY PRACTICAL THEOLOGY FOR FAMILIES?

Dorothy Day (1897–1980) is among the most inspiring of all contemporary Catholic figures. The bohemian journalist who converted to Catholicism and started the Catholic Worker movement in 1930 is compelling not only because of what she wrote but because of how she lived. It is one thing to speak of a preferential option for the poor and another to live simply among marginalized people day after day. Day tried to align every aspect of her life with her faith: the way she dressed and ate, the books she read and the music she listened to, where she lived, how she traveled, and the people with whom she spent her time. Although she has not yet been canonized a saint, because of her commitment to discipleship and the delight she brought to her life she is already an exemplar for many.[1]

In his influential book *Heroes, Saints, and Ordinary Morality*, Andrew Flescher defines morality as the struggle to be truly virtuous rather than living an ordinary life.[2] He suggests that readers should not dismiss the moral significance of figures like Dorothy Day by naming them as saints or heroes. Rather, "[w]e ought to read about heroes and saints because of their potential to serve as mentors for those interested in living a virtuous life."[3] More people will strive to live heroically because they will no longer be limited by low expectations of the ordinary.

Though there are good reasons for Christians to read about the saints, encouraging believers to follow the lead of extraordinary persons sidesteps some of the complexity of living a moral life. Flescher contends that when we fail to take heroes and saints seriously enough, we fail in virtue.[4] However, while a lack of virtue affects the ability to live well, other important concerns may also steer people to lead less than radical lives: uncertainties regarding how family commitments ought to reshape responsibility for social justice or how the effects of simple living compare to engagement in the economy, to name but a few. Modern prophets like Day inspire, but without the social analysis to consider particular choices, Christians are still left without moral guidance for all of the ordinary dilemmas that mark their daily lives.

Some contemporary theologians of the family have begun to undertake this kind of social analysis. In his book *Sex and Love in the Home,* David Matzko McCarthy comes at the ethics of ordinary life by analyzing family practices that sustain both families and communities. He contrasts the independent, upper-middle-class, "closed" suburban home where goods and services are purchased rather than exchanged with the "open" home where "ordinary practices of local interdependence are the substance of a complex system of interchange and a rich community life."[5] McCarthy explains that when people offer hospitality to other families' children, help others with home improvement projects, share extra baked goods, or trade produce from a garden, they are engaging in an informal, asymmetrical network of gift exchange that, unlike the money economy, creates interdependent relationships.[6] Keeping up these practices is essential, in his view, for building community and maintaining a Christian home that is more than a private haven.

McCarthy's focus on the home is controversial in the context of Christian ethics. Unlike theologians who speak of the family's mission to work for social justice in the world, McCarthy emphasizes what families can do by staying home. He realizes that focusing on practices such as snow shoveling and giving away second-hand clothes may seem mundane. Yet, with very particular descriptions of daily life that make up his contrast between the open and closed homes, he draws his readers' attention to the profound ways in which practices form a pattern of living, shape both adults and children into certain kinds of people, and constitute our most fundamental and enduring contribution to the world. This emphasis on everyday ethics is a welcome change from a Christian ethics of the extraordinary, and is one example of resonance between moral theology and practical theology. The concern with families and children also has been significant in practical theological scholarship, as illustrated by the multivolume Family, Culture, and Religion project led by Don S. Browning as well as work by practical theologians Pamela Couture, Bonnie Miller-McLemore, Joyce Mercer, Claire Wolfteich, and Annemie Dillen.[7]

More recent work in family ethics takes us even further by providing robust analysis of everyday family practices more akin to traditional ethical treatments of sex, divorce, and war.[8] This is precisely the sort of analysis that families need in order to make good judgments on the everyday dilemmas that mark their lives. A concern for practices unites family ethics and practical theology. Below, I present an argument for five practices that embody and sustain love and solidarity at the center of the family. I describe three of these practices that are central to my own family ethic, discuss some complications with two of the practices, and reflect on what theologians can learn about family from attending to everyday life. I offer this reflection with the hope that further dialogue between ethicists and practical theologians will yield better theology for those who love the saints and yet yearn for practical ways to live their faith in their homes.

I offer this reflection with the hope that further dialogue between ethicists and practical theologians will yield better theology for those who love the saints and yet yearn for practical ways to live their faith in their homes.

WHY PRACTICES OF RESISTANCE?

Intentional practices are necessary if Christian families are to live out their faith in a culture wedded to other truths. Because American family life is distorted by the lure of consumerism and the pressures of upward mobility, it is difficult for Christians to place love and solidarity at the center of their lives. To combat these pressures, I offer five practices: eating, tithing, making love, serving, and praying.[9] In the formulation of each practice, Catholic sacramental theology and social teaching are brought to bear on ordinary actions, social analysis is utilized to aid consideration of what is lacking in Christian family life, and hard questions are asked about the ethical significance of daily choices.

The language of practice is significant in the work of many contemporary writers, but few have been more influential in theological ethics than the philosopher Alasdair MacIntyre, who upholds the importance of actions that shape human persons in the context of their traditions.[10] Protestant ethicist Stanley Hauerwas places MacIntyre's work in a Christian context with a focus on discipleship. For Hauerwas, being a disciple of Christ means engaging in specific practices with a Christian community devoted to a particular way of life. The church, Hauerwas claims, must "be a people of virtue—not simply any virtue, but the virtues necessary for remembering and retelling the story of a crucified savior."[11] Those who want to be Christian must live deliberately out of step with the mainstream by adopting distinctive patterns of life.

Catholic theologians are also beginning to affirm the significance of practice.[12] According to Kieran Scott, "practices of resistance" can be "a protest against a meaningless, self-centered, commodity-driven life."[13] Building on John F. Kavanaugh's classic analysis of consumerism in *Following Christ in a Consumer Society*,[14] Scott outlines five cultural deficiencies and offers five practices of resistance. To combat a loss of interiority or self-knowledge, he suggests solitude and prayer. To counter the loss of solidarity, he commends "wasting time" on the covenantal relationships, giving those we love presence and attention. To combat injustice, he advises increasing our commitment to justice, beginning in the home. To counter the craving for consumption, he recommends throwing off cumber and embracing simplicity. To prevent a flight from vulnerability that prevents us from fully giving ourselves both to family and to those on the margins, he counsels compassion. In all five areas, the intent is to choose practices that will enable Christians to live the personal form—"a mode of perceiving and valuing men and women as irreplaceable persons whose fundamental identities are fulfilled in covenantal relationship."[15]

The work of practical theologians Craig Dykstra and Dorothy C. Bass places practices in the context of the Christian community. Dykstra and Bass define practice as an intentional, shared action, situated in the context of a tradition, ordinary in outward appearances but transcendent in its association with fundamental human goods.[16] When added to the more explicitly countercultural views of Hauerwas and other Christian ethicists, Bass and Dykstra's emphasis on tradition yields an understanding of practice that can be developed in Christian homes. Sex, eating, tithing, serving, and praying can be understood as essential practices of resistance embedded in the ordinary life of a Christian household committed to love and solidarity.

Practices for Families: Sex, Eating, and Serving

Sex may seem a particularly odd choice with which to begin. After all, what does sex have to do with resistance? Can sex be understood as a practice like prayer, fasting, or simplicity? Though it may seem odd to think about sex in marriage as a practice of resistance, there are good reasons for doing so. Admittedly, the Christian tradition has not often spoken of sex as a practice of love and solidarity.[17] A contemporary family ethic will necessarily leave behind much of the negativity that has marked Christian sexual ethics. However, we can bring forward recent theological affirmations of sex as an expression of self-giving love.[18] With this positive vision in hand, it will be possible to use practical reason to describe good sexual practice. We can then begin to imagine what sort of sex life married couples *could* have and ponder what goods they *ought* to seek. We can begin to see that fidelity to a practice of sex oriented to relationship could be a powerful response to the loss of solidarity and flight from vulnerability, key markers of consumer society.

A contemporary Christian sexual ethic rooted in the experience of men and women must assume the potential of sex to speak the commitment of marriage vows, not in explicit promises or earth-shattering experiences, but in the very ordinary repetition over time of a bodily act that says, "I still want to be with you. I will always want to be with you." Such a practice ought to be attentive to four goods basic to sex. The good of vulnerability requires a disciplining of desires within a relationship, a limitation designed to free attention for one particular other. We say, in effect, "I'm not going to any place or to anyone else. I'll pour my relational energy into you." Committed spouses are free to be increasingly vulnerable to one another over time. Good sexual practice will also involve self-sacrifice and self-love. True self-giving love can only come about through self-love that inspires a desire to be vulnerable. If both spouses do not desire pleasure for themselves, they are not fully loving themselves or connecting with their spouse. However, spouses who do not seek the pleasure of their partner fail to embrace a necessary measure of sacrifice that love requires. Both self-giving and self-seeking involve a kind of risk that engenders deep relationship.

Finally, bodily belonging is perhaps the most significant

good sought in married sex. Though couples share many bodily experiences, sex is unique to marital friendship and plays a key role in the development of one-flesh unity. If couples are faithfully committed to remaining connected, they will seek to maintain the sexual side of their life together. Honoring and nurturing sexual desire will bring them together bodily, emotionally, and spiritually. It will continue to open each spouse to the other, and that opening will not only nourish the communion of their married life together but will also prepare them to open themselves to others. Sex is a foundational practice for family ethics, the first practice of resistance to which married couples committed to love and solidarity ought to be faithful.

Eating, an ordinary practice that families engage in every day, can also become a practice of resistance. In this case, the tradition offers a prophetic word, calling families to express gratitude and honor the radical inclusivity of Jesus' table fellowship. Beginning a meal with grace connects families to God and one another and prepares them for a deeper commitment to social justice. L. Shannon Jung notes the importance of expressing gratitude in blessing: "Our own bounty must make us conscious of our undeserved situation of privilege. Calling this to mind should make us grateful, mindful eaters."[19] Expressing gratitude involves recognition that the goodness in our lives is not all of our own making. Neither is it all God's blessing. Those with abundance do not deserve all that they have any more than the many who live on less than two dollars a day deserve their lot in life. Paul criticizes the Corinthians for eating their memorials while others go hungry (1 Cor 11:17–28). There is something scandalous about eating while ignoring others' hunger.[20] With grace, families can recognize this scandal, give thanks for the privileges that are theirs, and express their solidarity with the truly needy. Communal consciousness of undeserved abundance can become a foundation for growth in solidarity.

Jesus' practice of eating with sinners is well established and many scripture scholars suggest that these meals are indications of what was central to his moral vision. In practicing inclusion, Jesus reveals his faith in a compassionate God who would not leave anyone out of the celestial banquet. As Elisabeth Schüssler Fiorenza claims,

> The power of God's *basileia* is realized in Jesus' table community with the poor, the sinners, the tax collectors, and prostitutes—with all those who "do not belong" to the "holy people," who are somehow deficient in the eyes of the righteous....Jesus' *praxis* and *vision* of the *basileia* is the mediation of God's future into the structures and experiences of his own time and people.[21]

In eating with sinners and outcasts, Jesus was revealing human compassion and modeling divine mercy. Christian families today ought to model this inclusive practice in their own homes, inviting their own saints and sinners to the table.

Serving is a practice most families already engage in but if it is to be a true practice of resistance rooted in Christian tradition, it should be directed to those most in need, rather than to others in what Dean Brackley calls "our middle class tribe."[22] Service to the poor is important because each human person has dignity and worth.[23] When people close to our homes are hungry, suffering from violence, or without shelter, of all the things we choose to do on a free evening or Saturday afternoon, service should have priority. As Kavanaugh says, "Social action is not the preserve of some special-interest group...because there are social conditions which minimize the very possibility of experiencing love, hope, and faith. Destitution, degrading prisons, world hunger, and armament are affairs of spirituality. The human spirit is at stake, not 'just' the body."[24] Those who are less needy can give hope to those who may have lost all hope.[25] Service has the potential to transform broken lives and thus it should command our energies.

Somehow, despite the imperatives from tradition and the reality of human need, families have often been excused from service. Perhaps they are asked to put together food baskets for Thanksgiving or adopt a family for Christmas, but most of the time the service families engage in is directed toward their own families, schools, and parishes. Because these groups are more and more homogeneous, the needy remain untouched on the other side of town. Families, it is thought, cannot be asked to bear another burden, and generally, they are not asked to do so. Kavanaugh challenges this norm by asking laypeople to tithe their time to the needy.[26]

There is a connection between service and growth in other areas of family life. Care for others, especially the poor, encourages an awareness of neediness. Stronger faith "emerges out of the conviction of one's own poverty and connectedness to that of others."[27] It is precisely the recognition of human vulnerability that comes in service to the marginalized that makes possible growth in communion.[28] As families serve together, they may find themselves more able to approach each other with humility, more ready to risk intimacy, more willing to welcome sinners like themselves to the table, and more conscious of their privilege and their need for prayer. Service is practice in love, a school of virtue with the potential to transform those who make it a part of their lives.

Sex, eating, and service are three of the five practices of resistance that form the core of a Christian ethic for families. They draw on the rich resources of the tradition as well as practical reasoning and experience to provide concrete ways for families to grow in love and solidarity through their everyday lives.

It's Complicated: Tithing and Praying

Practices of resistance are much more common in Christian communities other than families. Monks, priests, and nuns are more likely to embrace regular prayer and service. Radical communities associated with the Catholic Worker movement typically practice radical simplicity and just eating. Most families, whether poor, middle-class, or upper-class, are consumed in simply making sure that all members receive the care and attention they need.

I am arguing for much more intentionality in a family's practice of faith as a community and much more resistance to standard cultural ideas. This proposal is not without difficulties, including swimming against the tide of mainstream culture and respecting diversity among family members.

The difficulty of going against the culture by tithing 10 percent of one's income is real. Once a family makes choices about employment and housing, they are pulled into the culture associated with both. Certain things (e.g., club sports, SAT prep courses, family trips to Disneyland) appear normal in some contexts. Yet tithing requires a thorough questioning of consumerism—even consumerism that seems directed toward sustaining families.

A market economy is committed to growth and needs increasing consumption to thrive. Buying and having more thus seem to be unquestionable individual and social goods. In such a system, personal and social temperance is disrupted, so it becomes almost impossible to feel as though one has enough.[29] When families are asked in Catholic social teaching to give out of their excess, most feel they have little to give, and "the category of 'surplus' or of 'superfluous goods,' which one is obliged to distribute to the needy neighbor, effectively drops out."[30] Every time income goes up, perceived needs go up as well via what Christine Firer Hinze calls "reference group upscaling," thus, "amid unprecedented material abundance, people are afflicted by a pervasive sense of insufficiency."[31] A sense of never having enough makes it all but impossible to give very much away. Even though most acknowledge that they have too many things and care that many others go without, they feel powerless to act. Yet, if the church wants to take on consumer culture, "it can do so only by engaging consumer culture on the level of practice."[32]

Tithing is a practice with the power to check consumer culture. It does not require a rejection of all unnecessary goods. However, for most families, giving 10 percent or more of their income will mean reversing "reference group upscaling" by living more simply than those around them. The majority would find the practice to be a serious challenge. Advice on downscaling from those who manage to give more away has common themes. Families tend to trim their food bills, buy some things secondhand, reduce entertainment costs, do themselves what others pay to have done for them, and take care of what they have so that it lasts.[33] Giving 10 percent does not require radical change, but it does require taking on some sacrifice.

Those who advocate simple living almost always speak more often of the joys than of the difficulties.[34] Still, there are significant costs of maintaining a simpler lifestyle in order to tithe.[35] This complexity is important to acknowledge along with the freedom that is more commonly claimed. Greater freedom and greater struggle coexist when all economic choices become moral choices. Yet, some affirm that the struggle is ultimately worthwhile, saying, "We have gained as a family, if not exhilaration, then a deep sense of joy in sharing with our whole lives in God's kingdom work. We have known a greater communion with those who live simply not because they choose to, but because they must."[36]

Not all families enjoy this sort of communion among their members. Diversity within families makes all intentional practices more difficult. Prayer is especially problematic. The experience of contemporary families does not sit well with the advice from typical Christian prayer books.[37] Most of these books assume uniform Christian belief and imply that if families were sufficiently motivated, prayer would come to be a joyful practice. However, unity of belief is not as pervasive as one would think. At least 40 percent of Catholics today marry a spouse of a different Christian faith or a different religion.[38] Different levels of commitment are even more common. Even if they are able to pray with young children, parents may not have a strong foundation themselves, and if so it is unlikely that the experience will carry them through later stages of marriage. Many adults are less certain in their faith and less consistent in their practice than they would like to be. Children, too, are more complex than the family prayer literature allows. Although many accept the faith of their parents without question, today's

Catholic children are far less likely to sustain strong faith in adulthood.[39] Recognizing differences and limitations is crucial to approaching the practice of prayer realistically.[40]

Interreligious couples may be good models for all families who seek shared religious practice in spite of differences. Few couples are totally unified in belief and commitment. One spouse might be more religious, while another struggles with her faith. One might be drawn to traditional faith practices, while another finds God more easily outside the organized religion to which he belongs. One might be very comfortable as a lifelong adherent of the faith of his childhood, while another practices more cautiously, having converted before marriage. Or the convert's zeal is not matched by the faith of the cradle Catholic. Spouses do not always agree on matters of faith and may find faith to be a source of tension as often as a source of unity. Like interfaith couples, they will need to acknowledge the painfulness of holding different beliefs and desiring different practices, explore their differences, and find common ground on which to build a practice consistent with their respective faiths.[41] Yet, by refusing to abandon the practice despite the difficulties, by persisting in prayer while honestly acknowledging differences and doubts, families can strengthen their compassion for each other and for all who struggle.

The problems connected with intentional practices are real. Diversity makes coming to agreement challenging, and swimming against the tide of culture can be exhausting. Still, the available models of family life are lacking, and dissatisfaction with those is real, too. Knowing this makes working through the complexities of practices of resistance seems not only attractive but also necessary. The theory behind virtue ethics is that formation happens through practice.[42] A person becomes a runner by running, a swimmer by swimming, a guitarist by playing guitar. Similarly, we can become more animated by self-giving and solidarity through ordinary daily actions such as sex, service, eating, praying, and tithing. Though we may not think of ourselves as people capable of resistance, through practice, however imperfect, we hope to become more of what we want to be.

LEARNING FROM PRACTICE ABOUT FAMILY AND FAITH

Practice is never just practice. It is not simply the endpoint of ethics, the "answer" we come to after painstaking analysis. Rather, the practices we engage in teach us about the ideal we strive for and the beliefs we hold.[43] This is no less true about family ethics than anything else.

My own work on family ethics came out of a particular understanding of family and church influenced by Stanley Hauerwas and the generation of students he trained at Duke in the 1990s and 2000s.[44] My contribution to what might be called an ethics of radical Christian discipleship was to reflect on how to create and sustain a distinctively Christian home. The practices central to my work were designed for families who took discipleship seriously, and they came out of and influenced my own family's experience.

I still love that vision, but as my children grew up, it began to unravel. When my boys were younger, we read from the Bible or stories of saints before they left for school. We cooked at a Catholic Worker house. But as the boys got older, they began to resist. Prayer made less sense to them. They felt uncomfortable at the Catholic Worker. Though not opposed to some of our countercultural practices, none of them thought being distinctively Christian was particularly interesting. Children have their own ideas about what to believe and how to live. I should have known that. Even in 2003, when they were all under the age of seven, I wrote, "children are not just empty vessels into which we pour things."[45] Yet, I never imagined that my sons would find Jesus Christ to be a puzzling figure or that they would find very different heroes of their own. When I found my family ethic challenged by my experience of family, I knew I had to reconsider. My experience of living in an "interfaith" family has sparked theological rethinking.

Christian theologians throughout the history of the tradition have most often spoken about holy families headed by like-minded parents with obedient children or about the radical discipleship embodied by missionary couples who give up the distractions of ordinary family life to live the gospel. Much of contemporary Christian theology builds on one of these models. I am coming to believe that while these models may be very appropriate for families with like-minded people of faith, they may not be adequate for everyone.

Perhaps, then, Christians who find themselves in more mixed families can think about their church as their first family in faith and cultivate a vision of their family as a school of discipleship in which they work out their salvation even though others are involved in struggles of a different kind. If shared mission is impossible, perhaps it would be more realistic simply to be with "those you are stuck with" (Stanley Hauerwas's famous definition of family), respecting where each person is, asking not for total agreement but for companionship on the way, and agreeing to support each other in the quest for truth. Some families may be capable of the explicit, shared mission I have laid out above, but for those who are not, this more limited vision of "seeking with" may be more appropriate. We might even envision this as another family practice: living together in a loving community that respects, honors, and supports differences.

My hope is that both families of like-minded believers and more mixed families can still find in the Christian tradition an inspiring vision of commitment, communion, and service to others. The tradition has something beautiful and distinctive to offer, especially if we can acknowledge and work through the messiness of families as they really are. However strong or weak in faith, families need to share one another's burdens and help one another live in the imperfection of this world. Richard Gaillardetz writes powerfully of how married couples can experience God's presence not only in love and shared mission, but also in the continuing struggle to be one with a partner who is "always the wrong person."[46] Family is the place where most experience of the paschal mystery of dying and rising happens. In this context, practices of love and solidarity are always necessary, whether consciously chosen to cultivate resistance and build up faith or not.

Writing and living practical theology helped me realize that my vision of family needed more room for accommodation of difference and embrace of paschal mystery. Family, I have found, much like church, keeps asking for more; just when I think I have it figured out, it asks something else again. For me, at present, it is a community in which I can "seek with" others who may share my questions but not my vision of the kingdom. As I continue to ponder ethical questions and practices central to families, figuring out how to "seek with" is leading me to rethink everything I thought I knew and draw more from the resources of in the discipline of practical theology. As David Tracy writes in his essay in this volume, "Love, like theology, is both cataphatic and apophatic—ever greater understanding, ever greater mystery." Any good family ethic must embrace the mysteries of difference and finitude even as it points toward something more.

Notes

1. Jim Forest, *All Is Grace: A Biography of Dorothy Day* (Maryknoll, NY: Orbis Books, 2011).

2. Andrew Flescher, *Heroes, Saints, and Ordinary Morality* (Washington, DC: Georgetown University Press, 2003).

3. Ibid., 8.

4. Ibid., 10.

5. David Matzko McCarthy, *Sex and Love in the Home: A Theology of the Household*, 2nd rev. ed. (London, UK: SCM Press, 2004), 86.

6. Ibid., 93–94.

7. See Don S. Browning, Bonnie J. Miller-McLemore, Pamela D. Couture, and K. Brynolf Lyon, eds., *From Culture Wars to Common*

Ground, 2nd ed. (Louisville, KY: Westminster John Knox Press, 2000); Bonnie J. Miller-McLemore, *Also a Mother: Work and Family as Theological Dilemma* (Nashville, TN: Abingdon Press, 1994); Pamela D. Couture, *Child Poverty: Love, Justice, and Social Responsibility* (Atlanta, GA: Chalice, 2007); Joyce Mercer, *Welcoming Children: A Practical Theology of Childhood* (Atlanta, GA: Chalice, 2007); Claire E. Wolfteich, *Navigating New Terrain: Work and Women's Spiritual Lives* (Mahwah, NJ: Paulist Press, 2002); and Annemie Dillen and Didier Pollefeyt, eds., *Children's Voices: Children's Perspectives in Ethics, Theology and Religious Education* (Leuven, Belgium: Peeters, 2010).

8. See Julie Hanlon Rubio, "Family Ethics: Beyond Sex and Controversy," *Theological Studies* 74 (March 2013): 138–61.

9. These practices were first discussed in Julie Hanlon Rubio, *Family Ethics: Practices for Christians* (Washington, DC: Georgetown University Press, 2010).

10. Alisdair MacIntyre, *After Virtue: A Study in Moral Theory* (Notre Dame, IN: University of Notre Dame Press, 1984), especially chapter 14. Two of the most significant other authors who develop the category of practice are Pierre Bourdieu, *Outline of a Theory of Practice*, trans. Richard Nice (Cambridge, UK: Cambridge University Press, 1977); and Michel de Certeau, *The Practice of Everyday Life*, trans. Steven Rendall (Berkeley: University of California Press, 1984).

11. Stanley Hauerwas, *The Peaceable Kingdom: A Primer in Christian Ethics* (Notre Dame, IN: University of Notre Dame Press, 1983), 103.

12. Few Catholic moral theologians develop the concept of "practice" in a systematic way. Some exceptions are McCarthy, *Sex and Love in the Home*; David Cloutier, *Love, Reason, and God's Story: An Introduction to Catholic Sexual Ethics* (Winona, MN: Anselm, 2008); and John S. Grabowski, *Sex and Virtue: An Introduction to Sexual Ethics* (Washington, DC: Catholic University of America Press, 2003).

13. Kieran Scott, "A Spirituality of Resistance for Marriage," in *Perspectives on Marriage: A Reader*, ed. Kieran Scott and Michael Warren (New York: Oxford University Press, 2001), 403, 404.

14. John F. Kavanaugh, *Following Christ in a Consumer Society: The Spirituality of Cultural Resistance*, 25th Anniversary Edition (Maryknoll, NY: Orbis Books, 2006).

15. Scott, "A Spirituality of Resistance," 403.

16. Craig Dykstra and Dorothy C. Bass, "A Theological Understanding of Christian Practices," in *Practicing Theology: Beliefs and Practices in Christian Life*, ed. Miroslav Volf and Dorothy C. Bass (Grand Rapids, MI: William B. Eerdmans Publishing Company, 2002), 13–32.

17. For a brief summary of the difficulties presented by the tradition and the potential for moving beyond these difficulties, see Julie Hanlon Rubio, "Beyond the Liberal-Conservative Divide on Contraception: Wisdom of Practitioners of Natural Family Planning and Artificial Birth Control," *Horizons* 32, no. 2 (December 2005): 270–94.

18. Ibid. John Paul II's understanding of sex as total self-giving is fundamental to the potential for developing sexual ethics in the contemporary era.

19. L. Shannon Jung, *Sharing Food: Christian Practices for Enjoyment* (Minneapolis, MN: Fortress Press, 2006), 58.

20. David N. Powers, "Eucharistic Justice," *Theological Studies* 67, no. 4 (2006): 858–59.

21. Elisabeth Schüssler Fiorenza, *In Memory of Her: A Feminist Theological Construction of Christian Origins* (New York: Crossroad Publishing, 1989), 121.

22. Dean Brackley, *Call to Discernment in Troubled Times: New Perspectives on the Transformative Wisdom of Ignatius of Loyola* (New York: Crossroad Publishing, 2004), 37.

23. See *Gaudium et spes*, no. 27, accessed on August 30, 2013, http://www.vatican.va/archive/hist_councils/ii_vatican_council/documents/vat-ii_cons_19651207_gaudium-et-spes_en. html.

24. Kavanaugh, *Following Christ*, 136.

25. John Paul II, *Ecclesia in America*, no. 18, accessed on August 30, 2013, http://www.vatican.va/holy_father/john_paul_ii/apost_exhortations/documents/hf_jp-ii_exh_22011999_ecclesia-in-america_en.html.

26. Kavanaugh, *Following Christ*, 189.

27. Michael Warren, *Faith, Culture, and the Worshipping Community: Shaping the Practice of the Local Church* (Mahwah, NJ: Paulist Press, 1989), 66.

28. Kavanaugh, *Following Christ*, 204.

29. Christine Firer Hinze, "What is Enough? Catholic Social Thought, Consumption, and Material Sufficiency," in *Having: Property and Possession in Religious and Social Life*, ed. William Schweiker and Charles Matthewes (Grand Rapids, MI: William B. Eerdmans Publishing Company, 2004), 164.

30. Ibid., 169.

31. Ibid., 187, 186.

32. Ibid., 180.

33. See Ron J. Sider, ed., *Living More Simply: Biblical Principles & Practical Models* (Downers Grove, IL: InterVarsity Press, 1980), 59–107.

34. Ibid.

35. Ibid., 75.

36. Ibid.

37. See, for example, Jacquelyn Lindsey, *Catholic Family Prayer Book* (Huntington, IN: Our Sunday Visitor, 2001).

38. Michael G. Lawler, Gail Risch, and Lisa Riley, "Church Experience of Interchurch and Same-Church Couples," *Family Ministry* 13, no. 4 (Winter 1999): 36.

39. See William L. Portier, "Here Come the Evangelical Catholics," *Communio* 31 (Spring 2004): 48–51.

40. On this issue, practical theology is ahead of both popular prayer books and moral theology. See, for example, Mercer, *Welcoming Children*.

41. See Michael G. Lawler, *Marriage and the Catholic Church: Disputed Questions* (Collegeville, MN: Liturgical Press, 2002), 118–39.

42. See David Cloutier, *Love, Reason, and God's Story: An Introduction to Catholic Sexual Ethics* (Winona, MN: Anselm, 2008), for an accessible introduction to the concept of practice in virtue ethics and for application to sexual ethics.

43. On this point, see Craig Dykstra and Dorothy C. Bass, "A Theological Understanding of Christian Practices," in *Practicing Theology: Beliefs and Practices in Christian Life*, ed. Miroslav Volf

and Dorothy C. Bass (Grand Rapids: William B. Eerdmans Publishing Company, 2002), 13–32.

44. See William C. Mattison III, ed., *New Wine, New Wineskins: A Next Generation Reflects on Key Issues in Catholic Moral Theology* (Lanham, MD: Rowman & Littlefield, 2005); and Therese Lysaught and David Matzko McCarthy, eds., *Gathered for the Journey: Moral Theology in Catholic Perspective* (Grand Rapids, MI: William B. Eerdmans Publishing Company, 2007).

45. Julie Hanlon Rubio, *A Christian Theology of Marriage* (Mahwah, NJ: Paulist Press, 2003), 158.

46. Richard R. Gaillardetz, *A Daring Promise: A Spirituality of Christian Marriage* (Liguori, MO: Liguori Publications, 2007), 57–60.

Chapter 12

PRACTICES OF DIALOGUE

Ecclesiology and Practical Theology

Bradford Hinze

FROM PATERNALISM AND POLEMICS TO DIALOGUE

The Second Vatican Council marked a transition for the Catholic Church from a paternalistic approach to communication among members, and from a polemical approach to communication with other Christians, members of other religions, and adherents of other worldviews, to a dialogical approach both internally and externally. After the council, "dialogue" became a buzzword and provided a frequently invoked framework for understanding a range of church practices in which church members participated: personal prayer, liturgical prayer, catechesis, evangelization, works of mercy and work for justice, and discernment and decision-making in parish councils and in faith-based community organizations. This new semantics of dialogue contributed to a new practical grammar of the church, in which it was now assumed that practices of dialogue are necessary to realize the church's identity and mission.

Practices of Dialogue

Practices of dialogue are necessary to realize the church's identity and mission.

Before the Council, a one-way, monological approach to communication prevailed. Internally, information and directives flowed from centralized and higher levels of authority to those with no recognized authority: from Rome to local churches, from bishops to clergy, from clergy to laity. The hierarchy and clergy were envisioned as the teaching church, the trusted fathers charged to instruct the children of God, sons and daughters, the lay faithful, understood as the learning church. These fathers were conceived as teachers, leaders, and lawgivers; the children were those who obeyed.

The Council represented a genuine breakthrough to a dialogical ecclesiology, one that promoted collaboration, coresponsibility, and collegiality among all the baptized. Many would argue that, beginning in the mid-1980s, the incremental transition to dialogical practices initiated in the first decades after the Council met with countervailing forces undermining and restricting such changes. The fact remains, however, that since the Council great attention has been given to the development of conciliar and synodal models of collective discernment and decision-making at every level of the institution. The terms *conciliar* and *synodal* are derived from the terms *council* and *synod*, which were used since early Christianity to describe group decision-making processes about practices and beliefs in the church. Vatican II initiated alongside older forms of councils—ecumenical, national (plenary), and regional (provincial) councils—newer forms—parish and diocesan pastoral councils that bring together laypeople with priests or the local bishop and presbyteral councils that assemble diocesan clergy with their bishop. The Council established the synod of bishops as a vehicle of the universal church for representative bishops from around the world to deliberate about selected topics of concern for the universal church. Thus, at the Second Vatican Council emerged the retrieval and expansion of a conciliar and synodal vision of the church. This transformation was marked by the use of the words *dialogus* and *colloquium* in conciliar documents and led to the development of both structures of participation within the church and dialogical relationships with other Christians, other religions, and other worldviews.[1]

The Council's dialogical vision of the church included dialogue *ad extra* with "the people of our time," about their "joys and hopes, grief and anguish," especially with the poor or afflicted with whom the followers of Christ have special solidarity (*Gaudium et spes* 1).[2] With these words, the Council summoned the people of God to be attentive to the aspirations and laments of all people, both in the church and in contemporary society. Indeed, followers of Christ are mandated to cultivate an acute awareness of the complexities of this human condition: "With the help of the Holy Spirit, it is the task of the whole people of God, particularly of its pastors and theologians, to listen to and distinguish the many voices of our times and to interpret them in the light of God's word, in order that the revealed truth may be more deeply penetrated, better understood, and more suitably presented" (*Gaudium et spes* 44).[3] The truth of the gospel is made manifest not only in scripture and liturgy, but also in the words, deeds, and practices of individuals and communities. Among those practices, central even to the work of the church, are practices of dialogue—an important area of study for practical theology.

PRACTICES OF DIALOGUE IN THE CHURCH'S WORK FOR JUSTICE

One of the more compelling ways in which Catholic churches engaged in dialogue before and after the council has been in struggles against social injustice. In this arena, Catholics found a variety of ways to collaborate with other Christians and with adherents of other religious traditions and worldviews beginning in Europe. Groups of activists associated with the so-called Catholic Action movement were in the vanguard of campaigns for workers' rights, which were endorsed by Pope Leo XIII's encyclical *Rerum novarum* in 1891.[4] In this vein, in 1919 the Belgian priest Joseph Cardijn started the Young Trade Unionists, later renamed the Young Christian Workers, whose model, described by Cardijn as "see-judge-act," became a catalyst for the promotion of dialogue among bishops, clergy, and laity, and for Catholic involvement in the public realm.

The importance of dialogue, starting with one-on-one dialogues about people's griefs and anguish, hopes and joy, and moving on to small-group conversations and larger assemblies and rallies, was a bedrock conviction of Saul Alinsky, the mid-twentieth-century pioneer of the type of broad-based community organizing that came to influence many Catholics. Alinsky believed that people must learn to listen carefully to one another and identify with one another their aspirations, what frustrates them, and what angers them about society, and in so doing to determine the legitimate interests of individuals and eventually the common interests of the community. In Alinsky's own words:

> The first thing you've got to do in a community is listen, not talk, and learn to eat, sleep, breathe only one thing: the problems and aspirations of the community. Because no matter how imaginative your tactics, how shrewd your strategy, you're doomed before you even start if you don't win the trust and respect of the people; and the only way to get that is for you to trust and respect them. And without that respect there's no communication, no mutual confidence and no action. That's the first lesson any good organizer has to learn.[5]

Alinksy's insight into the role of dialogue in advancing civic engagement and grassroots democracy has been and remains the energizing force behind community organizing in the United States, in the United Kingdom, and around the world. Although no direct connection between Alinsky's model of community organizing and Catholic Action's see-judge-act has been established, these two approaches are among the most influential used by advocates of greater civic dialogue and grassroots democracy in the promotion of social justice.[6] Within the church this same insight into the importance of dialogue in promoting widespread participation has taken on its own forms in the promotion of synodality and conciliarity in parish and diocesan councils and synodal assemblies. Threading through all these developments is one central affirmation: dialogue plays a crucial role in the advancement of discernment and decision-making about shared aspirations and shared laments.

THE POWER OF DIALOGUE IN ACTION

A story of community organizing in the Bronx, New York, beginning in 2010, illustrates the power of dialogue in action. One of the members of Our Lady of Angels Catholic Parish, Ana Gilda Domínguez, originally from the Dominican Republic, was upset by the disrepair of her rented apartment and by similar complaints from her neighbors and the unwillingness of the building superintendent to address the problems. One day after Mass she approached her pastor, Father Tom Lynch. She told him about the terrible conditions in her apartment building.

Father Tom called Gabriel Pendas, a community organizer from the Northwest Bronx Community and Clergy Coalition who worked on housing issues, to ask Gabe to talk with Ana Gilda. The next day the two met, and within a week Ana Gilda also spoke with Allison Manuel (another community organizer from the Coalition who worked with the members of Our Lady of Angels Parish). Shortly thereafter, Ana Gilda attended her first meeting of the Community Angels, the faith in action committee of the parish, with Father Tom and Joan Apellaniz (now DeJesus), the leader of the group. At this meeting, the group explored what could be done to bring attention to the problems in these housing complexes. One proposal surfaced that seemed appealing:

hold a prayer vigil in front of Ana Gilda's building to draw attention to the problem. Joan, Gabe, and Allison brought this proposal to the parish council. The parish council was very supportive of the idea, and they talked about how best to rally parishioners and neighbors in these apartment buildings to join them in this effort.

To prepare for the prayer vigil, several meetings were held in Our Lady of Angels rectory to generate more widespread interest. Ana Gilda, Father Lynch, and members of the Community Angels were joined by Allison and Gabe and the parish council, other parishioners, members of the Coalition, and a growing number of disgruntled tenants. These small-group conversations brought together more disgruntled people, all residing in a group of ten apartment buildings owned by Milbank Real Estate. Gabe and Allison encouraged these residents to begin to form tenant associations to bring pressure to bear on the owners of Milbank in order to hold them accountable and to get their problems addressed. But it became clear that residents' difficulties would not be easily addressed. For more than a year Milbank had defaulted on its $35 million mortgage. At the same time the company was raising rents with the plan of urging tenants to leave so that the company could resell the units at a profit in an effort to gentrify the area, which would result in displacing the working-class and the working-poor families currently living in these buildings. Ana Gilda's initial dialogue with her neighbors and with Father Tom resulted in increased awareness of the problems with the Milbank Company and growing solidarity among the parishioners and in the neighborhood. Gabe began extending his organizing campaign by arranging with the help of Sergio Cuevas and Maggie Maldonado, joined by Juan Domínguez, Ana Gilda's son, to talk one on one with tenants and in groups to compile a list of problems in the apartment buildings.

To generate more interest in this campaign against Milbank Real Estate, Gabe and the Coalition produced flyers that described and pictured some of the problems found in Milbank buildings and listed the addresses of some of the tenement units. These were distributed to many local sites, including Catholic and Protestant Churches. The flyers included information about the Coalition's campaign and invited people to join together in a common struggle for change.

Gabe also laid out the problem at one of the monthly meetings of the Coalition's Clergy Caucus, composed of clergy representing Catholics, Lutherans, Presbyterians, Episcopalians, Methodists, Baptists, and Pentecostals. The clergy were eager to support the Coalition's campaign by mobilizing the members of their congregations.

For some time administrators in the Department of Housing Preservation and Development (HPD) had been receiving complaints about housing problems in the Northwest Bronx. However, they seemed unresponsive to the appeals made by tenant associations. It wasn't until Ana Gilda came forward and meetings took place in the rectory that tenants from the Milbank buildings were brought together to plan, first, the prayer vigil and, next, a strategy for challenging Milbank that this stalemate was broken.

On Wednesday, September 29, 2010, members of Our Lady of Angels Parish and neighbors and allies held their candlelit prayer vigil in front of Ana Gilda's building. The event took place after the 7:30 p.m. Mass. Parishioners attending the Mass, including members of the parish Cursillistas prayer group, walked over with Father Tom Lynch to Ana Gilda's building. The event brought together some thirty parishioners, including members of the faith in action committee, the parish council, parish members, and the Cursillistas, along with tenants from other Milbank buildings and members of the Coalition. Ana Gilda had inspired the service. Father Tom presided. The participants were largely Latinos/as and African Americans. They testified to the conditions of the building. Father Tom led the group in prayer, song, and a reading from the scriptures. He drew on one of his favorite themes in his words to the group: *We are the body of Christ. When one of us suffers, all of us suffer, when our brothers and sisters are suffering in these buildings, all of our parishioners and neighbors are suffering. We are called to care for one another.* The people prayed for one another and for a change in their conditions. In attendance were City Councilman Fernando Cabrera and Assemblyman Nelson Castro, who addressed the group in support of their cause.

After the vigil Gabe and Sergio wrote a letter to Vito Mustaciuolo, Deputy Commissioner of the Office of Enforcement and Neighborhood Services at HPD, with copies to Rafael Cestero, HPD Commissioner, and other municipal officials, describing the horrible conditions in the ten Milbank apartment buildings in the Bronx and requesting a meeting with HPD officials to discuss what could be done. The letter was signed by Father Tom, other members of the Clergy Caucus, and members of the Board of the Coalition. This triggered a response: Mustaciuolo was not pleased to receive this letter and seemed particularly upset that other officials were copied on the letter discussing these major housing violations in the Bronx. HPD was motivated to act.

At the end of October, one month after the prayer vigil, Vito Mustaciuolo and Rafael Cestero came and toured a couple of Milbank buildings. About one hundred tenants and community members were present. Juan Domínguez, Ana Gilda's son, led the public meeting in the lobby of their building. After Mustaciuolo and Cestero toured the building, Cestero committed his office to provide roof-to-cellar inspections of all the Milbank buildings. Gabe Pendas described what subsequently took place: "Each day a group of 3 to 4 inspectors went door-to-door cataloging the various violations ranging from broken carbon monoxide detectors to showers falling through the floor. They added over 1,300 violations in 3 weeks bringing the total violations on the portfolio to 4,392. This type of work inspired HPD to finalize and initiate a citywide program" to examine buildings with similar conditions.[7]

On January 13, 2011, in the gymnasium of Our Lady of Angels grade school, the Northwest Bronx Community and Clergy

Coalition held a press conference in which the Mayor of New York, Michael Bloomberg, Speaker of the City Council Christine Quinn, HPD Commissioner Rafael Cestero, Bronx Borough President Ruben Diaz Jr., and other elected officials stood side by side with members of the Clergy Caucus and the Coalition to announce the "Proactive Preservation Initiative" to address the many problems in multifamily units in New York City. Vito Mustaciuolo, the Deputy Commissioner of the Office of Enforcement of the HPD, was instrumental in calling for the news conference at this modest Catholic parish in the Northwest Bronx to announce this major citywide initiative. At one point during the press conference he turned to Father Tom and whispered, "Father, this is big, really big!"

At the gathering, the president of the Board of the Coalition, Desiree Pilgrim-Hunter, reviewed the reason why this event had come about—the laments of the tenants about their living conditions: "These tenants are living in buildings with no heat or hot water, peeling lead paint, ceilings collapsing because of water leaks, and molded walls that contribute to asthma and respiratory diseases."[8] The one-on-one dialogue of Ana Gilda with her neighbors and with Father Tom led to countless door-to-door, one-on-one conversations; parish councils; and small-group meetings in faith-in-action committees, in rectories with affected parishioners, and in apartment lobbies with newly formed tenant associations, along with prayer vigils, rallies, and protests. Their combined actions offer moving testimony to how grassroots parish councils and grassroots democratic organizations can join in fostering social action and bringing about meaningful change.

The public and legal pressure that was brought to bear on Milbank Real Estate resulted in the sale of their properties in 2011, when Steve Finklestein, a mortgage and deed holder landlord, bought the ten Milbank buildings. The terms of an agreement were reached between the tenants and Finklestein, who met in the rectory of Our Lady of Angels, now a recognized safe space. One dialogue culminated in another that brought to a hopeful end this episode.

A THEOLOGY OF DIALOGUE

The emergence of a multifaceted theology of dialogue during the twentieth century provided the backdrop for and lent credibility to local parishes' and communities' engagement in these practices of dialogue in the Bronx. The postconciliar advance of a dialogical vision of the Catholic Church was one complex facet of a much larger recovery of the dialogical dimensions at work in the broader Christian tradition. At the center of this renaissance was a compelling construal of the self-communicative and dialogical character of God's identity and mission. While modern deists considered God the transcendent and remote Creator of a moral world and atheists dismissed the notion of God as a mute fiction, preconciliar Catholics shaped by neo-Scholastic theology conceived of God as the sovereign One who creates the world, the Lawgiver who establishes the order of the world accessible through natural law and divine law, and the Judge who holds humanity accountable for adhering to this created order by nature and grace. Over the course of the twentieth century, however, new ways of thinking about God gave greater attention to the dialogical nature of the Triune God in creation, in the incarnation of the Word made flesh, and in the bestowal of the Spirit. Drawing on themes in phenomenology and existentialism, theologians began to speak of the human encounter with God through embodied corporeal and personalist engagement.

This fresh focus on the self-communicative and dialogical character of God was closely related to a mid-twentieth-century critique of the propositionalist approach to revelation and faith that had dominated neo-Scholasticism and the theological manuals during the late nineteenth and early twentieth centuries. A personalist philosophy and theology came to reshape the interpretation of the scriptures. Martin Buber's book *I-Thou,* which espoused a personalist and dialogical vision of the self, had a particularly profound impact on Catholics and Protestants in their approaches to revelation and to God's identity. The scriptures, these scholars pointed out, reveal a God who speaks and who listens; and faith was reconceived as a personal reception and response to the Word and the Spirit. This fresh approach to revelation and faith is in evidence in Vatican II's *Dogmatic Constitution on Divine Revelation (Dei verbum)*: "By revelation, then, the invisible God...from the fullness of his love, addresses men and women as friends, and lives among them, in order to invite and receive them into his own company" (*Dei verbum* 2).

Theological anthropology and ecclesiology were consequently recast in terms of personalism. The return to early Christian sources that animated the Council fathers retrieved a most apt focal point: humans are portrayed as created in the image of God. Likewise, the recovery of a range of images of the church as body of Christ, temple of the Holy Spirit, and the physical medium of sacramental communion all contributed to a persuasive personalist vision of the church. The return to the sources thus provided a convincing rhetoric for a relational and dialogical understanding of anthropology and ecclesiology. These developments culminated in the identity and mission of the human person and of the church being explored in light of the identity and mission of the Triune God, a communion of persons.

As scholars came to accentuate the dialogical character of the church it became particularly manifest in three of the most basic dimensions of the church's mission: in *liturgia* through communal ritual prayer; in *martyria* through witness, proclamation, and catechesis; and in *diakonia* through service to the poor, the sick, and the vulnerable. The church also entered into dialogue with those outside the church in the world: with people working in the sciences, the humanities, and the arts, with other Christians and people of other faiths, with agnostics and atheists, and with those working in civil society.

In the most important practical development for the activity of the church, during and after the council, dialogue was used in church synods and councils to engage in discernment and decision-making about the mission and strategic planning of parishes or dioceses. In every dimension of the church's practice, a renewed and reformed vision of the church emerged animated by one basic principle: collaboration, coresponsibility, and collegiality are accomplished by means of dialogue. Dialogue became the necessary instrument for breaking through cultures of paternalism and clericalism. Dialogue promotes the full and active participation of all the faithful in the life and mission of the church, which reflected their baptismal inheritance realized in new affirmation of the equality of all believers in the prophetic, priestly, and kingly offices of Jesus Christ through the anointing of the Spirit. In particular, prophetic discernment and decision-making responds to particular aspirations and laments of the community of faith and the wider society. The church is dialogical not only in fulfillment of its identity as a sacrament of the triune communion of persons in God, but also because it is called to be prophetic in discerning the signs of the times and receptive to the sense of the faithful in determining the mission of the local church.

The church is dialogical not only in fulfillment of its identity as a sacrament of the triune communion of persons in God, but also because it is called to be prophetic in discerning the signs of the times and receptive to the sense of the faithful in determining the mission of the local church.

LEARNING DIALOGICAL PRACTICES

Three sets of dialogical skills are central to dialogical practices: those pertaining to speaking, listening, and advancing a conversation that promotes collective discernment, decisions, and action.

Learning how to speak well requires avoiding two extremes. One extreme is when a person is unwilling to speak one's mind and convictions, unable to try to articulate what one is thinking or feeling. This unwillingness may be based on one's fear of rejection or ridicule, but it also might be based on a certain dismissive arrogance. Deficiencies in the formation of one's own viewpoint can also contribute to someone's silence. The other extreme is when one cannot stop speaking, when a person says whatever is on one's mind in a stream of consciousness that may not be judicious and well informed. The practice of speaking well requires the wisdom of knowing when to speak and when not to speak, knowing how to speak appropriately for a particular audience, knowing what is pertinent to the conversation and what is not, and knowing when to stop speaking.

Learning how to listen well requires cultivating hospitality—that is, finding ways to enable individuals or a group of people to feel welcome and at ease. This requires bracketing preconceived judgments and dismissive attitudes about people who are perceived as different based on their appearance, on their style of communication, or on some past episode or experience. Active listening requires attentive eyes and posture. Listening can be promoted by posing a question that generates a conversation. But once the other is speaking there is a need for silence and receptivity.

Michel Foucault, in a similar vein, commends the Stoics for their approach to speaking and listening, and the special attention they give to the practice and *ascesis* of silence. For Epictetus, "to speak properly we need *tekhne*, an art, whereas to listen we need experience, competence, diligent practice, attention, application, and so forth."[9] For Plutarch this means "we should keep as quiet as we can....It means, of course, that we should not speak when someone else is talking....We should not immediately convert what we have heard into speech. We should keep hold of it, in the strict sense, that is to say, preserve it and refrain from immediately converting it into words." By contrast, Plutarch speaks of the person who is "a chatterbox" and jokes that "the ear of a chatterbox...is not connected directly with his soul, but rather with his tongue....Everything the chatterbox receives through the ear immediately pours out, spills into what he says and, in spilling into what he says, what has been heard cannot have any effect on the soul itself."[10]

Learning to speak well and to listen well are the basic ingredients of dialogue. These skills are operative in the communication of information in education, manufacturing, and commerce, and in the communication of intimacy in friendship, family, and community. Beyond the aims of conveying information and intimacy, by generating knowledge, negotiating business transactions, or making promises with a loved one, dialogue also plays an important role in collective discernment and decision-making in civil society and in religious communities. In these contexts dialogue involves a conversation with a group of participants and requires that there be a space and time for open and free debate.

In the domains of synods and councils in churches and in various democratic associations, the skills of dialogue require as well that participants have the ability to track the dynamics of the conversation and to discover ways to move the conversation forward. One must identify areas of emerging consensus and important areas of disagreement. One must judge what debates are worthy of clarification and negotiations, what conflicts cannot be avoided or suppressed, and what are reasonable limits of *dissensus* in the group. One may be able to communicate in the idiom of intimacy or in the style of information, but the highest goal in a community is the ability to speak well and listen well in the interest of promoting wise discernment and decision-making that results in communal action. This is the language of a synodal community, or a democratic society focused on the common good.

HOW IS DIALOGUE TRANSFORMATIVE?

Practices of dialogue in the church and in civic society can be transformative. As we have seen in the case of the parish of Our Lady of Angels, the pastor, the parish council, and the faith in action committee learned to listen to the laments first voiced by Ana Gilda Domínguez about the problems with her apartment. Her laments were joined by those of others in the parish and in the neighborhood who were suffering from a similar plight. The people in this parish and neighborhood heeded, received, and responded to the growing laments surrounding housing issues in their neighborhood. They were mobilized to show their solidarity through collective action in prayer and protest. With the help of Gabe and other community organizers, they sharpened the issues involved and explored plans of action, and with other clergy and their church members, with tenant associations, and with the board of the Northwest Bronx Community and Clergy Coalition, a commitment was made to engage in social action against this injustice.

This collective action likewise resulted in the transformation of elected officials. The mayor, the city council president, borough representatives, political appointees in the Department of Housing Preservation and Development, and many others were called upon to heed these laments and to be held accountable. People in the parish and neighborhood, likewise, underwent a conversion about what kinds of problems can and should be addressed, what kinds of responses are possible, what solidarity in suffering and in collective action can achieve. As a result elected and appointed officials took notice, and governmental policies and procedures were changed. As Vito Mustaciuolo said, "This is big, really big."

Just as there are many other social laments that deserve widespread attention and collective action in such areas as housing, education, health care, and employment, there are other ecclesial laments that merit attention in parishes and dioceses. In commemoration of the nation's bicentennial in 1976, the U.S. bishops held a number of local meetings on a range of topics intended to provide the bishops with opportunities to listen to a wide variety of church members speak out about their concerns. This process culminated in the Call to Action Conference held in Detroit, Michigan, in 1976.[11] After hearing testimony from many people, those gathered took a vote in which members expressed the desire for further open discussion about the requirement of celibacy for priesthood, the male-only requirement for ordination, and the church's teachings on homosexuality and birth control. There were also calls for the church to deal more effectively and dialogically with racism, sexism, and militarism. Since 1976, similar groups around the world have voiced laments of church members on these issues.

Although there has not been widespread institutional change on most of these ecclesial matters, there have been instances of personal and communal transformation sparked by testimonies of and dialogue with victims of racism and sexism as well as the testimonies of experiences of prejudice and abuse suffered by gays and lesbians in the church. Dialogue in these situations has been the occasion not only for lamentations, but also for conversion, forgiveness, and reconciliation.

Practices of dialogue are also acutely needed in situations of conflict where resolution and perhaps mutual forgiveness are sought. There can be no hope of resolving conflict and promoting forgiveness without personal conversion and communal change, and these, in turn, cannot happen without forging awareness for dialogue. One thinks of horrible situations of civil strife in war-torn areas of South Africa, Northern Ireland, Guatemala, and the Middle East. Wherever there have been processes of collective reconciliation in such areas, there have invariably been opportunities for public lamentations and for dialogue. A clear instance of this collective reconciliation within the Catholic Church has been the postconciliar interfaith dialogue between Jews and Catholics.[12] These long-running efforts have resulted in Catholics changing how they pray, how they catechize, and how they preach the gospel. These changes could not have taken place without the painful, persistent exchanges between Catholics and Jews over a long period of time. Grievances still exist and further changes have been requested, but the commitment to ongoing interfaith dialogue offers a way forward. The same kind of interfaith dialogue and the promotion of mutual forgiveness and reconciliation are being pursued among Muslims and Catholics, and among other religious communities as well.

Accounts of dialogue with victims of exclusion and hatred reveal its powerful potential for acting as a means of personal and collective examination of conscience and of mutual accountability. Open dialogue in the church helps guarantee that it is *semper purificanda* and *semper reformanda*, and helps provide the basis for genuine ecclesial reform in service of the ongoing vitality of the church's tradition.

Surely, there are limitations and problems associated with dialogue and these must be acknowledged. But the identity and mission of the church cannot be realized without it.[13]

Notes

1. On Vatican II documents, see Ann Michele Nola, *A Privileged Moment: Dialogue in the Language of the Second Vatican Council 1962–1965* (Bern, Switzerland: Peter Lang, 2006); for the implementation of the documents, see Bradford E. Hinze, *Practices of Dialogue in the Roman Catholic Church: Aims and Obstacles, Lessons and Laments* (New York: Continuum, 2006); Bradford E. Hinze "The Reception of Vatican II in Participatory Structures of the Church: Facts and Friction," *Proceedings of the Canon Law Society of America Annual Convention* 70 (2009): 28–52.

2. Austin Flannery, ed., *Vatican Council II: The Basic Sixteen Documents* (Northport, NY: Costello Publishing Company; Dublin, Ireland: Dominican Publications, 1996).

3. Ibid.

4. On Catholic Action before and during Vatican II, see Giuseppe Alberigo and Joseph A. Komonchak, eds., *History of Vatican II*, vol. 1 (Maryknoll, NY: Orbis Books; Leuven, Belgium: Peeters, 1995), 78–80, 196–98. Before and during the council there was "sometimes quite [a] lively debate between what was called 'general' Catholic Action, Italian in origin, which took no account of special conditions of life in its parish-based mass-movements (men, women, young people, girls), and what was called 'specialized' Catholic Action, which was broken down into groups (workers, farmers, students, sailors…) and was national in structure" (78). On the role played by Cardinal Suenens and critical issues surrounding Catholic Action, see Giuseppe Alberigo

and Joseph A. Komonchak, eds., *History of Vatican II*, vol. 2 (Maryknoll, NY: Orbis Books; Leuven, Belgium: Peeters, 1995), 443–45. On Social Catholicism, see Paul Misner, *Social Catholicism in Europe: From the Onset of Industrialization to the First World War* (New York: Crossroad Publishing, 1991); and Adrien Dansette, *Religious History of Modern France: Under the Third Republic*, vol. 2 (New York: Herder and Herder, 1961).

5. "Interview with Saul Alinsky, Part Eight: Success Versus Co-optation," *Playboy Magazine*, 1972, posted at the *Progressive Report: Empower People, Not Elites*, accessed October 6, 2013, http://www.progress.org/2003/alinsky9.htm.

6. On the influence of Alinsky's methods on one influential Catholic organizer, see the story of Ernesto Cortes in Mary Beth Rogers, *Cold Anger: A Story of Faith and Power Politics* (Denton: University of North Texas Press, 1990); on the influence of Catholic Action on the development of the pastoral circle developed by Joe Holland and Peter Henriot in their book *Social Analysis: Linking Faith and Justice* (Maryknoll, NY: Orbis Books, 1983), see Joe Holland, "Introduction: Roots of the Pastoral Circle in Personal Experiences and Catholic Social Teaching," in *The Pastoral Circle Revisited: A Critical Quest for Truth and Transformation*, ed. Frans Jozef Servaas Wijsen, Peter Henriot, SJ, and Rodrigo Mejía (Maryknoll, NY: Orbis Books, 2005), 1–14.

7. Gabriel Pedras e-mail to supporters of the campaign against Milbank Real Estate, sent January 14, 2011.

8. Ibid.

9. Michel Foucault, *The Hermeneutics of the Subject: Lectures at the Collège de France 1981–1982* (New York: Picador, 2004), 240.

10. Ibid., 242.

11. On the Call to Action, see Hinze, *Practices of Dialogue*, 64–89.

12. See Bradford E. Hinze, "When Dialogue Leads to the Reform of Tradition," in *Tradition and Tradition Theories: An International Discussion*, ed. Torsten Larbig and Siegfried Wiedenhofer (Berlin, Germany: LIT Verlag, 2006), 336–55.

13. For a discussion of the limitations and problems associated with personalist, hermeneutical, and social models of

dialogue, see Bradford E. Hinze, "Dialogical Theology," *Kommunikative Theologie: Zugänge–Auseinandersetzungen–Ausdifferenzierungen//Communicative Theology: Approaches—Discussions—Differentiation*, ed. Matthias Scharer, Bradford E. Hinze, and Bernd Jochen Hilberath, Kommunikative Theologie–interdisziplinär //Communicative Theology—Interdisciplinary Studies (Vienna, Austria: LIT Verlag, 2010), 21–26.

CHAPTER 13

MISSIOLOGY AS PRACTICAL THEOLOGY

Understanding and Embodying Mission as Trinitarian Practice

STEPHEN BEVANS, SVD

MISSION AS TRINITARIAN PRACTICE

Mission is trinitarian practice: this is a core understanding that connects missiology and practical theology. To understand the nature of mission as a practice and to guide concrete practices of mission in the world, we have to begin with an understanding that God, in God's deepest self, is practice and that this "intra-trinitarian" practice is known only by the practices of the Trinity in the world's history. Trinitarian practices are known only when women and men in turn are caught up in trinitarian life, and so participate themselves in the practice of the Trinity. To seek to know what these practices are, and how they are to be practiced, takes us to the very heart of understanding the church's mission—indeed, into the very heart of theology. Knowing the trinitarian mystery catches Christians up into the trinitarian mission; reflective engagement in mission opens Christians up to the "depth of the riches and wisdom and knowledge of God" (Rom 11:33). In this sense, missiology is practical theology—aimed at understanding and embodying mission rightly as trinitarian practice.

Missiology is practical theology—aimed at understanding and embodying mission rightly as trinitarian practice.

God Is Practice

God is best described, many theologians are discovering today, not as a noun but as a verb. Of course, there is no way that God *can* be described—God is both incomprehensible and ineffable—but using the language of verb captures, if not God as such, the reality nevertheless that God, in revelation, offers to humanity God's very self and yet remains Mystery, so overwhelmingly close that God remains beyond grasping. God, as Aquinas said, is *actus purus*, pure activity, pure be-ing, "the 'Verb' in which all beings participate, live and move and have their being."[1] Or, to use other metaphors, God is, in Bonaventure's words, "self-diffusive love,"[2] a love, says Bonaventure's contemporary Mechtilde of Magdeburg, that is a "great outflow of divine love that never ceases."[3] God *as such* is a flow, a communion. The Father, in Mechtilde's words, is the "restless Godhead," a "flowing spring that no one can block." The Son is a "constantly recurring richness that no one can contain except the boundlessness which always flowed and shall ever flow from God, and which comes again in its fullness with his Son." The Spirit is "an unsuperable power of truth."[4] God is Be-ing, loving, flowing. God is practice—the practice of communion.

God Is the Practice of Communion

How do we know this? Not because, as Elizabeth Johnson says wryly, we are in possession of some kind of "high-powered telescope" that allows us to get God in its sights.[5] Rather, we know God from God's practices in history,[6] or, in other words, from God's practice of mission, the *missio Dei.*[7] Karl Rahner put it memorably: the "immanent Trinity" (God in God's self) is the "economic Trinity" (God revealing Godself in history), and vice versa.[8] Kathleen A. Cahalan, referring to Catherine LaCugna's seminal work on the Trinity, puts it in an even more succinct way: "who God is in essence is what God does."[9] What God does, as we know from the history of salvation, is to seek relationship, to draw humanity into communion with Godself and one another. The crucial move in trinitarian theology, says Edward Hahnenberg, is to recognize that God not only seeks communion, but is in essence communion, a relationship of persons.[10]

Trinitarian Practice in the World

What God is in Godself, God does in God's world. God's practice of communion in Godself overflows into God's first practice of mission, creation. From the very first nanosecond, the Spirit is sent into that creation, guiding and persuading, inspiring the evolution of the gasses, the formation of molecules, the development of the galaxies and their billions of planets, and calling forth life in all its abundance. The Spirit then commits itself to healing and reconciling what has been broken by selfishness and sin as self-conscious, free-willed humans emerge by living as a "secret presence"[11] among all cultures and religions.[12] God in all God's mystery was, as it were, "inside out" in the world.[13]

In the Judeo-Christian tradition, this immanent, always-present, life-giving, healing, and reconciling presence of God is imaged in the Old Testament by wind, breath, oil, water, a brooding bird—all concrete and yet illusive images. As Elizabeth Johnson writes, when we speak of the Spirit, "what we are actually signifying is God drawing near and passing by in vivifying, sustaining, renewing, and liberating power in the midst of historical struggle."[14]

"In the fullness of time" (Gal 4:4) the Word of God became flesh and gave the Spirit, as it were, a human face. If the Spirit is the way (or at least one way) that signified God's creating, healing, inspiring, reconciling, life-giving, challenging practices, Jesus of Nazareth is now God's *embodied* practice.[15] Now that Spirit that has pervaded the universe from the first instant of its creation is, as Johnson so beautifully puts it, "manifest in time in a concrete gestalt, the loving, gifting, and befriending first-century Jewish carpenter turned prophet."[16]

Jesus' ministry reveals in his own practice the practice of God. Jesus proclaims God's message of acceptance, forgiveness, reconciliation, inclusion, and commitment to justice ("good news to the poor"—Luke 4:18) in stunning parables (e.g., Luke 15; 18; Matt 20; 22)[17] and pithy and challenging teachings (e.g., Matt 5; Mark 8:34–38; 9:36; Luke 11:27; John 3:1–17). Jesus healed ("recovery of sight to the blind"—Luke 4:18) and drove out demons ("release to captives"—Luke 4:18; e.g., Matt 9:2–8; 9:27–31; Mark 6:30–44; Luke 8:26–39; John 4:46–54). These were all "parables in action," practices that concretized and demonstrated the message of his practice of preaching, and showing that the reign of God that Jesus preached was not only a spiritual reality, but a fully material and human reality as well. As Edward Schillebeeckx and others have pointed out, Jesus himself was a parable,[18] as by his own scandalous practices of personal freedom in interpreting the Law (e.g., Mark 2:23–27), fun-loving lifestyle (e.g., drinking wine—Matt 11:7–19), and inclusive behavior (e.g., Matt 9:9–13), he pointed to a God who is life, who cares for all, and who offers all inclusion and freedom.[19]

Participation in Trinitarian Practice

As Latino theologian Virgilio Elizondo has written, it was especially Jesus' practice of not being scandalized by anyone that was most scandalous to the religious leaders of his day, and was probably the biggest reason why they began quite early in his ministry to plot his death.[20] But Jesus' death on the cross was not the end. A few days after his crucifixion his disciples began to experience him as alive, as raised from the dead, and so vindicated in his radical, loving, and liberating practice of preaching, demonstrating, and witnessing to the reign of God. God's mission was not thwarted, but, as the disciples soon experienced, would continue in and through them. Gradually, painfully, amazingly, they discovered, the same Spirit that had anointed Jesus at his baptism had anointed them to share and continue his practice.[21] Not only is Christology "carried on by engaging in the practices of the Jesus-movement."[22] Carrying out these practices constitutes the church, which is thus "missionary by its very nature" (*Ad gentes* 2). Being Christian means participating in a missionary church, and such participation means engaging in trinitarian practice.

Mission in Today's World

Pope John Paul II in his encyclical *Redemptoris missio* distinguished three aspects of the church's evangelizing mission. There is first what he called mission *ad gentes*, or mission to or among peoples who have not yet accepted the gospel, or in situations where the church has not yet been fully established. This aspect he called mission in the proper sense of the word. Second, he spoke about the pastoral care of the faithful in places more fully evangelized. Third, he spoke of an "interim situation" in which Christians, once evangelized, have lost their faith, or live within cultures and worldviews that are devoid of religious sensibility. John Paul II called this the "New Evangelization" (33–34). Although he resisted somewhat the idea that a missionary situation exists now throughout the entire world (32), today, roughly a quarter-century later, the question can be asked again. In the face of a Christianity that now has its center of gravity in the Global South, in a world in which the population has shifted radically due to mass migrations of peoples, in a situation in which Christianity is, frankly, on the wane in the West, one might indeed declare a missionary situation.[23] While the distinctions might still, in some sense, obtain, the church in every situation needs to engage in a truly missionary practice, rooted in the practice of the Trinity. Mission today, however, is not an uncontested practice.

MISSION CONTESTED AND REFOCUSED

Mission Contested

The age of colonialism that peaked in the nineteenth century began to unravel after the First World War in 1918, and after the Second World War in 1945 its demise was accelerated. The rise of new nationalism, the renaissance of local religions in newly independent countries, and a newer consciousness of human rights gradually prompted a radical reassessment of missionary work. In the Catholic Church, but having influence well beyond it, the Second Vatican Council's teaching of the possibility of salvation outside the boundaries of Christian faith and the church, the recognition of the beauty and sacredness of all human cultures, and a fresh perspective on human dignity and freedom of conscience all served to plunge missionary work into a deep crisis. By the late 1960s, the very idea of mission was questioned. In both Protestant and Catholic camps, there was a call for a missionary moratorium.[24] Although articulated in the first decade of the twenty-first century, the forceful remarks of Native American theologian George "Tink" Tinker express clearly how mission in the past decades has been in contention: "Given the disastrous history of euro-western mission practices—to the cultures and the peoplehood of those missionized—it would seem that there are no missiological projects that we might conceive that would have legitimacy of any kind."[25]

Mission Reborn

Over against and in dialogue with the strenuous objections to Christian mission in the past half-century, there has been a gradual "rebirth" of the missionary movement in the Christian churches.[26] This rebirth is certainly grounded in Vatican II's *Decree on the Missionary Activity of the Church, Ad gentes* (1965), which attempted to point to the missionary nature of every local church and not to confine missionary practice to work in exotic (i.e., non-Western) places carried out by women and men with specialized vocations and training.[27] The Council clearly rooted missionary practice in trinitarian practice as well, recovering a perspective and motivation that had been lost for several centuries. In many ways, too, the Council reset the *way* missionary work was to be carried out: not with the morbid urgency of saving souls, but with the joyful motive of sharing the unsearchable riches of Christ, done in ways that model Jesus' practice of openness, listening, gentleness, and vulnerability. A rebirth of missionary practice came about as well as a new, more holistic understanding of mission, notably at the Medellín Conference of the Latin American Bishops in 1968, and the Extraordinary Synod of Bishops in 1971, where the ideas of liberation, justice, and solidarity with the poor were, the bishops realized, a "constitutive part of the preaching of the gospel."[28] Ten years after the promulgation of the Council's missionary decree, Paul VI published his apostolic exhortation *Evangelii nuntiandi* (1975) in which he called for an expansion of an understanding of mission to include justice issues and identified the "evangelization of cultures" as a legitimate missionary practice.[29] Gradually, too, the importance of interreligious dialogue came to be understood as integral to missionary practice, as evidenced in a Vatican document on dialogue and mission published in 1984 that included a list of five elements making up the practice of mission.[30] Pope John Paul II, in his 1990 encyclical *Redemptoris missio,* also expressed a multilayered, multivalent understanding of the church's missionary practice.

PROPHETIC DIALOGUE: THE *KIND* OF TRINITARIAN PRACTICE

Before focusing on the *kinds* of trinitarian practice, it is necessary to set out the "conditions for the possibility" of such practice: the basic attitude or spirituality—the *kind* of trinitarian practice—that underlies mission.[31]

Mission as Dialogue

First and foremost, the practice of mission today has to be rooted in a commitment to dialogue—not just as a practice, about which I reflect in the following section, but as a fundamental stance out of which any missionary practice needs to be done. Such a stance is rooted in the radical dialogical nature of God as such. Since God in history reveals Godself as working for communion, and since God in revelation reveals God's true and full self, God must be what God does: communion, relationship, dialogue. In addition, the *way* God reveals Godself is dialogical in nature.[32] If the Triune God carries out the divine mission *in* dialogue and *for* dialogue, so must those women and men baptized in the Trinity's name.

In the first place, then, those who engage in mission must be women and men who have hearts "so open," as novelist Alice Walker describes it, "that the wind blows through [them]."[33] Claude Marie Barbour explains such openness and vulnerability as "mission in reverse." Rather than arriving somewhere and right away serving or preaching or teaching, Barbour has insisted over forty years, the minister/missionary needs first to be evangelized by those whom she or he evangelizes. The people, she insists, must be the teachers before the missionary dares to teach. The first step of mission, then, is listening, docility (the ability to be taught), gentleness, the ability to bond in real relationships.[34] "Give us FRIENDS," was the heartfelt cry of the Indian churchman A. S. Azariah in his famous speech about missionaries at the 1910 Edinburgh World Mission Conference.[35]

Mission as Prophecy

Within—and only within—the context of dialogue, mission engages in prophecy, in all of its complex meaning. Prophecy, too, is a trinitarian practice, since "within" the Trinity God "speaks forth" the Word, and the Spirit is the very "breath" that proceeds from the depths of Holy Mystery. The Spirit in the world's history is the Spirit of truth and prophecy, and Jesus in his own ministry was recognized as a prophet. Prophecy is both "speaking forth" and "speaking out," and it is done in both word and deed.

"Speaking forth" entails speaking the future—not in the sense of predicting it, but assuring women and men of God's promises. It speaks forth the message of the gospel—clearly, relevantly, gently. "Speaking forth" is also in the witness of the community that shows by its life the truth of the message, the vitality and joy of what living the gospel means, giving a glimpse of the future fullness of God's reign.

"Speaking against" also means to speak forth the future—to warn people that there are dire consequences to living lives of selfishness, oppression of others, and self-indulgence. Christian prophets also speak out against any and all injustice—against any racism, sexism, marginalization, institutional violence. Mission as prophecy also entails personal and communal witness that is countercultural. Christians do not live for themselves, for success, for power; Christian communities are, in the words of Gerhard Lohfink, "contrast societies."[36] In some circumstances, for example, in the violence of the southern Philippines between Christians and Muslims, or in India between Christians and militant Hindus, even the willingness to dialogue is a prophetic act.

SIX ELEMENTS OF MISSION: THE *KINDS* OF TRINITARIAN PRACTICE

There are perhaps many ways by which we could speak of the trinitarian practices in which Christians in mission are engaged. Kathleen A. Cahalan anchors trinitarian practice in Jesus' mission and ministry and the Spirit's lavishing of charisms. She speaks of the ministry of teaching, preaching, care-giving, prayer and worship, of social mercy and justice, and of leadership and administration.[37] Terrence W. Tilley's "Christology as Reconciling Practice" takes the practice of reconciliation as the summation of Jesus' concrete practices of healing, teaching, forgiving, and inclusion: "The body of Christ, the Jesus movement, carries on the work by incarnating atonement."[38] In his more rhetorical approach to trinitarian theology David S. Cunningham writes evocatively of peacemaking, pluralizing, and persuading as the practices by which Christians join the Triune God in the divine mission and so come to a deeper trinitarian knowledge.[39] My own approach in the final section of this chapter is to reflect briefly on the six "elements" or "practices" that Roger Schroeder and I have set forth in *Constants in Context*: (1) witness and proclamation; (2) liturgy, prayer, and contemplation; (3) justice, peace, and the integrity of creation; (4) interreligious and secular dialogue; (5) inculturation; and (6) reconciliation.[40] It is through these practices that Christian disciples engage in trinitarian practice, and it is engaging in them that Christians come to a deeper knowledge of the trinitarian nature of God as such.[41] I first show the trinitarian roots of each, and then how each functions as a trinitarian practice in which Christians in mission participate and on which Christians reflect as they engage in practical theology.

Witness and Proclamation

From the very first instant of creation, God's Spirit witnessed as a "secret presence" (*Ad gentes* 9) in creation, a presence that prompted women and men of all ages to call on God and live lives in accordance with their consciences. The Spirit witnesses still. In his ministry as one sent from God, Jesus witnessed by his attitudes of mercy and patience toward sinners and the excluded to a new family of humankind and all creation that God had promised when God would fully reign. Participating in this trinitarian practice, Christians witness individually (consider someone like Mother Teresa), communally (e.g., the San Egidio Community, based in Rome but active worldwide), institutionally (the network of Catholic schools and hospitals throughout the United States), or with members of other Christian communities (e.g., the Taizé community in France).

The Spirit's proclamation is a silent one, "bearing witness with our Spirit" that we are indeed children of God (see Rom 16). But this silent witness finds voice in the incarnation of the Word, who calls women and men to reimagine who God is and what this world could be (see Mark 1:15), and on whom the Spirit descends to proclaim good news, bring healing, and work for liberation (see Luke 4:16–21). "Whenever God opens a door" (*Ad gentes* 13), Christians engaged in missionary trinitarian practice continue the joyful, liberating, inclusive, challenging message of Jesus. They do this in the classroom as teachers, as parents instructing children, as colleagues expressing their deepest religious convictions. They do it respectfully, giving the reason for their hope when asked (see 1 Pet 3:15–16). They do it using all the means of contemporary technology and communication available to them. They prophesy, but always in dialogue.[42]

Liturgy, Prayer, and Contemplation

The perfect communion among the persons of the Trinity, giving and receiving, is the pattern of all prayer, for prayer in its essence is being open to the will and action of God in one's life. The Spirit witnesses in women's and men's hearts, causing them to cry out "Abba," that great cry of confidence and love that Jesus himself used in his own prayer, prompted too by the Spirit (Luke 10:21–22). The Letter to the Hebrews images Jesus' life, death, and resurrection as priestly sacrifice, not offering this or that particular thing, but his very self (9:11–14; 10:5–10). And so "the liturgy is considered as an exercise of the priestly office of Jesus Christ," where he is present in word, in sacrament, and in the people gathered together by the Spirit in his name.[43]

Christians, baptized into trinitarian life, worship as priests, prophets, and kings (servants). The liturgy, Gregory Augustine Pierce points out, is an act of mission: "the Mass is never ended," he says.[44] It nourishes us for mission, inspires us for mission, and sends us out to worship God by our trinitarian practices in our lives. It is for such real worship, said my colleague Richard

Fragomeni, that Christians do liturgy in church.[45] Prayer for the world, and for the church's mission, is a powerful trinitarian practice, as evidenced by the fact that Thérèse of Lisieux, a cloistered Carmelite nun, was declared patroness of the church's missionary work in 1927 by Pope Pius XI. Prayer, like the practice of contemplation, opens us up to God's will and to see what is really going on among the women and men with whom we minister in mission.[46]

Justice, Peace, and the Integrity of Creation

There is no question that the God of the Bible is a God of justice and peace. Amos, for example, speaks a word of God's judgment against the rich women of Samaria "who oppress the poor, who crush the needy" (Amos 4:1). Micah feels himself filled with the power and spirit of God, "to declare to Jacob his transgression and to Israel his sin" (Mic 3:8). In Micah, too, we read the powerful words that what God requires of human beings is "to do justice, and to love kindness, and to walk humbly with your God" (Mic 6:8). Jesus' inclusive ministry revolves around the marginalized and sinful people of his time. The implications of his reconciling practice can only be interpreted as highly political. As José de Mesa and Lode Wostyn put it, "Jesus was engaged in a revolution—a revolution in religion, which was at the same time a revolution in politics and in everything else."[47] Brazilian theologian Leonardo Boff speaks of the Triune God as both model and agent of liberation, equality and justice in the world, and takes for his own the dictum of Orthodox theologians: "The Trinity is our social program."[48]

Denis Edwards writes of the Creator Spirit who is at work from creation's first instant. "The story of the Spirit," he writes, "begins not with Pentecost but with the origins of the Big Bang."[49] New Zealand theologian Neil Darragh suggests that, when thinking of the incarnation, we broaden our understanding to realize that, in becoming flesh, the Word became part of the earth, the cosmos.[50] In Christ, the Word takes on a body that, like everything else in the universe, is made of stardust.[51]

Christians baptized into the Trinity engage in the practices of working for justice, peacemaking, and ecological responsibility. Such practices are right at the heart of the church's mission and make concrete and visible the work of the Triune God. Whether as dramatic as the "Nuns on the Bus," or as simple as writing letters to members of Congress; as dramatic as the work of Father Roberto ("Bert") Layson working to end Muslim-Christian violence in the southern Philippines,[52] or as simple as contributing financially to groups like Pax Christi or similar peace and justice groups; as dramatic as planting a million trees on the devastated hillsides of Zimbabwe,[53] or as simple as recycling paper and glass, Christians embody trinitarian practices of justice, peacemaking, and the care of creation.[54]

Interreligious and Secular Dialogue

The Triune God is a God of dialogue, evidenced by the dialogical way that God has always worked in the history of salvation. God, writes the Scots theologian John Oman, never forces the divine mystery on us, but rather surrounds creation with gracious, persuading presence.[55] Denis Edwards reflects on how God's Spirit was present from the beginning, but always in a way that allowed evolution to take its course.[56] Jesus in the Gospels is remembered as a man of dialogue. "What do you want me to do for you?" he asks the blind man (Mark 10:51). In John 4 we read about Jesus' patient dialogue with the Samaritan woman, and we read also about how his dialogue with the Canaanite/Syrophoenician woman cut through Jesus' own religious prejudices (Mark 7:25–30; Matt 15:21–28).

As S. Mark Heim argues, trinitarian faith implies a willingness to dialogue with other religions since believing in the Trinity leads ineluctably to trinitarian practice. In dialogue with religions such as Hinduism, Buddhism, and Islam Christians not only have opportunities to testify to their own faith and learn about and be inspired by other religions; they can also be even more deeply enriched, even changed, through the other, in their own trinitarian faith.[57] Christians engage in dialogue when they simply live the "dialogue of life" or cooperate with other people of faith—or no faith—in actions for justice. They also practice dialogue when they engage in theological exchange interreligious conversations or a conversation in the "Courtyard of the Gentiles" as the 2012 Synod of Bishops suggests—or, like John Paul II and Benedict XVI on various occasions at Assisi, by praying in the same place together or sharing experiences of God. In these ways Christians participate in an essential trinitarian practice and work to make God's reign more visible in this world.[58]

Inculturation

Christians engage in practices of inculturation—the process of making the message and practice of the gospel relevant in particular contexts—because the practice of the Trinity is inculturated. The Holy Spirit is God's "secret presence" in the world, "and so, whatever good is found to be sown in the hearts and minds of women and men, or in the rites and cultures peculiar to various peoples" (*Ad gentes* 9) is indicative of that presence. Jesus "worked with human hands, He thought with a human mind, acted by human choice, and loved with a human heart."[59] As Austrian theologian Clemens Sedmak points out, Jesus was "somewhere." He was a product of his local Jewish culture and really communicated with people in his parables and other teachings. But at the same time, Sedmak says, he was critical of that culture, calling it to conversion.[60]

Trinitarian faith is commitment to inculturation. Christians in mission need to be as driven to be connected with the people among whom they live and minister as is the Triune God they sacrament as church. Inculturation is not easy. It demands deep listening, an ability to "let go" before "speaking out," a recognition that Christians in mission are always "entering into someone else's garden,"[61] an ability to challenge particular situations "with the light of the gospel, to set them free, and bring them under the dominion of God their Savior" (*Ad gentes* 11). Mission is, indeed, inculturated practice.[62]

Reconciliation

In today's violent world of wars in the Congo, interreligious violence in the Philippines, drive-by murders in U.S. cities, mass shootings, and shocking revelations about sexual abuse, Robert Schreiter writes that the Christian conviction of the possibility of reconciliation can be a particularly powerful expression of the gospel's "good news." In several of his many writings on the topic, Schreiter insists on two factors in the reconciliation process. First, reconciliation is not first a human act, but happens rather at God's initiative. God takes the first step in reconciling victim and perpetrator, opening the victim's heart to the possibility of forgiveness. Second, reconciliation does not take the victim back to a *status quo ante*, back to the past, but takes him or her *through* victimhood into a new way of being.[63] Schreiter says that this is the work of "God," but it would seem more appropriate to speak of the particular agent of reconciliation as the Holy Spirit because healing and surprising newness that takes place in reconciliation are always the signs of the Spirit's work. In the Second Letter to the Corinthians, the author looks back to Jesus' work and understands it as a work of reconciliation: "God was in Christ reconciling the world to God's self" (2 Cor 5:19).

> Reflection in turn will lead to more committed practice, as practitioners engage in a never-ending spiral of careful reflection that opens to transformed practice, a process at the heart of practical theology.

That work of reconciliation has been "entrusted to us" (2 Cor 5:19), making us Christ's ambassadors in the world (2 Cor 5:20). Christians can work for individual reconciliation (between victim and perpetrator), for cultural reconciliation (among Native

Americans, Australian Aboriginals), political reconciliation (after Apartheid in South Africa and after the genocide in Rwanda and Burundi), and even reconciliation within the church (women and victims of clergy abuse). But as they engage in these practices of reconciliation, Christians always need to be aware that they are only agents. The real work is done by the Triune God. More than a strategy, Schreiter writes, reconciliation is a spirituality.[64]

CONCLUSION: TRINITARIAN PRACTICE AND PRACTICAL THEOLOGY

Mission is trinitarian practice. As Christians reflect in faith on the *kind* and *kinds* of practice that mission is, they come to know more deeply the God who is always "drawing near and passing by"[65] in the world, calling women and men to greater communion, challenging them to more dedicated service, and overwhelming them with the mystery of acceptance and love. Reflection in turn will lead to more committed practice, as practitioners engage in a never-ending spiral of careful reflection that opens to transformed practice, a process at the heart of practical theology.

Notes

1. Elizabeth A. Johnson, *She Who Is: The Mystery of God in Feminist Discourse* (New York: Crossroad Publishing, 1992), 239.

2. Bonaventure, *De Trinitate* 3.16. See Ilia Delio, "Bonaventure's Metaphysics of the Good," *Theological Studies* 60, no. 2 (1999): 232.

3. Mechtilde of Magdeburg, *The Flowing Light of the Godhead*, trans. Frank Tobin, Classics of Western Spirituality 91 (Mahwah, NJ: Paulist Press, 1998), book 7, chap. 55: 323.

4. Mechtilde of Magdeburg, *The Flowing Light of the Godhead*, book 5, chap. 26: 207–8.

5. Johnson, *She Who Is*, 192.

6. Kathleen A. Cahalan, *Introducing the Practice of Ministry* (Collegeville, MN: Liturgical Press, 2010), 163.

7. The term *missio Dei* has a very rich and complex history and theology. For a brief summary and further references, see Stephen B. Bevans and Roger P. Schroeder, *Constants in Context: A Theology of Mission for Today* (Maryknoll, NY: Orbis Books, 2004), 289–91.

8. Karl Rahner, *The Trinity* (New York: Herder and Herder, 1970), 22.

9. Cahalan, *Introducing the Practice of Ministry*, 149, referring to Catherine Mowry LaCugna, *God for Us: The Trinity and Christian Life* (New York: HarperCollins, 1991).

10. Edward Hahnenberg, *Ministries: A Relational Approach* (New York: Crossroad Publishing, 2003), 85.

11. Second Vatican Council, *Decree on the Missionary Activity of the Church, Ad gentes* (1965), no. 9, accessed January 31, 2013, http://www.vatican.va/archive/hist_councils/ii_vatican_council/documents/vat-ii_decree_19651207_ad-gentes_en.html.

12. See Denis Edwards, *Breath of Life: A Theology of Creator Spirit* (Maryknoll, NY: Orbis Books, 2004), 43–49. On the Spirit active in cultures and religions, see John Paul II, encyclical letter *Redemptoris missio*, accessed February 4, 2013, http://www.vatican.va/holy_father/john_paul_ii/encyclicals/documents/hf_jp-ii_enc_07121990_redemptoris-missio_en.html.

13. See Stephen B. Bevans, "God Inside Out: Toward a Missionary Theology of the Holy Spirit," *International Bulletin of Missionary Research* 22, no. 3 (July 1998): 102–5.

14. Johnson, *She Who Is*, 127. For more extensive development of the Spirit as depicted in the Old Testament, see Christopher J. H. Wright, *Knowing the Holy Spirit Through the Old Testament* (Downers Grove, IL: InterVarsity Press, 2006).

15. Cahalan, *Introducing the Practice of Ministry*, 163.

16. Johnson, *She Who Is*, 150.

17. In interpreting this parable of the "unjust judge," I rely on the brilliant exegesis of the passage by my colleague Barbara E. Reid. See her *Parables for Preachers, Year C* (Collegeville, MN: Liturgical Press, 2000), 227–36.

18. Edward Schillebeeckx, *Jesus: An Experiment in Christology* (New York: Vintage Books, 1981), 156, 158.

19. For further reflection on Jesus' mission and ministry from the perspective of practice, see Terrence W. Tilley, "Part III: God's Reign in Practice," in *The Disciples' Jesus: Christology as Reconciling Practice* (Maryknoll, NY: Orbis Books, 2008), 127–89.

20. Virgilio Elizondo, "The Miracle of Conversion: Reflection on the Readings of the Third Sunday in Ordinary Time," in *Give Us This Day*, January 20, 2013 (Collegeville, MN: Liturgical Press, 2012), 205.

21. On this gradual development, see Bevans and Schroeder, *Constants in Context*, 10–31.

22. Tilley, *The Disciples' Jesus*, 2.

23. See Stephen B. Bevans, "Revisiting Mission at Vatican II: Theology and Practice in Today's Missionary Church," *Theological Studies* 74, no. 3 (September 2013): 261–83.

24. See Bevans and Schroeder, *Constants in Context*, 239–80. On the moratorium, see 251.

25. Tink Tinker, "The Romance and Tragedy of Christian Mission Among American Indians," in *Remembering Jamestown: Hard Questions About Christian Mission*, ed. Amos Yong and Barbara Brown Zikmund (Eugene, OR: Pickwick Publications, 2010), 27.

26. *Rebirth* is the term used by Robert J. Schreiter in "Changes in Roman Catholic Attitudes toward Proselytism and Mission," in *New Directions in Mission and Evangelization 2: Theological Foundations*, ed. James A. Scherer and Stephen B. Bevans (Maryknoll, NY: Orbis Books, 1994), 113–25. Schreiter speaks about periods of Certainty, Ferment, Crisis, and Rebirth in terms of attitudes toward mission in the twentieth century.

27. For this and what follows in this paragraph, see Stephen B. Bevans and Jeffrey Gros, *Evangelization and Religious Freedom:* Ad Gentes *and* Dignitatis Humanae (Maryknoll, NY: Orbis Books, 2009), 56–65.

28. 1971 Synod of Bishops, "Justice in the World," in *Catholic Social Thought: The Documentary Heritage*, ed. David J. O'Brien and Thomas A. Shannon (Maryknoll, NY: Orbis Books, 1992), 289.

29. Paul VI, apostolic exhortation *Evangelii nuntiandi* (1975), no. 20, accessed February 1, 2013, http://www.vatican.va/holy_father/paul_vi/apost_exhortations/documents/hf_p-vi_exh_19751208_evangelii-nuntiandi_en.html.

30. Secretariat for Non-Christians, "The Attitude of the Church toward the Followers of Other Religions: Reflections and Orientations on Dialogue and Mission," *Bulletin, Secretariatus Pro Non Christianis* 56, no. 13 (1984).

31. See Bevans and Schroeder, *Constants in Context*, 348–95; Stephen B. Bevans and Roger P. Schroeder, *Prophetic Dialogue: Reflections on Christian Mission Today* (Maryknoll, NY: Orbis Books, 2011), 19–55; Roger Schroeder, presidential address, "Proclamation and Interreligious Dialogue as Prophetic Dialogue," *Missiology: An International Review* 41, no. 1 (January 2013): 50–61. See *In Dialogue with the Word Nr 1* (Rome: SVD Publications, 2000), esp. 30–32.

32. Paul VI, encyclical letter *Ecclesiam suam* (1964), no. 70, accessed February 2, 2013, http://www.vatican.va/holy_father/paul_vi/encyclicals/documents/hf_p-vi_enc_06081964_ecclesiam_en.html.

33. Alice Walker, "A Wind through the Heart: A Conversation with Alice Walker and Sharon Salzberg on Loving Kindness in a Painful World," *Shambhala Sun* (January 1997): 1–5.

34. See Claude Marie Barbour, "Seeking Justice and Shalom in the City," *International Review of Mission* 73 (1984): 303–9; see also the festschrift in honor of Dr. Barbour: Stephen Bevans, Eleanor Doidge, and Robert J. Schreiter, ed., *The Healing Circle: Essays in Cross Cultural Mission* (Chicago, IL: CCGM Publications, 2000).

35. Brian Stanley, *The World Missionary Conference, Edinburgh 1910* (Grand Rapids, MI: William B. Eerdmans Publishing Company, 2009), 121–30. For a more expansive reflection on mission as dialogue, see Bevans and Schroeder, *Prophetic Dialogue*, 19–39.

36. See Gerhard Lohfink, *Jesus and Community* (Philadelphia, PA: Fortress Press, 1984). For a more extensive reflection on mission as prophecy, see Bevans and Schroeder, *Prophetic Dialogue*, 40–55.

37. Cahalan, *Introducing the Practice of Ministry*, 1–23, 69–98.

38. Tilley, *The Disciples' Jesus*, 236. See also 127–89.

39. David S. Cunningham, *These Three Are One: The Practice of Trinitarian Theology* (Malden, MA: Blackwell, 1998), 231–335.

40. See Bevans and Schroeder, *Constants in Context*, 350–51. The elements are reflected on in some detail in 532–95. For a shorter version, see Bevans and Schroeder, *Prophetic Dialogue*, 64–71; or Roger P. Schroeder, *What is the Mission of the Church? A Guide for Catholics* (Maryknoll, NY: Orbis Books, 2008), 112–26.

41. See Tilley, *The Disciples' Jesus*, 235–60; and Cunningham, *These Three Are One*, 1–16.

42. For fuller reflection on the practices of witness and proclamation, see Bevans and Schroeder, *Constants in Context*, 352–61.

43. Second Vatican Council, *Constitution on the Sacred Liturgy, Sacrosanctum concilium* (1963), no. 7, accessed February 2, 2013, http://www.vatican.va/archive/hist_councils/ii_vatican_council/documents/vat-ii_const_19631204_sacrosanctum-concilium_en.html.

44. Gregory Augustine Pierce, *The Mass Is Never Ended* (Notre Dame, IN: Ave Maria Press, 2007).

45. Richard Fragomeni, presentation on mission and liturgy, Mission Congress, Chicago, IL, October 2000.

46. For a more expansive development of these practices, see Bevans and Schroeder, *Constants in Context*, 361–68.

47. José de Mesa and Lode Wostyn, *Doing Christology: The Reappropriation of a Tradition* (Quezon City, Philippines: Claretian Publications, 1989), 109.

48. See Leonardo Boff, *Trinity and Society* (Maryknoll, NY: Orbis Books, 1988); see also Leonardo Boff, "Trinity," in *Mysterium Liberationis: Fundamental Concepts of Liberation Theology*, ed. Ignacio Ellacuría and Jon Sobrino (Maryknoll, NY: Orbis Books, 1993), 392; and Miroslav Volf, "'The Trinity is Our Social Program': The Doctrine of the Trinity and the Shape of Social Engagement," *Modern Theology* 14, no. 3 (July 1998): 403–23.

49. Edwards, *Breath of Life*, 171. Original in bold italics.

50. Neil Darragh, *At Home in the Earth: Seeking an Earth-Centered Spirituality* (Auckland, New Zealand: Accent Publications, 2000), 127–28.

51. See Edwards, *Breath of Life*, 13.

52. John Paul Lederach, "The Long Journey Back to Humanity: Catholic Peacebuilding with Armed Actors," in *Peacebuilding: Catholic Theology, Ethics, and Praxis*, ed. Robert J. Schreiter, R. Scott Appleby, and Gerard F. Powers (Maryknoll, NY: Orbis Books, 2010), 38–41.

53. See Marthinus L. Daneel, *African Earthkeepers: Wholistic Interfaith Mission* (Maryknoll, NY: Orbis Books, 2001).

54. For more expansive treatment of these elements, see Bevans and Schroeder, *Constants in Context*, 369–78.

55. John Wood Oman, *Vision and Authority, or, The Throne of St. Peter*, 2nd ed. (London, UK: Hodder and Stoughton, 1928), 225; see also Oman's *Grace and Personality* (Cambridge, UK: Cambridge University Press, 1917), 188.

56. Edwards, *Breath of Life*, 172.

57. S. Mark Heim, *The Depth of the Riches: A Trinitarian Theology of Religious Ends* (Grand Rapids, MI: William B. Eerdmans Publishing Company, 2001), 123–65.

58. For a more extensive treatment, see Bevans and Schroeder, *Constants in Context*, 378–85.

59. Second Vatican Council, *Pastoral Constitution on the Church in the Modern World, Gaudium et spes* (1965), no. 22, accessed on May 16, 2013, http://www.vatican.va/archive/hist_councils/ii_vatican_council/documents/vat-ii_cons_19651207_gaudium-et-spes_en.html.

60. See Clemens Sedmak, *Doing Local Theology: A Guide for Artisans of a New Humanity* (Maryknoll, NY: Orbis Books, 2002), 23–26.

61. See Bevans and Schroeder, *Prophetic Dialogue*, 72–87, 88–100.

62. For more expansive treatment of inculturation, see Bevans and Schroeder, *Constants in Context*, 385–89.

63. Robert J. Schreiter, "Globalization and Reconciliation: Challenges to Mission," in *Mission in the Third Millennium*, ed. Robert J. Schreiter (Maryknoll, NY: Orbis Books, 2001), 121–43.

64. Robert J. Schreiter, *The Ministry of Reconciliation: Spirituality and Strategies* (Maryknoll, NY: Orbis Books, 1998). For more extensive treatment, see Bevans and Schroeder, *Constants in Context*, 389–94.

65. Johnson, *She Who Is*, 124.

PART III

TEACHING AND RESEARCH

Chapter 14

PRACTICES OF TEACHING
A Pedagogy for Practical Theology

THOMAS GROOME

In the fall semester of 1981, I was a *very* young professor in the Theology Department at Boston College, and the great Johann Baptist Metz was a visiting scholar. He was teaching one course, using as primary text the recent English edition of his ground-breaking book, *Faith in History and Society: Toward a Practical Fundamental Theology*.[1] Appreciating Metz's explicit turn toward practical theology, and with much anticipation, I took his course; I was not disappointed. It was a rich experience to observe one of the most creative and historically committed theologians of our time at the cutting edge of his work.

The whole course could be well summarized by chapter 9 of *Faith in History and Society*. There, Metz calls for a paradigmatic shift "from a transcendental and idealistic" theology of Christian faith to a "narrative and practical" one. However, while he proposed such a radical shift in compelling ways, the irony was that his pedagogy throughout reflected far more a "transcendental and idealistic" approach than a "narrative practical" one. In other words, he lectured for an hour and forty minutes about great ideas and ideals, and for the last five asked if we had "any questions." I deliberately say above that I *observed* his course because I was never actively engaged, nor were my classmates, in the teaching–learning dynamic.

I tell this story with hesitation because I don't want it to be heard as a personal criticism of a great theologian. Metz was trained in the "transcendental and idealistic" mode of doing theology. In the process, he imbibed its corresponding pedagogy and likely never experienced an alternative way of teaching that would better reflect and more effectively promote a narrative practical theology. Rather than picking on a systematician, I note that practical theologians are equally challenged to employ a pedagogy that reflects and promotes the mode of "doing" theology that we propose. For practical theologians at least, our pedagogy is constitutive of our theology.

Of course, there are theological courses and contexts in which a presentation is entirely appropriate, and all the more so if it stimulates active engagement and leads on to conversation and personal appropriation by participants. But a purely didactic approach should not be the paradigmatic pedagogy of practical theologians. However, the still dominant "banking" mode of education (as Paulo Freire refers to it)[2] may dull our awareness that the nature and methods of practical theology demand a very different pedagogy to be fitting to our ends. Practical theologians need a pedagogy that promotes the "intended learning outcomes" of our theological discipline; otherwise, we defeat our own purposes.

Practical theology is a theological discipline in its own right; for now, I'll call it a way of *doing* theology within an historical context. In addition, practical theology functions as a collection of subdisciplines that share a practical intent and are typically realized within some faith community or instance of faith-based service. Here we can list pastoral care and counseling, homiletics, spiritual mentoring, worship, religious education/catechesis, and emerging hybrids such as faith-based social work, health care, and so forth. Thus, practical theology also functions as a unifying designation for many subdisciplines that enable faith communities to realize themselves and their commitments within their sociocultural contexts. In this essay I have in mind courses in practical theology as a distinct theological discipline and also in its subdisciplines. Such courses are taught in universities, theologates, seminaries, pastoral institutes, schools of theology and ministry, undergraduate courses in practical theology or its subdisciplines, and local programs (in a diocese, for example) that prepare catechists and pastoral leaders. I've taught them myself in a variety of those contexts.

Parenthetically, and given the intradisciplinary diversity within practical theology—primarily due to context—I make explicit at the outset my own situatedness. It greatly shapes how I do and teach practical theology. My teaching, mentoring, and research are done at Boston College's School of Theology and Ministry (STM). Boston College is a Catholic university in the Jesuit tradition and is highly esteemed as a major research-oriented university. Both Boston College's Catholic identity and its commitment to research and scholarship shape the life and curriculum of its School of Theology and Ministry. Likewise, the school is well named because its defining commitment is to both theology *and* ministry, or more precisely, to theology *for* ministry. The school's students include people preparing for Catholic priesthood, laypeople embracing vocations in ecclesial ministry, and people enrolled in dual degree programs (e.g., ministry and social work) who are preparing for faith-based service, often in nonecclesial contexts. The content and hermeneutical lens of the STM's curriculum is defined by Christian faith. As its mission statement envisions, "through the fostering of Christian faith and the promotion of justice and reconciliation" the school prepares its diverse student body "for service rooted in faith."

Within this context I do practical theology as a religious educator, intent to prepare graduates to maximize the faith-education potential of all ministries and faith-based service. Though my context is so particular, I'm convinced that I share common ground with at least a broad swath of practical theologians around our "intended learning outcomes." In this light, I make my pedagogical proposal, aspiring that it may be effective in other contexts as well.

THE INTENDED LEARNING OUTCOMES OF PRACTICAL THEOLOGY

Whenever our teaching/learning intent is *practice-oriented*, we need to employ a pedagogy that is likely to serve this purpose. This begs the question: What are the "intended learning outcomes"—to use educational language—of practical theology? Clarity about our ends is surely crucial to crafting the means of an effective pedagogy to promote our purposes. Note that the standard categories of intended learning outcomes in educational literature pertain to *knowledge* and *competency*. So what knowledge and competency do practical theologians intend by their teaching?

> Practical theology intends the learning outcome of reliable *knowledge*, spiritual *wisdom* for life, and the *arts* needed to render the services that enact Christian faith in the world.

I note at the outset that the *knowledge* intent of practical theology may well be what most lends it distinction as a theological discipline. In sum, it is threefold: practical theology intends the learning outcome of reliable *knowledge*, spiritual *wisdom* for life, and the *arts* needed to render the services that enact Christian faith in the world.[3] Here I must digress a little.

As often referred, Aristotle distinguished three *ways* of knowing, namely, *theoria*, *praxis*, and *poiesis*, with their corresponding *forms* of knowledge being *episteme*, *phronesis*, and *techne*.[4] They echo (though not precisely, see note 6) what we might call theoretical, practical, and artistic ways of knowing with their outcomes being scientific knowledge, practical wisdom, and the know-how to craft services or things. From my reading, Aristotle intended to distinguish these three as points of emphasis along the continuum of knowing and knowledge but not to separate them as if different enterprises. Yet, this is precisely what subsequent Western epistemology did, greatly favoring a *theoria*—theoretical—way of knowing, and dismissing practical wisdom and know-how as of no account, at least not to scholarship. This reductionism triumphed with the Enlightenment celebration of "certain ideas" that are presumed to transcend their historical context and to be objective from the perspective of the knowers. Such theory eschewed any practical or productive interest, though it might have some usefulness when "applied"—a one-way street.

If the late modern and postmodern movements have taught us anything, it is that all knowing and knowledge is influenced by its historical time and place and by the constitutive interest suggested by its context.[5] In the great summary phrase of Sandra Harding, "there is no view from nowhere."[6] This has prompted a shift away from prioritizing Aristotle's sense of theory as if it functions above the fray of history and attaining scientific certainty about unchanging truths.[7] Instead, in many quarters (the philosophy of education among them)[8] the movement has emerged to prioritize or at least reclaim a praxis way of knowing as reflection on life/experience, with its intended outcome of *phronesis*—practical wisdom. However, rather than continuing the old threefold separation, a contemporary praxis way of knowing can subsume both *theoria* and *poiesis*, promoting *episteme*, *phronesis*, and *techne* in an historically grounded and holistic epistemology.

Such an epistemology would seem imperative for practical theology, which surely intends people to have knowledge—social scientific and theological—and yet knowledge that is praxis-conscious and so appropriated as to reach beyond itself toward practical wisdom and the know-how to render ministry or service. Such a praxis-centered holistic way of knowing arises from reflection on life that is well informed by the best of available theory and disposes people to do what should be done or produced. Its knowledge is exemplified as practical wisdom for life that is informed by reliable theory and encourages the arts of living well.

A praxis way of knowing that subsumes both *theoria* and *poiesis*, and *phronesis* that includes both *episteme* and *techne*, is warranted by a contemporary rereading of Aristotle. For him, *praxis* is a unity of reflection/action; essentially, it is observation and reflection regarding life in the world. Aristotle, in fact, prioritized *praxis* by his constant insistence that all knowing begins from the data of the senses that are then brought by reflection to understanding, judgment, and decision. In sum, for Aristotle, all knowing begins from *praxis*. Then, he defined *phronesis* as "a truth-attaining rational quality concerned with action in relation to things that are good and bad for human beings."[9] Note that this wisdom-way of knowing *is* "truth-attaining" (theoretical if you will) and yet intends practice toward what is "good."

Likewise, even from Aristotle, we can propose the bond between *praxis/phronesis* and *poiesis/techne*. For him, both "right reason" and "right desire" are essential to choosing "the good" but desire ever depends on imagination—the work of *poiesis*—to make judgments and decisions.[10] Indeed, "the soul never thinks without a mental image."[11] In other words, prioritizing a praxis way of knowing as reflection on life in the world can engage the depths of theory and can resource people in the arts needed for service. In sum, a praxis epistemology offers the possibility of a holistic way of knowing that is theoretical, practical, and productive. More patently, it cumulatively intends truth, wisdom, and service.

Anticipating the section below on the method of practical theology, the intent of practical wisdom becomes the hermeneutical perspective that the practical theologian brings to theoretical resources (both the social scientific and theological), with the learning outcome being informed wisdom and know-how to get good things done. Concretely, in my context of educating people for Christian ministries and faith-based services, I intend a learning outcome of theologically and biblically well-informed graduates who are personally well formed in the spiritual wisdom of Christian faith and in how to encourage people and communities in such faith, and likewise are developing the various requisite arts of ministry—homiletics, education-in-faith, pastoral care, and so on. Though the latter *techne* intent is essential for people preparing for vocations in ministry, the service of Christian faith is the responsibility of every Christian. Indeed, the very praxis of faith and its wisdom must entail the services—especially to those in need—that should be rendered. As I elaborate below, Christian faith must not only be lived but be life-giving for all.

I can say, then, that my courses are thoroughly scholarly and theoretical (though students also take traditional theology and scripture courses), and likewise are geared to help participants develop the arts of ministry (which is more patently the agenda of their contextual education). These course aims are informed throughout by the overarching "learning outcome" of spiritual wisdom in Christian faith. The *competency* intended by a course in practical theology follows from its epistemology. In sum, practical theologians intend to inform and form people in the *habitus* of "doing" theology[12] while deliberately taking account of their historical circumstances.

I understand *habitus* as a personal disposition and competency of both mind and soul that unites theory, practice, and "know-how" to achieve ends that reflect knowledge, wisdom, and the arts of life. The intended *habitus* of practical theology, then, is to enable people to think theoretically about practices in pastoral and political contexts toward the ultimate end of spiritual wisdom that renders service. Our teaching should prepare practical theologians who can critically interpret present praxis, and, as appropriate, drawing on the social sciences to do so; reflect on it theologically; and enable people and communities to move toward the renewed praxis and services of their faith "for the life of the world" (John 6:51).

THE NATURE OF PRACTICAL THEOLOGY

While practical theology is a unifying discipline, it is also marked by great intradisciplinary diversity by way of its nature and methodology. There are many different paradigms of practical theology, due, in large part, to its various historical contexts. At a minimum, we can recognize ecclesial, academic, empirical, and narrative paradigms[13] and then various "forks in the road" by way of the object, method, agent, and audience of practical theology.[14] Jaco Dreyer argues persuasively against hegemony of any one paradigm of practical theology and likewise contra a pluralism of approaches that simply settles for fragmentation. Instead, he wisely calls for "a dialogic pluralist response to intradisciplinary diversity"[15] within practical theology, with the various paradigms finding enough common ground to learn from one another.

Without attempting to be hegemonic, I will lay out my own sense of the nature and method (following section) of practical theology that I try to practice in my context, precisely to encourage dialogue with other paradigms. These introductory comments are necessary in order to warrant and ground the pedagogy I propose. To begin with its nature, I appreciate R. Ruard Ganzevoort's proposal that all the paradigms of practical theology can find common ground by imagining our work as the "hermeneutics of lived religion."[16] I adjust his uniting summary according to my context. In sum and colored by my context, I understand the nature of practical theology as *the critical hermeneutics of lived and life-giving Christian faith*.

First, I favor the term *faith* over *religion* in describing the subject of practical theology. Anselm was correct in that all theology presupposes "faith" of some kind as its object of investigation. So, for practical theology to be theology—rather than an empirical study of religion—its subject matter must be "faith." In addition, faith is a broader term for what practical theology is to help realize in the world—beyond the personal lives and communities that claim a particular religion. For example, the Quaker and Mennonite religions have a faith-based influence for peacemaking far beyond their own communities of religious practice. Christian faith, especially, should be like the salt that savors everything (Matt 5:13) or the leaven that raises up all (Luke 13:21), whereas "religion" and its influence is more likely confined to its own community.

I also recognize *lived* faith to be faith that is realized, "done" within some historical context. The source and intent of practical theology is a faith that is known by its fruits (Matt 7:16) more than by its confessions. Christian faith must not only be lived but also must be *life-giving* for its participants, for their community, and for the common good of society. It must be a faith that encourages lived and life-giving discipleship to Jesus, who said that his purpose was "life in abundance" for all (John 10:10), with special favor for the least, the lost, and the last. The defining *telos* of such lived and life-giving faith is to realize God's reign of justice and peace for all, to promote doing God's will "on earth as in heaven" (Matt 6:10). As such, its arena is both ecclesial and sociocultural, and its concern is to incarnate life-giving Christian faith at every level of human existence—personal and interpersonal, communal and political.

Regarding *hermeneutics*, and following Ricoeur, I highlight that for practical theology this entails not only the task of *interpretation* but also of *explanation* and *application*.[17] In other words, even as practical theologians interpret texts, symbols, and situations, they *intend* the praxis of faith; they have an original interest in explanation and application, as well. In fact, interest in explanation and application will shape their interpretation, and vice versa.

Further, the *hermeneutics of faith* includes reflecting not only on explicit instances of Christian faith but on everything and anything in life, church, and world, *from the perspective and interest of lived and life-giving faith*. For example, the object of an exercise in practical theology might well be a current political issue that is reflected on and evaluated from the perspective of lived Christian faith and how Christians should be responding to it in life-giving ways within the public realm.

Here I follow Wilhelm Dilthey's broadening of hermeneutics beyond written texts; the hermeneutics of practical theology has as its focus what he called "the fullness of life,"[18] in other words, reflection on all of human experience or what I prefer to call "present praxis." In effect, its hermeneutic reaches beyond texts and symbols, sacred and otherwise, to *reflection on life* in the world, on what one is doing or what is being done or what is going on in any sociocultural context from the perspective of lived and life-giving faith. For example, an event of practical theology could well begin with a naming of and critical reflection on some present praxis of government policy (such as the Affordable Health Care Act,), doing so with the interest of lived and life-giving Christian faith.

Next, such reflection needs to be *critical* in that it attempts to uncover the sociocultural causes and consequences of the focused instance of present praxis. This critical reflection is the particular point of partnership of practical theology with the social sciences and social theory. All present praxis is already theory-laden, and the social sciences can enable the practical theologian to uncover the social, cultural, and historical causes and consequences of present praxis. Practical theologians' hermeneutics should be *critical*, too, in that practical theologians should become self-conscious of how their location and sociocultural context shapes their own hermeneutics of present praxis. Given the contextuality of our work, our best hope of objectivity is awareness of our own subjectivity.

Then, because practical theology is a "hermeneutics of lived and life-giving *faith*," its critical reflection must also focus on and be in conversation with the normative sources of some particular faith tradition in order to evaluate present praxis and enhance it toward more faithful praxis and service of said faith. For Christians, these sources are Scripture and Tradition. Note again that as practical theologians approach the core texts and symbols of Christian faith, our hermeneutics have the interests from the beginning of explanation and application as well as interpretation. This original interest in explanation and application is crucial to maintaining *theoria*, praxis, and *poiesis* in a unified and holistic epistemology.

The intended outcome of such hermeneutics, then, is not simply theoretical clarity but begins with the intention of renewed and deepened praxis of Christian faith, and not only as personal improvement or ecclesial enhancement but "for the life of the world" (John 6:51). In Christian terms, the ultimate intent is the realization of God's reign of justice, peace, and fullness of life for all (John 10:10). From a Christian perspective, *lived and life-giving Christian faith* is the originating interest, the departure point, the perspective along the way, and the intended *telos* of the "journey" of practical theology.[19]

To summarize, then, and looking to its pedagogy, I understand the nature of Christian practical theology as critical reflection on some present praxis of faith or on a generative theme (Freire's term) of life in the world that is germane to Christian faith. This critical reflection is to be done informed by the social sciences as relevant, and in light of the normative sources of Scripture and Tradition, themselves critically interpreted in conversation with present praxis (more below), with a view to renewed and deepened living of Christian faith toward personal, communal, and social transformation for God's reign.

A FAVORED METHOD OF PRACTICAL THEOLOGY: PRAXIS TO THEORY TO PRAXIS

Regarding the method of practical theology, I stand on a large swath of common ground that favors a methodology that proceeds from praxis to theory to (more faithful) praxis of Christian faith. I share this preferred approach with many other scholars and it most readily suggests a constitutive pedagogy.[20]

In this *praxis to theory to* (renewed) *praxis* dynamic, critical reflection on present praxis, as I stated above, does well to engage the insights of the social sciences and whatever scholarly sources can enhance its hermeneutics of the focused aspect of life in the world. In that the reflection on praxis engages the social sciences, social theory, and so forth, it is already drawing on scientific knowledge and holding together both praxis and theory. So, the reflection that begins with present praxis should be informed as appropriate by the social sciences for a deeper understanding of the causes and consequences of the focused praxis theme. However, Christian practical theologians must turn to their own indigenous faith, namely, scripture and tradition as understood in contemporary scholarship. Practical theologians bring their spiritual wisdom interest to interpreting these sources, to glean their potential for the practice and services of Christian faith for our time and place. Here again, as practical theologians interpret scripture and tradition, we hold together our interest in theory, practical wisdom, and the arts needed to render the services of Christian faith. For practical theologians, then, scripture and tradition are not simply "theory" in the purely theoretical sense. Rather, they are the normative sources of practical spiritual wisdom and service that constitute Christian faith and identity; they mandate how Christians personally and communally are to live their faith and enact its services in the midst of the world.

For this reason, I prefer to name such Christian "theory" with the less theoretical terms of Christian story and vision. I use these as dual symbols for all that Christian faith offers, demands, and promises to the lives of adherents.[21] To approach Christian faith as an overarching narrative of God's saving work in human history while imagining a constant horizon of ever more faithful discipleship and service—this is precisely what unleashes Christianity's potential for the ethical, prophetic, and mystical.[22]

In moving from present praxis to Christian story and vision, the intent of the practical theologian, from beginning to end, is the ever more faithful realization of the values and fruits of lived Christian faith. Our intentions may be to explicitly encourage a personal and communal praxis of faithful Christian living (e.g., in a catechetical context) or it can be to propose Christian values and services in the public realm—for the common good of all (e.g., regarding health care). This begs the question of the relationship between present praxis and Christian story and vision; as Ganzevoort notes, there are varying senses of the "epistemic status" of praxis and of its "role in practical theology."[23]

My proposal is that practical theologians are to mediate a critical correlation of praxis and theory as a dialectical hermeneutics toward the wisdom of Christian living and service. By this I mean that present praxis and Christian story and vision are to mutually inform and challenge each other to invite to ever more faithful living and realizing of Christian faith.[24] In this *dialectical* hermeneutics, there will be aspects of present praxis that are affirmed, challenged (even opposed), and enhanced by Christian faith. Likewise, present praxis can bring its affirmations, challenges, and deepened insights to the truths, practical wisdom, and service of Christian faith.

SOME "CATHOLIC" CONVICTIONS

The pedagogy I propose for practical theology is undergirded by a number of deep convictions; they need to be embraced by practical theologians who would employ such a pedagogy. They are implied by my description of practical theology above, but here I make them explicit with a view to its pedagogy. I can think of more,[25] but here I name three convictions that seem central: (1) that God's revelation continues to unfold through the ordinary and everyday of life (why else turn to present praxis as a theological *locus*?); (2) that Christian faith is to be realized as a way of life and service—forming people's identity as disciples (which explains the whole intent of practical theology, from beginning to end); and (3) that practical theology cannot settle for "understanding" alone; it must push people toward judgment and decision about the wisdom and service of Christian faith, as well. (À la Anselm, theology entails "faith seeking understanding"—but the practical theologian must also ask, "and then what?").

In this collection of Catholic perspectives on practical theology, I note that Catholicism persuasively encourages all three of these convictions. However, they can be readily embraced by Christian theologians of any denomination; these are "catholic" convictions.

(1) Revelation Through the Everyday

Catholicism is marked by its embrace of scripture and tradition as dual media of God's one revelation. Vatican II's *Dogmatic Constitution on Divine Revelation* (*Dei verbum*) summarized an enduring Catholic conviction, "that Sacred tradition and Sacred Scripture form one sacred deposit of the word of God, committed to the Church" (10). The classic Catholic appreciation for tradition points to the deeper conviction that God's revelation continues to unfold, albeit in essential continuity with sacred scripture. Echoing a favorite sentiment of Pope John XXIII, the Council taught that Christians "have the duty of scrutinizing the signs of the times and of interpreting them in the light of the Gospel."[26] But why attend to "the signs of the times"? Because, as the *Catechism of the Catholic Church* states, "the great book of creation and that of history" is "the page on which the 'today' of God is written" (2705). We turn to present praxis, then, not simply as a methodological or pedagogical ploy to get people interested (though it should do as much), but because Christians need to constantly "scrutinize" and respond to God's self-disclosure in present praxis—where the "today of God is written"—as well as through the normative Christian story and vision.

(2) Christian Faith as a Way of Life—An Identity as Disciples

As noted already, lived and life-giving Christian faith is *the* material of practical theology. Without piling on Gospel quotes, surely the intent of Jesus' whole public mission was that people would come to live and bear fruit as disciples—to follow *the way* in his footsteps. He even took it to the extreme of saying, "whoever does the will of God is my brother and sister and mother" (Mark 3:35). Without falling back into Reformation polemics, this was an issue that distinguished the Reformers from the classic Catholic position regarding the "works of faith." The Reformers made a much needed contribution by emphasizing faith as a trusting relationship with God in Jesus Christ. Catholicism wisely retained its traditional emphasis that "faith without works is dead" (James 2:26). A theology that begins and ends with the interest and intent of lived and life-giving faith is surely consonant with the praxis-like emphasis of Catholic Christianity.

(3) *A Dynamic of Attending, Understanding, Judging, and Deciding*

It may be stretching a point to claim that there is a distinctive Catholic epistemology. In so far as Aquinas is the third most important figure in the Catholic pantheon (after Jesus and Paul), we can recognize his insistence that all knowing begins with sense data as at least suggesting that Catholics favor a turn to present praxis as the starting point of knowledge, practical wisdom, and effective service. Further, Thomas's emphasis (echoing Aristotle) that knowledge must reach beyond understanding toward judgment and decision is a helpful alternative to Immanuel Kant's dichotomy between theoretical and practical reason.

Bernard Lonergan, inspired by Aquinas, has done the most to articulate a wisdom way of knowing that moves from attending to data, to understanding it, and thence to judgments regarding what is understood and decisions about what to do with what we understand and judge.[27] As such, beginning with present praxis and intending the learning outcome of renewed praxis seems entirely consonant with what we'll stretch a little and call a "Catholic" epistemology. Again, this conviction is readily shared by practical theologians. Indeed, these dynamics of cognition are prompted, says Lonergan, "by the eros of the human spirit for meaning."[28]

A PROPOSED PEDAGOGICAL APPROACH

In light of all of the above, I now make my pedagogical proposal. For some forty years, I've been attempting to develop, articulate, and practice a pedagogy that invites people from naming and critically reflecting on present praxis to a dialectical encounter with Christian story and vision, in order to encourage a lived Christian faith or at least to learn *from* Christian faith for oneself and for the common good. I have written about it formally as a "shared Christian praxis approach."[29] More recently I've proposed it with the more user-friendly description of *bringing life to faith and faith to life.*[30]

In sum:

1. *A shared Christian praxis approach encourages a teaching-learning community of active participation, conversation, and presentation*; in other words, the context is a teaching–learning community;
2. ...*in which people share their critical reflections on their own lives in the world around a generative theme of life or of life-in-faith*; this echoes Freire's notion of "generative" in that the praxis theme for reflection must be of real interest, import, and consequence to participants' lives;[31]
3. ...*in which people are given access to the truths, spiritual wisdom, and services of Christian story and vision regarding the theme*; this is the prime moment of interpreting, explaining, and proposing the symbols of Christian faith as relevant to the generative theme;
4. ...*in which people are encouraged to place their own reflections on present praxis (their own stories and visions) in dialogue and dialectic with the truths, spiritual wisdom, and services of Christian story and vision*; the key here is that people come to make judgments for themselves and personally appropriate Christian faith for their lives and sociocultural context;

5. ...*and in which people come to decisions and commitments that enact Christian faith;* such integration of present praxis and Christian story and vision into renewed and realized faith is the intention from beginning to end.

I have organized the *shared Christian praxis approach* more deliberately around a focusing activity and five pedagogical movements. By way of example, I imagine a class in practical theology that focuses on the generative theme of health; the U.S. Affordable Health Care Act (AHCA) is the specific focus. My second example is an instance of religious education with a group of adolescents reflecting on their praxis of faith in Jesus. These diverse examples suggest that a *shared Christian praxis approach* can be effective both in practical theology toward the public realm and in its subdisciplines within an ecclesial context. Know also that all the pedagogical moves can be implemented in myriad different ways besides what I describe here.

Focusing Activity—Establishing the Curriculum Around a Life/Faith Theme

Here the practical theologian's intent is twofold: (1) to engage people's interest and dispose them to become active participants in the teaching–learning event, and (2) to focus them on the praxis of some generative theme of life, of faith, or of life-in-faith. As noted already, I borrow the notion of "generative theme" from Freire. In sum, it means to situate a topic for attention within an instance of present praxis, and to do so in ways likely to engage participants with a theme of pressing interest to their life in the world.

For example, attention to the AHCA might begin with establishing the vital importance that everyone be insured for adequate health care, that it is essential for the common good and of deep interest to all. There might also be a review of the chief characteristics and provisions of the AHCA legislation. By contrast, a unit on Jesus with adolescents might have them imagine themselves on the road to Caesarea Philippi with Jesus (Matt 16:13–20), readying them to express who *their* Jesus is and what he means for their own life-praxis.

Movement One (M1)—Naming Present Praxis

Here, the practical theologian encourages participants to express themselves around the generative theme as reflected in their present lives and situations. They can express what they do or see others doing, their own feelings or thoughts or interpretations, and/or their perception of what is going on around them in their sociocultural context. Their expressions can be mediated through any means of communication—spoken words, writing, art, and so forth.

For example, people could be invited to take their own initial positions on the AHCA, or to indicate how they view the present state of health care in our country, its cost, its exclusivity, and so on. With the young adults, the catechist might invite as follows: Imagine Jesus putting the question to you, "Who do *you* say that I am?" How do you respond? What difference does he make for your life? (naming their own praxis of discipleship to Jesus).

Movement Two (M2)—Reflecting Critically on the Theme of Life/Faith

The intent here is to encourage participants to reflect critically on the praxis they described in M1. Depending on the theme, critical reflection can engage reason, memory, imagination, or a combination of them. Such reflection can be both personal and sociocultural. The invitation is not only to reflect on a theme of present praxis but also to have participants probe their own interpretations of it.

Regarding the AHCA, there could be a huge draw here from the social sciences, including statistics on health care in our country, who has access and who is denied, the politics involved, and so on. The teenagers might reflect on "Who or what has shaped my image of Jesus?" and "What difference do I imagine Jesus can make in my life?" (their own christological stories and visions).

Movement Three (M3)—Accessing the Wisdom of Christian Story and Vision Apropos the Generative Theme

Here, the pedagogical task is to offer an informed and critical (discerning) hermeneutic of the Christian story and vision around the particular theme. The key is that participants have ready access to the truths, wisdom, and services of Christian faith and what it might mean for their own lives and for the life of the world—the vision.

So, the practical theologian in M3 might lay out core aspects of Catholic social teaching regarding health care, people's rights thereto, and the responsibility of society to honor those rights, with commentary on the AHCA in this light. With the teenagers, M3 is the most overtly catechetical moment; now is the time to lay out a portrayal of Jesus, appropriate to age level, highlighting both who Jesus is from the perspective of Christian faith and what it means to live as a disciple of Jesus (i.e., both story and vision).

Movement 4 (M4)—Dialectical Hermeneutic Between Present Praxis and Christian Story and Vision

Now, the teaching-learning intent is that people judge for themselves what the truths, wisdom, and services of Christian faith might mean for their everyday lives, to personally recognize and appropriate the faith for who they are and how to live. This movement epitomizes the dialectical hermeneutics between present praxis and story and vision regarding the generative theme; the key is to invite participants to discern how these two sources—their lives and Christian faith—affirm, challenge, and enhance each other.

In our health care example, the intent of such dialectical hermeneutics is to recognize how Catholic social teaching affirms or is challenged by the AHCA and, vice versa, how the AHCA realizes or is challenged by Catholic social teaching. With the teenagers, the reflective activities might invite participants to express their developing image of Jesus as they take the instruction of M3 to heart, what discipleship and Christian service might ask of them now, and how their own lives can help clarify what it means for young people today to live as disciples of Jesus.

Movement Five (M5)—Making Decisions in Light of Christian Faith

Participants are invited to choose how to respond to the truths, wisdom, and services of Christian faith as pertaining to the generative theme of the occasion. Decisions can be cognitive, affective, or behavioral—what people choose to believe now (renewed by the process), how they might relate with God or others, or the ethics and service by which to live. The decisions might be personal or communal or for the implementation of Christian values in their public realm.

For example, decisions might be what faith-based stance to take on the issue of affordable health care in our country, what to do and favor regarding health care for the common good of all. For the adolescents, M5 might invite decisions like, "If a young person today professes faith in Jesus, what practically and productively could this mean for her or his life?" or, if in a more confessional context, "Do you want to live as a disciple of Jesus?" and if so deciding, then "so what?"

POST NOTE

While there is a logic to the sequencing of these movements—from life to Christian faith to renewed faith for life—let me emphasize that the movements often combine, recur, or go backward and forward, and one cycle can prompt the beginning of another. In fact, more important than the movements are the commitments that undergird them and the imperative that these commitments be embraced—however crafted and in whatever sequence—by the pedagogy of the practical theologian.[32]

I propose that some such pedagogy is demanded by the nature and method of practical theology, at least as I understand and practice it in my context. It is most likely to promote the intended learning outcomes of developing the *habitus* of "doing" theology in historical circumstances and of promoting practical spiritual wisdom and service in people's personal lives, in their communities of faith, and in the public realm.

Notes

1. Johann Baptist Metz, *Faith in History and Society: Toward a Practical Fundamental Theology* (New York: Seabury Press, 1980).

2. See Paulo Freire, *Pedagogy of the Oppressed* (New York: Seabury Press, 1970).

3. The section that follows echoes the conversation between Jaco S. Dreyer and Bonnie J. Miller-McLemore about whether practical theology should have the intent of *phronesis* alone or of *episteme*, as well. I include *techne* and say that all three should be intended learning outcomes of practical theology. See Jaco S. Dreyer, "Practical Theology and Intradisciplinary Diversity: A Response to Miller-McLemore's 'Five Misunderstandings about Practical Theology,'" *International Journal of Practical Theology* 16, no. 1 (2012): 34–54.

4. Aristotle's best summary is found in *Nicomachean Ethics*, book 6. My references are to the Loeb Classical Library edition: Aristotle, *Nicomachean Ethics*, trans. H. Rackham (Cambridge, MA: Harvard University Press, 1934). My own more in-depth treatment can be found in *Sharing Faith: A Comprehensive Approach to Religious Education and Pastoral Ministry* (San Francisco, CA: HarperSanFrancisco, 1991), 42–49.

5. For example, see Jürgen Habermas, *Knowledge and Human Interests* (Boston, MA: Beacon Press, 1971), esp. 168ff.

6. This is a common theme in Sandra Harding's writings; see, for example, *Whose Science? Whose Knowledge? Thinking from Women's Lives* (Ithaca, NY: Cornell University Press, 1991), 311.

7. This is an instance of how Aristotle's terms have been greatly revised since his time. For example, he understood scientific knowledge as "a mode of conception dealing with universals and things that are of necessity." *Nicomachean Ethics*, book 6, chap. 6: 1, 341. By contrast, and at least since the seventeenth century (Francis Bacon, Galileo Galilei, et al.), scientific knowledge arises from developing and then testing hypotheses through systematic observation, experimentation, and modification according to the resultant data.

8. Here one readily thinks of John Dewey's "reconstruction of experience," of Maria Montessori's emphasis on "sensory reflection," and of Paulo Freire's "critical reflection on present praxis" as the foundation of all knowledge.

9. Aristotle, *Nicomachean Ethics*, book 6, chap. 5: 4, 337.

10. Here I reference Aristotle's treatment of imagination in *On the Soul* (*De Anima*), book 3, chap. 3: 155–63.

11. Ibid., book 3, chap. 7: 177.

12. *Theologia habitus* is a medieval notion, revived in our time by Edward Farley; see his *Theologia: The Fragmentation and Unity of Theological Education* (Eugene, OR: Wipf & Stock, 2001; 1st ed.: Philadelphia, PA: Fortress Press, 1983).

13. See Dreyer, "Practical Theology and Intradisciplinary Diversity," 35. Of course, I know of no practical theologian who fits neatly into any of these categories. For myself, and as indicated by my statement of context, my own work is both ecclesial and academic, and I've long emphasized the role of a hermeneutical and narrative approach to practical theology.

14. R. Ruard Ganzevoort, "Forks in the Road When Tracing the Sacred: Practical Theology as Hermeneutics of Lived Religion," presidential address to the International Academy of Practical Theology, Chicago, IL, March 8, 2009, R. Ruard Ganzevoort Web site, accessed September 30, 2013, http://www.ruardganzevoort.nl/pdf/2009_Presidential.pdf.

15. See Dreyer, "Practical Theology and Intradisciplinary Diversity," 49.

16. See Ganzevoort, "Forks in the Road."

17. See Paul Ricoeur, *Interpretation Theory: Discourse and the Surplus of Meaning* (Forth Worth: Texas Christian University Press, 1976), esp. 74–91.

18. Dilthey's phrase quoted in Richard Palmer, *Hermeneutics* (Evanston, IL: Northwestern University Press, 1969), 105.

19. Here I echo Ganzevoort's metaphor of practical theology as "traveling." See "Forks in the Road," 3.

20. I first recommended this "praxis to theory to praxis" approach in my *Christian Religious Education* (San Francisco, CA: HarperCollins, 1980). Many other leading scholars of practical theology also favor it; see, for example, Don S. Browning, *A Fundamental Practical Theology: Descriptive and Strategic Proposals* (Minneapolis, MN: Fortress Press, 1991); Richard R. Osmer, *Practical Theology: An Introduction* (Grand Rapids, MI: William B. Eerdmans Publishing Company, 2008).

21. For further elaboration of my use of story and vision, see my *Will There Be Faith* (San Francisco, CA: HarperCollins, 2012), esp. 289–93.

22. For space, I cannot elaborate here but I reference the essays of David Tracy and Roberto S. Goizueta in this volume.

23. Ganzevoort, "Forks in the Road," 9.

24. For more detailed discussion of "dialectical hermeneutics," see my *Sharing Faith*, 223–40, 256–62.

25. See my *Will There Be Faith*, 296–97.

26. Second Vatican Council, *Pastoral Constitution on the Church in the Modern World*, no. 4.

27. Lonergan's description of the dynamics of authentic cognition is most readily accessible in *Method in Theology* (New York: Seabury Press, 1972), esp. chap. 1. For my own elaboration on the implications of Lonergan's "dynamics of cognition," see *Sharing Faith*, 116–21.

28. Lonergan, *Method in Theology*, 13.

29. My most complete account of a *shared Christian praxis approach* can be found in *Sharing Faith*, chaps. 5 to 10; see chap. 4 for a summary statement.

30. See Groome, *Will There Be Faith*, esp. chaps. 8 and 9.

31. Building a praxis-based pedagogy around the "generative themes" of people's lives is a central aspect of Freire's approach.

See Paulo Freire, *Pedagogy of the Oppressed* (New York: Seabury Press, 1970).

32. For a listing of these commitments, see Groome, *Will There Be Faith*, 334–36.

CHAPTER 15

RESEARCH IN PRACTICAL THEOLOGY

Methods, Methodology, and Normativity

ANNEMIE DILLEN AND ROBERT MAGER

In their introduction to the discipline, Stephen Pattison and James Woodward identify fourteen characteristics of practical theology. Among other aspects, it is "related to experience," "unsystematic," "truthful and committed," "contextual and situationally related," "reflectively based," and "dialectical."[1] Practical theology seeks to hold different poles together: theory and practice, tradition and experience, reality and ideal, description and prescription, written texts and texts of life, theology and other disciplines, religious community and society. Pattison and Woodward also describe practical theology as being skillful and demanding. This becomes clear if one tries to imagine how the bridges between all the mentioned poles could be established.

In this chapter, we offer a *methodological* reflection on various *methods* used in practical theological research and on the metaquestions that these methods provoke. In other words, the focal point of our reflection will be the bridges between the aforementioned poles. We cannot give an extensive overview or introduction to all possible practical theological methods, but we evoke some of them in order to show which theological questions can be raised, and we take initial steps to answer them.

FOUNDATIONAL PRINCIPLES

To clarify the stance we take on methodological issues, a few preliminary remarks must be made about key terms such as *practical theology, methods, methodology, practices, experiences,* and *context.*

Practical Theology

"Practical theology" is a paradoxical phrase. If we consider its etymological roots, it refers altogether to speech (or discourse), to reason and science (*logos*), to action or practice (praxis), and to God (*theos*). One's understanding of practical theology and its methods depends largely on the relations one establishes between these terms: science of human actions related to God (i.e., ecclesial practices), discourse about God's actions in the world, practices of doing theology, and so forth. This can create much confusion about the nature, goals, and means of practical theology, though many rather tend to celebrate the diverse possibilities that are thus made possible. The paradox is intrinsic to the two terms themselves: as *logos,* theology is in itself a form of action (thus the common phrase "the practice of theology"); conversely, human practices necessarily entail forms of speech and thought. So practical theology is not reducible to "theory about practice": it is also a form of practice about practice, and an encounter of different forms of speech and thought. Many methodological challenges of practical theology stem from this paradox.

As noted in the introduction to this volume, Bonnie Miller-McLemore distinguishes four ways in which the term *practical theology* is used: as a scientific discipline, a way of life, a method, and a "curricular area of subdisciplines."[2] In this chapter, we focus on the first and the third meanings, that is, on the scientific endeavor and its methods. This is not to deny the fundamental importance of the theological language developed within the life of faith itself. Speech, thought, and action are intertwined at all levels in the faith experience. Nor do we underestimate the development of *reflective practice*. But we focus here on the scientific endeavor of practical theology as it methodically studies given practices.

Another distinction can be made within practical theology between pastoral training (or fieldwork education) and academic research. Pastoral training and fieldwork education involve the acquisition and development of different know-how or skills, most of which refer to given "methods": nondirective counseling, group animation, narrative preaching, and others. The methods for academic research are of another nature, and they will be the ones at stake here.[3]

The image of a triangular pyramid illustrates the focus of this essay.[4] A first face refers to reflection in action—for instance, the reflection of chaplains in the course of their work. A second face involves the methods and techniques related to the practices, such as nondirective counseling methods. A third form of reflection refers to the theories legitimizing practices or practical/pastoral theologies—for instance, narrative theory. In this essay, we focus on the fourth face, namely, the meta-reflection on methodology and the relationship between theory and practice. All four faces are closely related to one another, and each one could be the "bottom" in this model, depending on the way the pyramid is placed.

Methods, Methodology, and Other Terms

Method is understood here as a systematic mode of inquiry; *methodology* is the reflection on methods. Any given method involves different research *procedures* (interviews, focus groups, polls, verbatim). Methods may maintain close links with certain *approaches* or *perspectives* (feminist theology, psychoanalysis, critical pedagogy); they often refer to established *models* or to full-fledged *theories* (narrative theory, Thomism, Marxian analysis).

In the literature, such distinctions are not always present. For instance, when one encounters a reference to *hermeneutics* or to *theological reflection*, it is not always clear if this refers to a theory, a model, a method, or concrete procedures. As a rule, the *methodological* reflection of a given research must make clear which approaches, models, or theories are in the background or put to the test, and which procedures will concretely be used to explore reality. Methods are complex constructs that must not be confused with simple series of procedures: the elaboration of a research method makes sense inasmuch as it is consistent with the goals of the research, its core question, and the theoretical horizon that is privileged. We describe methods of data collection and analysis and of building theories in relation to these data.

Practices, Experiences, Contexts

Practical theology can refer to practices, but also to experiences, phenomena, and situations. It is mainly focused on actions, on what people do. But these actions involve motives, intentions, meanings, and thus experiences. They are performed in certain situations, milieus, and contexts. They form patterns that others may perceive as phenomena. All these dimensions come together under the umbrella notion of *practice*. We do not want to focus here on the debate between those who consider practical theology as an action-focused science and those who see it as an observational science of lived religion. In this contribution, *practice* includes actions, experiences, forms of lived religion, phenomena, and anything thus related to what people do in life. Artistic expression can also fall under this broad term of *practices*.

Contexts play an important role both as a dimension of the studied practices and in the making of the studies themselves. Practical theology is done in various contexts: at universities, in seminaries, and in grassroots movements. Each context may influence the choice of potential methods. For instance, participant observation might be much easier in the context of a grassroots movement than quantitative empirical research. In some universities, empirical research is encouraged by financial structures and by the way "objective" scientific knowledge is conceived; in others, it is hindered by ethical, administrative, or financial procedures.

Nevertheless, in all these contexts, one way or the other, theologians deal with the relationship between the study of practices and theological theory. Two examples will help us to illustrate possible methods and related methodological questions.

FIRST CASE: THE STUDY OF HOSPITAL CHAPLAINCY

Practices and Methods of Inquiry

Chaplains in Catholic hospitals visit patients, prepare rituals, preside in prayer and liturgical services, attend team meetings, write about their tasks for hospital magazines, and perform many other duties. For hospital boards, it is not always clear what chaplains do and what the Catholic character of a hospital means. The chaplains may feel pressured to justify their work. As reflective practitioners, they develop and share many ideas; they might seek assistance from academic theologians to reflect more formally on what they are doing and why, or to help them meet standards of quality for their work. Practical theological research may help in various ways.

From a traditional perspective, practical theological research could strive to improve sacramental and liturgical practices in hospitals. A hermeneutical study of literature (most often church documents) would be performed in dialogue with the experiences of chaplains. Another procedure might be a content analysis of church documents and liturgical books. Codes and categories would then be used to structure and analyze the texts.

Content Analysis
Content analysis is generally understood as thematic analysis of written, audio, and video data. These sources can also be submitted to other forms of analysis (semiotic, psychoanalytic, metaphorical, etc.).

- Klaus Krippendorff, *Content Analysis: An Introduction to Its Methodology* (New York: Sage, 2012).
- Kimberly A. Neuendorf, *The Content Analysis Guidebook* (New York: Sage, 2012).

In a pluralized and detraditionalized Western context, the inquiry must be enlarged beyond the rituals issue. Many chaplains also want to demonstrate how the spiritual care they offer (focused on dialogue with patients but encompassing rituals and sacraments) is an essential part of holistic care, aiming at the general wellbeing of patients. Various other methods and approaches can be employed, either quantitative or qualitative, depending on the specific *research question*. When turning to empirical methods, the approval of the research by an ethical committee of the hospital or research institution will most probably be necessary.

Empirical Research

There has been much development of empirical theological research in the past decades, especially in the English-, Dutch-, and German-speaking countries.

- Chris Hermans and Mary Elizabeth Moore, eds., *Hermeneutics and Empirical Research in Practical Theology* (Leiden, Netherlands: Brill, 2004).
- Heinz Streib, Astrid Dinter, and Kerstin Söderblom, eds., *Lived Religion: Conceptual, Empirical and Practical-Theological Approaches* (Leiden, Netherlands: Brill, 2008).

Quantitative empirical research into the spirituality of patients or caregivers is used when the researchers want to have representative data that can be generalized among the whole population. Researchers using quantitative methods want to know how specific features or practices are spread in a certain group of people. An adequate research question, divided into subquestions, should be formulated. The researchers then look for a hypothesis that can be validated by the research or be further explored, depending on the state of the art of the research domain. A questionnaire with its own constructed scales, or with already validated scales, should be made. Various tryouts will be needed in order to check if the questionnaire is measuring the concepts and ideas about spirituality in a valid and reliable way.

If one wants to know what themes are frequently discussed in pastoral relationships, questionnaires should be distributed among chaplains to ensure that a representative number of people complete the questionnaire. Types of qualitative research, such as videotaped conversations or verbatim (quasi-literal transcripts of a pastoral conversation), may help this form of quantitative research in giving the basis for the construction of a written questionnaire that seeks to determine which topics arise in pastoral conversations.

The quantitative research concerning the outcome of pastoral care can be complemented by an intervention study. This means that a form of intervention is undertaken, such as participation in a ritual or a meeting with a chaplain. Afterward the outcome of the intervention can also be measured and compared with the initial data about spirituality.

Qualitative Empirical Research

Qualitative empirical research may take many shapes, depending on the chosen approach or method: grounded theory, phenomenology, ethnomethodology, narrative analysis.

- John Swinton and Harriet Mowat, *Practical Theology and Qualitative Research* (London, UK: SCM Press, 2006).
- Norman K. Denzin and Yvonna S. Lincoln, *The Sage Handbook of Qualitative Research* (New York: Sage, 2011).
- John W. Creswell, *Research Design: Qualitative, Quantitative, and Mixed Method Approaches* (New York: Sage, 2003).

Quantitative research could be complemented with qualitative empirical research in the form of open or semistructured interviews. Patients could be asked about their spiritual wellbeing, spiritual needs, or experiences with chaplains. Caregivers could also be interviewed, individually or in a group.

Qualitative methods have traditionally been underestimated in the social sciences and also in practical theology. More recently, however, there has been more and more interest in qualitative methods as they help researchers to deepen their understanding of a phenomenon/practice, its underlying ideas, and its various interpretations. Qualitative methods are helpful for theory building or for the exploration of new realities.

A suitable form of qualitative research in the context of hospital chaplaincy would be the observation or videotaping and analysis of what chaplains do. A discourse analysis of the images, or of a verbatim or written report about the pastoral encounters, can help the researchers to learn about the relationships between what is said and not said, about the intonation, gestures, hidden meanings, specific words that are used, and so on. These methods are used, for instance, to study power dynamics and ethical issues in pastoral conversations, to analyze the body language of chaplains, or to explore their way of asking questions.

In other settings, qualitative empirical research can be broadened into narrative biographical research, where a small group of people are asked for their life stories.[5] Such a method is well suited for chronological research about realities such as the experiences of various generations within the church or faith transmission.

In addition to empirical research, more reflective theoretical research, in dialogue with practitioners, is possible.[6] It may develop critical views on the urge to measure everything. It may also reflect theologically on the relevance of faithfully guiding people when they are no longer attractive to other caregivers.

Methodological Issues

A few questions may be raised about the specific methods evoked so far. A first question is whether one method promises more objectivity than another. Generally speaking, we prefer to speak about *intersubjectivity*—as researchers who aim for neutrality or objectivity often overlook their own subjectivity. Of course, it is important to avoid subjective biases and ideological influences, and to proceed with research questions that are as open as possible: the researcher should not have the right answer already in mind when she or he launches the research. But even if careful attention is paid to these open research questions and to adequate methods and approaches, we should continue to question the researcher's beliefs, interests, and intentions: How do they interact with the actors' beliefs, interests, and intentions? What are the researcher's blind spots?

This is particularly important when practical theologians are involved in the practices or experiences they study. First, practical theological research should be more than a legitimization of one's own practices and views, and should rather lead to critical and methodologically elaborated reflections on these practices. By choosing an appropriate approach, method, and procedure to set up the research, the theologian allows for the emergence of new questions and perspectives. Conversely, the researcher's involvement with and experience of the practices can be helpful for the discernment and recognition of these new insights.

Second, methods are not value-free. In choosing a given method, often borrowed from the social sciences, it is important to reflect on its anthropological and philosophical assumptions and to assess them theologically. Traditionally, at least three possible relationships between the social sciences and (practical) theology can be distinguished.[7] Social sciences can be seen as *ancillae theologiae*: they assist theology, but in the end theological norms prevail, at the risk of censuring dimensions of the scientific endeavor and thus short-circuiting the research process. Social sciences can also function as a *Fremdprophetie*, a prophetic challenge coming from outside of theology (such as psychoanalysis, critical theory, and so forth), which calls theology into question at the risk of paralyzing it. Both perspectives are unidirectional. A third relationship is required that involves some form of mutual challenge and enrichment.

Neither the social sciences nor classical theological positions are free from subjective and contextual influences. In our example, one can ask whether the researchers will pay attention to the cultural, socioeconomic, or ethnic context of the patients, the chaplains and the other caregivers, and the (sometimes hidden) power issues at stake in these contexts. Feminist, womanist, or postcolonial approaches teach us to be alert to hidden perspectives. In the context of a Catholic hospital, one can also ask how various understandings of Catholicism play a role.

Another question has to do with the strategic use of the data. Results of quantitative empirical research on the spirituality of patients might be used in various ways. Various elements may influence the interpretation: not only the researcher's theological position, but possibly also his or her ecclesial status (priest, religious, lay), his or her own experience of suffering, aspects of social class, and so on. When asking if a mean score of 3 on a 5-point Likert scale on spiritual needs is high or low, one might consider what kind of questions have been asked, how spirituality is defined, and who has answered the questions. Maybe those with the greatest needs were not able to answer the written questionnaire.

Finally, any given research aims at understanding the practice at stake, improving it, or both. Not all research is geared toward a transformation of the practice. When it is, various ideas, assumptions, and values play a role in the way we interpret what a "better" praxis might be. What are, then, the criteria by which to judge whether a transformation is "good"?[8] What might be the side or down effects of the proposed "improvement"? Who might be excluded or victimized by it?

SECOND CASE: STUDYING THE SPIRITUALITY OF SOCIAL ACTIVISTS

A second example will allow for a few additional suggestions of practical theological research methods and prompt us to make other methodological comments.

Practices and Methods of Inquiry

Social activism is quite a large label, covering different forms of commitment aiming at bettering the world on the basis of values such as equality, freedom, peace, or justice. Social activists can be found in community agencies, political parties, nonprofit organizations, environmental groups, labor unions, international cooperation organizations, feminist groups, and the like.

As pragmatic as they may be, social activists are driven by values, beliefs, dreams, utopias, or ideologies. Many of them acknowledge that their commitment rests on spiritual foundations, however diverse, and on whichever way they understand *spirituality*. In a world that claims to be led by rationality and where the great utopias of the past century are dead or severely wounded, spiritual issues are not easily and openly addressed. In a highly secularized society like Quebec (Canada), which is still in the process of purging its Catholic heritage, theologians are often looked at with suspicion. But many social organizations want to reflect on their mission, explore their core values, or expand their vision. Their staff often struggles with discouragement, loss of hope, or burnout. They want to reflect on commitment, resilience, and hope, but at a distance from any given religious context.

Different types of practical theological research are conceivable here. The researcher could position him- or herself as an expert, using classical procedures (interviews, surveys, focus groups) to explore the spiritual underpinnings and expressions of social activism, interpreting the results in light of the relevant literature, and producing a paper for the benefit of the academic world. In research of this type, the phenomenon is objectified, as it is in most experimental researches, and the beneficiaries of the research are mainly members of the scientific community.

Other methodological approaches would be more concerned with the respect of social activists as *subjects*, or with their organizations as beneficiaries of the research. Thus *action research* conceives any study as a collaborative process between the professional researchers and the actors themselves of the phenomenon under study—often considered as "coresearchers." The knowledge of these actors about their own practice and experience is deemed primary to the research, not only as "data," but also as a driving force and guide for the research process itself. The study is then designed and realized by a team of academics and practitioners; its outcome must necessarily benefit the actors and their organization. The Action Research—Church and Society (ARCS) agency at the Heythrop Institute in London (United Kingdom) has especially worked along such lines, developing what they call "theological action research."[9]

Action Research

There are many forms of action research or cooperative inquiry, all of which converge around the idea of concrete problem solving involving the actors of an organization or a milieu concerned with this problem.

- Helen Cameron et al., *Talking about God in Practice: Theological Action Research and Practical Theology* (London, UK: SCM Press, 2010).
- Peter Reason and Hilary Bradbury, *Handbook of Action Research* (New York: Sage, 2008).

In approaching the spiritual motivations of social activists, one could take a more *phenomenological* stance, characterized by the precise description of their experience and the search for its constituent elements. "Its bracketing of presuppositions and commitment to description distinguish phenomenology from positivist, postpositivist, constructivist, critical, and relativistic approaches. Phenomenology is more hospitable, accepting, and receptive in its reflection on 'the things themselves' and in its care not to impose order on its subject matter."[10] French theologian Étienne Grieu conducted an extensive study along those lines, whereby he listened to the life stories of militant Christians and showed how they evolved around the central notion of filiation.[11]

Phenomenological Research
Phenomenological research aims at producing thick descriptions of experiences as they are voiced by the actors themselves. It has developed from a philosophical trend into various research methods incorporating hermeneutical elements.

- Hans-Günter Heimbrock, "From Data to Theory," *International Journal of Practical Theology* 9 (2005): 273–99.

Beyond insightful description, another approach could aim at elaborating a theory of the spiritual concerns of secular social activists. *Grounded theory*, as developed by Barney G. Glaser and Anselm L. Strauss, would engage in a series of observations and interviews. These are analyzed to identify the key concepts they embody. These concepts are in turn progressively organized into a theoretical construct. The analysis of subsequent inquiry materials adds elements to the theory, amending it up to a saturation point.

Grounded Theory
Grounded theory is a form of theory building proceeding from the ground up. It is particularly appropriate for the analysis of new phenomena, for which no existing theory can be invoked.

- Barney G. Glaser and Anselm L. Strauss, *The Discovery of Grounded Theory* (New York: Aldine, 1967).
- H.J.C. Pieterse, "Metatheoretical Decisions for the Grounded Theory Research of Sermons on Poverty and to the Poor as Listeners," *Nederduitse Gereformeerde Teologiese Tydskrif* 51, nos. 3–4 (2010): 104–13.

Methodological Issues

Practical theology usually deals with ministerial practices, church life, or faith commitments. But this second example goes beyond the religious sphere to deal with secular practices. Admittedly, the theological interest for the spirituality of social activists still keeps us close to religious matters, but the example could have gone beyond that to address other issues such as poverty, exploitation, segregation, or the like. This raises questions about the exact nature of the practical theological endeavor.

Sketching roughly the scene of practical theology, we could distinguish three types of research:

1. Religious study of religious/spiritual matters
2. Religious study of secular matters
3. Scientific study of religious/spiritual matters.

These three types represent different stances and endeavors. The first type (religious study of religious/spiritual matters) is "typical" of the work done in pastoral theology and training. The second type (religious study of secular matters) corresponds to a fundamental Christian claim: the risen Christ reigns over the whole universe and his Spirit infuses all aspects of life. Thus every life dimension, either societal or individual, can be reflected on from a Christian stance: there is space and legitimacy for "public theologies."[12] In turn, the third type of practical theology (scientific study of religious/spiritual matters) is much influenced by the academic environment in which most practical theologians work, and which is dominated by the modern scientific paradigm.

The potential pitfalls of each type of practical theology may be obvious, but they are nonetheless not always avoided. Religious studies of religious/spiritual matters can stay locked in religious schemes and concepts, neglecting to examine seriously the concrete human dimensions of the practices at stake. Religious studies of secular matters can adopt a judgmental stance and remain draped in truth and principles, without properly recognizing the novelty, complexity, and ambiguities of most human affairs and ethical issues. Conversely, scientific studies of religious/spiritual matters can be quite methodical in their analyses of concrete phenomena, but this may be at the price of losing sight of the theological inquiry as *fides quaerens intellectum*.

Our second example also shows how the orientation of a research project is much influenced by the way the issue of *subjectivity* is handled. This can be illustrated by a debate between Johannes A. van der Ven[13] and Hans-Günter Heimbrock.[14] Van der Ven held that empirical methods are neutral scientific methods that deliver exact and empirically valid knowledge concerning experiences of "lived religion." Heimbrock, however, suggested that reality as such can never be grasped and that experience is always already interpreted. Heimbrock's phenomenological method acknowledges the subjective nature of all experience and helps people to become aware of their ceaseless perceptive involvement in the experiential process. Although his phenomenological approach has a more contextual and life-world oriented character than van der Ven's, it remains rather theoretical and does not mention the practical need to take into account the social context and the identity of the research subjects and the researcher, or issues such as gender, age, class, and race.

As a whole, the design of any given practical theological project must tackle a few pivotal questions. This process might need some time to mature. These questions deal with:

1. The *object* (or topic): What will this research be about *exactly*? This object needs to be as precise as possible for the research to be fruitful and not to wander in all directions. In practical theology, it will normally be a concretely located practice or experience rather than a theme. As the object is usually related to concrete persons, it is an important task for practical theologians to treat these persons as subjects (even if they are considered as research objects).

2. The *problem*: Why must this object be put under study rather than left alone? What needs to be solved or better known? From whose point of view does this appear problematic? A review of the relevant literature must be performed to identify and assess previous studies on the matter.

3. The research *question*: What question needs to be answered, be it partially, by the research? This aspect of the research design requires special care. The question must be clear, precise, and specific. It must be theological in nature. It must not be a fake question or a rhetorical one, a conviction in disguise. It will normally be an open question, calling for development (and thus starting with "what," "how," "in which cases," "under which conditions," etc.), rather than a closed question (answerable by "yes" or "no").

4. The *subject*: Who is doing this research? Why? Driven by which convictions, interests, motives, commitments, agenda? For the sake of which institution? Practical theology has to dissipate once and for all the illusion of the objective and bias-free researcher. The research engages a subject (the researcher) with an object (the practice), in such a way that both may evolve and change.

5. The *theory*: What is the theological framework behind this research? Which theories (trends, works, authors, concepts) are concerned? Which approaches will be chosen, and why?

6. The *hypothesis*: We rarely approach any object without theoretical assumptions or previous knowledge. This may prompt us to follow the scientific experimental procedure and to formulate a hypothesis that will be put to the test. But this is not always useful. Many researchers prefer to put aside or to suspend the assumptions and any previous knowledge, and thus any hypothesis, to pay better attention to the phenomenon at stake and to welcome unexpected insights.

7. The *goals*: The main goal of any research is to answer the question, but this general goal needs to be spelled out in a few concrete objectives. This helps to surface any underlying agenda and to trace the limits of the research.

8. The *method*: Only then does the method per se come into play. The choice of any given method rests on the

previous elements, and especially on the goals of the research. The *methodos* is the way (Greek *odos*, "way," "journey") that we choose to follow on the conviction that it may lead to a better knowledge or to some solution. It will normally be composite and adapted to each research project.

9. The *outcome*: What kind of discourse does the research project aim to produce (scientific paper, large audience document, expert advice, online manual, pedagogical project, artistic work, etc.)? What is the targeted audience? Marcel Viau of Université Laval (Canada) has written extensively on the practical theological discourse as *artifact*, and made us more aware of the aesthetical, rhetorical, and pragmatic aspects of the theological endeavor.[15]

The design of a research project thus comprises multiple factors, which can be schematized this way:

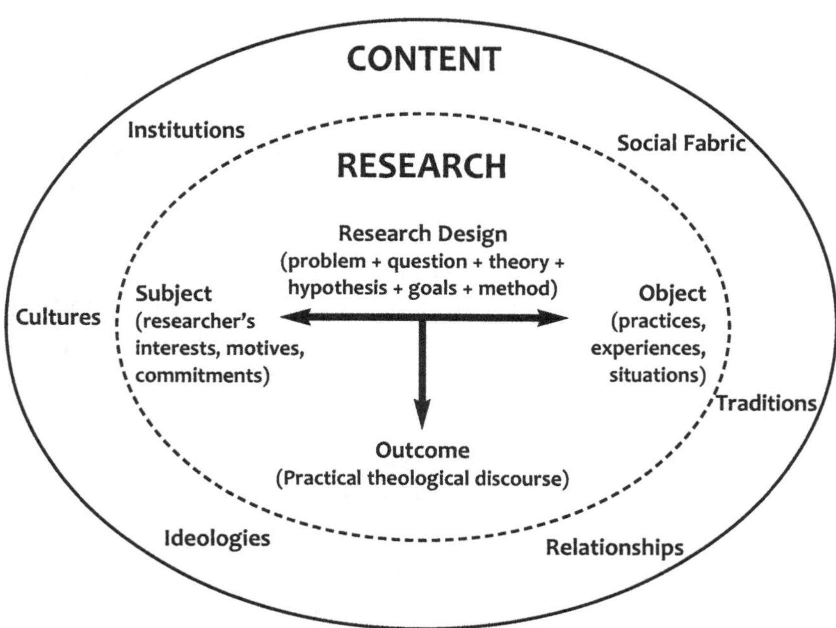

THEOLOGICAL REFLECTION ON METHODOLOGY

Our reflection so far leads to two fundamental practical theological questions about methodology: the theological status of practice and issues of normativity.

Practice as Locus Theologicus

Various authors speak of *the* practical theological method, or of "practical theology as a method." They usually refer to a three-step process that is spelled out in different ways: see-judge-act; observation (step 1), evaluation/analysis (step 2), and stimulating new practices (step 3); or, in the words of Rolf Zerfass, (old) praxis 1, practical-theological theory, and (new) praxis 2.[16]

The third step, the stimulation of new practices, is not always central because of the complex situation of practical theology between church, world, and academia. This third step is valued when the church or society is in need of strategic—pastoral—innovations (praxis 2). But the demands of academia—especially academic grants—often prompt practical theology to show its scientific character by focusing more on the description and analysis of practices (praxis 1).

Good practical theology will combine an in-depth analysis of praxis 1 and sufficient attention to praxis 2. In doing so, at least four dangers must be avoided. First, practical theology should avoid becoming simply "applied theology," whereby practices and experiences do not really influence theological understanding. Second, the study of practices may influence theoretical-theological thinking but lack concern for the integration of this renewed theory into practices.[17] Third, an approach in which practices are only analyzed sociologically, psychologically, or in any other way and not really discussed theologically can hardly be called practical theology. Fourth, research on practices that are deemed prophetic must resist the temptation of sacralizing them, and remain focused on a process of critical investigation.

If and when these pitfalls are avoided, practice may prove to be a fundamental *locus theologicus*, a source for theological thinking (see also Griffith's chapter in this volume). This requires a form of inter- or intradisciplinarity between the social sciences and theology.[18] Various theological reasons might be given to support these claims. We refer to elements within the Catholic tradition and theology; however, these elements are not restricted to Catholic approaches.

The Catholic principle of sacramentality[19] suggests that in theory everything can refer to God, especially also within daily life. This means that God's grace is not limited to the seven sacraments. All human practices and experiences are potential grounds for experiencing God. Joyful moments, liberating processes, hardships, and painful situations are all open in principle to faith journeys and theological reflection. Love and abuse, cooperation and oppression, caring and suffering: good and evil are often inextricably woven together in the fabric of human experiences, and this is where God is celebrated, called for, or denied existence. The fabric of life is the fabric of practical theology.

Another theological basis is the optimistic creation anthropology and the focus on grace within the Catholic tradition. Every human person is born with the potential of doing good. She or he is born into a sinful world and is affected by original sin, which means, among other things, that she or he may also be corrupted by sinful powers in the world, which leads to sinful actions. But the original goodness of creation, the potential and original openness of human beings to transcendence, and the practical effects of conversion and grace are crucial to Catholic anthropology. Human practices refer us to the goodness of creation and may thus also lead to discovering the Creator. Acting in the world may be "mystagogical."[20]

In the same way, the Second Vatican Council encourages us to "scrutinize the signs of the times" and to "interpret them in the light of the Gospel" (*Gaudium et spes* 4). Positive here is the attention to the world, which is to be taken seriously. However, the "interpretation in light of the Gospel" has often led to a one-sided theological-ethical critique of contemporary practices. This chapter fosters an ongoing interpretation, aiming toward an open future, where ideas and criteria may again be criticized. If truth is not considered a closed box but one of the eschatological aims of an open search,[21] practices may also challenge provisional theological interpretations and thus foster a mutual, critical, interactive process. In the course of history this has often proven to be the case, leading to important theological developments.

The Second Vatican Council (*Lumen gentium*) has also renewed the Catholic perception of the *sensus fidelium*. Even though recent teachings have insisted on its necessary accordance with the teaching of the magisterium,[22] the concept of *sensus fidelium* underlines the relevance of the sense of faith of ordinary people. Practical theologians study this sense of faith in a very broad and open way, as a flair for the ways of God in the world, not only as a source of consensus (or dissent) with the magisterium.

Other foundations are well established in the Christian tradition. The belief in a God who is always greater than our thoughts and expressions has led to different forms of apophatic theology. It may encourage theologians not to remain affixed to the past or in a closed tradition, but to continue searching for ways in which God is expressed in practice, time and again, knowing that none of these forms will ever fully disclose who God is.

Christians might, however, look especially to experiences of those who have been marginalized by the mainstream theological or social tradition. The preferential option for the poor is a principle in Catholic social thought that not only influences concrete practices but is also relevant in guiding the practical theological research.

Christians also believe that though they may hear the voice of the Holy Spirit, they "do not know where it comes from or where it goes" (John 3:8). In the process of developing theology in a mutual critical exchange with the analysis of practices, practical theologians believe in the guidance of the Spirit; they also believe that it may prompt them to take seemingly desert roads (Acts 8:26).

Some authors argue that practical theology is essentially concerned with the practices of God in human contexts. There is a risk here of short-circuiting practical theology as a scientific endeavor. Strictly speaking, a "practice of God" or an "action of God" can only be acknowledged within a human experience or practice. "Practices of God" is an analogical phrase. Practical theology is about human practices inasmuch as these allow or lead to assertions about God or godly matters. Only such human practices can be observed, analyzed, and reflected on within a practical theological approach, and they then require a methodical treatment.

Issues of Normativity

The second question centers on issues of normativity.[23] In practical theology, the study of practices and the normative reflection are clearly interrelated.[24] The question is how this is done, and whether theology and practices are both validated in their own right.

There is a substantial consensus that practical theology aims at some form of correlation between praxis and theory/tradition. The correlation method introduced by Paul Tillich,[25] in which existential questions drawn from human experience are correlated with theological answers offered by the Christian tradition, is well known. David Tracy has criticized Tillich's unidirectional method and introduced a mutually correlative and critical model that brings experience into a conversation with the Christian tradition and other sources of knowledge.[26] Don Browning elaborated this model for practical theology.[27] In Richard Osmer's four-step scheme, "mutually critical correlation" takes place during the interpretative and normative tasks (subsequent to the descriptive-empirical task and preceding the pragmatic task).[28]

Although mutually critical correlation is widely accepted in practical theology, some critiques have called into question the search for continuity between experiences and theological thinking.[29] Neo-orthodox thinkers such as John Milbank have criticized theology's engagement with the social sciences and argued for refocusing on Tradition in its radical orthodoxy.[30] This position counters the basic assumptions of practical theology, where elaborating the relationship between the social sciences, the contemporary world, and theology is the core element of the discipline. This critique tends to overlook the practical foundation of Tradition, the demands of hermeneutical soundness, and the ongoing need for relevance. However, "correlational strategies" can indeed be questioned in certain ways. While they might tend to focus on the continuity between the secular world and dimensions of Christian faith, postmodern thinkers will underline aspects of discontinuity and difference. They will thus criticize forms of dominance or one-sided approaches that do not attend to the victims of society.

On the methodological level, one of the remaining problems concerning the mutually critical correlation is the way to make it truly correlational. Many researches end up being either mostly inductive or mostly deductive. An inductive method starts with practice, with concrete examples, with case studies, or with empirical data; a deductive method will emphasize and apply theoretical/theological principles to practice. Most practical theologies claim to be inductive, as the inductive method fits well into the praxis-theory-praxis scheme, or at least into the first half of it. But their theological interpretations often have a deductive bent, when Scripture or church doctrine is referred to as given truths or norms to which practices are confronted.

In a similar way, methods of inquiry adopt either a (more inductive) theory-developing setup or a (more deductive) theory-testing setup.[31] Quantitative methods are used more as theory testing and tend to have a more deductive character. In other approaches, a combination of deduction and induction takes place, for example, when interviews are analyzed with the help of sensitizing concepts derived from the literature. Furthermore, when using the qualitative method of content analysis for large amounts of text, such as diaries or books, a more inductive or a more deductive approach are both possible, depending on how the categories for analysis are developed (from the text itself or from existing theories).[32]

The challenge is to honor the experiences and practices of people on the one hand, and the theological traditions on the other hand. How can one avoid the manipulation of either practices or theories in order to come up with a harmonious theory or solution to an issue? An inductive approach seems to focus on the practices and experiences of people, but it might actually interpret them in a way that does not take them seriously, by linking them too easily with general theological concepts. Conversely, theological traditions may receive insufficient attention in an inductive approach; one should avoid the risk of letting the social sciences colonialize theology.[33]

In addition to inductive or deductive approaches, some authors evoke an *abductive* way of bringing theory and praxis into relation with each other.[34] The abductive approach is used to integrate theory and praxis in some forms of religious education[35] or pastoral care,[36] but it may also enrich our reflection on practical theology methodology. Instead of emphasizing "what is" (induction) or "what should be" (deduction), theological reflection as abduction centers on "what could be." Abductive reflection departs from existing frameworks of interpretation and allows these to interact both with new knowledge from practice/experience and with alternative interpretations, so that what was previously present but hidden in the practices/experiences comes to light, revealing in fact new dimensions. Abductive reasoning opens up a hermeneutical scope of multiple interpretations in which religious traditions can also provide frameworks for interpretation, ones that could be meaningful for the understanding of actual experiences. Central to this way of doing research are the multiple relations (multicorrelation)[37] and the self-awareness/self-critique of too simplistic question-answer schedules and of contextual factors that influence the interpretation.

Neither practices nor theories/traditions should be considered plainly normative. Conversion—change of mind, of heart, of practice, of vision, in such a way that the subject is healed—is what the God experience is about. It implies continuity with the past as well as discontinuity toward a new future. In practical theological research, both practices and theories/traditions are critically challenged to evolve. As Christian life itself, the research process is centered on the redemptive transformation of the subject and of his or her world. The church as a whole is *semper reformanda* and *semper purificanda* (see, for example, *Lumen gentium* 8).

FIVE BASIC PRINCIPLES

We conclude this chapter with five basic principles for practical theological methodology.

1. Attention to practice or experience is at the heart of practical theology and demands a methodical study of that practice or experience, whatever approach or method is chosen to realize this study.
2. Any practical theological study has to deal with two areas of meaning: one inherent to the practice or experience being examined, and one invoked by the researcher. Practical theological methodology is extensively determined by the way in which these two areas are made to interact.
3. The methodology of any practical theological endeavor should be closely related to the goals of the research and its key theological question. It should also be consistent with its theological framework and perspectives.
4. To paraphrase Marshall McLuhan: *the method is the message*. Practical theological methods are not neutral: they are full of theological assumptions and convictions; they serve specific goals and interests. Any methodology has to be aware of these factors, and to be critical about them.

5. Practice is not only the starting point of practical theology: it is also its final destination. Practice must benefit from a practical theological research, in terms of better knowledge and/or in terms of improved practice.

Practical theological methods are not denominational. Like other Christians, Catholic practical theologians have very good reasons to stay close to practices and experiences themselves, to take them as a starting point for their theology. The Catholic tradition has developed from an ongoing interaction between new experiences/practices and existing theories/beliefs, both challenging each other. To the extent that Catholics have a perspective on Tradition and truth that is open to change and to the complex interaction between continuity and discontinuity (see the chapter by Terrence W. Tilley), they will be able to support various Catholic practical theologies.

Notes

1. Stephen Pattison and James Woodward, "An Introduction to Pastoral and Practical Theology," in *The Blackwell Reader in Pastoral and Practical Theology*, ed. Stephen Pattison and James Woodward (Oxford, UK: Blackwell, 2000), 1–22.

2. Bonnie J. Miller-McLemore, "Introduction: The Contributions of Practical Theology," in *The Wiley-Blackwell Companion to Practical Theology*, ed. Bonnie J. Miller-McLemore (Oxford, UK: Wiley-Blackwell, 2012), 4–14.

3. However, some researchers interpret their method of doing research as a form of pastoral practice. See, for example, Mary Clark Moschella, *Ethnography as a Pastoral Practice: An Introduction* (Cleveland, OH: The Pilgrim Press, 2008).

4. For a similar image, see Corja Menken-Bekius and Henk Van der Meulen, *Reflecteren kun je leren* (Kampen, Germany: Kok, 2007).

5. Stephanie Klein, *Theologie und Empirische Biographieforschung* (Stuttgart, Germany: Kohlhammer, 1994).

6. For an overview of various models of practical theological reflection, see Elaine L. Graham, Heather Walton, and Frances Ward, *Theological Reflection: Methods* (London, UK: SCM Press, 2005).

7. Stefan Gärtner, "Pastoraltheologie? Praktische Theologie!" in *Katholische Theologie Studieren*, ed. Andreas Leinhäupl-Wilke and Magnus Striet (Münster, Germany: LIT Verlag, 2000), 320–36.

8. See Elaine L. Graham, *Transforming Practice: Pastoral Theology in an Age of Uncertainty* (Eugene, OR: Wipf & Stock, 2002; 1st ed.: London, UK: Mowbray, 1996).

9. Accessed August 12, 2013, http://www.heythrop.ac.uk/research/heythrop-institute-religion-and-society/arcs-project.html.

10. Frederick J. Wertz, "Phenomenological Research Methods for Counseling Psychology," *Journal of Counseling Psychology* 52 (2005): 167–77, at 175.

11. Étienne Grieu, *Nés de Dieu* (Paris, France: Cerf, 2003).

12. Elaine L. Graham and Anna Rowlands, eds., *Pathways to the Public Square*, International Practical Theology 1 (Münster, Germany: LIT Verlag, 2003).

13. Johannes A. van der Ven, *Entwurf einer Empirischen Theologie* (Kampen, Germany: Kok, 1990).

14. Hans-Gunter Heimbrock, "Reconstructing Lived Religion," in *Religion: Immediate Experience and the Mediacy of Research*, ed. Hans-Gunter Heimbrock and Christopher P. Scholtz (Göttingen, Germany: Vandenhoeck & Ruprecht, 2007), 133–57.

15. Marcel Viau, "Doing Practical Theology in an Age of Pluralism," in *Pathways to the Public Square*, ed. Elaine L. Graham and Anna Rowlands (Münster, Germany: LIT Verlag, 2006), 11–29; Marcel Viau, *Practical Theology* (Leiden, Netherlands: Brill, 1999). See also R. Ruard Ganzevoort, "The Social Construction of Revelation," *International Journal of Practical Theology* 8 (2006): 1–14.

16. Rolf Zerfaß, "Praktische Theologie als Handlungswissenschaft," in *Praktische Theologie heute*, ed. Ferdinand Klostermann and Rolf Zerfaß (Munich, Germany: Kaiser, 1974), 164–77.

17. Bonnie J. Miller-McLemore, "The 'Clerical Paradigm': A Fallacy of Misplaced Correctness?" *International Journal of Practical Theology* 11, no. 2 (2007): 19–38, at 28.

18. Johannes A. van der Ven, "Perspektiven der Praktischen Theologie," *ET-Bulletin* 2, no. 1 (1991): 64–94.

19. Susan A. Ross, *Extravagant Affections* (New York: Continuum, 1998), 34–42.

20. Henk Meeuws, *Diaconie* (Gorinchem, Netherlands: Narratio, 2011), 360–66.

21. See Annemie Dillen and Didier Pollefeyt, "Catechesis Inside Out," *The Person and the Challenges* 1 (2011): 151–77.

22. Benedict XVI, "Speech to the International Theological Commission," December 7, 2012.

23. See also Hans-Georg Ziebertz, "Normativity and Empirical Research in Practical Theology," *Journal for Empirical Theology* 15 (2002): 5–18; Johannes A. van der Ven and Michael Schrerer-Rath, eds., *Normativity and Empirical Research in Theology* (Leiden, Netherlands: Brill, 2004).

24. Johannes A. van der Ven, "An Empirical or a Normative Approach to Practical-Theological Research?" in *Normativity and Empirical Research in Theology*, ed. Johannes A. van der Ven and Michael Schrerer-Rath (Leiden, Netherlands: Brill, 2004), 101–35.

25. Paul Tillich, *Systematic Theology*, vol. 1 (London, UK: SCM Press, 1951). For the evolution of this position, see, for example, Edward Schillebeeckx, "Correlation Between Human Question and Christian Answer," in *The Understanding of Faith*, ed. Edward Schillebeeckx (London, UK: Sheed & Ward, 1974), 78–101.

26. David Tracy, *Blessed Rage for Order* (New York: Seabury Press, 1975); David Tracy, "The Foundations of Practical Theology," in *Practical Theology: The Emerging Field in Theology, Church, and World*, ed. Don S. Browning (San Francisco, CA: Harper & Row, 1983), 61–83.

27. Don S. Browning, *A Fundamental Practical Theology: Descriptive and Strategic Proposals* (Minneapolis, MN: Fortress Press, 1991). On correlation, see also Martina Blasberg-Kuhnke, "Theologie studieren als Praxis," *International Journal of Practical Theology* 3 (1999): 52–68.

28. Richard R. Osmer, *Practical Theology: An Introduction* (Grand Rapids, MI: William B. Eerdmans Publishing Company, 2008), 4.

29. Lieven Boeve, *God Interrupts History* (New York: Continuum, 2007).

30. John Milbank, *Theology and Social Theory: Beyond Secular Reason* (London, UK: Wiley-Blackwell, 2006).

31. See Frans Jozef Servaas Wijsen, "The Practical-Theological Spiral," in *The Pastoral Circle Revisited: A Critical Quest for Truth and Transformation*, ed. Frans Jozef Servaas Wijsen, Peter Henriot, SJ, and Rodrigo Mejía (Maryknoll, NY: Orbis Books, 2005), 108–26, 114.

32. Stephanie Klein, "Methodische Zugänge zur sozialen Wirklichkeit," in *Handbuch praktischer Theologie*, vol. 1, ed. Herbert Haslinger (Mainz, Germany: Grundlegungen, 1999), 248–59.

33. Stefan Gärtner, "Praktische Theologie als Pastoraltheologie?" *International Journal of Practical Theology* 13 (1997): 1–21, at 5.

34. Charles S. Peirce, "How to Make Our Ideas Clear," in *The Nature of Truth*, ed. Michael P. Lynch (Cambridge, MA: MIT Press, 2001), 193–209.

35. C. A. M. Hermans, "Abductive Hermeneutics," in *Hermeneutics and Religious Education*, ed. Herman Lombaerts and Didier Pollefeyt (Leuven, Belgium: Peeters, 2004), 95–120.

36. R. Ruard Ganzevoort and Jan Visser, *Zorg voor het verhaal* (Zoetermeer, Netherlands: Meinema, 2007), 213–16.

37. Didier Pollefeyt, "The Difference of Alterity," in *Responsibility, God and Society*, ed. Johan De Tavernier (Leuven, Belgium: Peeters, 2008), 305–30.

CHAPTER 16

CATHOLIC VOICES AND VISIONS IN PRACTICAL THEOLOGY

Contributions and Future Directions

CLAIRE E. WOLFTEICH

As noted in the introduction, this book centers on dual aims: to make a substantial Catholic contribution to scholarship in practical theology and to explore the import of practical theology for Catholic theology and theological education. Because practical theology in Catholic contexts is "both concentrated in a discipline of 'practical theology' and simultaneously diffused throughout the theological disciplines" (Cahalan and Froehle), we need to cast a wide net that encompasses philosophical, systematic, and moral theologians. Here one finds important work on practice. Some of this scholarship is known in practical theological circles; much of it is not.

> The project of "Catholic practical theology" should be understood as a dialogical contribution to a larger discourse.

While practical theology as a discipline has been shaped strongly by Protestant scholars, it is clear that practical theology actually does have a long pedigree and deep roots in Catholic tradition as well. Continuing to surface the distinctive forms of Catholic practical theology is an important task. So, too, one can identify the increasingly significant influence of Catholic scholars on the discipline of practical theology and the mutual exchange of scholars across traditions (see, for example, the influence of David Tracy on Don S. Browning, James W. McLendon on Terrence W. Tilley). Consolidating and advancing Catholic work in practical theology cannot be done in a vacuum but rather in lively engagement with a wide range of scholarship. Thus, the project of "Catholic practical theology" should be understood as a dialogical contribution to a larger discourse. Pluralism does not eliminate the import of tradition-specific study. Rather, attention to the particularities of traditions becomes the ground for the dialogue. Particularity is situated within the fluid and hybrid identities of contemporary cultures; the complexity of identity is part of what we study.

Religious and cultural practice is rightly a critical focus of theological study, research, and teaching. That is a clear assumption of practical theology and a central argument of this book. In exploring Catholic contributions, note an important observation: while the turn to practice reflects a broad contemporary move across fields of scholarship—seen, for example, in moral philosophy, cultural theory, and sociology—Catholic theologians advance significant *theological* arguments for the import of practice. These arguments have deep roots in the Catholic tradition and imagination, including convictions about revelation, sacramentality, incarnation, theological anthropology, grace, the *sensus fidelium*, and the nature of tradition itself. Here is a significant point of contribution to the larger discipline of practical theology and a point for critical engagement across traditions.

Moreover, practical theology must be named as part of the lived faith of the community, not limited to academic scholarship but also a dimension of everyday practice, parish life, popular religion, lay movements, struggles for justice, and the organic practices of family life, spiritual direction, community organizing, pastoral ministry. Ideally, these two forms of practical theology—in the academy and as exercised in everyday faith life—mutually inform and correct each other. We have in the rich traditions of Catholic social teaching and social action important examples of practical theology that must be named and studied. In the struggles of African American, Asian, and Latino/a Catholics for empowerment and agency within church and society, there is living practical theology. This too must be analyzed and mined for practical wisdom. Catholic theologies of labor and the "domestic church" clearly assert that practices of work and family life deserve theological attention. As sites of humanization and dehumanization, these spheres of everyday lay life are key areas for practical theology. The practical theology that takes place "on the ground" can be guided by scholarship and good teaching, even as academic study and theological education must not remain distant from the concerns, questions, and wisdom of laity.

PRACTICAL THEOLOGY IN CATHOLIC CONTEXTS OF THEOLOGICAL EDUCATION

Authors in this volume advance a strong theological rationale for practical theology within Catholic theology and theological education. Practical theology may not be perceived as a "traditional" part of the Catholic curriculum—but this book argues persuasively that practical theology is actually essential to *traditio*, the passing on of a tradition. *Invitation to Practical Theology* aims to provide a much-needed resource in practical theology that is grounded in Catholic theology and attentive to issues of practice in Catholic contexts. Such resources are needed in pastoral formation programs, which already work with practical theological methods and texts. This kind of resource is also needed more broadly for theology and ethics courses. Tilley understands practice as the "ground out of which theory grows" and argues thus that "practical theology can be construed as the context out of which systematic theology arises" (see ch. 5). At the same time, several authors note the power of systematic theology within the structures of Catholic theology (see Cahalan and Froehle, Goizueta). What are the implications for Catholic theology and theological education? The vitality and continued development of practical theology requires institutional support, pedagogical shifts, and sustained collaboration among scholars in systematic, moral, and practical theologies. For example, the typical separation between practical theology (located primarily in centers of pastoral formation) and systematic theology (located in robust departments of theology) risks depriving Catholic theology of sustained attention to pastoral ministry and parish life and risks depriving pastoral theology of essential dialogue partners in systematic theology and theological ethics. Moreover, the separation tends to reduce practical theology to pastoral formation—whereas the scope of practical theology actually includes a much broader study of religious and cultural practice. Some theological schools and research institutions already seek to bridge these gaps. This dialogue should be encouraged along with greater scholarly collaboration across disciplines and institutions. It also is vital to recognize practical theology as an academic discipline with significant scholarly resources for Catholic theology at this time.

This book ought to be the beginning, rather than the end, of conversation. How can we develop "practical theological agency" (Copeland) through theological education, parish life, and community action? What new courses and adult education programs might be imagined? How can we integrate practical theological pedagogies (Groome) into existing courses and programs? How are narratives, art, ritual, contextual learning, and spiritual practice understood as part of the pedagogical process? One can imagine fruitful possibilities for interdisciplinary ventures to extend this work in teaching and research—for example, team teaching and research design that bring together systematic theologians, practical theologians, moral theologians, and social scientists around concrete issues of practice. This requires institutional collaboration and greater funding for practical theological research. Doctoral-level training in practical theology in Catholic contexts also is hugely underdeveloped, certainly in comparison with PhD programs in practical theology in ecumenical schools of theology such as Vanderbilt, Emory, or Boston University. How will we adequately form the next generation of theological educators and pastoral leaders without more opportunities for doctoral-level training in practical theology?

A recent conference of the International Academy of Practical Theology (2013) included a meeting of a working group on Catholic Approaches in Practical Theology. The room was full—with Canadian, American, German, Dutch, Spanish, Indian, and Croatian Catholic theologians around the table. The energy was high: this is a conversation and a research area that is ripe for further development. It was clear at the meeting that those around the table share many points of commonality (e.g., the theological arguments for a turn to practice) and also work across some significant differences as well (university contexts, seminary contexts, more religious contexts, more secular contexts, strict use of empirical methods, more hermeneutical and other approaches). This is not a monolithic conversation, by any means. It is one that stands to contribute high-level scholarship for theology. Indeed, a volume that consolidates, analyzes, and advances Catholic practical theology research on an international level is another important project for the future.

In the remainder of this chapter, I highlight several specific points that are significant regarding future directions and further contributions of Catholic scholarship in practical theology. First, I note the import of both empirical and aesthetic-poetic approaches, and then I give particular attention to some critical aspects of the dialogue between spirituality studies and practical theology.

EMPIRICAL METHODS IN THEOLOGICAL RESEARCH

Despite attention to practice and culture, one does not see among American Catholic theologians the level of empirical theological research that has become prominent in recent decades within the international field of practical theology, particularly among English, Dutch, and German practical theologians (as described by Dillen and Mager). Lynn Bridgers notes that "a school of empirical studies has emerged as a critical aspect of practical theology in Catholic contexts outside the United States."[1] Yet the same is not the case among American Catholic theologians. This gap should be considered in the further development of Catholic approaches in practical theology. Will empirical methods gain more traction as a dimension of American Catholic theology and ethics? Will more attention to practical theology stimulate that development? Catholic ethicist Emily Reimer-Barry, who uses ethnographic methods in studying HIV-positive women, writes: "Catholic magisterial teachings tend to be suspicious of the use of sociological methods in theological research."[2] She calls ethnography, which can bring marginalized voices into the theological conversation, an important but "underutilized" method. So, too, sociologist Robert Orsi, well known for his studies of popular Catholic devotions, calls ethnography an essential part of religious scholarship:

> For a scholar of religion to go among living people practicing the idioms of their religions in the ordinary and extraordinary circumstances of their days is more than one methodological choice among others in the study of religion. To be present in disciplined attentiveness in all the places where human beings come face to face with their gods and with each other...I now believe is the necessary condition for developing knowledge about religion.[3]

American Catholic work in practical theology would be enhanced by fuller engagement with a wide range of empirical theological methods. The relevance of empirical research to practical theology has been convincingly demonstrated by, for example, Dutch Catholic scholar Johannes van der Ven, one of the foremost practical theologians of recent decades. In describing his empirical theological method, van der Ven expressly notes that it is one among several relevant practical theological methods that include historical, systematic, hermeneutical, ideology-critical, and linguistic approaches. Still, he argues for the importance of "enriching the methodological apparatus...into the direction of empirical methodology" in order to accomplish the task of practical theology, which he identifies as "reflecting on the people's praxis from the viewpoint of God's revelatory praxis in a way that is as scientific as possible."[4] Catholic practical theology could well enrich the methodological apparatus—critically engaging with empirically oriented scholarship in practical theology, such as the work of Johannes van der Ven, Chris Hermans, Leslie Francis, Richard Osmer, Mary Elizabeth Moore, Pete Ward, Chris Scharen, Mary Clark Moschella, Mary McClintock Fulkerson, Tom Beaudoin, and Jeff Astley.[5] As Dillen and Mager make clear, the normative dimensions of methodology must always be critically addressed. One of the challenges, moreover, will be to keep in fruitful tension the various approaches in practical theology, such that an empirical approach does not come to dominate the discourse at the expense of other forms of theological inquiry.

IMPORTANCE OF AESTHETICS AND POETICS

For Tracy, listening to the "hints and guesses" all around us—especially in art and poetry—is a primary task of practical theology. Goizueta makes key conceptual arguments about the aesthetic nature of praxis, finding in *flor y canto* an important corrective to instrumentalist understandings of praxis.[6] So too, aesthetic practice emerges as a key dimension of African American and Latino/a pastoral action and agency (Copeland; Cervantes, Deck, and Johnson-Mondragón). Here is a place for Catholic contribution to and dialogue with the larger field of practical theology, in which social scientific approaches have tended to eclipse nascent movements toward aesthetics and poetics.

Building on prior Catholic work—such as Norbert Mette's call for "the conceptual development of a practical theological theory of action which explicitly includes the aesthetic dimension"[7] and Terry Veling's exploration of practical theology as a mystical-prophetic poetic dwelling in the world[8]—Catholic theology and imagination can advance the place of aesthetics and poetics in practical theology. There would be fruitful intersection here with efforts to rethink the relationship between *phronesis* and *poiesis*—seen, for example, in Heather Walton's work in poetics and practical theology.[9] Similarly, Catholic theologies (e.g., Latino/a, African American, and feminist theologies) could contribute to efforts to weave a "poetics of resistance" into pastoral theology.[10] The study of aesthetics is important for generating theological theories of action that reflect the lived experience of diverse cultural communities, as Goizueta shows. So also Gerard Hall notes the importance of poetry and art in the emergence of practical theology in the context of Australia and Oceania.[11] In short, Catholic scholarship lends more weight to the significance of aesthetics and poetics in practical theology. There are natural connections too between mysticism, aesthetics, and poetry—for example, in practices of "unsaying"[12] (Michel de Certeau), in the mystics' turn to poetry to name the "unlanguageable."[13] These mystical-poetic-aesthetic trajectories are underdeveloped in the wider discourse of practical theology, though also areas of building energy.

ADVANCING THE CONVERSATION BETWEEN SPIRITUALITY AND PRACTICAL THEOLOGY

It is clear from this volume that spirituality is integral to Catholic visions of practical theology. The argument for practical theological attention to spiritual traditions, texts, and practices is not solely a Catholic argument, by any means, but it is one that emerges across chapters and disciplinary orientations, and has much to contribute to practical theology more broadly. From Tracy's mystical-aesthetic corrective of practical theology's emphasis on prophetic ethics, to Ruffing's discussion of spiritual direction as practical theology, to Griffith's analysis of spiritual practice, to Bevans's turn to the mystic Mechtilde in his argument for mission as trinitarian practice, spirituality is integral to Catholic approaches in practical theology. As Cahalan and Froehle note, spirituality has long been a central site for Catholic forms of practical theology.

Catholic pastoral action and "practical theological agency" are rooted in spirituality. Copeland freely combines research, liturgical life, and spiritual gifts in the same sentence as she describes the practical theological agency of black Catholics. Cervantes, Deck, and Johnson-Mondragón note that at the heart of the Prophets of Hope model for *pastoral juvenil hispana*, developed by Instituto Fe y Vida, is "a biblically based, christocentric spirituality that animates and guides all pastoral and formative actions." Hinze describes the role of prayer in faith-based community organizing in the Bronx. Scholarship should reflect the integral place of spirituality in Catholic practice and theology.

In previous publications,[14] I have explored significant points of intersection between spirituality studies and practical theology. I also have argued that practical theology—so shaped by dialogue with the social sciences, ethics, and hermeneutic philosophy—needs a similarly deep engagement with spiritual traditions, texts, and practices. Practical theology should be at the forefront of reintegrating or remembering spirituality and theology, still divided in many ways since the unfortunate splitting of spiritual and Scholastic theology in the Middle Ages. This must be a central task of practical theology—as Jon Sobrino wrote, "spirituality is not merely a dimension of theology, it is an integral dimension of the whole of theology."[15] While some in practical theology see any mention of spirituality as diminishing the properly scientific character of practical theology as an academic discipline, my perspective mirrors that of Gustavo Gutiérrez in arguing: "All authentic theology is spiritual theology. This fact does not weaken the rigorously scientific character of theology; it does, however, properly situate it."[16] By emphasizing the relevance of spiritual and mystical theologies to practical theology more broadly, I am not arguing for a subdiscipline of practical theology but for an animated and transforming understanding of the *theological* character of practical theology.

I would note three clarifying points. First, increased attention to spirituality does not mean an uncritical embrace of spiritual traditions. For example, it is complex and even deeply problematic to undertake the retrieval and reconstruction of mystical theologies, which, some have argued, are caught in a "patriarchal imaginary."[17] Any conceptualization of practical theology as "mystical theology" needs to recover the liberative, socially transformative potential of mystical experience and practice while carefully studying and deconstructing mysticism's oppressive social construction (as analyzed, for example, in Grace Janzten's work on gender, power, and mysticism).[18] This is a significant practical theological task and research focus with important implications for contemporary theology and lived faith. Practical theologians would bring all the critical and constructive resources of the academy to the task.

Second, the mystical dimension of practical theology complements or even intensifies—rather than subverts—the public, prophetic orientation of practical theology (as Tracy also argues). The understanding of spirituality and, more specifically, of mysticism, advanced here is not a privatistic spirituality divorced from social concern. Scholars such as Mark McIntosh, Janet K. Ruffing, and Aristotle Papanikolau have made a strong case that mystical theology can contribute to the shaping of public bodies of practice, to ecclesial-social-cultural-political transformation.[19] To envision practical theology as mystical theology, then, is not to set back practical theology's important movement toward public theology. Practical theology rightly focuses attention on, for example, poverty, globalization, religious diversity and conflict, HIV-AIDS, secularization, urban life (all themes of recent conferences of the International Academy of Practical Theology).[20] Mystical practical theologies would be informed by "political mysticism"—what Johann Baptist Metz described as "a mysticism of open or opened eyes." This is a "mysticism that especially makes visible all invisible or inconvenient suffering...pays attention to it and takes responsibility for it, for the sake of a God who is friend to human beings."[21]

Similarly, I have argued that if mystical theology is not to serve as a rationale for otherworldly disengagement or as an elitist mechanism of silencing and hierarchizing spiritual experience and practice, then it must be understood in relationship to everyday life of the laity. Overemphasis on practices of contemplation and extraordinary mystical experience can serve to distance women, for example, from the quotidian practices that make up so much of our spiritual landscapes—the spiritual-bodily knowing that emerges from practices of caring for and learning from children; from daily labor in domestic or market spheres; from ordinary community and ecclesial participation.[22] As Rubio articulates well, family practices are indeed an important context for organic practical theology and a worthy focus of practical theological research. To highlight the salience of the quotidian as site for religious experience and theology, we can turn both to church teaching (e.g., on labor, family, and lay holiness) and to sociological studies of "lived religion," such as Nancy Ammerman's work on religion in everyday life.[23] I would resist any attempt to set up "mystical practical theologies" in a way that would further distance women (or men) from these theological and spiritual loci—resonating here with Elaine Graham's affirmation of "the kitchen table" as a legitimate site for practical theologizing.[24] Edward Schillebeeckx described mysticism as "an intense form of the experience of God...essentially the life of faith, and therefore not a separate sector in Christian life to which only a few, or individuals are called."[25] Similarly, Karl Rahner wrote: "In the days ahead, you will either be a mystic (one who has experienced God for real) or nothing at all."[26] In many ways, however, we still need to work at a constructive mystical theology of everyday life, particularly one attentive to issues of gender, race, and ethnicity. This is an excellent task ahead for practical theology.

Finally, mystical theology opens up interesting pathways for a cutting edge of practical theology–interfaith approaches and critical engagement with secular cultures. Spirituality scholarship is greatly expanding the conversation—with major publications on spirituality across traditions, including Christian, Jewish, Islamic mysticism, and research on forms of "secular spirituality." This is work that practical theology needs to engage. Mystical understandings of practical theology are not rendered obsolete by pluralism—in fact, practical theologians attentive to mysticism test the capaciousness of public theology to critically engage these most intensely religious witnesses and visions. Practical theological research on spirituality also is highly salient in secularizing contexts, where new forms of "spirituality" may thrive amid a decline in institutional religion, raising important questions for theology. Practical theology has much to gain through dialogue with spiritual/mystical traditions and practices—and here Catholics (alongside Orthodox Christians and many others) have much to contribute.

GOING FORWARD

Catholic approaches in practical theology are rich and multivalent. We have significant resources on which to draw and also much work ahead. The time is ripe for a more concerted focus on practical theology as a rigorous field of research that bridges academy, church, and culture. It is important to build those disciplinary bridges so as to discover and advance the significant work being done among diverse kinds of scholars. So too, we need to claim institutional space for practical theology in Catholic contexts of theological education. Yet the most compelling reason for opening this conversation, in my view, is the need to address pressing practical questions of how we live our faith in the current ecclesial and cultural situation. These questions drive and animate scholarship, demanding renewed study of practice and faithful visions for transformed communities.

Notes

1. Lynn Bridgers, "Roman Catholicism," in *The Wiley-Blackwell Companion to Practical Theology*, ed. Bonnie J. Miller-McLemore (Oxford, UK: Wiley-Blackwell, 2012), 574.

2. Emily Reimer-Barry, "The Listening Church: How Ethnography Can Transform Catholic Ethics," in *Ethnography as Theology and Ethics*, ed. Christian Scharen and Aana Marie Vigen (London, UK: Continuum, 2011), 98.

3. Robert Orsi, "Doing Religious Studies With Your Whole Body," *Practical Matters* 2 (Spring 2013): 1–6.

4. Johannes A. van der Ven, "An Empirical Approach in Practical Theology," in *Practical Theology—International Perspectives* (Frankfurt am Main, Germany: Peter Lang), 328, 323.

5. See, for example, Jeff Astley and Leslie Francis, eds., *Exploring Ordinary Theology: Everyday Christian Believing and the Church* (Farnham, UK: Ashgate, 2013); Mary McClintock Fulkerson, *Places of Redemption: Theology for a Worldly Church* (New York: Oxford University Press, 2007); Mary Clark Moschella, *Ethnography as a Pastoral Practice: An Introduction* (Cleveland, OH: The Pilgrim Press, 2008); Johannes A. van der Ven, *Practical Theology: An Empirical Approach* (Leuven, Belgium: Peeters, 1998); Pete Ward, ed., *Perspectives on Ecclesiology and Ethnography* (Grand Rapids, MI: William B. Eerdmans Publishing Company, 2012).

6. See also Roberto S. Goizueta, *Caminemos Con Jesús: Toward a Hispanic/Latino Theology of Accompaniment* (Maryknoll, NY: Orbis Books 1995).

7. Norbert Mette, "Practical Theology: Theory of Aesthetics or Theory of Action?" in *Creativity, Imagination, and Criticism: The Expressive Dimension in Practical Theology*, ed. Paul Ballard and

Pamela D. Couture (Cardiff, UK: Cardiff Academic Press, 2001), 61. See also discussion in Robert Mager, "Action Theories," in *The Wiley-Blackwell Companion to Practical Theology*, ed. Bonnie J. Miller-McLemore (Oxford, UK: Wiley-Blackwell, 2012).

8. Terry A. Veling, *Practical Theology: On Earth As It Is In Heaven* (Maryknoll, NY: Orbis Books, 2005), 210.

9. Heather Walton, "Practical Theology and Poetics," in *The Wiley-Blackwell Companion to Practical Theology*, ed. Bonnie J. Miller-McLemore (Oxford, UK: Wiley-Blackwell, 2012), 173–82.

10. Bonnie J. Miller-McLemore, "The Subject and Practice of Pastoral Theology as a Practical Theological Discipline: Pushing Past the Nagging Identity Crisis to the Poetics of Resistance," in *Liberating Faith Practices: Feminist Practical Theologies in Context*, ed. Denise M. Ackerman and Riet Bons-Storm (Leuven, Belgium: Peeters, 1998), 175–98. Note also Rebecca S. Chopp's comments: "Feminist theology includes poetic revisioning, aesthetic production, and imaginative construction." Rebecca S. Chopp, *Saving Work: Feminist Practices of Theological Education* (Louisville, KY: Westminster John Knox Press, 1995), 109.

11. Gerard V. Hall, "Australia and Oceania," in *The Wiley-Blackwell Companion to Practical Theology*, ed. Bonnie J. Miller-McLemore (Oxford, UK: Wiley-Blackwell, 2012), 548.

12. Michel de Certeau, "Mystic Speech," in *The Certeau Reader*, ed. Graham Ward (Oxford, UK: Blackwell, 2000), 188–206.

13. Mark Burrows, "'Raiding the Inarticulate': Mysticism, Poetics, and the Unlanguageable," in *Minding the Spirit: The Study of Christian Spirituality*, ed. Elizabeth Dreyer and Mark Burrows (Baltimore, MD: Johns Hopkins University Press, 2004), 341–61.

14. See Claire E. Wolfteich, "'Practices of Unsaying': Michel de Certeau, Spirituality Studies, and Practical Theology," *Spiritus: A Journal of Christian Spirituality* 12 (2012): 161–71; Claire E. Wolfteich, "Spirituality," in *The Blackwell Companion to Practical Theology*, ed. Bonnie J. Miller McLemore (Oxford, UK: Wiley-Blackwell, 2012), 328–36; Claire E. Wolfteich, "Animating Questions: Spirituality and Practical Theology," *International Journal of Practical Theology* 13 (2009): 121–43. See also Claire E. Wolfteich and Jörg Schneider, "A Comparative Research

Conversation: American Catholic and German Protestant Spirituality Studies," *International Journal of Practical Theology* 17, no. 1 (August 2013): 100–30.

15. Jon Sobrino, *Spirituality of Liberation: Toward Political Holiness,* trans. Robert R. Barr (Maryknoll, NY: Orbis Books, 1988), 49. See also the Russian Orthodox Vladimir Lossky's assertion: "There is...no Christian mysticism without theology; but above all, there is no theology without mysticism....Mysticism is...the perfecting and crown of all theology...theology *par excellence."* Vladimir Lossky, *The Mystical Theology of the Eastern Church* (Crestwood, NY: St. Vladimir's Press, 1976), 9.

16. Gustavo Gutiérrez, *We Drink from Our Own Wells: The Spiritual Journey of a People* (Maryknoll, NY: Orbis Books, 1984), 37.

17. Luce Irigaray, quoted in Beverly Lanzetta, *Radical Wisdom: A Feminist Mystical Theology* (Minneapolis, MN: Fortress Press, 2005), 22.

18. Grace Jantzen, *Power, Gender and Christian Mysticism* (Cambridge, UK: Cambridge University Press, 1995).

19. See Mark A. McIntosh, *Mystical Theology: The Integrity of Spirituality and Theology* (Malden, MA: Blackwell, 1998); Janet K. Ruffing, ed., *Mysticism & Social Transformation* (Syracuse, NY: Syracuse University Press, 2001); Aristotle Papanikolaou, *The Mystical as Political: Democracy and Non-Radical Orthodoxy* (Notre Dame, IN: University of Notre Dame Press, 2012).

20. See Edward Foley, ed., *Religion, Diversity, and Conflict,* International Practical Theology 15 (Münster, Germany: LIT Verlag, 2011); Wilhelm Gräb and Lars Charbonnier, eds., *Secularization Theories, Religious Identity, and Practical Theology,* International Practical Theology 7 (Münster, Germany: LIT Verlag, 2009); Hans-Georg Ziebertz and Friedrich Schweitzer, eds., *Dreaming the Land: Theologies of Resistance and Hope,* International Practical Theology 5 (Münster, Germany: LIT Verlag, 2007); Elaine L. Graham and Anna Rowlands, eds., *Pathways to the Public Square,* International Practical Theology 1 (Münster, Germany: LIT Verlag, 2005); Pamela D. Couture and Bonnie J. Miller-McLemore, eds., *Poverty, Suffering and HIV/AIDS* (Cardiff, UK: Cardiff Academic Press, 2003).

21. Johann Baptist Metz, *A Passion for God: The Mystical-Political Dimension of Christianity* (New York: Paulist Press, 1998), 162–63.

22. On this point, see Claire E. Wolfteich, "Standing at the Gap: Reading Classics and the Practices of Everyday Life," *Spiritus: A Journal of Christian Spirituality* 10, no. 2 (2010): 250–55. See also Claire E. Wolfteich, "It's About Time: Rethinking Spirituality and the Domestic Church," in *The Household of God and Local Households*, ed. Thomas Knieps-Port le Roi, Gerard Mannion, and Peter De Mey (Leuven, Belgium: Peeters, 2012), 127–44.

23. Nancy T. Ammerman, *Sacred Stories, Spiritual Tribes: Finding Religion in Everyday Life* (Oxford, UK: Oxford University Press, 2013), and Nancy T. Ammerman, ed., *Everyday Religion: Observing Modern Religious Lives* (Oxford, UK: Oxford University Press, 2007).

24. Elaine L. Graham, "A View from a Room: Feminist Practical Theology from Academy, Kitchen or Sanctuary?" in *Liberating Faith Practices: Feminist Practical Theologies in Context*, ed. Denise M. Ackerman and Riet Bons-Storm (Leuven, Belgium: Peeters, 1998), 129–52.

25. Edward Schillebeeckx, *Church: The Human Story of God* (New York: Crossroad Publishing, 1990), 69.

26. Karl Rahner, "Mysticism of Everyday Life," in *The Practice of Faith: A Handbook of Contemporary Spirituality* (New York: Crossroad Publishing, 1986 [1983]), 84.

CONTRIBUTORS

Stephen Bevans, SVD, is the Louis J. Luzbetak Professor of Mission and Culture at Catholic Theological Union. He is past president of the American Society of Missiology and a past member of the board of directors of the Catholic Theological Society of America.

Kathleen A. Cahalan is Professor of Theology at St. John's School of Theology in Collegeville, Minnesota, and Project Director of the Collegeville Institute Seminars. She is a past president of the Association of Practical Theology, a member of the International Association of Practical Theology, and a board member of the Louisville Institute.

Carmen María Cervantes is the Executive Director of the Instituto Fe y Vida (Institute for Faith and Life), the mission of which is to empower young Hispanics for leadership in church and society. Dr. Cervantes also is the cofounder and past president of the National Catholic Council for Hispanic Ministry and the National Organization of Catechesis for Hispanics.

M. Shawn Copeland is Professor of Systematic Theology at Boston College. She is a former president of the Catholic Theological Society of America and former convenor of the Black Catholic Theological Symposium.

Allan Figueroa Deck, SJ, holds the Casassa Chair of Social Values in the Theological Studies Department of Loyola Marymount

University. He is the past executive director of the National Catholic Council for Hispanic Ministry (NCCHM) and was the first executive director of the Secretariat of Cultural Diversity in the Church of the United States Conference of Catholic Bishops.

Annemie Dillen is Associate Professor of Empirical Theology in the Faculty of Theology and Religious Studies at Katholieke Universiteit, Leuven, Belgium. Focusing in pastoral theology, childhood studies, and ethics, she is a member of the International Academy of Practical Theology.

Edward Foley is the Duns Scotus Professor of Spirituality and Professor of Liturgy and Music at Catholic Theological Union. He is past president of the North American Academy of Liturgy, founder and originating member of the executive committee of the Catholic Academy of Liturgy, and served on the executive committee of the International Academy of Practical Theology.

Bryan Froehle is Professor of Practical Theology at St. Thomas University in Miami and the PhD Program Director for the Practical Theology Program there. He has served at the executive director for the Center for Applied Research in the Apostolate (CARA) and a researcher and consultant for the United States Conference of Catholic Bishops, the National Federation of Priests' Councils (NFPC), and the National Organization for Continuing Education for Roman Catholic Clergy (NOCERCC). He is a member of the International Academy of Practical Theology.

Roberto S. Goizueta is the Margaret O'Brien Flatley Professor of Catholic Theology at Boston College. He is past president of the Catholic Theological Society of America and the Academy of Catholic Hispanic Theologians of the United States.

Colleen M. Griffith is Associate Professor of the Practice of Theology and Faculty Director of Spirituality Studies at the School of Theology and Ministry, Boston College. She also directs the Post-

Masters Certificate Program in the Practice of Spirituality and is a member of the International Academy of Practical Theology.

Thomas Groome is the Chair of the Department of Religious Education and Pastoral Ministry and Professor of Theology and Religious Education at the School of Theology and Ministry, Boston College. He is a member of the International Academy of Practical Theology.

Bradford Hinze is Professor of Theology at Fordham University. He is Vice President of the Catholic Theological Society of America, past president of the College Theology Society, and past president of the International Network of Societies for Catholic Theology.

Ken Johnson-Mondragón is Director of Research and Publications at the Instituto Fe Y Vida (Institute for Faith and Life), the mission of which is to empower young Hispanics for leadership in church and society.

Robert Mager is Professor of Systematic and Practical Theology, Head of Studies, and Director of the Doctoral Program in Practical Theology at the Faculté de théologie et de sciences religieuses, Université Laval, Québec, Canada. He serves on the Executive Committee of the International Academy of Practical Theology.

Julie Hanlon Rubio is Associate Professor of Christian Ethics and Director of the MA Program in Theology at St. Louis University. She has served as a board member of the Society of Christian Ethics and coconvenor of its Women's Caucus.

Janet K. Ruffing, RSM, is Professor in the Practice of Spirituality and Ministerial Leadership at Yale Divinity School and Professor Emerita of Spirituality and Spiritual Direction at Fordham University. She was a founding member of Spiritual Directors

International, has chaired the mysticism group for the American Academy of Religion (AAR), and is past president of the Society for the Study of Christian Spirituality.

Terrence W. Tilley is the Avery Cardinal Dulles, SJ, Professor of Catholic Theology and the former Chair of the Department of Theology at Fordham University. He is a past president of the Catholic Theological Society of America and the College Theology Society. He also served as president of the Society for Philosophy of Religion.

David Tracy is the Andrew Thomas Greeley and Grace McNichols Greeley Distinguished Service Professor Emeritus of Catholic Studies and Professor of Theology and the Philosophy of Religions at the University of Chicago Divinity School.

Claire E. Wolfteich is Associate Professor of Practical Theology and Spirituality Studies at Boston University School of Theology, where she also is cofounder and codirector of the Center for Practical Theology. She has served as president of the International Academy of Practical Theology and as president of the Association of Practical Theology.

BIBLIOGRAPHY

Acuña, Clodomiro L. Siller. *Para comprender el mensaje de María de Guadalupe*. Buenos Aires, Argentina: Editorial Guadalupe, 1989.

Alberigo, Giuseppe, and Joseph A. Komonchak, eds. *History of Vatican II*. 2 vols. Maryknoll, NY: Orbis Books; Leuven, Belgium: Peeters, 1995.

The Alliance for the Certification of Lay Ecclesial Ministers. *Revised National Certification Standards for Lay Ecclesial Ministers and National Certification Procedures*. Accessed March 5, 2013. http://www.lemcertification.org/standards.htm.

Ammerman, Nancy T., ed. *Everyday Religion: Observing Modern Religious Lives*. Oxford, UK: Oxford University Press, 2007.

———. *Sacred Stories, Spiritual Tribes: Finding Religion in Everyday Life*. Oxford, UK: Oxford University Press, 2013.

Aristotle. *Nicomachean Ethics*. Trans. H. Rackham. Loeb Classical Library. Cambridge, MA: Harvard University Press, 1934.

Ashley, James Matthew. *Interruptions: Mysticism, Politics, and Theology in the Work of Johann Baptist Metz*. Notre Dame, IN: University of Notre Dame Press, 1998.

Astley, Jeff. *Ordinary Theology: Looking, Listening, and Learning in Theology*. Explorations in Pastoral, Practical, and Empirical Theology. Aldergate, UK: Ashgate, 2003.

Astley, Jeff, and Leslie Francis, eds. *Exploring Ordinary Theology: Everyday Christian Believing and the Church*. Farnham, UK: Ashgate, 2013.

Bamat, Tom, and Jean Paul Wiest. *Popular Catholicism in a World Church: Seven Case Studies in Inculturation*. Maryknoll, NY: Orbis Books, 1999.

Barron, Robert. *The Priority of Christ: Toward a Postliberal Catholicism*. Grand Rapids, MI: Brazos Press, 2007.

Bass, Dorothy C., ed. *Practicing Our Faith*. San Francisco, CA: Jossey Bass, 2010 [1997].

Bass, Dorothy C., and Craig Dykstra, eds. *For Life Abundant: Practical Theology, Theological Education, and Christian Ministry*. Grand Rapids, MI: William B. Eerdmans Publishing Company, 2008.

Bell, Catherine. *Ritual Theory, Ritual Practice*. New York: Oxford University Press, 1992.

Bergoglio, Jorge Mario. "Religiosidad Popular como Inculturación de la Fe." In *Testigos de Aparecida*. Vol. 2. Bogota, Colombia: CELAM, 2008.

Bevans, Stephen B., SVD. *An Introduction to Theology in Global Perspective*. Maryknoll, NY: Orbis Books, 2009.

Bevans, Stephen B., and Jeffrey Gros. *Evangelization and Religious Freedom:* Ad Gentes, Dignitatis Humanae. Maryknoll, NY: Orbis Books, 2009.

Bevans, Stephen B., and Roger P. Schroeder. *Constants in Context: A Theology of Mission for Today*. Maryknoll, NY: Orbis Books, 2004.

Boeve, Lieven. *God Interrupts History*. New York: Continuum, 2007.

Boff, Leonardo. *Trinity and Society*. Maryknoll, NY: Orbis Books, 1988.

Boisen, Anton. *Religion in Crisis and Custom: A Sociological and Psychological Study*. New York: Harper, 1955.

Boone, Kathleen. *The Bible Tells Them So: The Discourse of Protestant Fundamentalism*. Albany: State University of New York Press, 1989.

Boulaga, F. Eboussi. *Christianity without Fetishes: An African Critique and Recapture of Christianity*. Translated by Robert Barr. Maryknoll, NY: Orbis Books, 1984.

Bourdieu, Pierre. *Outline of a Theory of Practice*. Translated by Richard Nice. Cambridge, UK: Cambridge University Press, 1977.

Brackley, Dean. *Call to Discernment in Troubled Times: New Perspectives on the Transformative Wisdom of Ignatius of Loyola*. New York: Crossroad Publishing, 2004.

Bradshaw, Paul. "Did Jesus Institute the Eucharist at the Last Supper?" In *Issues in Eucharistic Praying in East and West*, edited by Maxwell E. Johnson, 1–19. Collegeville, MN: Liturgical Press, 2010.

Bridgers, Lynn. "Roman Catholicism." In *The Wiley-Blackwell Companion to Practical Theology*, edited by Bonnie J. Miller-McLemore, 567–86. Oxford, UK: Wiley-Blackwell, 2012.

Brother Emmanuel of Taize. *Love, Imperfectly Known: Beyond Spontaneous Representations of God*. Translated by Dinah Livingston. New York: Crossroad Publishing, 2011.

Browning, Don S. *A Fundamental Practical Theology: Descriptive and Strategic Proposals*. Minneapolis, MN: Fortress Press, 1991.

———, ed. *Practical Theology: The Emerging Field in Theology, Church, and World*. San Francisco, CA: Harper & Row, 1983.

Browning, Don S., Bonnie J. Miller-McLemore, Pamela D. Couture, and K. Brynolf Lyon, eds. *From Culture Wars to Common Ground*. 2nd ed. Louisville, KY: Westminster John Knox Press, 2000.

Budde, Michael L. *The Two Churches: Catholicism and Capitalism in the World System*. Durham, NC: Duke University Press, 1992.

Burke, Margaret Ellen. "Social Sin and Social Grace." *The Way Supplement* 85 (Spring 1996): 40–54.

Burke, Raymond. "The Discipline Regarding the Denial of Holy Communion to Those Obstinately Persevering in Manifest Grave Sin." *Periodica De Re Canonica* 96 (2007): 3–58.

Burrows, Mark. "'Raiding the Inarticulate': Mysticism, Poetics, and the Unlanguageable." In *Minding the Spirit: The Study of Christian Spirituality*, edited by Elizabeth Dreyer and Mark Burrows, 341–61. Baltimore, MD: Johns Hopkins University Press, 2004.

Butler, Judith. *Gender Trouble*. New York: Routledge, 1990.

Bynum, Caroline Walker. *Holy Feast and Holy Fast: The Religious Significance of Food to Medieval Women*. Berkeley: University of California Press, 1987.

Cahalan, Kathleen A. *Introducing the Practice of Ministry*. Collegeville, MN: Liturgical Press, 2010.

———. "Locating Practical Theology in Catholic Theological Discourse and Practice." *International Journal of Practical Theology* 15, no. 1 (2011): 1–21.

Cahill, Lisa Sowle. "The Atonement Paradigm: Does It Still Have Explanatory Value?" *Theological Studies* 68, no. 2 (2007): 418–32.

Castillo, Ana, ed. *Goddess of the Americas: Writings on the Virgin of Guadalupe*. New York: Riverhead Books, 1996.

Chadwick, Owen, ed. and trans. *Western Asceticism*. Philadelphia, PA: Westminster Press, 1958.

Chopp, Rebecca S. "Practical Theology and Liberation." In *Formation and Reflection: The Promise of Practical Theology*, edited by Lewis S. Mudge and James N. Poling, 120–38. Minneapolis, MN: Fortress Press, 1987.

———. *Saving Work: Feminist Practices of Theological Education*. Louisville, KY: Westminster John Knox Press, 1995.

Clebsch, William A. *Christianity in European History*. New York: Oxford University Press, 1979.

Cloutier, David. *Love, Reason, and God's Story: An Introduction to Catholic Sexual Ethics*. Winona, MN: Anselm, 2008.

Compendium of the Social Doctrine of the Church. Rome, Italy: Pontifical Council for Justice and Peace, 2004.

Concluding Document of the Fifth General Conference of the Bishops of Latin America and the Caribbean. Aparecida Conference, 2007. Washington, DC: USCCB Publications, 2008.

Conclusions: First National Encounter for Hispanic Youth and Young Adult Ministry. Washington, DC: USCCB Publications, 2008.

Congar, Yves, OP. *Tradition and Traditions: An Historical and a Theological Essay*. Translated by Michael Naseby and Thomas Rainborough. New York: Macmillan, 1967.

Conroy, Maureen. *Looking into the Well: Supervision of Spiritual Directors*. Chicago, IL: Loyola University Press, 1995.

Copeland, M. Shawn. *Enfleshing Freedom: Body, Race, and Being*. Minneapolis, MN: Fortress Press, 2010.

———. "Tradition and the Traditions of African American Catholicism." *Theological Studies* 61, no. 4 (December 2000): 632–55.

Couture, Pamela D. *Child Poverty: Love, Justice, and Social Responsibility*. Atlanta, GA: Chalice, 2007.

Couture, Pamela D., and Bonnie J. Miller-McLemore, eds. *Poverty, Suffering and HIV/AIDS*. Cardiff, UK: Cardiff Academic Press, 2003.

Curtain, Philip. *The Atlantic Slave Trade, A Census*. Madison: University of Wisconsin Press, 1969.

Daneel, Marthinus L. *African Earthkeepers: Wholistic Interfaith Mission*. Maryknoll, NY: Orbis Books, 2001.

Dansette, Adrien. *Religious History of Modern France: Under the Third Republic*. Vol. 2. New York: Herder and Herder, 1961.

Darragh, Neil. *At Home in the Earth: Seeking an Earth-Centered Spirituality*. Auckland, New Zealand: Accent Publications, 2000.

Davis, Cyprian. *The History of Black Catholics in the United States*. New York: Crossroad Publishing, 1990.

de Certeau, Michel. "Mystic Speech." In *The Certeau Reader*, edited by Graham Ward, 188–206. Oxford, UK: Blackwell, 2000.

———. *The Practice of Everyday Life*. Translated by Steven Rendall. Berkeley: University of California Press, 1984.

De La Torre, Miguel A., and Edwin David Aponte. *Introducing Latino/a Theologies*. Maryknoll, NY: Orbis Books, 2001.

de Mesa, Jose, and Lode Wostyn. *Doing Christology: The Reappropriation of a Tradition*. Quezon City, Philippines: Claretian Publications, 1989.

De Tavernier, Johan, ed. *Responsibility, God and Society*. Leuven, Belgium: Peeters, 2008.

Deck, Allan Figueroa. "A Latino Practical Theology: Mapping the Road Ahead." *Theological Studies* 65 (2004): 275–97.

———. "Toward a New Narrative for the Latino Presence in U.S. Society and the Church." *Origins* 42, no. 29 (December 20, 2012): 458–64.

Dillen, Annemie, and Didier Pollefeyt, eds. *Children's Voices: Children's Perspectives in Ethics, Theology and Religious Education*. Leuven, Belgium: Peeters, 2010.

Dodd, C. H. *The Parables of the Kingdom*. New York: Scribner, 1961.

Dreyer, Elizabeth. *Manifestation of Grace*. Collegeville, MN: Michael Glazier, 1990.

Dreyer, Jaco S. "Practical Theology and Intradisciplinary Diversity: A Response to Miller-McLemore's 'Five Misunderstandings about Practical Theology.'" *International Journal of Practical Theology* 16, no. 1 (2012): 34–54.

Dykstra, Craig, and Dorothy C. Bass. "A Theological Understanding of Christian Practices." In *Practicing Theology: Beliefs and Practices in Christian Life*, edited by Miroslav Volf and Dorothy C. Bass, 13–31. Grand Rapids, MI: William B. Eerdmans Publishing Company, 2001.

Ecclesia Dei. Accessed May 18, 2012. http://www.vatican.va/holy_father/john_paul_ii/motu_proprio/documents/hf_jp-ii_motu-proprio_02071988_ecclesia-dei_en.html.

Edwards, Denis. *Breath of Life: A Theology of Creator Spirit*. Maryknoll, NY: Orbis Books, 2004.

———. *Ecology at the Heart of Faith: The Change of Heart that Leads to a New Way of Living on Earth*. Maryknoll, NY: Orbis Books, 2006.

———. *The Human Experience of God*. New York: Paulist Press, 1983.

Edwards, James C. *The Authority of Language: Heidegger, Wittgenstein and the Threat of Philosophical Nihilism*. Tampa: University of South Florida Press, 1990.

Edwards, Janice. *Wild Dancing: Embraced by Untamed Love*. Sea Cliff, NY: Brookville Books, 2012.

Egbulem, Nwaka Chris. *The Power of Afrocentric Celebrations: Inspirations from the Zairean Liturgy*. New York: Crossroad Publishing, 1996.

Eliot, T. S. *The Complete Poems and Plays*. New York: Harcourt, Brace and Company, 1950.

Elizondo, Virgilio. *Guadalupe: Mother of the New Creation*. Maryknoll, NY: Orbis Books, 1997.

———. *La Morenita: Evangelizer of the Americas*. San Antonio, TX: Mexican American Cultural Center Press, 1980.

Elizondo, Virgilio, Allan Figueroa Deck, and Timothy Matovina, eds. *The Treasure of Guadalupe*. Lanham, MD: Rowman & Littlefield, 2006.

Elizondo, Virgilo, and Timothy Matovina, eds. *Mestizo Worship: A Pastoral Approach to Liturgical Ministry*. Collegeville, MN: Liturgical Press, 1998.

Ellacuria, Ignacio, and Jon Sobrino, eds. *Mysterium Liberationis: Fundamental Concepts of Liberation Theology*. Maryknoll, NY: Orbis Books, 1993.

Encuentro 2000: Many Faces in God's House. Washington, DC: USCCB Publications, 2000.

Encuentro and Mission. Washington, DC: USCCB Publications, 2002.

Endean, Philip, ed. *Karl Rahner: Spiritual Writings*. Modern Spiritual Masters. Maryknoll, NY: Orbis Books, 2004.

Espin, Orlando O. *The Faith of the People: Theological Reflections on Popular Catholicism*. Maryknoll, NY: Orbis Books, 1997.

Espinosa, Gastón. "The Impact of Pluralism on Trends in Latin American and U.S. Latino Religions and Society." *Perspectivas* (Fall 2003): 13–21.

———. "The Pentecostalization of Latin American and U.S. Latino Christianity." *Pneuma: The Journal of the Society for Pentecostal Studies* 26, no. 2 (2004): 266.

Fact Sheet 2010. Stockton, CA: Instituto Fe y Vida, 2010.

Faggioli, Massimo. *True Reform: Liturgy and Ecclesiology in Sacrosanctum Concilium*. Collegeville, MN: Liturgical Press, 2012.

———. *Vatican II: The Battle for Meaning*. Mahwah, NJ: Paulist Press, 2012.

Fanon, Franz. "On National Culture." In *The Wretched of the Earth*, translated by Richard Philcox. New York: Grove Press, 2004 [1963].

Farley, Edward. *Theologia: The Fragmentation and Unity of Theological Education*. Eugene, OR: Wipf & Stock, 2001; 1st ed.: Philadelphia, PA: Fortress Press, 1983.

Fiorenza, Elisabeth Schüssler. *In Memory of Her: A Feminist Theological Construction of Christian Origins*. New York: Crossroad Publishing, 1989.

Fischer, Mark F. *The Foundations of Karl Rahner: A Paraphrase of the Foundations of Christian Faith, with Introduction and Indices*. New York: Crossroad Publishing, 2005.

Flannery, Austin, ed. *Vatican Council II: The Basic Sixteen Documents*. Northport, NY: Costello Publishing Company; Dublin, Ireland: Dominican Publications, 1996.

Flescher, Andrew. *Heroes, Saints, and Ordinary Morality*. Washington, DC: Georgetown University Press, 2003.

Foley, Edward. "Engaging the Liturgy of the World: Worship as Public Theology." *Studia Liturgica* 38, no. 1 (2008): 31–52.

———, ed. *Religion, Diversity, and Conflict*. International Practical Theology 15. Münster, Germany: LIT Verlag, 2011.

———. "Which Jesus Table? Reflections on Eucharistic Starting Points." *Worship* 82, no. 1 (2008): 41–52.

Forest, Jim. *All Is Grace: A Biography of Dorothy Day*. Maryknoll, NY: Orbis Books, 2011.

Foucault, Michel. *The Hermeneutics of the Subject: Lectures at the Collège de France 1981–1982*. New York: Picador, 2004.

Freire, Paulo. *Pedagogy of the Oppressed*. New York: Seabury Press, 1970.

Fulkerson, Mary McClintock. *Changing the Subject: Women's Discourses and Feminist Theology*. Minneapolis, MN: Fortress Press, 1994.

———. *Places of Redemption: Theology for a Worldly Church*. New York: Oxford University Press, 2010 [2007].

Gadamer, Hans Georg. *Truth and Method*. Translated and edited by Garrett Barden and John Cumming. New York: Crossroad Publishing, 1975.

Gaillardetz, Richard R. *A Daring Promise: A Spirituality of Christian Marriage*. Liguori, MO: Liguori Publications, 2007.

Ganzevoort, R. Ruard. "Forks in the Road When Tracing the Sacred: Practical Theology as Hermeneutics of Lived Religion." Presidential address to the International Academy of Practical Theology, Chicago, IL, March 8, 2009. R. Ruard Ganzevoort Web site, Accessed September 30, 2013. http://www.ruardganzevoort.nl/pdf/2009_Presidential.pdf.

Ganzevoort, R. Ruard, and Jan Visser. *Zorg voor het verhaal*. Zoetermeer, Netherlands: Meinema, 2007.

García, Richard A. "Changing Chicano Historiography." *Reviews in American History* 34 (2006): 521–28.

García-Rivera, Alejandro. *St. Martin de Porres: The "Little Stories" and the Semiotics of Culture*. Maryknoll, NY: Orbis Books, 1995.

Gaudium et spes. Accessed August 30, 2013. http://www.vatican.va/archive/hist_councils/ii_vatican_council/documents/vat-ii_cons_19651207_gaudium-et-spes_en.html.

Geertz, Clifford. *The Interpretation of Cultures*. New York: Basic Books, 1973.

Geffré, Claude, and Gustavo Gutiérrez. *The Mystical and Political Dimension of the Christian Faith*. New York: Herder and Herder, 1974.

Gerkin, Charles. *An Introduction to Pastoral Care*. Nashville, TN: Abingdon Press, 1997.

Gilroy, Paul. *The Black Atlantic: Modernity and Double Consciousness*. Cambridge, MA: Harvard University Press, 1993.

Goizueta, Roberto S. *Caminemos, Con Jesús: Toward a Hispanic/Latino Theology of Accompaniment*. Maryknoll, NY: Orbis Books, 1995.

Gomez, José H. "Immigration Reform After the Election." *Origins* 38 (November 13, 2008): 363–66.

Gonzalez, G. M. James. "Of Property: On 'Captive' 'Bodies,' Hidden 'Flesh,' and Colonization." In *Existence in Black: An Anthology of Black Existential Philosophy*, edited by Lewis R. Gordon, 129–36. New York: Routledge, 1997.

Gould, Emily Clark, and Virginia Meacham. "The Feminine Face of Afro-Catholicism in New Orleans, 1727–1852." *The William and Mary Quarterly* (April 2002): 409–48.

Gräb, Wilhelm, and Lars Charbonnier, eds. *Secularization Theories, Religious Identity, and Practical Theology*. International Practical Theology 7. Münster, Germany: LIT Verlag, 2009.

Grabowski, John S. *Sex and Virtue: An Introduction to Sexual Ethics*. Washington, DC: Catholic University of America Press, 2003.

Graham, Elaine L. *Transforming Practice: Pastoral Theology in an Age of Uncertainty*. Eugene, OR: Wipf & Stock, 2002; 1st ed.: London, UK: Mowbray, 1996.

———. "A View from a Room: Feminist Practical Theology from Academy, Kitchen or Sanctuary?" In *Liberating Faith Practices: Feminist Practical Theologies in Context*, edited by Denise M. Ackerman and Riet Bons-Storm, 129–52. Leuven, Belgium: Peeters, 1998.

———. "Why Practical Theology Must Go Public." *Practical Theology* 1, no. 1 (2008): 1–17.

Graham, Elaine L., and Anna Rowlands, eds. *Pathways to the Public Square*. International Practical Theology 1. Munster, Germany: LIT Verlag, 2005/6.

Graham, Elaine L., Heather Walton, and Frances Ward. *Theological Reflection: Methods*. London, UK: SCM Press, 2005.

Grieu, Étienne *Nes de Dieu*. Paris, France: Cerf, 2003.

Griffith, Colleen M. "Spirituality and the Body." In *Bodies of Worship: Explorations in Theory and Practice*, edited by Bruce T. Morrill, 67–83. Collegeville, MN: Liturgical Press, 1999.

Groome, Thomas H. *Christian Religious Education*. San Francisco, CA: HarperCollins, 1980.

———. *Sharing Faith: A Comprehensive Approach to Religious Education and Pastoral Ministry*. San Francisco, CA: HarperSanFrancisco, 1991.

———. *Will There Be Faith*. San Francisco, CA: HarperCollins, 2012.

Groome, Thomas H., and Colleen M. Griffith, eds. *Catholic Spiritual Practices: A Treasury of Old and New*. Brewster, MA: Paraclete Press, 2012.

Gutiérrez, Gustavo. *We Drink from Our Own Wells: The Spiritual Journey of a People*. Maryknoll, NY: Orbis Books, 1984.

Habermas, Jürgen. *Knowledge and Human Interests*. Boston, MA: Beacon Press, 1971.

Hahnenberg, Edward. *Ministries: A Relational Approach*. New York: Crossroad Publishing, 2003.

Hall, Gerard V. "Australia and Oceania." In *The Wiley-Blackwell Companion to Practical Theology*, edited by Bonnie J. Miller-McLemore, 544–54. Oxford, UK: Wiley-Blackwell, 2012.

Hall, Gwendolyn Midlo. "The Formation of Afro-Creole Culture." In *Creole New Orleans: Race and Americanization*, edited by Arnold R. Hirsch and Joseph Logsdon, 58–87. Baton Rouge: Louisiana State University Press, 1992.

Harding, Sandra. *Whose Science? Whose Knowledge? Thinking from Women's Lives*. Ithaca, NY: Cornell University Press, 1991.

Haslinger, Herbert, ed. *Handbuch Praktische Theologie*. Vol. 1. Mainz, Germany: Grundlegungen, 1999.

Hauerwas, Stanley. *The Peaceable Kingdom: A Primer in Christian Ethics*. Notre Dame, IN: University of Notre Dame Press, 1983.

Heim, S. Mark. *The Depth of the Riches: A Trinitarian Theology of Religious Ends*. Grand Rapids, MI: William B. Eerdmans Publishing Company, 2001.

Heimbrock, Hans-Gunter, and Christopher P. Scholtz, eds. *Religion: Immediate Experience and the Mediacy of Research*. Gottingen, Germany: Vandenhoeck & Ruprecht, 2007.

Heitink, Gerben. *Practical Theology: History, Theory, Action Domains*. Studies in Practical Theology. Grand Rapids, MI: William B. Eerdmans Publishing Company, 1999.

Hiltner, Seward. *Preface to Pastoral Theology*. Nashville, TN: Abingdon Press, 1979.

Hinze, Bradford E. "Dialogical Theology." In *Kommunikative Theologie: Zugänge–Auseinandersetzungen–Ausdifferenzierungen //Communicative Theology: Approaches—Discussions—Differentiation*, edited by Matthias Scharer, Bradford E. Hinze, and Bernd Jochen Hilberath, 21–26. Kommunikative Theologie–interdisziplinär// Communicative Theology—Interdisciplinary Studies. Vienna, Austria: LIT Verlag, 2010.

———. *Practices of Dialogue in the Roman Catholic Church: Aims and Obstacles, Lessons and Laments*. New York: Continuum, 2006.

———. "The Reception of Vatican II in Participatory Structures of the Church: Facts and Friction." *Proceedings of the Canon Law Society of America Annual Convention* 70 (2009): 28–52.

———. "When Dialogue Leads to the Reform of Tradition." In *Tradition and Tradition Theories: An International Discussion*, edited by Torsten Larbig and Siegfried Wiedenhofer, 336–55. Berlin, Germany: LIT Verlag, 2006.

Hinze, Christine Firer. "What is Enough? Catholic Social Thought, Consumption, and Material Sufficiency." In *Having: Property and Possession in Religious and Social Life*, edited by William Schweiker and Charles Matthewes. Grand Rapids, MI: William B. Eerdmans Publishing Company, 2004.

Hobsbawm, Eric, and Terence Ranger, eds. *The Invention of Tradition*. Cambridge, UK: Cambridge University Press, 1983.

Holland, Joe, and Peter Henriot. *Social Analysis: Linking Faith and Justice*. Maryknoll, NY: Orbis Books, 1983.

Ingham, Mary Beth, CSJ. *Rejoicing in the Works of the Lord: Beauty in the Franciscan Tradition*. St. Bonaventure, NY: Franciscan Institute Publications, St. Bonaventure University, 2009.

———. *Scotus for Dunces: An Introduction to the Subtle Doctor*. St. Bonaventure, NY: Franciscan Institute Publications, St. Bonaventure University, 2003.

Jantzen, Grace. *Power, Gender and Christian Mysticism*. Cambridge, UK: Cambridge University Press, 1995.

John Paul II. *Ecclesia in America*. Accessed August 30, 2013. http://www.vatican.va/holy_father/john_paul_ii/apost_exhortations/documents/hf_jp-ii_exh_22011999_ecclesia-in-america_en.html.

Johnson, Elizabeth A. *Friends of God and Prophets*. New York: Continuum, 1999.

———. *She Who Is: The Mystery of God in Feminist Discourse*. New York: Crossroad Publishing, 1992.

Johnson, Mark. *The Body in the Mind*. Chicago, IL: University of Chicago Press, 1990.

Johnson, Maxwell E. *The Virgin of Guadalupe: Theological Reflections of an Anglo-Lutheran Liturgist*. Lanham, MD: Rowman & Littlefield, 2002.

Johnson-Mondragón, Ken. "Pastoral Care for the Second Generation." Instituto Fe y Vida Research and Resource Center for Hispanic Youth and Young Adult Ministry, *Fe y Vida Insights*, January 30, 2013. Accessed February 5, 2013. http://www.feyvida.org/research/second-generation/.

Jung, L. Shannon. *Sharing Food: Christian Practices for Enjoyment*. Minneapolis, MN: Fortress Press, 2006.

Kaplan, Sara. "Souls at the Crossroads, Africans on the Water: The Politics of Diasporic Melancholia." *Callaloo* 30, no. 2 (Spring 2007): 511–26.

Karris, Robert. *Luke: Artist and Theologian*. New York: Paulist Press, 1985.

Kavanaugh, John F. *Following Christ in a Consumer Society: The Spirituality of Cultural Resistance*. 25th Anniversary Edition. Maryknoll, NY: Orbis Books, 2006.

Klein, Stephanie. *Theologie und empirische Biographieforschung*. Stuttgart, Germany: Kohlhammer, 1994.

Kokx, Stephen C., and Nicholas C. Lund-Molfese. "An Analysis of the Formative Years of the Catholic Campaign for Human Development." Washington, DC: USCCB, Secretariat of Justice and Peace, 2010.

Komonchak, Joseph, Mary Collins, and Dermot Lane, eds. *The New Dictionary of Theology*. Wilmington, DE: Michael Glazier, 1987.

Laird, Martin. *A Sunlit Absence: Silence, Awareness, and Contemplation*. New York: Oxford University Press, 2011.

Lanzetta, Beverly. *Radical Wisdom: A Feminist Mystical Theology*. Minneapolis, MN: Fortress Press, 2005.

Lash, Nicholas. *Believing Three Ways in One God: A Reading of the Apostles Creed*. Notre Dame, IN: University of Notre Dame Press, 2010.

Lawler, Michael G. *Marriage and the Catholic Church: Disputed Questions*. Collegeville, MN: Liturgical Press, 2002.

Lawler, Michael G., Gail Risch, and Lisa Riley. "Church Experience of Interchurch and Same-Church Couples." *Family Ministry* 13, no. 4 (Winter 1999): 36–46.

Leckey, Dolores R. *Laity Stirring the Church: Prophetic Questions*. Philadelphia, PA: Fortress Press, 1987.

Leinhaupl-Wilke, A., and M. Striet, eds. *Katholische Theologie Studieren*. Munster, Germany: LIT Verlag, 2000.

Liebert, Elizabeth. "Supervision as Widening the Horizons." In *Supervision of Spiritual Directors: Engaging the Holy Mystery*, edited by Mary Rose Bumpus and Rebecca Bradburn Langer, 125–45. Harrisburg, PA: Morehouse Publishing, 2005.

Lindsey, Jacquelyn. *Catholic Family Prayer Book*. Huntington, IN: Our Sunday Visitor, 2001.

Liturgiam authenticam. Accessed May 18, 2012. http://www.vatican.va/roman_curia/congregations/ccdds/documents/rc_con_ccdds_doc_20010507_liturgiam-authenticam_en.html.

Lohfink, Gerhard. *Jesus and Community*. Philadelphia, PA: Fortress Press, 1984.

Lombaerts, Herman, and Didier Pollefeyt, eds. *Hermeneutics and Religious Education*. Leuven, Belgium: Peeters, 2004.

Lonergan, Bernard. *Method in Theology*. New York: Seabury Press, 1972.

———. "Response of the Jesuit as Priest and Apostle in the Modern World." In *A Second Collection by Bernard J. F. Lonergan*, edited by William F. J. Ryan and Bernard J. Tyrrell, 165–88. Philadelphia, PA: Westminster Press, 1974.

Lossky, Vladimir. *The Mystical Theology of the Eastern Church*. Crestwood, NY: St. Vladimir's Press, 1976.

Lubac, Henri de. *Corpus Mysticum: The Eucharist and the Church in the Middle Ages*. Edited by Laurence Paul Hemming and Susan Frank Parsons. Translated by Gemma Simmonds. Notre Dame, IN: University of Notre Dame Press, 2006.

Lysaught, Therese, and David Matzko McCarthy, eds. *Gathered for the Journey: Moral Theology in Catholic Perspective*. Grand Rapids, MI: William B. Eerdmans Publishing Company, 2007.

MacIntyre, Alasdair. *After Virtue: A Study in Moral Theory*. Notre Dame, IN: University of Notre Dame Press, 1984.

Mackey, James P. *The Modern Theology of Tradition*. London, UK: Darton, Longman & Todd, 1962.

Madariaga, Oscar Rodríguez. "Una Conversión Pastoral." In *Testigos de Aparecida*, vol. 1, 411–25. Bogota, Colombia: CELAM, 2008.

Mager, Robert. "Action Theories." In *The Wiley-Blackwell Companion to Practical Theology*, edited by Bonnie J. Miller-McLemore, 255–65. Oxford, UK: Wiley-Blackwell, 2012.

Majozo, Estella Conwill. *Libation: A Literary Pilgrimage through the African-American Soul*. New York: Harlem River Press, 1995.

Matovina, Timothy. *Guadalupe and Her Faithful: Latino Catholics in San Antonio, From Colonial Origins to the Present*. Baltimore, MD: Johns Hopkins University Press, 2005.

———. *Latino Catholicism: Transformation in America's Largest Church.* Princeton, NJ: Princeton University Press, 2012.

———. "Latino Contributions to Vatican II Renewal." *Origins* 42, no. 29 (December 20, 2012): 465–71.

Mattison, William C., III, ed. *New Wine, New Wineskins: A Next Generation Reflects on Key Issues in Catholic Moral Theology*. Lanham, MD: Rowman & Littlefield, 2005.

McCarthy, David Matzko. *Sex and Love in the Home: A Theology of the Household.* 2nd rev. ed. London, UK: SCM Press, 2004.

McClendon, James Wm., Jr. *Biography as Theology, Truly Our Sister: A Theology of Mary in the Communion of the Saints.* New York: Continuum, 2003.

———. *Systematic Theology*. Vol. 1, *Ethics*. Nashville, TN: Abingdon Press, 2002 [1986].

———. *Systematic Theology*. Vol. 2, *Doctrine*. Nashville, TN: Abingdon Press, 1994.

McDermott, Brian O. *What Are They Saying about the Grace of Christ?* New York: Paulist Press, 1984.

McGuire, Meredith B. "Why Bodies Matter: A Sociological Reflection on Spirituality and Materiality." In *Minding the Spirit: The Study of Christian Spirituality*, edited by Elizabeth A. Dreyer and Mark S. Burrows, 118–34. Baltimore, MD: Johns Hopkins University Press, 2005.

McIntosh, Mark A. *Mystical Theology: The Integrity of Spirituality and Theology*. Malden, MA: Blackwell, 1998.

Meeuws, Henk. *Diaconie*. Gorinchem, Netherlands: Narratio, 2011.

Mercer, Joyce. *Welcoming Children: A Practical Theology of Childhood.* Atlanta, GA: Chalice, 2007.

Merleau-Ponty, Maurice. *Phenomenology of Perception*. Translated by Colin Smith. London, UK: Routledge & Kegan Paul, 1962.

"Message to the People of God From the XIII Ordinary General Assembly of the Synod of Bishops." Synod of Bishops on the New Evangelization, Rome, Italy, October 26, 2012, Proposition 13. Accessed February 15, 2013. http://www. zenit.org/en/articles/message-to-the-people-of-god-from-the-xiii-ordinary-general-assembly-of-the-synod-of-bishops.

Mette, Norbert. "Practical Theology: Theory of Aesthetics or Theory of Action?" In *Creativity, Imagination, and Criticism: The Expressive Dimension in Practical Theology*, edited by Paul Ballard and Pamela D. Couture, 49–63. Cardiff, UK: Cardiff Academic Press, 2001.

Metz, Johann Baptist. *Faith in History and Society: Toward a Practical Fundamental Theology*. New York: Seabury Press, 1980.

———. *A Passion for God: The Mystical-Political Dimension of Christianity*. New York: Paulist Press, 1998.

Milbank, John. *Theology and Social Theory: Beyond Secular Reason*. London, UK: Wiley-Blackwell, 2006.

Miles, Margaret R. *Practicing Christianity: Critical Perspectives for an Embodied Spirituality*. New York: Crossroad Publishing, 1988.

Miller-McLemore, Bonnie J. *Also a Mother: Work and Family as Theological Dilemma*. Nashville, TN: Abingdon Press, 1994.

———. "The 'Clerical Paradigm': A Fallacy of Misplaced Concreteness?" *International Journal of Practical Theology* 11, no. 2 (2007): 19–38.

———. "The Contributions of Practical Theology." In *The Wiley-Blackwell Companion to Practical Theology*, edited by Bonnie J. Miller-McLemore, 1–20. Oxford, UK: Wiley-Blackwell, 2012.

———. "Embodied Knowing, Embodied Theology: What Happened to the Body?" *Pastoral Psychology* (January 13, 2013): 1–16. Accessed May 1, 2013. http://link.springer.com/article/10.1007/s11089-013-0510-3, DOI 10.1007/s11089-013-0510-3.

———. "The Subject and Practice of Pastoral Theology as a Practical Theological Discipline: Pushing Past the Nagging Identity Crisis to the Poetics of Resistance." In *Liberating Faith Practices: Feminist Practical Theologies in Context*, edited by Denise M. Ackerman and Riet Bons-Storm, 175–98. Leuven, Belgium: Peeters, 1998.

———, ed. *The Wiley-Blackwell Companion to Practical Theology*. Oxford, UK: Wiley-Blackwell, 2012.

Miner, Harold. "Body Ritual Among the Nacirema." *The American Anthropologist* 58 (1956): 503–7.

Misner, Paul. *Social Catholicism in Europe: From the Onset of Industrialization to the First World War*. New York: Crossroad Publishing, 1991.

Moreman, Shane T. *Performativity and the Latino/a-White Hybrid Identity: Performing the Textual Self*. PhD diss., University of South Florida, 2005.

Moschella, Mary Clark. *Ethnography as a Pastoral Practice: An Introduction*. Cleveland, OH: The Pilgrim Press, 2008.

Murdoch, Iris. *The Fire and the Sun: Why Plato Banished the Artists*. Oxford, UK: Clarendon Press, 1977.

———. *Metaphysics as a Guide to Morals: Writings on Philosophy and Literature*. New York: Viking Press, 1992.

Nabhan-Warren, Kristy. "Blooming Where We're Planted: Mexican-Descent Catholics Living Out Cursillo de Cristiandad." *U.S. Catholic Historian* 28 (Fall 2010): 99–125.

National Pastoral Plan for Hispanic Ministry. Washington, DC: USCCB Publications, 1987.

Nearon, Joseph. *Theology: A Portrait in Black, Proceedings of the 1978 Black Catholic Theological Symposium*. Edited by Thaddeus J. Posey. Pittsburgh, PA: The Capuchin Press, 1980.

Nebel, Richard. *Santa María Tonantzín, Virgen de Guadalupe: Continuidad y transformación religiosa en México*. Mexico City, Mexico: Fondo de Cultura Económica, 1995.

Newman, John Henry Cardinal. *Essay on the Development of Christian Doctrine*. London, UK: Basil, Montague, Pickering, 1878. Accessed September 24, 2013. http://archive.org/ stream/a599872600newmuoft#page/n5/mode/2up.

Nola, Ann Michele. *A Privileged Moment: Dialogue in the Language of the Second Vatican Council 1962–1965*. Bern, Switzerland: Peter Lang, 2006.

Nora, Pierre. "Between Memory and History: Les Lieux de Mémoire." In *History and Memory in African-American Culture*, edited by Genevieve Fabre and Robert O'Meally, 284–300. New York: Oxford University Press, 1994.

Norris, Kathleen. *Amazing Grace: A Vocabulary of Faith*. New York: Riverhead Books, 1998.

O'Brien, David J., and Thomas A. Shannon, eds. *Catholic Social Thought: The Documentary Heritage*. Maryknoll, NY: Orbis Books, 1992.

Oman, John Wood. *Grace and Personality*. Cambridge, UK: Cambridge University Press, 1917.

———. *Vision and Authority, or, The Throne of St. Peter*. 2nd ed. London, UK: Hodder and Stoughton, 1928.

Orsi, Robert. "Doing Religious Studies With Your Whole Body." *Practical Matters* 2 (Spring 2013): 1–6.

Osmer, Richard R. *Practical Theology: An Introduction*. Grand Rapids, MI: William B. Eerdmans Publishing Company, 2008.

Palmer, Richard. *Hermeneutics*. Evanston, IL: Northwestern University Press, 1969.

Papanikolaou, Aristotle. *The Mystical as Political: Democracy and Non-Radical Orthodoxy*. Notre Dame, IN: University of Notre Dame Press, 2012.

Pauw, Amy Plantinga. "Attending to the Gaps Between Beliefs and Practices." In *Practicing Theology: Beliefs and Practices in Christian*

Life, edited by Miroslav Volf and Dorothy C. Bass, 33–49. Grand Rapids, MI: William B. Eerdmans Publishing Company, 2001.

Pecklers, Keith. *The Unread Vision*. Collegeville, MN: Liturgical Press, 1998.

Perrin, David M. *Studying Christian Spirituality*. New York: Routledge, 2007.

Pew Research Center. *Changing Faiths: Latinos and the Transformation of American Religion*. Washington, DC: Pew Hispanic Center, 2007.

Phan, Peter C. "Method in Liberation Theologies." *Theological Studies* 61 (2000): 40–63.

———. *Vietnamese-American Catholics*. New York: Paulist Press, 2005.

Phelps, Jamie T. "African American Culture: Source and Context of Black Catholic Theology and Church Mission." *Journal of Hispanic/Latino Theology* 3, no. 3 (February 1996): 43–58.

———, ed. *Black and Catholic: The Challenge and Gift of Black Folk, Contributions of African American Experience and Thought to Catholic Theology*. 2nd ed. Milwaukee, WI: Marquette University Press, 2002.

Pierce, Gregory Augustine. *The Mass Is Never Ended*. Notre Dame, IN: Ave Maria Press, 2007.

Pinn, Anthony. *Varieties of African American Religious Education*. Minneapolis, MN: Augsburg Fortress Press, 1998.

Polanyi, Michael. *Knowing and Being*. London, UK: Routledge, 1969.

———. *The Tacit Dimension*. Gloucester, MA: Peter Smith, 1983.

Portier, William L. "Here Come the Evangelical Catholics." *Communio* 31 (Spring 2004): 48–51.

Powers, David N. "Eucharistic Justice." *Theological Studies* 67, no. 4 (2006): 856–78.

Preaching the Mystery of Faith: The Sunday Homily. Pastoral Statement on Preaching at the Sunday Liturgy by the U.S. Bishops. Washington, DC: USCCB Publications, 2012.

Putnam, Robert D., and David E. Campbell. *American Grace: How Religion Divides and Unites Us*. New York: Simon and Schuster, 2010.

———. "The Changing Face of American Catholicism." Memo to the U.S. Conference of Catholic Bishops, Washington, DC, May 22, 2008.

Rahner, Karl. *Foundations of Christian Faith*. Translated by William Dych. New York: Seabury Press, 1978 [1976].

———. *The Practice of Faith: A Handbook of Contemporary Spirituality*. New York: Crossroad Publishing, 1986 [1983].

———. "Reflection on the Experience of Grace." In *Theological Investigations*. Vol. 3, translated by Karl-H. Kruger and Boniface Kruger, 86–90. Baltimore, MD: Helicon Press, 1967.

———. *Theological Investigations, IX, 1965–1967*. New York: Herder and Herder, 1976.

———. *The Trinity*. New York: Herder and Herder, 1970.

Rahner, Karl, SJ, and Heinz Schuster, eds. *The Pastoral Mission of the Church. Concilium: Theology in the Age of Renewal*. Vol. 3. Glen Rock, NJ: Paulist Press, 1965.

Ramsey, Ian T. *Christian Discourse: Some Logical Explorations*. London, UK: Oxford University Press, 1965.

Reid, Barbara E. *Parables for Preachers, Year C*. Collegeville, MN: Liturgical Press, 2000.

Reimer-Barry, Emily. "The Listening Church: How Ethnography Can Transform Catholic Ethics." In *Ethnography as Theology and Ethics*, edited by Christian Scharen and Aana Marie Vigen, 97–117. London, UK: Continuum, 2011.

Reiser, William, SJ. *Seeking God in All Things: Theology and Spiritual Direction*. Collegeville, MN: Liturgical Press, 2004.

Ricoeur, Paul. *Interpretation Theory: Discourse and the Surplus of Meaning*. Forth Worth: Texas Christian University Press, 1976.

Rodriguez, Edmundo, SJ. "The Hispanic Community and Church Movements: Schools of Leadership." In *Hispanic Catholic Culture in the United States*, edited by Jay Dolan and Allan Figueroa Deck, SJ, 206–39. Notre Dame, IN: University of Notre Dame Press, 1994.

Rodriguez-Holguin, Jeanette. *Our Lady of Guadalupe: Faith and Empowerment Among Mexican American Women*. Austin: University of Texas Press, 1994.

Rogers, Mary Beth. *Cold Anger: A Story of Faith and Power Politics*. Denton: University of North Texas Press, 1990.

Ross, Susan A. *Extravagant Affections*. New York: Continuum, 1998.

Rubio, Julie Hanlon. "Beyond the Liberal-Conservative Divide on Contraception: Wisdom of Practitioners of Natural Family Planning and Artificial Birth Control." *Horizons* 32, no. 2 (December 2005): 270–94.

———. *A Christian Theology of Marriage*. Mahwah, NJ: Paulist Press, 2003.

———. "Family Ethics: Beyond Sex and Controversy." *Theological Studies* 74 (March 2013): 138–61.

———. *Family Ethics: Practices for Christians*. Washington, DC: Georgetown University Press, 2010.

Ruffing, Janet K. "An Integrated Model of Supervision in Training Spiritual Directors." *Presence* 9, no. 1 (February 2003): 24–30. Reprinted in *The Soul of Supervision: Integrating Practice and Theory*, edited by Margaret Benefiel and Geraldine Holton, 153–64. Harrisburg, PA: Morehouse Publishing, 2010.

———, ed. *Mysticism & Social Transformation*. Syracuse, NY: Syracuse University Press, 2001.

———. *Spiritual Direction Beyond the Beginnings*. New York: Paulist Press, 2000.

———. *To Tell the Sacred Tale: Spiritual Direction and Narrative*. New York: Paulist Press, 2011.

Rush, Ormond. *The Eyes of Faith: The Sense of the Faithful and the Church's Reception of Revelation*. Washington, DC: Catholic University of America Press, 2009.

Ryle, Gilbert. *The Concept of Mind*. Chicago, IL: University of Chicago Press, 2000.

Schatzki, Theodore R. *Social Practices: A Wittgensteinian Approach to Human Activity and the Social*. Cambridge, UK: Cambridge University Press, 1996.

Scherer, James A., and Stephen B. Bevans, eds. *New Directions in Mission and Evangelization 2: Theological Foundations*. Maryknoll, NY: Orbis Books, 1994.

Schillebeeckx, Edward. *Christ: The Experience of Jesus as Lord*. Translated by John Bowden. New York: Crossroad Publishing, 1981.

———. *Church: The Human Story of God*. New York: Crossroad Publishing, 1990.

———. *The Eucharist*. Translated by N. D. Smith. New York: Sheed and Ward, 1968.

———. *Jesus: An Experiment in Christology*. Translated by Hubert Hioskins. New York: Vintage Books, 1981.

Schneiders, Sandra. "A Hermeneutical Approach to the Study of Christian Spirituality." In *Minding the Spirit: The Study of Christian Spirituality*, edited by Elizabeth A. Dreyer and Mark S. Burrows, 49–60. Baltimore, MD: Johns Hopkins University Press, 2005.

Schön, Donald A. *Educating the Reflective Practitioner: Toward a New Design for Teaching and Learning in the Professions*. San Francisco, CA: Jossey-Bass, 1990.

Schreiter, Robert J., CPPS. *Constructing Local Theologies*. Maryknoll, NY: Orbis Books, 1985.

———. *The Ministry of Reconciliation: Spirituality and Strategies*. Maryknoll, NY: Orbis Books, 1998.

———, ed. *Mission in the Third Millennium*. Maryknoll, NY: Orbis Books, 2001.

———. *The New Catholicity: Theology Between the Global and the Local*. Maryknoll, NY: Orbis Books, 1997.

Schreiter, Robert J., R. Scott Appleby, and Gerard F. Powers, eds. *Peacebuilding: Catholic Theology, Ethics, and Praxis*. Maryknoll, NY: Orbis Books, 2010.

Schwartz, Barry. "Iconography and Collective Memory: Lincoln's Image in the American Mind." *The Sociological Quarterly* 32, no. 3 (Autumn 1991): 301–19.

Scott, Kieran. "A Spirituality of Resistance for Marriage." In *Perspectives on Marriage: A Reader*, edited by Kieran Scott and Michael Warren, 397–410. New York: Oxford University Press, 2001.

Searle, John. *Making the Social World: The Structure of Human Civilization*. New York: Oxford University Press, 2010.

Sedmak, Clemens. *Doing Local Theology: A Guide for Artisans of a New Humanity*. Maryknoll, NY: Orbis Books, 2002.

Shea, John. *Experiences of the Spirit*. Chicago, IL: Thomas More Press, 1983.

———. *Stories of Faith*. Chicago, IL: Thomas More Press, 1980.

Sheldrake, Philip E. *Explorations in Spirituality: History, Theology, and Social Practice*. New York: Paulist Press, 2010.

Sider, Ron J., ed. *Living More Simply: Biblical Principles & Practical Models*. Downers Grove, IL: InterVarsity Press, 1980.

Smith, Ted A. "Theories of Practice." In *The Wiley-Blackwell Companion to Practical Theology*, edited by Bonnie J. Miller-McLemore, 244–54. Oxford, UK: Wiley-Blackwell, 2012.

Sobrino, Jon. *Spirituality of Liberation: Toward Political Holiness*. Translated by Robert R. Barr. Maryknoll, NY: Orbis Books, 1988.

Stanley, Brian. *The World Missionary Conference, Edinburgh 1910*. Grand Rapids, MI: William B. Eerdmans Publishing Company, 2009.

Streck, Valburga Schmiedt. "Brazil." In *The Wiley-Blackwell Companion to Practical Theology*, edited by Bonnie J. Miller-McLemore, 525–33. Oxford, UK: Wiley-Blackwell, 2012.

Sweeney, James, Gemma Simmonds, and David Lonsdale, eds. *Keeping Faith in Practice: Aspects of Catholic Pastoral Theology*. London, UK: SCM Press, 2010.

Thiel, John. *Senses of Tradition: Continuity and Development in Catholic Faith*. New York: Oxford University Press, 2000.

Thompson, Robert Farris. *Flash of the Spirit: African and Afro-American Art and Philosophy*. New York: Random House/Vintage Books, 1984.

———. "Recapturing Heaven's Glamour: Afro-Caribbean Festivalizing Arts." In *Caribbean Festival Arts: Every Little Piece of Difference*, edited by John W. Nunley and Barbara A. Bettelheim. Seattle: University of Washington Press, 1988.

Thompson, Robert Farris, and Joseph Cornet. *The Four Moments of the Sun: Kongo Art in the Two Worlds*. Washington, DC: National Gallery of Art, 1981.

Tilley, Terrence W. *The Disciples' Jesus: Christology as Reconciling Practice*. Maryknoll, NY: Orbis Books, 2008.

———. *Faith: What It Is and What It Isn't*. Maryknoll, NY: Orbis Books, 2010.

———. *History, Theology, and Faith: Dissolving the Modern Problematic*. Maryknoll, NY: Orbis Books, 2006.

———. *Inventing Catholic Tradition*. Eugene, OR: Wipf & Stock, 2011; 1st ed.: Maryknoll, NY: Orbis Books, 2001.

———. *Story Theology*. Wilmington, DE: Michael Glazier, 1985.

———. *The Wisdom of Religious Commitment*. Washington, DC: Georgetown University Press, 1995.

Tillich, Paul. *Systematic Theology*. Vol. 1. London, UK: SCM Press, 1951.

Tracy, David. *The Analogical Imagination: Christian Theology and the Culture of Pluralism*. New York: Crossroad Publishing, 1981.

———. *Blessed Rage for Order*. New York: Seabury Press, 1975.

Treviño, Roberto. *The Church in the Barrio: Mexican American Ethno-Catholicism in Houston*. Chapel Hill: University of North Carolina Press, 2006.

USCCB Committee on Catholic Education, Subcommittee on Certification for Ecclesial Ministry and Service. Accessed March 28, 2013. http://www.usccb.org/certification.

Van der Ven, Johannes A. "An Empirical Approach in Practical Theology." In *Practical Theology—International Perspectives*, 323–39. Frankfurt am Main, Germany: Peter Lang, 1999.

———. *Practical Theology: An Empirical Approach*. Leuven, Belgium: Peeters, 1998.

Vasquez, Manuel A. *More Than Belief: A Materialist Theory of Religion*. New York: Oxford University Press, 2011.

Veling, Terry A. *Practical Theology: On Earth As It Is In Heaven*. Maryknoll, NY: Orbis Books, 2005.

Volf, Miroslav. "Theology for a Way of Life." In *Practicing Theology: Beliefs and Practices in Christian Life*, edited by Miroslav Volf and Dorothy C. Bass, 245–63. Grand Rapids, MI: William B. Eerdmans Publishing Company, 2002.

Volf, Miroslav, and Dorothy C. Bass, eds. *Practicing Theology: Beliefs and Practices in Christian Life*. Grand Rapids, MI: William B. Eerdmans Publishing Company, 2002.

Walton, Heather. "Practical Theology and Poetics." In *The Wiley-Blackwell Companion to Practical Theology*, edited by Bonnie J. Miller-McLemore, 173–82. Oxford, UK: Wiley-Blackwell, 2012.

Ward, Pete, ed. *Perspectives on Ecclesiology and Ethnography*. Grand Rapids, MI: William B. Eerdmans Publishing Company, 2012.

Warren, Michael. *Faith, Culture, and the Worshipping Community: Shaping the Practice of the Local Church*. Mahwah, NJ: Paulist Press, 1989.

———. *Youth, Gospel, Liberation*. San Francisco, CA: Harper and Row, 1987.

Webb, Raymond J. "Muslims, Christians, Dreaming: The Importance of Place." In *Dreaming the Land: Theologies of Resistance and Hope*, edited by Hans-Georg Ziebertz and Friedrich Schweitzer, 41–50. Berlin, Germany: LIT Verlag, 2007.

Wijsen, Frans Jozef Servaas, Peter Henriot, SJ, and Rodrigo Mejía, eds. *The Pastoral Circle Revisited: A Critical Quest for Truth and Transformation*. Maryknoll, NY: Orbis Books, 2005.

Wittgenstein, Ludwig. *Philosophical Investigations*. 3rd ed. Translated by G.E.M. Anscombe. New York: Macmillan, 1958.

Wolfteich, Claire E. "Animating Questions: Spirituality and Practical Theology." *International Journal of Practical Theology* 13 (2009): 121–43.

———. "It's About Time: Rethinking Spirituality and the Domestic Church." In *The Household of God and Local Households*, edited by Thomas Knieps-Port le Roi, Gerard Mannion, and Peter De Mey, 127–44. Leuven, Belgium: Peeters, 2012.

———. *Navigating New Terrain: Work and Women's Spiritual Lives*. Mahwah, NJ: Paulist Press, 2002.

———. "'Practices of Unsaying': Michel de Certeau, Spirituality Studies, and Practical Theology." *Spiritus: A Journal of Christian Spirituality* 12 (2012): 161–71.

———. "Spirituality." In *The Blackwell Companion to Practical Theology*, edited by Bonnie J. Miller McLemore, 328–36. Oxford, UK: Wiley-Blackwell, 2011.

———. "Standing at the Gap: Reading Classics and the Practices of Everyday Life." *Spiritus: A Journal of Christian Spirituality* 10, no. 2 (2010): 250–55.

———. "Time Poverty, Women's Labor, and Catholic Social Teaching: A Practical Theological Exploration." *Journal of Moral Theology* 2, no. 2 (June 2013): 40–59.

Wolfteich, Claire E., and Jörg Schneider. "A Comparative Research Conversation: American Catholic and German Protestant Spirituality Studies." *International Journal of Practical Theology* 17, no. 1 (August 2013): 100–30.

Woodward, James, and Stephen Pattison, eds. *The Blackwell Reader in Pastoral and Practical Theology*. Oxford, UK: Blackwell, 2000.

Wright, Christopher J. H. *Knowing the Holy Spirit Through the Old Testament*. Downers Grove, IL: InterVarsity Press, 2006.

Yeats, William Butler. *The Poems: A New Edition*. Edited by Richard J. Finneran. New York: Macmillan, 1983.

Yong, Amos, and Barbara Brown Zikmund, eds. *Remembering Jamestown: Hard Questions About Christian Mission*. Eugene, OR: Pickwick Publications, 2010.

Zhenhua, Yu. "Embodiment in Polanyi's Theory of Tacit Knowing." *Philosophy Today* 52 (Summer 2008): 126–35.

Ziebertz, Hans-Georg, and Friedrich Schweitzer, eds. *Dreaming the Land: Theologies of Resistance and Hope*. International Practical Theology 5. Münster, Germany: LIT Verlag, 2007.

INDEX

Italic page references indicate photographs and graphs.